Trails of the
Wild Selkirks

South of the Canadian Border

Dennis Nicholls

KEOKEE BOOKS

Sandpoint, Idaho

Cover photos:

Front – Hunt Peak towers over Fault Lake with a carpet of glacier lilies in the foreground. Photo by Leland Howard.

Back – The Lions Head as seen from Lookout Mountain in the Selkirk Crest. Photo by Dennis Nicholls.

The photographs in this book were taken by Dennis Nicholls and Jim Mellen, unless otherwise noted.

Copyright © 2004 by Dennis Nicholls

All rights reserved. No part of this book may be reproduced in any manner without the express written consent of the publisher, except in the case of brief excerpts in critical reviews and articles.

Keokee Books is an imprint of Keokee Co. Publishing, Inc.

Published by:
Keokee Co. Publishing, Inc.
P.O. Box 722
Sandpoint, ID 83864
(208) 263-3573

www.keokeebooks.com

ISBN 1-879628-23-6

Things can change. We want to be accurate as possible, but the vagaries of natural forces and human activity can bring many changes to trails in short periods of time. If you find any information in this guidebook is inaccurate or out of date, please let us know and we'll correct it in future editions ... and send you a big thank-you, to boot.

Also by Dennis Nicholls
Trails of the Wild Cabinets

Foreword

No animal has gone extinct in the Selkirk Mountains in 10,000 years. Grizzlies, lynx, bald eagles, transient wolves, even the exceedingly rare woodland caribou: They're all still there in mountains that rise Alps-like into thickly timbered slopes, high meadows, pebble-bed-clear streams, glacially striated rock faces and cliff amphitheaters around snowmelt cold lakes. And there are groves of ancient cedar and larch, even valleys into which rubber tires and metal bulldozer tracks have never rolled.

On a few of the trails during the busiest summer weekends, you might pass fellow hikers now and then, but on most routes you're likely to go all day, or even days, without encountering anyone. If you haven't seen them yet, these are the mountains you've been looking for. Here, what you see out your tent flap or while pausing to catch your breath on a ridge top lives up to the paradise you've been imagining since you can remember. If you already know the Selkirks, you know they are a place that makes you glad you also are a living animal; that makes you feel you've discovered paradise. You know they are a natural habitat where that other rare species, your human heart, can find what it too needs to keep from going extinct.

Amazingly, this wild country is just minutes outside the cities of Spokane and Coeur d'Alene, and literally at the edge of town from Sandpoint to Bonners Ferry, Priest River to Newport to Metaline Falls, along with several other small communities. You can steal away here to hike for an hour in your sneakers, or you can head out for a full-pack expedition lasting weeks.

Whatever the ambition or frequency of your visits, though, this book is an essential companion. It is the definitive guide to the area, clearly describing trails, terrain, points of interest and trailhead approach roads. It even lists suitability for mountain bikes and horses, and availability of water. But more importantly, in this book long-time hiking junkie Dennis Nicholls guides you into the spirit of this place with beautiful essays on the Selkirks, hiking and mountain life in general, with a sense of humor and good cheer in his trail advice and with a voice throughout that expresses the same exuberance and love that brought him, and now you, here.

Though the Selkirks have been a part of my life since the beginning, it was with Dennis that I first saw much of the high, remote country he introduces here to you. And now, as I sit at my desk and read *Trails of the Wild Selkirks*, both his precise directions and his mountain-loving heart take me back up there with him again. I can think of no one better to take you there, whether it be in person or in the pages of this book.

– Jonathan Johnson, Professor of Creative Writing
Eastern Washington University, Cheney, Washington

The Selkirk Mountain Range: South of the Canadian border

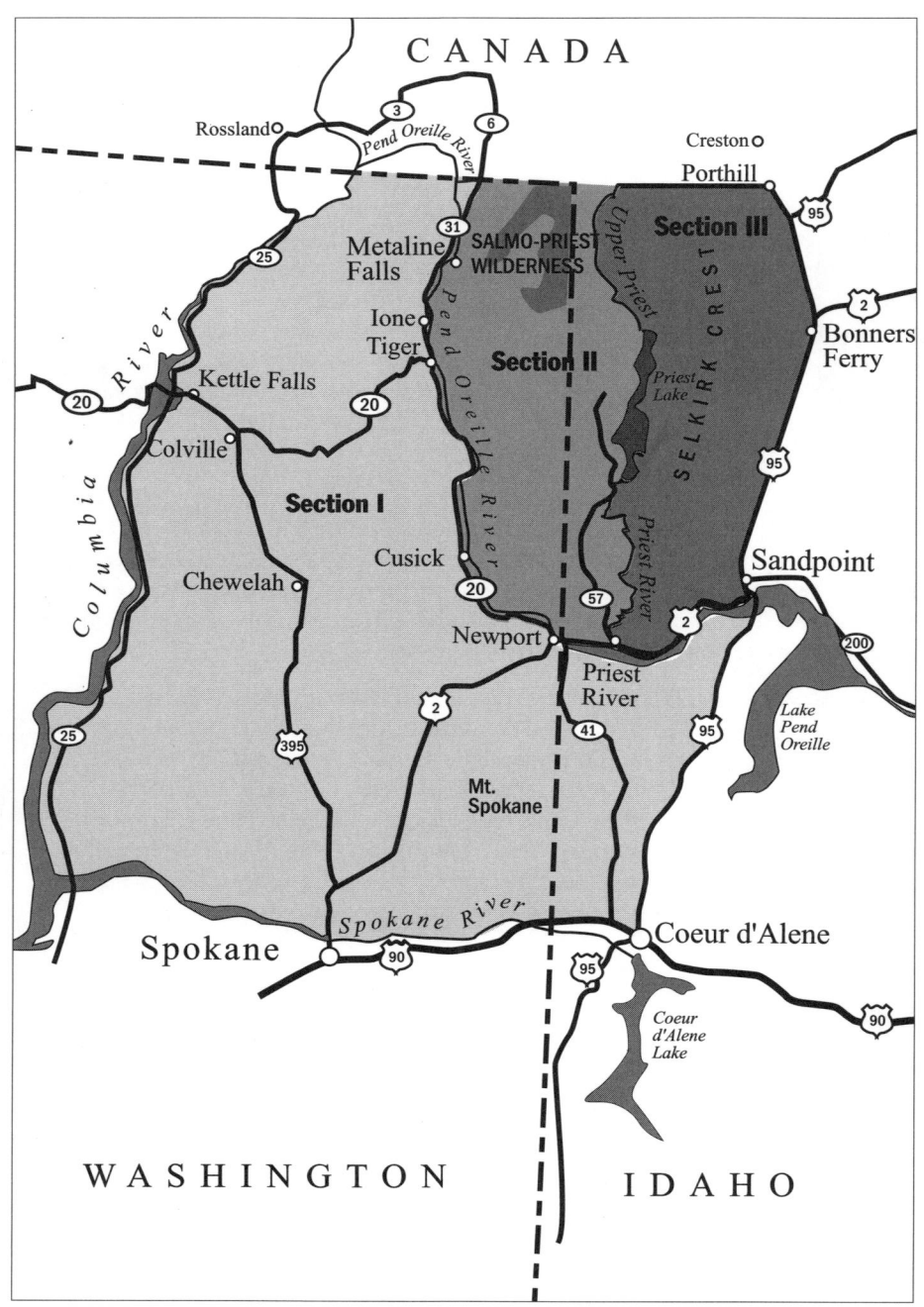

Contents

Acknowledgements 9
Introduction – *Initiation* 11
About this Guide 18
Features Chart 22
Discovering the Selkirk Mountains 26
Conservation – Our Fragile Home 40

Section I: Between the Columbia River and Pend Oreille River

The Lay of the Land 43
Abercrombie Mountain to Gillette Ridge **45**
    Flume Creek Trail No. 502 47
    Abercrombie Mountain Trail No. 117 48
    North Fork Silver Creek Trail No. 119 51
    South Fork Silver Creek Trail No. 123 52
    Sherlock Peak Trail No. 139 54
    Meadow Creek Trail No. 125 and Big Meadow Lake Trail No. 120 57
    Gillette Ridge Trail No. 131 and Mount Rogers Loop Trail No. 130 60
    Crawford State Park and Gardner Cave 62
Little Pend Oreille Lakes to Newport **64**
    Little Pend Oreille National Wildlife Refuge 65
    Little Pend Oreille Lakes Trails System 68
    Frater Lake Trail No. 150 and Lake Leo Trail No. 155 69
    Granite Peak Trail No. 145 70
    Springboard Trail No. 149 and Rufus Trail No. 148 72
    Sherry Trail No. 147 74
    Crystal Falls Viewpoint 75
    Batey-Bould Trails System 77
    Tacoma Peak Trail No. 309 78
    Upper Wolf Trail and Lower Wolf Trail Nos. 304 and 305 80
Spokane Area **82**
    Riverside State Park and the Spokane River Centennial Trail 83
    Spokane House and Little Spokane River Natural Area Trail 85
    Lake Roosevelt National Recreation Area and Fort Spokane 88
    Mount Spokane State Park 91
Essay – *Aladdin* 93

Section II: Pend Oreille-Priest Divide

The Lay of the Land 97
Salmo-Priest Wilderness and Upper Priest River **99**
    Continental Trail No. 28 101
    Upper Priest River Trail No. 308 102
    Little Snowy Lookout Trail No. 14 and Little Snowy Top Trail No. 349 . .104

Salmo Basin Trail No. 506 and Salmo Cabin Trail No. 531 107
　　　Salmo Divide Trail No. 535 109
　　　Shedroof Divide Trail No. 512 110
　　　Shedroof Cutoff Trail No. 511 112
　　　Thunder Creek Trail No. 526 113
　　　Jackson Creek Trail No. 311 117
　　　Hughes Fork Trail No. 312, Thunder Mountain Trail No. 313
　　　　and Bench Creek Trail No. 319 118
　　　Hughes Ridge Lookout Trail No. 314 120
　　　Upper Hughes Trail No. 315 and Cabinet Pass Trail No. 317 121
　　　Crowell Ridge Trail No. 515 124
　　　Slate Creek Trail No. 525 126
　　　Halliday Trail No. 522 127
　　　Red Bluff Trail No. 553 128
　　　North Fork Sullivan Creek Trail No. 507 129
Essay – *Longevity* 131

Sullivan Lake to Blacktail Mountain .133
　　　Mill Pond Flume Trail No. 520 and Mill Pond Trail No. 550 135
　　　Elk Creek Trail No. 560 136
　　　Sullivan Lakeshore National Recreation Trail No. 504 and
　　　　Sullivan Nature Trail No. 509 139
　　　Noisy Creek Trail No. 588 140
　　　Hall Mountain Trail No. 540 and
　　　　Hall-Grassy Divide Trail No. 533 144
　　　Grassy Top National Recreation Trail No. 503 145
　　　Muskegon Lake Trail 149
　　　Huff Lake Trail 150
　　　Huff Lake Interpretive Site 151
　　　Roosevelt Trail No. 266, Zero Creek Trail No. 256,
　　　　Little Grass Mountain Trail No. 265 and
　　　　Boulder Mountain Trail No. 293 153
　　　Granite-Roosevelt Trail No. 301 and Cedar Grove Trail No. 301A 155
　　　Blacktail Mountain Trail No. 292 158

Kalispell Rock to Pioneer Park 160
　　　Kalispell Rock Trail No. 370 162
　　　Kalispell Rock-North Baldy Trail No. 103 .163
　　　Stateline Trail No. 162 165
　　　Squaw Valley Trail No. 164 166
　　　Icy Springs Trail No. 197 167
　　　Hanna Flats National Recreation Trail No. 600 170
　　　North Fork Lamb Creek Trail No. 204 and Camp 15 Trail No. 232 171
　　　Binarch Creek Trail No. 220 172
　　　Browns Lake Trail No. 320 175
　　　South Skookum Lake Trail No. 138 176
　　　Bead Lake Trail No. 127 179

Newport Geophysical Trails 181
　　　Nok-OSH-Kol Heritage Trail at Pioneer Park 182
　The Priest Lakes and Lower Priest River **183**
　　　Upper Priest Lake Trail No. 302 185
　　　Centennial Trail No. 58 186
　　　Navigation Trail No. 291 and Portage Trail 188
　　　Plowboy Mountain Trail No. 295 189
　　　Priest Lakeshore National Recreation Trail No. 294 192
　　　Kalispell-Reeder Bay Trail No. 365 193
　　　Lakeview Mountain Trail No. 269 196
　　　Beach Trail No. 48 197
　　　Kalispell Island Trail No. 49 199
　　　Woodrat Trail No. 235 and Bulldog Point Trail No. 274 200
　　　Chipmunk Rapids National Recreation Trail No. 192 201
　　　Peewee-Steep Creek Trail Nos. 175, 176, 177, 178, 179 204
　　　Vinther-Nelson Cabin National Historic Site 205

Section III: Selkirk Crest

The Lay of the Land 207
　The North End – Shorty Peak to Myrtle Creek **209**
　　　Italian Ridge Trail No. 95 211
　　　Red Top Trail No. 102 212
　　　Smith Creek-Red Top Ridge Trail No. 21 214
　　　West Fork Mountain Trail No. 347 216
　　　Smith Creek Trail No. 17 and Smith Ridge Trail No. 18 218
　　　Long Canyon Creek Trail No. 16 221
　　　Parker Ridge Trail No. 221 224
　　　Parker Creek Trail No. 14 226
　　　Fisher Peak Trail No. 27 229
　　　Pyramid Pass Trail No. 13 230
　　　Pyramid-Ball Lakes Trail No. 43 232
　　　Big Fisher Lake Trail No. 41 233
　　　Pyramid Trail No. 7 235
　　　Russell Mountain Trail No. 12 and Russell Ridge Trail No. 92 236
　　　Burton Peak Trail No. 9 240
　　　Snow Creek Falls Trail 241
　　　Myrtle Falls Trail 242
　　　Myrtle Peak Trail No. 286 245
　　　Two Mouth Lakes Trail No. 268 246
　　　Upper Myrtle Creek Trail No. 6 248
　　　Kootenai National Wildlife Refuge 250
　Essay – *Gifts* 253

　The South End – Harrison Lake to Caribou Lake **256**
　　　Bottleneck Lake Trail No. 187 258
　　　Snow Lake Trail No. 185 259

Roman Nose Lakes Trail No. 165 260
Harrison Lake Trail No. 217 264
Beehive Lakes Trail No. 279 265
Chimney Rock Trail No. 256 266
Fault Lake Trail No. 59 268
Caribou Lake Trail No. 58 271
Mickinnick Trail 272
Essay – *Lost Summer: 1967* 274

Priest Lake State Forest 278
Trapper Creek Trail 281
Mollies Lake and The Mollies Trail 282
Lookout Lake and Lookout Mountain Trail .283
Devil Falls Trail 287
The Wigwams Trail 288
Upper Standard Lake Trail 290
Goblin Knob Trail 291
Mount Roothaan Trail 293
Hunt Lake Trail 295
Hunt Creek Falls Trail 296
Essay – *Caribou Conundrum* 298

North of the Border: A Hike in West Arm Provincial Park 302

Appendices
Appendix 1: Leave No Trace and Outdoors Ethics 307
Appendix 2: Who to Contact 309
Appendix 3: Family Fun Hikes 313
Appendix 4: Accessibility Guide for Americans with Disabilities 315
Appendix 5: The National Recreation Trail System 318
Appendix 6: Idaho Centennial Trail and Pacific Northwest Trail 319
Appendix 7A: Mileage Chart 322
Appendix 7B: Mileposts 323
Appendix 8: Index by Trail Name 328
Appendix 9: Index by Trail Number 332

Acknowledgements

The easy part of writing a book like this is in getting out on the trail and hiking, sometimes with companions, sometimes without. I am usually a loner when it comes to hitting the trail, but there were days when I hiked with different folks who helped make those days much more enjoyable. My thanks goes to folks like Jim and Sandii Mellen, Taneesha Smith, Jack Ferrell and Kitty Meredith, the Monday Hikers and Tuesday Trekkers, Judy Hutchins, Anna Rhodes, Barb Perusse, Duke and Grace, and Mindy Ferrell for taking time to enjoy the high country with me.

Taneesha Smith and the author on Roman Nose

My favorite week was when my oldest brother, Archie, came from Virginia to hike with me. For four days and three nights we had West Fork Cabin and the surrounding backcountry to ourselves. A summer of hiking is not complete without having Archie along for at least a few days.

At the Priest Lake Ranger Station, I said I wanted to hike every trail in that area and I was told, "Oh, you want to talk to Wayne." A lot of information about trails in the Selkirks, especially those in the Upper Priest, came from Wayne Kopischke. Not many know the enormous trails system of that area as intimately as he does.

I was thankful for input from Cris Currie and the Friends of Mount Spokane, and for the use of their park map and a photo by Cris.

How many people do you know who would give 160 acres to the government in exchange for developing a public hiking trail for all to use? That is exactly what Mick and Nicky Pleass of Sandpoint, Idaho, have done and the brand-new "Mickinnick Trail" is the result. Mick has

The Monday Hikers

passed on, but Nicky still hits the trails practically every day. Thank you for doing this. It will be a great thing for the community and for everyone who will share, for a few moments at least, the same love for the Great Outdoors you have shared with all of us. Smiles and a hug go to Jan Griffitts who helped me get information about this trail.

Like I said, hiking is the best part of doing a book like this, but back in the offices of Keokee Co. Publishing, the real work that went into producing this book was done by Laura White, Billie Jean Plaster and Trish Gannon. Billie Jean and Trish did a lot of editing and proofreading. But special thanks to Laura for helping make this a great hiking guide. It's all in the presentation, and she has presented my miles and months of hiking magnificently in these pages.

And of course, at the bottom of it all is Chris Bessler, the publisher, who believed this book was worth the effort and the expense. Thanks for the opportunity, Chris.

– Dennis Nicholls
Noxon, Montana
May 2004

Introduction

Initiation

Leave this afternoon or wait until morning? That was the big question facing me one day in mid-June 2003. Friends Jim and Sandii Mellen had offered to guide me into Fault Lake and introduce me to Idaho's Selkirk Mountains. It's not like they really needed an introduction, but I had not hiked much in those mountains, spending most of my hiking hours for the past 20 years in Montana's Cabinets. So I was pretty excited about spending several days up close and personal with the Selkirks, with Jim and Sandii as my unofficial guides.

We were going to hike in together, but I thought I had too much writing to do because of the previous week's hiking I had done around Lake Pend Oreille. I felt I should catch up on those trail entries before embarking upon a new set of trails. Jim and Sandii were not about to let my distractions deter them from heading to the lake, so we agreed I would meet them that evening or the following morning at the lake. From the dejected tone of my voice, they figured it would be the following morning.

By early afternoon, however, I had had my fill of sitting at the computer while the sun scooted from behind clouds periodically to taunt me with visions of alpine meadows full of spring wildflowers and ripples on the cold dark waters of Fault Lake. I decided leaving immediately for Idaho was the best course of action.

I grabbed my pack, made sure I had everything I would need (and then some) for four or five days, and out the door I went. Two hours later, having passed Edna and Buck's Tavern (alas, it burned down in Winter 2004), along the Upper Pack River and successfully, if not reluctantly, resisting the urge to drop in for some refreshment, I drove into the parking area at the Fault Lake trailhead and pulled up next to the Mellens' white Subaru. The sun was already low in the sky despite the summer solstice. "Plenty of time," I muttered under my breath. Six miles lay between the lake and me, and with a glance at the sun hovering just above the treetops, I wondered if I really did have enough time to make it before darkness settled upon the land.

The trail followed an old roadbed for the first several miles, making the hike much easier than I anticipated, except for when towering thickets of tag alder arched overhead and branches entwined to block out the sky. It was like entering a tunnel of translucent green. Still I stumbled on, shifting the heavy pack from side to side, mentally noting I would need to rearrange things to better balance the load.

As dusk slowly settled over the high basin into which I climbed, I couldn't help but pause and relish the beauty surrounding me. A fire in 1967 had burned hotly through here, and the young forest evolving from the ashes was still in its infancy. Head-high saplings of Engelmann spruce, subalpine fir and whitebark pine dotted the ridges and slopes of the basin. Spring beauties and glacier lilies splashed white and yellow and hints of pink and lavender among the tussocks of beargrass carpeting the ground. Directly in front of me to the west rose the sheer walls of the Selkirk Crest. Cradled in a higher valley fractured by a gigantic crack in the granite shimmered Fault Lake. Jim and Sandii should be there, perhaps watching as I followed the meandering trail through the meadows.

They were indeed watching, but not for me. Jim was hoping to see a bear or moose in those meadows and said he did not spot me until I was negotiating the final steep pitch to the lip of the lake. He was perched on a granite boulder at the edge of a flat bench on the north side of the lake. Sandii was nearer their camp on that same bench overlooking the lake with Hunt Peak rising black into the purple twilight of the sky. We greeted each other warmly, and they both remarked they had not expected me until morning. Though that had been the plan in the back of my mind originally, I argued that it seemed silly to spend another night at home when all I had to do was drive two hours and hike three more to spend a night in the high country with friends. They couldn't argue with that.

The author with Sandii and Jim Mellen on Hunt Peak

The moon rose into the clear sky, about three quarters full. It passed above Pack River, then tethered itself to the dark outline of Hunt Peak by a string of glistening stars. Its reflection shimmered on the surface of the lake, casting a mesmerizing spell on the evening. I had erected my tent on a ledge just below Jim and Sandii, but I sat with them on cold rock while the night unfolded in the heavens above Fault Lake.

We turned in when the frigid breeze slanting down from the snow-covered rim on the ridgeline above us became too cold to tolerate any longer. I lay in my sleeping bag gazing through the mesh window in the roof of my North Face Polaris tent. The stars laughed merrily while the wind whispered a lullaby. Wait until morning, indeed! What a great decision it had been to leave that afternoon. I slept more soundly on the cold, hard ground that night than if I had been curled up beneath the quilt on my bed at home.

During the wee hours of the night, a bank of clouds rolled in and the wind picked up. The morning dawned dreary-looking but dry. A rocky pinnacle southeast of the lake lured me into a brief but invigorating hike. The climb got my heart to pumping, but the coarse granite made for great traction, and I loped from boulder to boulder pretending I was a mountain goat. My footing felt as sure as it must feel for one of those great monarchs of the crags, and I sprang up the slope to a wind-whipped point of rocks. In a deep basin to the south lay McCormick Lake, still embraced by icebergs floating on its slate gray waters. To the north Gunsight Mountain pierced the scuttling clouds and disappeared into a fog of ice crystals. What a fine day, I grinned, for exploring the high country. Oh yes, I could handle the task of wandering about these mountains for the next four or five months, exploring trails, spying on wildlife, feeling the sap of the wilderness flow through my veins.

I threw my arms up and raised my hands toward the sky, practically laughing out loud at the envious prospect of living in the wilds of northern Idaho and northeastern Washington most of the summer. Then the wind smacked me in the face and bit my fingertips with cold teeth. I started back toward camp, my own teeth clattering uncontrollably, and snagged the end of a log with the toe of my right boot and floundered face first into a pile of moose turds. But you know what? I never stopped laughing.

Back at camp we ate breakfast, had a hot drink, then started out on the day's excursion. A leisurely ascent up the slope north of the lake eventually took us to a pass from which we could see Hunt Lake on the west side. The gentler flank of the mountain climbed northward to Gunsight, but the route we took, the near vertical cliff overgrown with brush and gnarly trees, attained the top of a snow-covered ridge south of the pass. From here several spikes of granite jutted from the ridgeline all the way out to Hunt Peak. We went that way, though the wind tried to blow us off the east side into the abyss at the bottom of which churned the windy surface of Fault Lake.

At the summit of Hunt Peak, gale-force winds tore at our clothing. Heavy gray clouds rolled through the sky just above our heads. The wind chill made it feel more like February than June. Patches of snow, despite the relative scarceness of snow the previous winter, lay in depressions and on the leeward side of stones and ridges all about us. It could have been taken as a miserable day, but we were ecstatic at being on top of a 7,000-foot peak so near to summer. All of the south side of Hunt Peak and the ridges and basins stretching clear to Jeru Peak and Sundance Mountain were burned by that 1967 wildfire, which resulted in vast meadows of grasses, sedges and wildflowers frequented by deer and elk, bears, moose and other animals of the backcountry. The sight of it all reminded me of the alpine tundra I hiked across in the Colorado Rockies 30 years ago. It was a breathtaking moment, both because of the view and the wind.

We strode east, walking easily through a forest of charred snags. At a rounded point overlooking McCormick Creek, Caribou Ridge and the rustic lodge situated on its shoulder far away, we stepped off the top and descended to the glacial waters of McCormick Lake. Jim likes to swim in every lake he hikes to, but he resisted the urge here. Winter still clung just a bit too frigidly to this remote basin. Soon we were back at our camp at Fault Lake, tired but thrilled with the day's adventures.

The next morning conditions had improved and we discussed where to go next and, lightheartedly, I suggested we hike from right where we were to

Beehive Lake, 15 miles to the north and more than a dozen peaks and valleys away.

Jim's face lit up like a kid's upon hearing Santa's reindeer on the roof. He said, "Let's do it." I said, "Well, okay, if you think we can." And Sandii was quite happy to hike out to the trailhead and drive farther up Pack River and meet us at Beehive Lake that evening.

Little did I realize that my real initiation to hiking in the American Selkirks was about to commence.

Jim and I, packs strapped to our backs, retraced our steps from the previous day toward the pass above Hunt Lake and kept going up. Gunsight is a formidable-looking mountain and is the highest along the south half of the Selkirk Crest, yet the ascent to its summit from Fault Lake is actually a piece of cake. We reached the flat, forested expanse of McCormick Ridge, which slides eastward from a boulder field tumbling off the flank of the mountain. Here we stopped and consulted the topographic map on Jim's GPS unit. Invaluable in charting our progress through the trackless mountains, its maps were really of little use since the screen was hardly any bigger than a thumbnail. We eyed the countryside, studying the cliffs that fell away into the upper valleys of the West Branch of Pack River. We couldn't find a route, so we left our packs for a climb to the top.

Mount Roothaan and Chimney Rock from Gunsight Mountain

The view was absolutely spectacular, but we were a little worried and unsure about following the broken ridgeline to the north. Returning to our packs, we studied McCormick Ridge stretching gently beneath the rising sun. It looked so easy, so flat. We decided to take it as far as we could, then drop down to Chimney Creek, cross the trail to Chimney Rock and climb back up toward Silver Dollar Peak.

Mistake. Big mistake.

McCormick Ridge indeed was flat. The pleasant walk along its game trails jostled my spirits to a new high – for all of a half-mile. Then the earth fell away into a canyon that seemed miles below us, straight down. We wandered for a while until we found what appeared to be a safe way down, and over the edge we went. It was steep but not unusually difficult, and I was still feeling good about the world and where exactly we were in it at that moment, but our feet took us to more cliffs and the brush got thicker and taller. Rhododendron, alder, vine maple, skunkbrush, mountain ash, the thorny stems of gooseberries – it was a veritable jungle we had stumbled into and there was no turning back. Believe me, I tried. The brush simply flung me farther down the dizzyingly steep slope. Now I was clinging for dear life to the very limbs and branches I was already coming to despise. And my pack, that unwieldy 50 pounds of gear swaying from my shoulders, scared me. My balance was all out of whack.

Jim had taken a route along the base of one of the sheer rock walls we had descended while I wallowed in a green, chaotic sea of leaves and limbs. We finally met up again, and the descent looked easier across the face of some granite slabs. Near the bottom, one tricky maneuver to get off the granite and back into the brush nearly pulled me over backwards. I grabbed a handful of fir boughs to steady me and the heavy pack swinging from my shoulders, and stepped across a gap in the rock onto a slanted, smooth surface that dropped several feet into beargrass hiding deep holes and sharp projectiles.

The rugged Selkirk Crest

I made it and the breath I had been holding for several minutes exploded in a sigh of relief.

The relief was short-lived, however. We got across the West Branch and climbed over a low hill full of brush to the next stream, Chimney Creek. The hillside rising above it was steep but not so brushy. Huckleberry bushes, mostly, and downed logs greeted us for several hundred vertical feet, then suddenly there was a trail. Aha! The trail to Chimney Rock. Now, which way do we go? Since going down was inherently easier than going up – even though we were faced with having to go up eventually – we chose down.

Umm, second big mistake.

It seemed like we followed the trail for a mile, dropping elevation like leaves falling from a cottonwood in autumn. When we finally crossed a stream and decided to climb again, we must have been more than a thousand feet below the next ridge blocking our way to Beehive Lake. Up we went, up and up and up. And finally we were on the crest of a ridge sloping gently from Silver Dollar – with

Introduction   15

a sheer cliff slicing deeply into the next canyon just on the other side.

By now I was getting tired. Fatigue wracked my body and shivers rippled through my extremities. Jim-the-Man-of-Steel-Legs-and-Iron-Lungs seemed unaffected by the exertion, but I needed to rest. The day had advanced well into the afternoon, and we still had a very long way to go so the rest stop was brief. We found a way down and passed along the eastern shore of one of the most picturesque little lakes I had ever seen, the basin encompassing it still full of snow and ice. And there yet again was another climb.

This time when we reached the ridgeline, still something like two and a half air miles from Beehive Lake and probably 112 miles over and around the high mountains in front of us, I knew I was done in. We wandered up the ridge looking for a way down. At one point Jim indicated a place that dropped off into the murky darkness engulfing the basin and suggested we could make it down that, maybe. I told Jim I was at the end of my endurance and I wasn't going down anything. At the next patch of snow we came to, since our water was virtually gone, I would have to make camp.

He acknowledged that with the waning daylight, it probably would be best to find a campsite. With any luck he'd be able to raise Sandii on the portable radios they both carry when backpacking, so she wouldn't worry about us.

Up the ridge, we continued looking for a flat place to lay our sleeping bags and a patch of last year's snow. At 7,100 feet, below a jumble of angular rocks that surely seemed to block any further progress, we found the spot. I was so overjoyed I could have sung "America the Beautiful" right then and there, but I was too tired to carry a tune.

We counted our lucky stars as the sun set in a blaze of color that bathed the Western sky and as the first faint twinkles of starlight flickered in the east. I sat down and could barely move while Jim explored our high-country bivouac. He later said that nearby was an easy way down into the next valley and a route that would then transport us across a wide-open expanse of rock, meadows and snow to the approach to Twin Peaks. That night, before succumbing to the satisfying, fatigue-induced sleep that hard hiking brings on, I vaguely wondered if he told me that just so I would sleep well without nightmares of rocks bruising my shins, brush clawing at my legs and tree limbs slapping me across the face.

That evening Jim was able to get Sandii on the radio and tell her of our plight. We had gone as far as we could, but would not make the lake before the next day. We thought noon, perhaps, but we thought wrong.

Jim escaped nearly being trampled by a mule deer during the night. Otherwise, our campsite had been perfect. The rocks in front of us indeed prevented further progress along the ridge, but Jim had not been lying about the way down into the headwaters of Thor Creek. Refreshed from the night's rest and some nourishment, it was easy trekking into the basin that swept up to a grassy meadow draped over a pass south of the twins. We rock-hopped and pranced our way to the bottom edge of that carpet of beargrass, to be rewarded with the music of fresh water and the most spectacular display of glacier lilies either of us had ever seen. The climb from there to the summit of the south twin was a walk in the park. We couldn't see Beehive Lake yet. It lay deep in a granite-lined pocket below the north twin. A broad saddle connected the two spires, and it looked easy enough to traverse.

It turned out to be not quite so easy. The ridgeline was comprised of broken, sharp rocks cloaked with dense, stunted subalpine fir growing thickly in every crevice. On the east, cliffs dropped sharply into a rocky bowl and on the west, the impenetrable tangle of trees and boulders tore at our naked legs. But finally, sometime well past noon, we reached the top of the north twin at an elevation of 7,607 feet according to a USGS marker set in stone at its summit. Below was the magnificent basin holding the sky blue waters of Beehive Lake. Farther east was the granite dome of The Beehive itself. The beauty of this place surpassed my wildest, most hopeful expectations. The fatigue, the bruises, the blood were all forgotten at the top of this part of the world.

With reluctance we finally began the arduous descent to the lake. I looked and would have sworn there was no way down, but Jim knew a route from a journey here 10 years before. He was right; there was a route, and we hiked across vast snowfields, over boulders and among flowery meadows lined with rushing streams full of snowmelt. A wilder place, I imagined, could not be found in the Selkirks anywhere.

My initiation in the American Selkirks was completed on the shoreline of Beehive Lake at the camp Sandii had set up the day before. We shared hot soup and crackers, granola and the experiences of having traveled cross-country through some of the most challenging terrain imaginable. Jim took a dip in the frigid waters of the lake. I settled for dipping my feet, though later, in the midst of a sweltering summer, I was happy to grasp opportunities for jumping into high mountain lakes. Jim put it this way, "Think, Dennis, have you ever regretted plunging into a pristine wild mountain lake afterward?"

No, Jim, I haven't. And neither have I regretted those two memorable days when you and I scrambled our way from Fault Lake to Beehive Lake. Thanks for the introduction to the Selkirks. It began a summer of some of the finest hiking of my life.

I hope all those reading this book share in the thrills, the adventures and the simple satisfaction of exploring one of the great places on Earth – the wild Selkirks.

About this Guide

A popular way to venture into unknown mountains is with a guide. Many people will pay big money to get a close-up look at, and an explanation of, wild things. It enhances the wilderness experience when a guide can expound on the character of the landscape and the habits of the creatures living there. But sometimes the most enjoyable and rewarding way to experience the Great Outdoors is on your own, or with a friend, exploring wild places, making your own discoveries and uncovering secrets. Then the wilderness truly comes alive, and the sense of satisfaction is deeper and more meaningful.

But where to start? Where does one go to find those wild landscapes and animals, the secrets whispered on the wind in the trees? There are many places in the world awaiting your own personal discovery. Maybe it just takes getting pointed in a certain direction, and, instead of a guide, perhaps a guidebook can provide all the direction you need. Such is this book. *Trails of the Wild Selkirks* hopefully contains enough information about the Selkirk Mountains, including where to go for more information, that you will want to explore these mountains for yourself, as I did during the spring, summer and fall of 2003.

I had hiked a little in the Selkirks before that year, but not much, so the opportunity to spend six months exploring the trails throughout this magnificent mountain range was a very welcome opportunity. I covered some 1,300 miles on something like 130 trails, and the knowledge and experiences gained along those miles and on those trails are conveyed in the pages of this book. This is not an exhaustive guide. There are more trails in the Selkirks than you will find described here, but this guide covers most of the best trails, plus some of the worst trails, just enough to whet your appetite. *Trails of the Wild Selkirks* is a great place to start becoming familiar with this range of mountains in northern Idaho and northeastern Washington.

Grizzly, black bear ... or Sasquatch?

Trails Description

Well more than 130 trails are described in this book. Three or four dozen others are mentioned in one place or another, but because they have been abandoned or have not been maintained in a long time, detailed descriptions for those were not included. A format for describing all the others follows the outline below.

Trail: the name and number (if there is one) of the trail.

ACCESSIBLE: indicates a trail that meets some level of accessibility standards for people with disabilities.

Family Fun Hike: denotes trails that are suitable for people of all ages, from young children to the elderly, provided they are reasonably healthy and in good condition.

Destination: identifies where a trail goes.

Best Suited For: lists whether the trail is suited to hiking, horseback riding, mountain biking or all three.

How Much Use: A Little * A Little More * A Lot * A Lot More * Excessive. The level of use will be bold and in all **CAPS**.

What's it like? This is a description of what to expect along the trail.

USGS Map: identifies the topographic map or maps on which to find the trail.

Trailhead: directions to the start of the trail. (Sometimes a trail can be accessed from more than one location.)

Trail Length: distance in miles from one end of the trail to another, sometimes including distances to specific landmarks along the trail, or the combined distance with other trails to a particular destination.

Trail Condition: poor, fair, good or excellent, depending on the amount of brush, blowdown and other obstacles found in or along the trail, the trail width, its relative steepness and the condition of the tread.

Elevation: the elevation of the trail at its starting point, high (or low) point and its end, or destination.

Estimated Duration of Hike: a subjective estimate as to how long it can be expected to hike a trail.

Sweat Index: a cutesy way of saying how difficult or easy a hike might be.

Mountain Bike Sweat Index: expresses the difficulty of a trail for a mountain biker using the International Mountain Biking Association rating system.

Best Features: some of the highlights encountered on the trail.

Availability of Water Along the Trail: where and how much water might be expected along a trail, keeping in mind that water is more plentiful in spring and early summer than late summer and early fall. Some streams with water in June might be dry in August.

Stream Crossings: the number and complexity of streams crossed by a trail.

Campsites: conveys whether developed or primitive campsites are present near or along a trail.

Precautions: points out any special hazards that should be noted.

Alternate Hikes: explains if any trails connect to the trail in the description.

Wildlife Sightings: remarks about animals seen while hiking any given trail.

Wild Notes: more remarks about animals, plants or special habitats found along a trail.

The primary focus of this guide is on hiking, since that is what I do. Virtually every trail discussed in this book is open to horses, and the majority of trails are open to mountain bikes, though many are so rugged they may not be suitable for pedal power. Horsemen and bicyclists should judge for themselves the suitability of these trails for rides.

A lot of trailheads in the Selkirks are clearly marked and easy to find, but many are poorly signed, not signed at all, obscure or difficult to locate. The directions to trailheads in this book are fairly precise, but it always helps to refer to detailed maps and to ask for assistance from trails people with the Forest Service. Trails on the Priest Lake State Forest can be particularly difficult to find since not a one is signed.

There is a lot of mixed ownership in this range. Most trails are on federally owned, public land, but some start or pass through private lands for which permission from landowners has been obtained, so always respect private property.

The details offered in these pages about each hike come from maps, signs, Forest Service booklets or pamphlets, conversations with others and, most of all, my own hiking experiences. Every trail described in this book was hiked between May and December of 2003, with a few exceptions. The snow just finally got too deep for the last few trails I wanted to explore, so I relied on other information rather than firsthand experience. Mistakes, especially in distances and elevations, are almost inevitable. I took great care to be as accurate as possible, but don't be surprised if, for instance, a trail is a mile longer or shorter than I say it is.

If you are looking for a particular kind of experience when exploring the Selkirks, check the Features Chart following this section on pages 22-25. It is a quick reference on where to find waterfalls, fire lookouts, hikes with points of historical significance, and other information that can help you select a hike that most interests you.

Quantifying the level of difficulty for a hike is based on three criteria: distance, elevation gained and condition of trail. It is also subjective and depends largely on each hiker's abilities. The author assumes most people utilizing this guide have done some hiking and are in reasonably good health. Each person should be aware of their limitations and judge for themselves just how hard a hike might be based on the information you will find in this guide.

The levels of difficulty used in this book are expressed in "The Sweat Index," mainly because it's just no fun simply saying "easy," "difficult," or "insanely crazy." Well, "insanely crazy" as a level of difficulty might be fun, but nonetheless, the ratings I have used are defined in the table below.

The Sweat Index: level of difficulty

1. No Sweat: An easy hike that practically anyone of any ability can do. Example: Sullivan Lakeshore National Recreation Trail No. 504.

2. Break a Sweat: A moderate hike that will probably make you breathe heavy and sweat a little, but you will think it was a piece of cake. Example: Caribou Lake Trail No. 58.

3. Buckets of Sweat: A difficult hike where you will likely sweat profusely during the day and will probably want to go to bed early that night, weary from a pleasant day in the mountains. Example: West Fork Mountain Trail No. 347.

4. Bathed in Sweat: The kind of strenuous hike that will more than likely test your endurance and tax your strength, but at the end of the day you may well wipe the salty sweat stinging your eyes and exclaim, "That was a dandy!" Example: Chimney Rock Trail No. 256.

There is another category in this book where a trail is noted to be "accessible." That means it is a barrier-free trail accessible to people in wheelchairs or with other ambulatory challenges. For more about these trails, see the "Accessibility Guide for Americans with Disabilities" in the Appendices on page 315.

Precautions

In the Selkirk Mountains, as for hiking in any mountainous terrain, there are some things to watch out for. They include:

- Sunburn – use sunscreen or wear clothing that covers exposed skin, including hats and/or sunglasses to shield your eyes.
- Snow blindness – wear sunglasses when hiking in snow on bright days.
- Extreme weather conditions any time of the year – always pack sufficient extra clothing and have waterproof matches and shelter available.
- Hypothermia – don't sweat so much that you lose body heat faster than your body can replace it; that is very dangerous.
- Insects – biting and stinging insects are common, especially in spring and early summer; wear appropriate clothing and have insect repellent handy.
- Wildlife – hikers and other outdoors enthusiasts are not the only creatures in these mountains. Always give animals a wide berth or leave an area entirely if animals you encounter don't leave; remember, you are the visitor here.
- Bears – the Selkirk Mountains harbor both black bears and grizzly bears. Learn to distinguish between them and familiarize yourself with techniques on how to hike and camp safely in bear habitat.
- Dehydration – it's simple: if you don't drink enough water, you dehydrate, and that is bad. Always drink plenty of water when hiking.
- Availability of Water – with upwards of 100 inches of precipitation annually in much of the Selkirks, you can expect to find water in lots of places, but it is always wisest to filter it, boil it or otherwise treat it before drinking.

One final note: With decreased funding from Congress for recreation projects, it has become necessary for agencies to seek funding in other ways. Thus was born, at least for Washington and Oregon, the Northwest Pass. It is essentially a parking permit required to leave your vehicle at certain trailheads and recreation sites. There are places in this book that require a pass for use of parking areas. The Nok-OSH-Kol Heritage Trail at Pioneer Park is one example. The passes cost $30 for a year, available at ranger station or various private vendors. Some Idaho recreation officials warn this system may also be coming to the Panhandle.

Trails of the Wild Selkirks Features Chart

Many people like to plan hikes for particular reasons: They want to go to a mountaintop, visit a lake, picnic by a waterfall, increase the likelihood of seeing wildlife. There are as many reasons for hiking as there are hikers. This section of *Trails of the Wild Selkirks* offers a quick glance at the features that can be found along many of the trails described in this book. These features are in the following categories:

- Waterfall – identifies significant waterfalls located along or near a trail.

- Lake – many of the trails covered in this book provide access to high mountain lakes.

- Mountaintop – if the trail does not go to a lake, then it likely climbs to the summit of a high peak; and sometimes it does both.

- Historical – a few trails harbor sites of historical significance, such as mining sites or old homesteads.

- Lookout/Cabin – some mountain tops have forest fire lookout towers on them, a few of which are still manned. There are also some cabins in the range, with a few available for use.

- Old Growth – because the Selkirks are home to fast-growing forests, the timber industry has thrived here for over a hundred years. However, some spectacular stands of old-growth forest still remain, as well as some remarkable individual trees that are worth mentioning.

- Wildfire – Forest fires play a major role in the shaping of the environment, and there are areas of significant burns in the past 10 years that offer excellent opportunity for viewing and studying the effects of wildfire.

*Sweat Index Key
1. No Sweat
2. Break a Sweat
3. Buckets of Sweat
4. Bathed in Sweat

Trail Features

Trail Name & No.	Miles One Way	Sweat Index*	Waterfall	Lakes	Mountaintop	Historical	Lookout/Cabin	Old Growth	Wildfire	Page Number

Section I: Between the Columbia River and Pend Oreille River

Trail	Miles	Sweat	Waterfall	Lakes	Mtntop	Historical	Lookout/Cabin	Old Growth	Wildfire	Page
Flume Creek Trail No. 502	4	4			x					47
Abercrombie Mountain Trail No. 117	3.5	4			x					48
North Fork Silver Creek Trail No. 119	5.9	5			x					51
South Fork Silver Creek Trail No. 123	7	4(1)								52
Sherlock Peak Trail No. 139	3.5	3			x					54
Big Meadow Lake Trail No. 120	1.5	2(1)		x						57
Meadow Creek Trail No. 125	1.5	2(1)		x						57
Gillette Ridge Trail No. 131	12.1	3			x			x		60
Mount Rogers Loop Trail No. 130	1.4	3			x					60
Frater Lake, Lake Leo Trail Nos. 150, 155	10	3(1)		x						69
Granite Peak Trail No. 145	9	4			x					70
Springboard Trail No. 149	2.4	3					x			72
Rufus Trail No. 148	3.8	3								72
Sherry Trail No. 147	3.8	2(1)								74
Crystal Falls Viewpoint	0.1	2	x							75
Batey-Bould Trails System	38.2	4		x	x	x				77
Tacoma Peak Trail No. 309	6	4			x					78
Upper and Lower Wolf Trails	5	2(1)								80
Spokane River Centennial Trail	37	2(1)	x			x				83
Little Spokane River Natural Area Trail	6	3				x				85
Old Kettle Townsite Trail	1	2(1)				x				89
St. Paul's Mission Trail	.25	2(1)				x				89
Sentinel Trail at Fort Spokane	2	2(1)				x				90
Mount Spokane State Park	100	2-4			x	x		x		91

Section II: Pend Oreille-Priest Divide

Trail	Miles	Sweat	Waterfall	Lakes	Mtntop	Historical	Lookout/Cabin	Old Growth	Wildfire	Page
Continental Trail No. 28	2.5	3	x					x	x	101
Upper Priest River Trail No. 308	8.1	3						x		102
Little Snowy Lookout Trail No. 14	0.7	4			x	x	x			104
Salmo Basin Trail No. 506 and Trail 531	8.8	4				x		x		107
Salmo Divide Trail No. 535	3	2(1)								109
Shedroof Divide Trail No. 512	22	4			x	x		x	x	110
Shedroof Cutoff Trail No. 511	1.7	3						x		112
Thunder Creek Trail No. 526	5	4						x	x	113
Jackson Creek Trail No. 311	5.6	4				x		x	x	117
Hughes Fork Trail No. 312	7.5	5						x	x	118
Hughes Ridge Lookout Trail No. 314	0.75	2			x	x	x			120
Upper Hughes Trail No. 315	9.1	4			x					121
Cabinet Pass Trail No. 317	1.3	4						x		121
Crowell Ridge Trail No. 515	7.8	4			x	x				124
Slate Creek Trail No. 525	4.3	3								126
Halliday Trail No. 522	4.2	3								127
Red Bluff Trail No. 553	5.2	3								128
North Fork Sullivan Creek Trail No. 507	5.3	4			x					129
Mill Pond Flume Trail No. 520	0.6	2(1)	x	x		x				135
Mill Pond Trail No. 550	0.75	2	x	x		x				135
Elk Creek Trail No. 560	2.1	3	x	x						136
Sullivan Lakeshore National Rec. Trail No. 504	4.1	3		x		x		x		139

Trail Features

Trail Name & No.	Miles One Way	Sweat Index*	Waterfall	Lakes	Mountaintop	Historical	Lookout/Cabin	Old Growth	Wildfire	Page Number
Sullivan Nature Trail No. 509	0.6	3								139
Noisy Creek Trail No. 588	5.3	5		x						140
Hall Mountain Trail No. 540	2.5	3			x					144
Hall-Grassy Divide Trail No. 533	5.1	4			x					144
Grassy Top National Recreation Trail No. 503	7.8	4			x					145
Muskegon Lake Trail	0.1	2(1)		x			x			149
Huff Lake Trail	0.1	2(1)		x						150
Roosevelt Trail No. 266	4.5	4			x			x		153
Granite-Roosevelt Trail No. 301	1.5	3(1)	x			x		x		155
Cedar Grove Trail No. 301A	0.25	2(1)				x		x		155
Blacktail Mountain Trail No. 292	2	4			x					158
Kalispell Rock Trail No. 370	2.5	3			x	x				162
Kalispell Rock-North Baldy Trail No. 103	8	4			x		x			163
Stateline Trail No. 162	9	4			x					165
Squaw Valley Trail No. 164	5.5	4			x					166
Icy Springs Trail No. 197	10	4			x					167
Hanna Flats National Recreation Trail No. 600	0.25	2(1)				x		x	x	170
N. F. Lamb Creek Trail No. 204	4	3	x							171
Binarch Creek Trail No. 220, Trail 232	3.5	3								172
Browns Lake Trail No. 320	1	2(1)		x				x		175
South Skookum Lake Trail No. 138	1.3	2		x						176
Bead Lake Trail No. 127	6.4	3(1)		x				x		179
Newport Geophysical Trails	6.6	2								181
Nok-OSH-Kol Heritage Trail at Pioneer Park	0.3	2(1)				x				182
Upper Priest Lake Trail No. 302	4.3	3		x		x		x		185
Centennial Trail No. 58	5	2		x						186
Navigation Trail No. 291	8.1	2		x				x		188
Portage Trail	0.3	2(1)		x				x		188
Plowboy Mountain Trail No. 295	6	4			x					189
Priest Lakeshore National Rec. Trail No. 294	7.6	2		x						192
Kalispell-Reeder Bay Trail No. 365	4.5	3								193
Lakeview Mountain Trail No. 269	5.3	4			x					196
Beach Trail No. 48	9	2(1)		x		x				197
Kalispell Island Trail No. 49	2.5	2		x						199
Woodrat Trail No. 235, Bulldog Pt. Trail No. 274	7	3								200
Chipmunk Rapids National Rec. Trail No. 192	10.4	2								201
Peewee-Steep Creek Trails	18	4			x					204
Vinther-Nelson Cabin National Historic Site	1	2		x		x				205

Section III: Selkirk Crest

Trail Name & No.	Miles One Way	Sweat Index*	Waterfall	Lakes	Mountaintop	Historical	Lookout/Cabin	Old Growth	Wildfire	Page Number
Italian Ridge Trail No. 95	2.6	3			x	x	x			211
Red Top Trail No. 102	8.5	4		x	x					212
Smith Creek-Red Top Ridge Trail No. 21	3.2	4			x	x		x		214
West Fork Mountain Trail No. 347	3.5	4		x	x	x	x	x		216
Smith Creek Trail No. 17, Trail No. 18	8	4			x	x		x		218
Long Canyon Creek Trail No. 16	12	4						x		221
Parker Ridge Trail No. 221	16.5	5		x	x	x	x			224
Parker Creek Trail No. 14	4	3				x				226
Fisher Peak Trail No. 27	7	5			x					229
Pyramid Pass Trail No. 13	2.9	3								230
Pyramid-Ball Lakes Trail No. 43	2.5	2		x						232

Trail Features

Trail Name & No.	Miles One Way	Sweat Index*	Waterfall	Lakes	Mountaintop	Historical	Lookout/Cabin	Old Growth	Wildfire	Page Number
Big Fisher Lake Trail No. 41	5.2	4		x						233
Pyramid Trail No. 7	4	4						x		235
Russell Mountain Trail No. 12	3	4			x	x		x		236
Russell Ridge Trail No. 92	4	4			x					236
Burton Peak Trail No. 9	2.6	3			x	x	x			240
Snow Creek Falls Trail	0.5	2	x					x		241
Myrtle Falls Trail	0.1	2(1)	x							242
Myrtle Peak Trail No. 286	4.5	4		x	x					245
Two Mouth Lakes Trail No. 268	4	4		x						246
Upper Myrtle Creek Trail No. 6	4.5	4		x				x		248
Kootenai National Wildlife Refuge Trails	3	2		x					x	250
Bottleneck Lake Trail No. 187	3.3	3		x						258
Snow Lake Trail No. 185	5.6	4	x	x					x	259
Roman Nose Lakes Trail No. 165	4.1	3(1)		x					x	260
Harrison Lake Trail No. 217	2.3	3		x						264
Beehive Lakes Trail No. 279	4.4	4		x						265
Chimney Rock Trail No. 256	6	5	x							266
Fault Lake Trail No. 59	6.5	4	x	x					x	268
Caribou Lake Trail No. 58	1.5	2		x						271
Mickinnick Trail	3.5	4								272
Trapper Creek Trail	2.5	3		x						281
Mollies Lake and The Mollies Trail	2.5	4		x	x				x	282
Lookout Lake/Lookout Mtn Trail	3	4		x	x	x	x			283
Devil Falls Trail	1.75	2	x							287
The Wigwams Trail	2	3			x					288
Upper Standard Lake Trail	4.5	3		x				x		290
Goblin Knob Trail	7	5			x					291
Mount Roothaan Trail	2.5	3			x					293
Hunt Lake Trail	1	3		x					x	295
Hunt Creek Falls Trail	0.5	2(1)	x							296

*Sweat Index Key

1. No Sweat
2. Break a Sweat
3. Buckets of Sweat
4. Bathed in Sweat

Discovering the Selkirk Mountains

Between Pack River Flats 10 miles east of Sandpoint, Idaho, and Chalk Grade Flat 12 miles southwest of Colville, Washington, is a distance of some 85 miles, if you could walk it in a flat, straight line. But you can't because there are four rivers, countless streams and dozens of mountains in the way, not to mention numerous lakes. Such a trek, however, would take you through the heart of the Selkirk Mountains, or at least the American portion of the Selkirks.

This book is about the Selkirk Mountains in the United States, but you see, the Selkirks are a gigantic range of mountains extending from the Spokane River in Washington to Kinbasket Lake in British Columbia, Canada. That's a distance of 300 miles. Those 85 miles from flat to flat represent the widest segment of this magnificent expanse of mountainous terrain. And what are the four rivers you would encounter on such a walkabout? The Pend Oreille, the Priest, the Little Pend Oreille and the Colville. Those are a few of the streams that help define this mountain range.

The Selkirk Crest harbors some of the most rugged terrain in the Selkirk Mountains

The Selkirks is one of many ranges comprising the Rocky Mountains strung along the spine of the North American continent. Oriented on a north-south axis, about two-thirds of the Selkirks' 13,000 square miles are in Canada. The other third straddle the north end of the Washington-Idaho state line. It is a staggering landscape of spectacular peaks, glacial lakes, dark coniferous forests and grassy hills thick with ponderosa pine, all the way from Mount Spokane (5,851 feet) to Mount Sir Sandford (11,590 feet).

South of the border are 3 million acres of national forests, wildlife refuges, state lands, corporate timberlands, Indian reservations and private holdings. The trails that traverse some of those 3 million acres are what this book is about.

Boundaries

On the west side of the Selkirk Mountains, their entire length from north to south, the range is bordered by the Columbia River where it flows out of Kinbasket Lake and over Mica Dam into Lake Revelstoke. For another 100 miles, nearly from Revelstoke to Castlegar, the river is impounded as Upper and Lower Arrow Lakes. Below that, it flows freely into Stevens County, Washington, on its long journey to the Pacific Ocean. The southerly limit of this landmass is marked by the Spokane River, which flows from Lake Coeur d'Alene in Idaho to its confluence with the Columbia River in Washington. Here the mighty Columbia is personified as Franklin D. Roosevelt Lake.

Moving north from Lake Coeur d'Alene, the southeastern boundary of the Selkirks follows the Purcell Trench to Bonners Ferry, Idaho, which sits on the banks of the Kootenai River. The Purcell Trench is a great tectonic rift in the Rocky Mountains that stretches over 200 miles. The Kootenai River joins with Kootenay Lake to form the eastern boundary in British Columbia, splitting the Selkirks apart from the Purcell Mountains. (In the States the spelling is "Kootenai," and in Canada it is "Kootenay.") The boundary then continues upstream along Duncan Lake and the Duncan River. Here the boundary between the Selkirks and the Purcells is somewhat obscure. These twin ranges come together in the jumble of glaciated peaks amassed in Glacier National Park at the headwaters of the Spillimacheen River flowing to the east and the Illecillewaet River flowing to the west, both tributaries to the upper Columbia and both nearly impossible to pronounce. The Columbia then flows northwesterly into Kinbasket Lake at the northern tip of the range. In Canada, the Selkirks average about 40 miles in width. The Canadian border slices through these mountains for 50 miles from the Kootenai River at Porthill, Idaho to the Columbia River a little ways north of Northport, Washington. From that international boundary, the Selkirks fan out in a southerly direction into the diminishing hills and open ponderosa pine forests of northeastern Washington and the granitic batholith of northern Idaho.

The Selkirks are also known for their temperate rain forests

Surrounding the Selkirks are eight other mountain ranges. The heart of the Rocky Mountains forms the Continental Divide northeast of Kinbasket Lake. The Columbia Mountains stretch northward across the river from Mica Creek. Along the west side in Canada are the Monashee Mountains and the Christina Range. In Washington the Selkirks are flanked by the Kettle River Range west of the Columbia River.

In Idaho, the Purcell Trench is the meeting place of several ranges, including the Cabinets, the Coeur d'Alenes and the Bitterroots. Lake Pend Oreille is embedded within the northwest corner of mountains where the Bitterroots and the Coeur d'Alenes come together. The lake is nearly encircled by an outpost of hills severed from the main range perhaps by movements within the earth's crust and by the action of catastrophic flooding associated with the draining of Glacial Lake Missoula during the Pleistocene Ice Age thousands of years ago.

North of the Kootenai River in Idaho and Montana and west of Kootenay Lake in British Columbia are the Purcell Mountains, the twin range to the Selkirks. Beyond the southern extremity of the Selkirks, south of the Spokane River, are the fertile farmlands of the Palouse.

Aside from straddling an international border, the American Selkirks also sprawl across two states, five counties, two national forests and two Indian reservations (the Spokane and Kalispel). There are also state lands, corporate timberlands and private lands throughout the range.

Geology

The material forming the bedrock of much of the Selkirk Mountains is relatively young in geologic terms. The east half of the Selkirk Range south of the international border is granitic, originating some 135 million years ago during a particularly active period deep inside the earth's crust. This igneous intrusion pushed its way into stratified beds of sedimentary rock laid down perhaps as long as a billion years ago, or overrode the ancient lakebed deposits altogether. Granite monoliths such as Chimney Rock, Harrison Peak, Roman Nose and other features dominate the high Selkirks.

Other areas in the Selkirks are sedimentary in origin or a mix of igneous and sedimentary rocks. For instance, at the north end of the Selkirk Crest, which is virtually all granite, layers of sedimentary rock surface on the northeast flank of Parker Ridge. Much of the Salmo-Priest Wilderness is covered in layered sedimentary rock, but farther south along the Pend Oreille-Priest Divide, like at Kalispell Rock and Hungry Mountain, there's that granite again. And even farther south and a bit west,

Headwall of Kent Creek from The Wigwams

especially near the Columbia River, basalt is common, indicating the volcanic action that affected this area millennia ago.

The substrate underlying the Selkirks and surfacing as peaks, domes and rocky outcrops is complex. Why, there is even a limestone cavern near Metaline Falls, Washington. More recent geologic forces, however, have shaped the surface of the land. Glaciers, and not just the tongues of alpine ice churning downslope from the craggy heights of the jagged peaks, but the great Cordilleran Ice Sheet swept down from the Arctic and encased most of the Selkirks in a frozen mass as recently as 10,000 or 12,000 years ago. The leading edge of this mantle of ice ceased its southern march in Idaho between present-day Sandpoint and Coeur d'Alene at what is now referred to as the Purcell Lobe. Perhaps as thick as 2,000 feet, the ice choked entire valleys and created at the toe of the ice sheet huge lakes such as Glacial Lake Missoula, Glacial Lake Bonneville and the biggest of them all, Glacial Lake Agassiz.

The ice retreated after thousands of years, grinding river bottoms into U-shaped valleys and scouring deep holding basins for the bodies of water known today as Lake Pend Oreille (the largest lake in Idaho and the fifth deepest lake in North America), Lake Coeur d'Alene, Priest Lake and Sullivan Lake, along with dozens of other smaller lakes especially common in the southern part of the range.

Landscapes and Climate

The climate of the Selkirk Mountains is decidedly maritime, meaning the Pacific Ocean is the greatest influence on the weather. That, in turn, means a great deal of precipitation falls on these mountains, and most of it comes in the form of snow. The northern latitude combined with the oceanic moisture that typically streams into the region results in conditions ripe for heavy snowfall and plenty of rain. In the high country, snow can fall in any month of the year.

Nonetheless, the climate varies considerably within the region. Spokane, Washington, for instance, at the southernmost tip of the range, receives about 15 inches of precipitation annually while Sandpoint, Idaho, gets about double that. Areas within the Priest River drainage may receive almost double that yet again. Snowfall tends to be light farther south, but much of the Selkirk uplands and sheltered valleys usually experience heavy snow during the winter months. Farther north into Canada, snowfall is even heavier. In fact, snow is such an integral part of the climate and the landscape of the Selkirks, there are no less than half a dozen ski resorts located throughout the range.

Yet, even though snow is so prolific, the seasonal extremes in temperatures are fairly mellow, more so south of the border. The mercury may well drop to 20 degrees below zero or rise to 100 scorching degrees, but as a rule winters are mild and summers are pleasant compared to many locations in the Northern Rockies. Such a moderate climate helps make for an inconceivable variety of habitats, ranging from the impressive old-growth forest at the Roosevelt Grove of Ancient Cedars northwest of Priest Lake to the sagebrush hills of the Spokane Indian Reservation along the Columbia.

Across this whole landscape one phenomenon has recurred over the past 10,000 years – fire. That has never been more evident than in 1967 when historic wildfires swept through northern Idaho, including the monster known as the Sundance Fire. Ignited by lightning on the flank of Sundance Mountain northwest of Sandpoint, Idaho, it consumed more than 55,000 acres, most of that in a matter of hours when it made a spectacular 16-mile run that threatened to overrun the town of Bonners Ferry.

Other years and decades have seen fire as well. There may be a great deal of moisture in these mountains, but the seasonal drought in July and August coupled with lightning flashing across the peaks is a recipe for wildfire. Much of the interior of the Selkirks burned in the 1890s and the Roaring '20s saw a great deal of flame, especially 1926 when 80,000 acres were scorched on the west side of Priest Lake. Even the 1930s had substantial fire. Since early in the 20th century, though, when the famous Great Fire of 1910 wreaked havoc across the Inland Northwest, man has battled wildfire in almost every instance.

These days, 2003 may be viewed as a bad fire year because of the 600 acres burned in Hunt Creek, the 4,000 acres scorched in Myrtle Creek and other smaller blazes, but firefighters have become so good at their job that fire has nearly been eliminated from the forests when compared to historic trends. The need for fire on the landscape has become apparent in recent years, and land management agencies are learning to use fire as a tool to help meet forest management goals.

Topography

Contributing to the variety of landscapes in the Selkirks are the immense extremes in elevation. The most graphic illustration is in the far north end of the range at Revelstoke, British Columbia, which is situated on the shores of the Columbia River at 1,494 feet above sea level. About 35 miles to the east is Mount Dawson, an enormous mountain topping 11,123 feet. Another 15 miles to the north is Mount Sir Sandford rising to more than 11,500 feet, making for a difference of more than 10,000 vertical feet from river bottom to mountaintop.

Farther south in the range, the mountains are lower, though hardly any less rugged. The most striking area of peaks in all the Selkirks may well be found in Valhalla Provincial Park northwest of Nelson, B.C., but south of the West Arm of Kootenay Lake, the terrain takes on a definite softer look. Only one or two peaks south and west of the Kootenay River in B.C. exceed 8,000 feet, while the American portion of the Selkirks has no 8,000-footers at all.

Still, the American Selkirks, which are the focus of this book, are inarguably a marvelous collection of majestic peaks, wild valleys and fabulous lakes. In fact, all of the largest natural lakes in the Selkirks are clustered in the southeastern corner, while 18 mountain summits rise to more than 7,000 feet. This end of the mountain range can be broken into three sections: the Selkirk Crest; the Pend Oreille-Priest Divide; and the lands between the Columbia and Pend Oreille rivers.

The Selkirk Crest is the most rugged and wildest of the American Selkirks and harbors many of the highest peaks south of Canada. The highest named mountain south of the border is Parker Peak northwest of Bonners Ferry, Idaho. It measures 7,670 feet. A close neighbor, Smith Peak four miles to the southwest, reaches 7,653 feet. There are two unnamed peaks northeast of Big Fisher Lake that surpass both of these mountains at 7,682 feet and 7,709 feet.

The Pend Oreille-Priest Divide forms the centerpiece of the American Selkirks, the crown jewel of which is the Salmo-Priest Wilderness. This divide is a narrow, compact ridge of mountains between the Priest River and the Pend Oreille River. The highest summit in this section is Snowy Top at 7,572 feet, located barely a mile south of Canada.

West of the Pend Oreille River are the southwestern foothills of the Selkirk Mountains. The terrain broadens in a wedge of hilly land tucked between the Columbia River and the Pend Oreille River. National Forest lands and their proliferation of trails end at the Colville River, a tributary to the Columbia. This entire landscape is less than 6,000 feet in elevation except for the extreme north end where Abercrombie and Hooknose mountains both exceed 7,000 feet. South and west of the Colville River, there are no national forest lands, nor are there in the entire Little Spokane River basin. But there are some interesting sites with trails and other points of interest worth mentioning in these pages.

Priest Lake is by far the largest lake in the Selkirks at 19 miles from north to south and five miles across at its widest point from Kalispell Bay to Hunt Creek. It covers more than 20,000 surface acres and is 360 feet deep. Other large lakes in the area include Upper Priest Lake, Sullivan Lake, Calispell Lake and Bead Lake. There are also dozens of small alpine lakes dotting the high terrain of the Selkirk Crest from Saddle Lake to Keokee Lake.

Human History

The Selkirk Mountains were named for the Fifth Earl of Selkirk, Thomas Douglas (1771-1820). Hailing from Selkirk County in southern Scotland, he worked for the North West Company in Montreal and was a peer of David Thompson, the Welsh fur trader and geographer who was the first white man to explore much of the region. The Earl never actually made it to the Rockies, but this range of mountains was named in his honor, quite possibly by Thompson himself.

When Jaco Finlay, on a scouting excursion for David Thompson in 1806, stepped across the Continental Divide at what is now known as Howse Pass, he peered down the Blaeberry River and across the upper Columbia River at the shocking peaks of Canada's Glacier National Park. Of course, he didn't know these names then, but he knew he had found a way over the mountains and into a rich new region for the fur trade. He made sketches and returned to Thompson's trading post at Rocky Mountain House on the North Saskatchewan River.

During the ensuing years, Thompson and his men made it over the "Height of Land" where Jaco had stood and descended for the first time into the upper Columbia River valley. They established a post called Kootanae House and eventually circled the Purcell and Selkirk mountains to the south, making contact with native tribes and opening this remote country up to fur trapping. It was 1809 before Thompson crossed into what would become Montana and Idaho on the Kootenai River as he continued to search for a route to the sea.

This historic photo of the Mill Pond Flume is on display at the Mill Pond Historical Site near Metaline Falls, Washington

Native tribes populated virtually all this region, from the Colville and Kalispel Indians in the southwest to the Pend Oreille Indians around the lake of the same name to the Kootenay and Salish peoples along the upper Columbia and Kootenay rivers. Many other tribes moved back and forth through this region as well, sometimes warring with each other, often trading goods with one another, or on their way to particular hunting grounds.

By and large, the early explorers were well received by the natives, but trappers and hunters, who ventured first into the Selkirks, were soon followed by miners, loggers and settlers. Even Jesuit priests came to northern Idaho in the very early days. Father Peter DeSmet busied himself with bringing Christianity to the natives around "Kaniksu" Lake from 1844 to 1846. That was a name given the lake Father DeSmet later called Roothaan Lake, after his Jesuit superior in Rome. The word Kaniksu is thought to have meant "black robe," indicating the natives gave it that name after the priests arrived in the region. The name eventually evolved into Priest Lake, but a high peak rising to the east, Mount Roothaan, has held its name.

The discovery of gold in the 1860s in British Columbia brought thousands of miners through northern Idaho and adjacent Washington. In the latter years of the 19th century, some of the miners liked the look of the terrain south of the border and began prospecting throughout these mountains. The Continental Mine above the Upper Priest River operated into the 1960s, and over by Metaline Falls a limestone deposit was developed in the early 1900s. Today, a lead and zinc mine is operating a couple miles north of Metaline Falls.

The real boom cycle for the region, however, came about with the advent of the railroads. By the 1880s railroad tracks had been laid to Sandpoint, Spokane and other towns scattered along the area's rivers, and timber was being cut at a rapid rate. Communities were growing and enjoying a bustling economy. Mining was a factor in the settlement of the area but not as much as the forests so rich in big timber. The fur trade had died out. With the invasion of sawyers and crosscut saws, an era that lasted 50 years began. Log drives down every river brought wood to the mills that had sprung up. The first recorded log drive on Priest River, which ushered the giant whitepine, cedar and other species downstream, took place in 1901. At the height of this fervor to raze the magnificent forests of the Selkirk Mountains, 50,000 cedar poles and 125 million board feet of logs were herded downriver in 1931 by men known as "river pigs."

By the 1930s and the onslaught of the Depression, much of the country had plunged into economic gloom. A bright spot was the creation of the Civilian Conservation Corps (CCC) and the subsequent construction boom across the mountainous West. Numerous camps sprung up in the Selkirks, and, in a period of just a few years, the CCC had built hundreds of miles of trails and roads and erected dozens of structures. The presence of most of the hiking trails today in this range can be credited to the work of thousands of men 70 years ago.

Though logging is still an important part of the region's economic pulse, it has diminished in recent years, and a greater emphasis is being placed on tourism and recreation. Mining is still alive here, too, as evidenced by the re-opening of the Pend Oreille lead and zinc mine near Metaline Falls. In addition, the Selkirk Mountains south of the Canadian border have become a mecca for retired people. The region's natural beauty attracts new settlers from coast to coast. With the growth of ski resorts, guest ranches, bed and breakfast inns and other tourist-related businesses, the recreation industry is booming in the American Selkirks, and it has a system of hiking trails rivaled by few areas anywhere on earth.

Lookouts and Cabins

While hiking the trails to many of the mountaintops throughout the Selkirks, one thing became overwhelmingly apparent. At one time there were a lot of lookouts in these mountains. Following the devastating and deadly fire of 1910, the fledgling U.S. Forest Service decided it needed to extinguish every wildfire as quickly as possible in order to protect the vast timber resources cloaking the mountainsides. So by the late 1920s, a massive effort was under way to place men on the tops of mountains who would then search for the telltale signs of fire in the forest: a bolt of lightning, a wisp of smoke and the crackling of flames.

Over the next 20 years, an enormous building project witnessed the erection

Sullivan Mountain Lookout

of more than 220 lookouts in the Selkirks alone. In fact, nowhere on Earth had as many lookouts per square mile as northern Idaho. And in northeastern Washington, more than 90 percent of the mountain peaks had a lookout on them. The men staffing these structures, which were sometimes nothing more than a platform in a high tree and at other times an elaborate tower with living accommodations, had the responsibility of spotting a fire and, if at all possible, single-handedly battling the blaze until it was out.

The era of the lookout diminished as rapidly as it grew. With the evolution of planes and helicopters and the improvement of communications by leaps and bounds, the need for a solitary man on a distant peak all but disappeared. And so did the lookouts. A few still survive intact, and some are still used for the purposes of spotting fires and providing communication links to remote areas in the forest. But more often than not, a trek to many mountaintops in the Selkirks today will reveal some weathered concrete footings, wire, bolts, broken glass and decaying boards.

Today, the active lookouts that remain in the Selkirks include Lookout Mountain, Sundance Mountain, Gisbourne Mountain, Indian Mountain, South Baldy and Hughes Ridge. Several others are still standing, such as West Fork Mountain, Shorty Peak, Salmo Mountain, Sullivan Mountain and Little Snowy Top. It makes for an interesting step back in time to visit one of these lookouts.

The best source of information on the history of lookouts, not only in the Selkirks but throughout the Pacific Northwest, is Ray Kresek's book, *Fire Lookouts of the Northwest*.

Of equal interest are the numerous cabins to be discovered in the Selkirks. Miners and trappers built them and so did the Forest Service. Some of them are what is left of old homesteads. Hardly any of the old cabins remain intact. For the most part a few rotting logs, boards and piles of debris is what you will see where once a remote cabin provided shelter for some hearty soul.

Only four cabins that I know of in the Selkirks are still useable. The cabin at

Hughes Meadow is used by smoke-chasers during times of active wildfires. It is off limits to the public. West Fork Cabin, northwest of Bonners Ferry, Idaho, burnt to the ground in 1998, but the community and Forest Service rebuilt it essentially as it was before, this time placing it on a foundation and putting a metal roof on it. This cabin is the most remarkable of them all. It is open to the public on a first-come, first-served basis and has a couple of bunks, a table and chairs and a wood-stove. Another cabin open to the public is near Big Meadow Lake west of Ione, Washington, and is a replica of the Hess Homestead and other like structures built around the turn of the 20th century. It is not as remote as West Fork Cabin but still has a similar character. The third cabin open to the public is at Frater Lake west of Tiger, Washington. It is essentially a warming hut for wintertime use, but it is a rather elaborate warming hut. The log cabin faces Frater Lake less than a half-mile off Highway 20.

You may be surprised where you will run into the remains of someone's hard work and sweat. Salmo Cabin on the South Salmo River in the Salmo-Priest River might be the most remote, though that title might be challenged by the dilapidated structure on Cutoff Peak at the north end of the Selkirk Crest. There is also a rotting cabin on Russell Mountain, and at the north end of Upper Priest Lake a trail quietly skirts the remains of Coolin's Cabin.

These and others make for interesting discoveries in the Selkirks, and they remind us of a time when the land was truly wild. It was rough pioneering in the Selkirk Mountains, but memories last longer than rotting timbers. As you encounter these historic places on your journeys, remember to respect the memory of those who struggled in this vast wilderness. Don't disturb the sites or remove any trinkets or keepsakes. Leave everything as you find it for the enjoyment of those who will follow. It is sites like the sheepherder's cabin in Parker Creek that link us to the past and instill hope for the future.

Communities and Access

The Selkirk Mountains are home to perhaps half a million people, though half of them live in or around Spokane, Washington, far and away the largest city on the fringes of this range. There are nearly three dozen communities scattered through the Washington Selkirks, including Colville, which is home to the headquarters of the Colville National Forest. Another forest headquarters is located in Coeur d'Alene, Idaho, on the extreme southeast fringe of the range. The Idaho Panhandle National Forests are managed from this location. The other major communities in Idaho adjacent to the Selkirks are Sandpoint, Priest River and Bonners Ferry.

In Canada the largest communities on the fringes of the Selkirks are Revelstoke, Nelson, Castlegar, Trail and Creston. They all have fewer than 10,000 people each, as the more rugged Canadian Selkirks are perhaps somewhat less hospitable to lots of people.

On the American side of the border, access into the Selkirk Mountains is excellent. Highways 2 and 395 north from Spokane tie in with other primary routes such as Highway 20 between Colville and Newport and Highway 31 north from Tiger to Metaline Falls and the Canadian line. Highway 2 continues east and north from Newport into Idaho to Priest River. From there one of the most popular routes into the Selkirks is Highway 57 north to Priest Lake, Nordman and the southern edge of the Salmo-Priest Wilderness.

Staying on Highway 2 from Priest River takes you to Sandpoint; then heading north on Highway 95 takes you to the junction with the Pack River Road, another popular access route into the heart of the Selkirks. North of the Pack River, several routes off Highway 95 provide good access into the highlands of the Selkirk Crest before you reach Bonners Ferry, and past it as you proceed north to the border.

North of the border, Trans Canada Highway 1 traverses Glacier National Park from Revelstoke to Golden. This may well be the most scenic drive anywhere in the Selkirks. Highway 23 provides access to Mica Creek at the base of the gargantuan Mica Dam in the shadow of Mount Chapman, a peak rising to more than 10,000 feet. South of Revelstoke, Highway 23 continues to Nakusp and Highway 6, which winds through the mountains all the way to Nelson on the West Arm of Kootenay Lake, and to Ymir and Salmo on the North Fork of the Salmo River. Highway 3 passes through Stagleap Provincial Park and connects Highway 6 to the town of Creston that resides on the banks of the Kootenay River a short way north of the international boundary.

From almost all these highways are forest roads leading deep into the mountains and to dozens of trailheads, especially in the United States. A century of road building and logging has resulted in an abundance of narrow dirt tracks into all parts of the range.

Wilderness and Wildlife

Though man's incursion into the Selkirks has escalated over the past 200 years, native wildlife populations remain largely intact. There are some notable exceptions. Beaver is what first lured the white man here and at one time these creatures of rivers, lakes and ponds were nearly trapped out of existence. Being the resilient critters they are, however, they survived and flourished and now support what is largely a sporting industry for recreational trappers.

Wolves, too, were exterminated, at least south of the border, and if they were not really exterminated, they were reduced in numbers to

The rarest of mammals in the continental United States is the woodland caribou. This antler was found in the Priest Lake State Forest

just an occasional transient passing through from the north. But the gray wolf was placed on the United States' endangered species list and has been the object of a concerted effort to preserve the species, not to mention an object of great controversy. Though there are no known packs established in the Selkirks at this time, these animals have spread rapidly throughout adjacent western Montana and are sighted more and more frequently in northern Idaho.

Another predator showing up on the endangered species list and that is present in the Selkirks is the grizzly bear. A large part of the Selkirk Crest and Pend Oreille-Priest Divide between the Pend Oreille River and the Kootenai and Pack rivers is identified as a Grizzly Bear Recovery Zone. Grizzlies inhabit approximately 5 percent of their former range in the continental United States, and the Selkirk Mountains are a small portion of that habitat. It is one of half a dozen areas in the United States where wildlife biologists feel grizzlies can survive if given adequate room to live and rear their young. It is thought 30 to 40 grizzlies inhabit the Selkirk Mountains. Grizzlies are not to be confused with another type of bear in these mountains; the much more common black bear, which is not always black and can brown or chocolate. Accurate identification of these two animals is essential, since black bears can be hunted while grizzlies, in the lower U.S., cannot.

The rarest mammal in the "Lower 48" can be found in the American portion of the Selkirks and nowhere else south of the 49th parallel. It is the woodland caribou. Also on the endangered species list, this close relative of the more familiar Arctic barren-ground caribou was likely never abundant in the continental United States. At one time woodland caribou were known in the northern forests of New England and along the border in northern Minnesota as well as in the remote backcountry straddling the boundary between Canada and Washington, Idaho and northwestern Montana. There have been no confirmed sightings of caribou in Montana for decades, but this elusive, gentle ungulate is still seen occasionally in the mountains just north of Sandpoint. Recent surveys have determined perhaps only 40 to 50 of these animals exist in all the Selkirks, and for the most part they hang out in British Columbia, only dropping south from Stagleap Provincial Park into the United States from time to time. It is doubtful that a resident herd inhabits the Selkirks south of the border at this time.

Other species found in the Selkirks include elk, white-tail deer, mule deer, moose, bighorn sheep and mountain goats. The most plentiful of those are white-tails, though moose are also abundant. During the season of hiking I enjoyed in 2003, I never once saw a mountain goat or a bighorn sheep, but they are present in the range. Other predators include mountain lion, bobcat, Canada lynx and smaller animals like marten, fisher and wolverine. Bird life is rich in the Selkirk Mountains, including a host of hawks, owls, grouse and waterfowl.

The area's waters are full of fish with cutthroat trout inhabiting many high mountain lakes and streams. The larger lakes and rivers are home to a wide variety of fish, only a few of which are native. Those species include bull trout and white sturgeon, both of which appear on the federal endangered species list. Sturgeon are found in the Kootenai River below Libby Dam in Montana and Idaho. The greatest remaining stronghold for bull trout in the entire nation may

Wolves still survive — or at least range into — the Selkirks

well be Lake Pend Oreille and its tributaries, despite dams on the Clark Fork River that have blocked their migratory patterns for half a century.

And speaking of Lake Pend Oreille, the world-record Gerard rainbow trout (also known as kamloops), weighing in at over 37 pounds, came from these waters. Another large fish that has been pulled from these waters was a mackinaw, or lake trout, in 1996. It weighed more than 43 pounds and is still the largest trout to ever come out of the lake.

Not much of the Selkirk Mountains south of the border remain undeveloped in some way in the 21st century. Almost every drainage has a road system; mining or logging or both has taken place on most every hillside. After the fur industry dwindled, these were the activities that helped establish communities and supported families in this region. Mining is next to nonexistent now, and timber management, at least on public lands, has diminished significantly over the past 10 years. Two reasons for that is the desire on the part of society to protect wildlife habitat and the realization that water quality needs to be safeguarded by protecting watersheds.

Today, some areas are set aside specifically for those purposes and others. In 1984 the United States Congress created the Salmo-Priest Wilderness in the extreme northeast corner of Washington. It encompasses 39,937 acres of rugged mountains crowned by the 7,309-foot summit of Gypsy Peak. It generally lies along two main ridgelines wrapping around the headwaters of Sullivan Creek and the South Salmo River. Wild areas adjacent to the wilderness include the Upper Priest River, Grassy Top Mountain, through which a national recreation trail wends, and the highlands of Abercrombie Mountain (7,308 feet) west of the Pend Oreille River.

The most spectacular terrain of the American Selkirks is found along the Selkirk Crest between Sandpoint and Bonners Ferry, Idaho. The greatest concentration of high peaks is found here with more than a dozen exceeding 7,000 feet. These granitic uplands harbor a host of sparkling alpine lakes, and through the valleys and across the ridges are hundreds of miles of trails.

Across the landscape in the United States are numerous areas that have been proposed for wilderness designation by one party or another. Wilderness advocates have identified almost 300,000 additional acres that could be protected that way. Included in those proposals are 56,000 acres that could be added to the Salmo-Priest, 50,000 acres from Little Grass Mountain to Grassy Top and 40,000 acres on Abercrombie and Hooknose, among others. Legislation designed to protect these areas and more as wilderness called the Northern Rockies Ecosystem Protection Act has been before Congress for several years. In 2003 the bill had more than 170 sponsors.

Not to be forgotten are the vast wildlands in the Canadian portion of the Selkirks, where the wildest and most dramatic terrain is to be found. North of the border are such gems as Canada's Glacier National Park, Mount Revelstoke National Park, the Valhallas, Kokanee Glacier, West Arm and Stagleap.

Recreation

Fishing. Hunting. Camping. Boating. Off road four-wheeling. Skiing. Swimming. Horseback riding. Mountain biking. Rock climbing. These are all activities for which people flock to the Selkirk Mountains, but this book is primarily about another form of recreation – hiking. Trails are scarcer north of the border, but across the Kaniksu National Forest in Washington and Idaho, which these days is administered by the Colville and Idaho Panhandle national forests, there is an expansive system of trails. The American Selkirks are laced with nearly 200 trails. These trails are not all maintained the same; some will be in excellent shape, and others will be poorly marked and crowded with brush. Some will be gentle meanders through a shady forest, and others will be brutal climbs to sweeping, mountaintop panoramas. Throughout the region there are hikes suitable to people of all abilities, and there are trails for various types of enjoyment.

Horseback riding is a good way to see the Selkirks, as this rider on Sherlock Peak can attest

It is important that all trail users share the great outdoors with others in attitudes of respect and common courtesy. Some trails are specifically designated for hikers alone, but others are open to mountain bikes or horses, and still others are identified for motorized use, so those who dig dirt bikes and four-wheelers can enjoy their sport. It is big country out there and there is room enough for us all. Share the trail.

Camping opportunities abound along these trails, from developed campsites with RV hookups and paved access to semi-primitive sites with picnic tables and fire pits to primitive backcountry sites for which "Leave No Trace" practices are essential to preserving the wild character of the landscape. Just remember to always pack out whatever you pack into the forest. Enjoy yourselves, have fun and leave it better than when you found it. The abundant natural resources of the Selkirk Mountains have served people in a variety of ways for two centuries, and for Native Americans much longer than that. Timber and minerals, fish and game, sustenance, both physical and spiritual, have met peoples' needs for centuries. Those needs are still being met today for anyone willing to venture into the mountains.

From the easy nature trail at Hanna Flats west of Priest Lake to the miles and miles of narrow rugged tread in Long Canyon northwest of Bonners Ferry, the wild Selkirks beckon to be explored.

Conservation

Our Fragile Home

Food. Water. Clothing. Shelter. Those are pretty much the basic elements of survival for us humans. Take care of the necessities and the rest of life falls into place, like recreation, for instance. People love to play and where we play is often at the beach or in the mountains. Who doesn't enjoy a summer day on the water or on a high peak? As long as we've got food and water and can come home to a change of clothing, we're as happy as, say, a moose standing chest deep in lily pads at Lookout Lake, or a bear with its nose in an anthill, or a pileated woodpecker perched on the side of a giant, old, decadent cedar crawling with luscious insects.

Spiders often spin their delicate webs across trails, like this one on the South Fork of Silver Creek

This brings to mind what we are not always mindful of. We can leave our shelters, carry food and drink with us, and go spend a day or a week or even just a few hours in our favorite playgrounds and then go home again without a second thought for moose, bear, woodpecker or any other creature whose homes we just invaded for a bit of fun. You see, when we head to the lake or to the mountains, we enter a world where wild creatures live, where natural processes have shaped the way things are for thousands of years. In little over a century, though, we have dramatically altered those processes and things aren't shaped quite the same way they were before we went out to play.

Since the last shards of ice melted after the continental glaciers receded, life evolved in the Selkirks with very little interference from man. Forests grew, fires burned and animals adapted to their favorite habitats. Do you realize that in some isolated parts of the Selkirks only four or five generations of trees have come and gone in the last 10,000 years? I have read that some of the ancient cedars along the Upper Priest River and in the Salmo Basin could be as much as 2,000 years old, and one report even suggested the largest and most enduring might approach 3,000 years of age. If so, that tree's great grandfather may have witnessed the melting of the northern ice.

Then our ancestors came along in 1880 or thereabouts and built railroads and cities and went to work digging for precious minerals and felling whole stands of timber. Roads were pushed into just about every remote corner of the mountains, trails were constructed, and in no time we had access to virtually every stream, lake and peak. It is that access we enjoy today when we go recreating.

Jan Griffitts and Nicky Pleass, both low impact hikers, attempt to move a boulder above Fault Lake

The remarkable thing is, despite the rapid development and harvest of natural resources and our insatiable lust for outdoor frolics, the wild animals that inhabited this landscape persisted, for the most part. We have roads and trails going everywhere, we have taken out many of the big old trees, filled in too many spawning beds with sediment, built our homes in the choicest feeding areas, and put campgrounds and picnic tables and toilets at every lake, but still the animals have survived; some just barely, though.

Which brings me to the point I am trying to make. It is up to all of us individually to do what it will take to ensure animals have adequate food, water, clothing and shelter – in a word, habitat. We have made such inroads into the forests and valleys of the Selkirk Mountains that many wild residents are on the verge of dying off altogether here: woodland caribou, grizzly bears, Canada lynx, bull trout. And who's to say what disappears next, if they go? Elk? Mule deer? Cutthroats? We are loving the Selkirks to death, and though many natural resources are renewable, they don't renew at a speed that can keep up with the frantic pace of human activity.

When I told Pat Hart I was writing a book on the trails of the Selkirk Mountains, she was a bit less than enthusiastic about it. Pat works for the U.S. Forest Service and is responsible for the trails in the Bonners Ferry Ranger District. She has witnessed the exponential increase in human activity in these mountains and has seen firsthand the degradation that has taken place because too many of us are careless. She insisted that at the least I tell people how fragile this ecosystem is. It is a special place in the "Lower 48," and if we trample and trash it into submission, there will be nowhere left in the continental United States for animals like the woodland caribou.

What can we do? It's pretty simple, really. Consider you are going to someone else's home and treat it with respect. Pick up your trash and the trash of other less-considerate people. Give animals a wide berth, and don't intimidate them or cause them unnecessary stress. They have enough to deal with just trying to survive the rigors of life in the wild. Be careful what you do next to streams and lakes. Water is the very source of life, not just for wild inhabitants but for ourselves as well. If you and I aren't careful to keep it clean and pure, who will? Utilizing established trails is great, but be aware erosion is easy to cause by cutting switchbacks or taking motorized equipment where it doesn't belong.

Courtesy and respect, for one another and for the landscape we love so much to explore and utilize for our own pleasures: Those are pretty much the basic elements for the survival of the wild Selkirk Mountains, its forests and wildlife. If we each do our part, we just might be able to recreate to our hearts' content in this place of unparalleled beauty and mystique.

• • •

Want to get involved? Here are some regional conservation groups.

Alliance For the Wild Rockies
P.O. Box 8731
Missoula, MT 59807
(406) 721-5420
www.wildrockiesalliance.org

Idaho Conservation League
P.O. Box 9783
Moscow, ID 83843
(208) 882-1010
www.wildidaho.org

Inland Northwest Land Trust
35 W. Main Ave., Ste. 210
Spokane, WA 99201
(509) 328-2939 or (208) 255-4997
www.inlandnwlandtrust.org

Kettle Range Conservation Group
P.O. Box 150
Republic, WA 99166
(509) 747-1663
www.kettlerange.org

The Lands Council
423 W. First Ave., Ste. 240
Spokane, WA 99201
(509) 838-4912
www.landscouncil.org

North Idaho Audubon Society
P.O. Box 3028
Bonners Ferry, ID 83805
(208) 267-5842

Selkirk Conservation Alliance
P.O. Box 1809
Priest River, ID 83856
(208) 448-2971
www.scawild.org

Upper Columbia River Sierra Club
P.O. Box 413
Spokane, WA 99210
(509) 838-9022
www.idaho.sierraclub.org/uppercol/index2.html

Section I:

Between the Columbia River and Pend Oreille River

The Lay of the Land

The mightiest of western rivers in North America drops south out of Canada into the northeast corner of Washington State. Traveling in a southwesterly direction, the Columbia is already a huge river when it enters the United States. It drains whole regions of the Canadian Rockies, all of the northern Selkirks and Purcells, the Monashees and other mountain ranges stretching northward into the vast Canadian wilderness. Its first named tributary in the States is Tom Bush Creek, a brook barely two miles long. But just north of the border, in British Columbia, a large river in its own right joins the Columbia.

Barely a mile above the 49th parallel, after 110 miles in the United States, the Pend Oreille River makes a hairpin turn west and flows into Canada's Columbia without a passport. For 80 miles it flows practically due north, and then it is as though the Pend Oreille got tired of bucking the trend of most other rivers in the region of heading south, west, or at least northwest and chose to spill its waters into the Columbia.

Folded into the landscape encompassed by the Columbia and Pend Oreille rivers is a portion of the Selkirk Mountains that doesn't get a lot of attention from recreationists, especially hikers. From Newport, Washington on the Idaho state line, where the Pend Oreille first turns northward, to Fort Spokane where the Columbia absorbs the current of the Spokane River, is a distance of a hundred miles. At the Canadian line, the two rivers are 13 miles apart. Inside that giant triangle is a region of prairies, ponderosa pine forests, rivers, lakes and hills that all seem to squeeze into a point at Abercrombie Mountain. This is the highest summit in the Selkirks between the Columbia River and the Pend Oreille River at 7,308 feet.

Most of the south end of this area is outside public ownership, and there aren't a great many places to hike. The major exception to this is at Mount Spokane State Park, which has 100 miles of hiking trails. Otherwise, the area is home to the Spokane Indian Reservation, Lake Roosevelt National Recreation Area, David Thompson's Spokane House and small communities scattered across the sparsely wooded rolling hills. Interestingly, the Colville River, much like its nearby cousin the Pend Oreille, flows northward and slightly west to its confluence with the Columbia near Kettle Falls, Washington. Barely 2 miles southwest of Newport, the Little Spokane River exits from a small lake and drives nearly due south until it turns west to join its big brother, the Spokane.

In the middle of all this is the Little Pend Oreille River. It drains the central part of this section of the Selkirks in a southwesterly fashion into the Colville. East and north of this stream is where national forest lands begin to dominate the landscape, and though that means countless miles of logging roads and countless acres of clear-cuts, it also means trails and some pristine nuggets of backcountry that remain wild.

The primary route through the heart of this country is Washington State Highway 20, also known as the Tiger Highway. It crosses the Columbia at Bens Spring west of Kettle Falls, passes through Colville and snakes up into the mountains surrounding the Little Pend Oreille Lakes. At Tiger Meadows the highway heaves over a low divide and descends to the historic town site of Tiger and bends south along the Pend Oreille River to Usk, Cusick and Newport. In Colville the Aladdin Highway (County Road 9435) and the Deep Creek-Boundary Highway (County Road 9445) provide access to the west side of this section all the way to Silver Creek. At Tiger, Highway 31 ventures north to Ione, Metaline and Metaline Falls. Connecting Usk to Chewelah is a beautiful mountain road called Flowery Trail. On this route is located 49 Degrees North Ski Resort. Along the southernmost edge of this section of the Selkirks are the Spokane River and Interstate 90 connecting the large cities of Coeur d'Alene, Idaho and Spokane, Washington. Access northward from Spokane is on Highway 2 to Newport or Highway 395 to Colville.

Compared to other parts of the American Selkirks, this section does not contain a lot of hiking opportunities, but some great ones are still out there and one of the largest recreational trail systems found anywhere is here – the Batey-Bould and Little Pend Oreille ORV trails network. More than 135 miles of trails make up this network, and though all are open to motorized users (mostly dirt bikes, though some of it is also suitable for ATVs), many of these miles are terrific for horseback riders, mountain bikers and hikers as well.

Other than Abercrombie and Hooknose mountains, no other peaks surpass 7,000 feet here, and the majority are well under 6,000 feet. One of the largest unspoiled chunks of wildlands in the American Selkirks is in this section, spreading south of Sherlock Peak to Hooknose Ridge, encompassing more than 40,000 acres.

From the ski area on Chewelah Mountain to the Little Pend Oreille National Wildlife Refuge, from Gillette Ridge to Big Meadow Lake, from Tacoma Peak to the Abercrombie-Hooknose Proposed Wilderness, there is some mighty fine hiking to be discovered between the Columbia River and the Pend Oreille River in the Selkirks.

Abercrombie Mountain to Gillette Ridge

The northwestern-most corner of the American Selkirks lies along a narrow, jagged spine of high country that rivals any other part of the range for sheer, rugged beauty. Rising steeply above the Pend Oreille River and Boundary and Box Canyon dams is a ridge stretching from Baldy Mountain (one of four "Baldys" in the range) to Hooknose Ridge. At the height of this ridge are Hooknose Mountain (7,210 feet) and Abercrombie Mountain (7,308 feet). A system of five trails converges on these and other peaks, making up an area that has been lobbied for years for wilderness designation as the Abercrombie-Hooknose Wilderness. One trail climbs from the east side and the other four from the west.

Along the Pend Oreille River are other exceptional points of interest, including Crawford State Park and Gardner Cave, the viewpoints at both dams and a mountain goat viewing area just north of Metaline.

South of this block of wild land is the much tamer but certainly as beautiful Big Meadow Lake. Here you will find the only paved trail in all the Selkirks. Due west of that is the timbered uplands of Gillette Ridge and Mount Rogers. The trails are not plentiful here, but the destinations are spectacular.

Hooknose Mountain peeks above a dilapidated homestead near Metaline, Washington

Trails: Flume Creek No. 502, Abercrombie No. 117

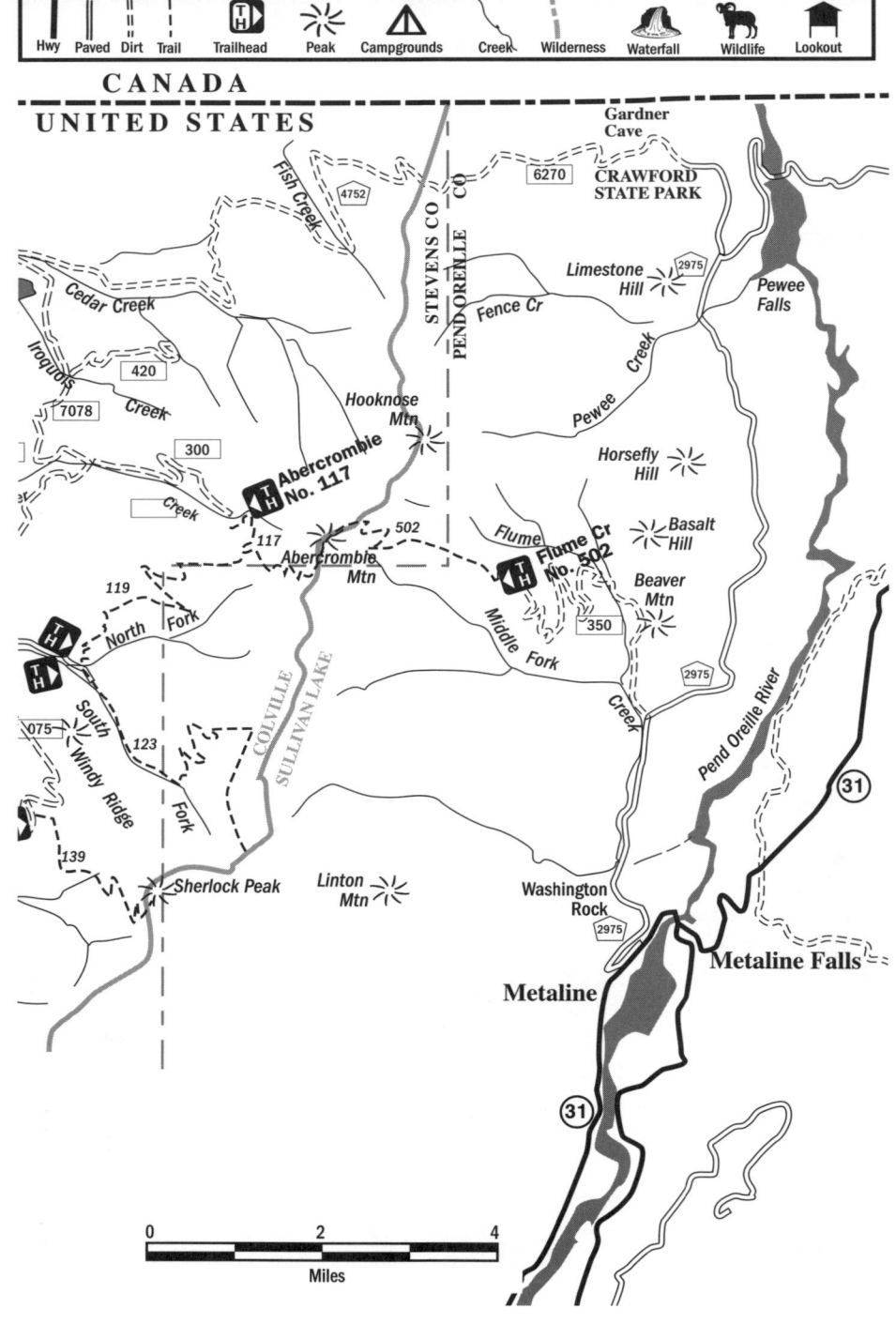

Flume Creek Trail No. 502

Destination: Abercrombie Mountain, 7,308 feet. *Map, page 46.*

Best Suited For: hiking, horseback riding, mountain biking

How Much Use: A Little * A Little More * **A LOT** * A Lot More * Excessive

What's it like? This is a truly magnificent trail. It starts out on an old roadbed for a short way along the north side of a ridge but soon gains the ridge top in a forest of lodgepole pine. The trail is quite flat here. Through the trees are filtered views of Hooknose Mountain. Soon the trail turns upslope at a gentle grade and climbs toward Abercrombie Mountain, the summit of which can be seen from time to time as you gain elevation.

Flume Creek drains the east side of Abercrombie Mountain

At the first big switchback, a space was leveled out long ago for a campsite near a seasonal brook, but it looks like the site has not been used much in recent years. Perhaps most campers continue to the top of the main ridge where another site is well used and the views are spectacular. However, there is no water nearby. The trail continues across the open east flank of Abercrombie, affording excellent views of the Pend Oreille Valley, the Salmo-Priest Wilderness and the Selkirk Crest far to the east. This trail ends at a junction high on the mountain, but Trail 117 goes the final 200 or 300 yards to the glorious top. From here you can see as far north as Kokanee Glacier and the Valhallas in British Columbia and westward to the Kettle River Range. But look south as well – nearly all of the American Selkirks are visible stretching into the hazy distance.

USGS Map: Abercrombie Mountain

Trailhead: At milepost 13.1 on Highway 31 less than one-half mile north of Metaline, Washington, turn on Boundary Road No. 2975 and go 3.7 miles to Road 350. Turn by an old dilapidated house on a curve and proceed across a powerline corridor. It is 7.5 miles to the end of the road and the trailhead. This is a narrow, rough road where you hope not to meet an oncoming vehicle. There is parking for three to five vehicles.

Trail Length: 4 miles one-way

Trail Condition: good

Elevation: Trailhead – 5,120', High Point/Low Point – 7,020' (junction with Trail 117), End – 7,308' (Abercrombie Mountain on Trail 117)

Estimated Duration of Hike: 2 to 3 hours up, 1.5 to 2.5 hours down

Sweat Index: buckets of sweat (difficult)

Mountain Bike Sweat Index: bathed in sweat (strenuous)

Best Features: rugged mountaintop, extraordinary vistas

Availability of Water Along the Trail: none (maybe a trickle in a small draw about 2 miles up early in the hiking season)

Stream Crossings: none

Campsites: A couple of campsites are located at the trailhead; an old site apparently not used much these days (it is kind of brushy) is located 2 miles up the trail on a switchback near a seasonal brook; and a good site is on the ridge top about 3 miles up the trail.

Alternate Hikes: This trail connects to Trail 117 on the south shoulder of Abercrombie Mountain a couple hundred yards from the top. A great off-trail hike from the campsite at the 3-mile mark takes you to the summit of Hooknose Mountain, 7,210 feet.

Wild Notes: Speaking of Hooknose – what an odd name, huh? Well, from Boundary Dam Road north of Metaline, the reason for the name is pretty obvious. Though from on top the summit's ridgeline seems rather straight and flat, from the valley below the cliff dropping steeply off the north face of the mountain accentuates a point of granite that hooks over the basin far below.

Abercrombie Mountain Trail No. 117

This is a Family Fun Hike

Destination: Abercrombie Mountain, 7,308 feet. *Map, page 46.*

Best Suited For: hiking, horseback riding, mountain biking

How Much Use: A Little * A Little More * **A LOT** * A Lot More * Excessive

What's it like? Abercrombie Mountain would probably like the U.S. Geological Survey to re-measure its elevation to be certain it's not really the highest peak in northeastern Washington. It misses that mark by a mere 12 inches, as Gypsy Peak in the Salmo-Priest Wilderness to the east eclipses its height by one foot. This trail is the shortest access to the summit of this magnificent high peak. It follows an old skid road that climbs quite steeply through an old overgrown clearcut to the ridgetop for 1.4 miles. From there it is level to slightly downhill for several hundred

Abercrombie Mountain

yards, crossing a shallow notch before beginning its brutal ascent into the sky. It is not all that bad, though. The trail switchbacks through sparse timber onto the shoulder of the mountain, then snakes along the steeply rising ridge to its rocky pinnacle. The views in every direction become increasingly fantastic. About one-quarter mile from the top is a junction with Trail 502. Note an old wooden sign nailed to a snag perhaps 50 feet to the east. At the top you will find a rock shelter and the remains of a forest fire lookout tower. It will be difficult to decide in which direction to look first. Hooknose Mountain (7,210 feet) is right in front of you to the northeast, and Sherlock Peak is just down the ridge to the south for close-ups. But beyond those mountains are the endless ridges of the Selkirks to the east, past the Pend Oreille River, the Salmo-Priest Wilderness, all the way to the Selkirk Crest. The Selkirk's most famous landmark, Chimney Rock, can even be seen from here. Westward you will gaze out over the Columbia River Valley to the Kettle River Range, and you won't be able to help but notice the Canadian border slicing across the hills to the northwest. The ascent from the trailhead to the ridge and the junction with Trail 119 is tough, but hardcore mountain bikers utilize this route for a terrific ride that forms a loop of almost 16 miles, over 7 miles of which are single-track heaven.

USGS Map: Abercrombie Mountain

Trailhead: In downtown Colville, Washington, turn east on Third Avenue (also Highway 20) and go just over a mile. Turn north on Aladdin Road (County Road No. 9435) and go approximately 23 miles to Deep Lake-Boundary Road No. 9445 and go northeast about 7 miles to Silver Creek. Turn east and go 1.9 miles to Road 7078 and take it and Road 300 for a total of 7 miles to the trailhead. The parking area will accommodate four to six vehicles, but it is a tight turnaround for trailers.

Trail Length: 3.5 miles one-way

Trail Condition: good

Elevation: Trailhead – 5,000', High Point/Low Point – 5,830' (junction with Trail 119), End – 7,308'

Estimated Duration of Hike: 2 to 3 hours up, 1.5 to 2.5 hours down

Sweat Index: buckets of sweat (difficult)

Mountain Bike Sweat Index: bathed in sweat (strenuous)

Best Features: high peaks, great views, proposed wilderness

Availability of Water Along the Trail: Several streams contain good water along the first three-quarters of a mile, but there is none after that.

Stream Crossings: two easy hops across small streams

Campsites: none

Alternate Hikes: Trail 119 connects to this trail about 1.4 miles from the trailhead. It descends to Silver Creek. Trail 502 from the Middle Fork of Flume Creek ties in with this trail near the summit.

Trails: North Fork Silver Creek No. 119, South Fork Silver Creek No. 123, Sherlock Peak No. 139

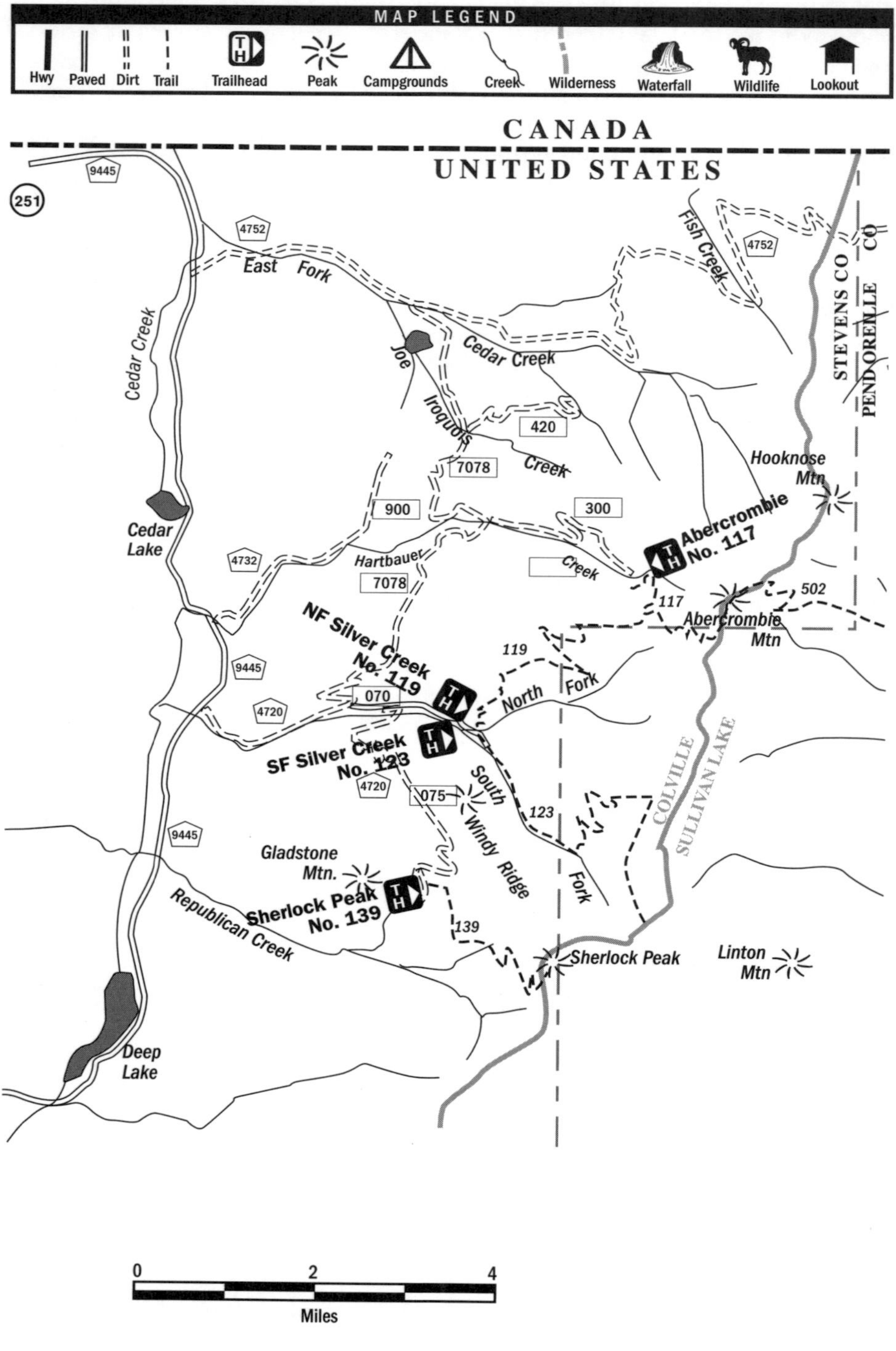

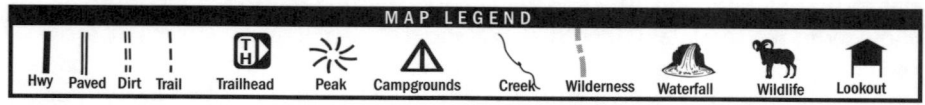

North Fork Silver Creek Trail No. 119

Destination: Abercrombie Mountain, 7,308 feet, via Trail 117. *Map, page 50.*

Best Suited For: hiking, horseback riding, mountain biking

How Much Use: A Little * A Little More * **A LOT** * A Lot More * Excessive

What's it like? Unlike its twin trail up the South Fork of Silver Creek, this trail launches a sustained climb as soon as it crosses over the North Fork. Whereas Trail 123 spends a couple of miles in the creek bottom, this trail rises sharply onto the brushy hillside overlooking the North Fork. Big, old-growth ponderosa pines and Douglas firs are scattered across this open mountainside for a couple of miles. Meadows full of ninebark and snowberry afford great views of the surrounding countryside. At times thickets of skinny Douglas fir saplings crowd out everything, including the views, but

In the North Fork of Silver Creek, looking at Sherlock Peak

they don't last. And they are replaced higher on the slope by fabulous groves of aspens. Aspens are, in fact, common along much of the way, but particularly notice the stand of pure aspen about 3 miles up the trail. It is truly beautiful. A half-mile farther is a small spring that might have enough flow for replenishing water bottles. A curious oddity maybe 4.5 miles up the trail is an old wooden gate affixed to a couple of trees. Perhaps at one time it was meant to prevent cattle from heading down the trail. And not far from that is an obvious trail junction on a switchback, but this is not the trail you want to take. Continue around the switchback. It is still nearly another mile to the junction with Trail 117. There must have been an older trail here that traversed the mountainside because I saw it in several places. But it has been abandoned and partially obliterated. Finally, on the ridgeline nearly 6 miles and over 2,800 feet later, you will come to the well-signed junction with Trail 117. From there it is 1.8 miles (and another 1,300 vertical feet) to the summit of Abercrombie. I might have rated Trail 119 unsuitable for mountain bikes until I saw the tracks of several bikes in the dusty tread. Apparently hardy bikers take Trail 117 to its junction with 119, then take it down to Silver Creek.

USGS Map: Abercrombie Mountain

Trailhead: In downtown Colville, Washington turn east on Third Avenue (also

Highway 20) and go just over a mile. Turn north on Aladdin Road (County Road No. 9435) and go approximately 23 miles to Deep Lake-Boundary Road No. 9445 and go northeast about 7 miles to Silver Creek. Take that road 3.2 miles to its end and the Silver Creek Trailhead. This is a large, partially developed site with camping, picnic tables, a vault toilet and hitching posts.

Trail Length: 5.9 miles to the junction with Trail 117; 7.7 miles to Abercrombie Mountain

Trail Condition: good

Elevation: Trailhead – 3,230', High Point/Low Point – 3,230'-5,830', End – 5,830' (junction with Trail 117)

Estimated Duration of Hike: 3.5 to 4.5 hours up, 3 to 4 hours down

Sweat Index: bathed in sweat (strenuous)

Mountain Bike Sweat Index: bathed in sweat

Best Features: high peaks, wonderful aspen groves, fabulous views, proposed wilderness

Availability of Water Along the Trail: one tiny trickle might have water late in summer about 3.5 miles up

Stream Crossings: none after the footbridge over the North Fork of Silver Creek

Campsites: The trailhead has several primitive, though partially developed, campsites.

Precautions: This area is open range for cattle.

Alternate Hikes: 5.9 miles from the Silver Creek trailhead this trail connects to Trail 117, which then climbs to the top of Abercrombie Mountain. Just below the summit Trail 117 connects to Trail 502, which comes in from the Middle Fork of Flume Creek on the east side of the mountain.

South Fork Silver Creek Trail No. 123

ACCESSIBLE: The Silver Creek Trailhead is a rustic, but accessible facility with lots of parking, a handicapped-accessible vault toilet and picnic tables. The first few hundred yards of Trail 123 may also be accessible to some disabled people.

Destination: Gunsight Pass. *Map, page 50.*

Best Suited For: hiking, horseback riding

How Much Use: A Little * A Little More * **A LOT** * A Lot More * Excessive

What's it like? The first 2 miles along the South Fork of Silver Creek is a magnificent walk through a beautiful forest of birch and aspen, larch, Douglas fir and cedar. The creek flows noisily nearby. The trail climbs gradually among lodgepole pine and, like its nearby neighbor, Trail 139, the forest floor is covered with thimbleberry bushes in places. The timber is dense, so there are no panoramic views until about the 6-mile mark where a spur trail branches off to a vista point. For almost one-quarter mile, the trail descends a ridge to a rocky outcropping with a marvelous view of the South Fork, Gunsight Pass and Sherlock Peak. The main trail continues for another mile or so from that junction to a high spot above the pass where a barely discernible trail sneaks off through the brush toward Abercrombie Mountain. Down in the pass 200 feet below, the official trail ends but another primitive trail continues out toward Sherlock Peak. Mountain bikers would enjoy the first 2 miles of this trail and maybe the hardiest bikers would find the challenge of the other 5 miles interesting as well.

Looking toward Gunsight Pass below Sherlock Peak

USGS Map: Abercrombie Mountain

Trailhead: In downtown Colville, Washington turn east on Third Avenue (also Highway 20) and go just over a mile. Turn north on Aladdin Road (County Road No. 9435) and go approximately 23 miles to Deep Lake-Boundary Road No. 9445 and go northeast about 7 miles to Silver Creek. Take that road 3.2 miles to its end and the Silver Creek Trailhead. This is a large, partially developed site with camping, picnic tables, a vault toilet and hitching posts. Note that a sign at a fork 1.9 miles up Silver Creek Road erroneously identifies this trail as No. 129.

Trail Length: 7 miles one-way

Trail Condition: good

Elevation: Trailhead – 3,230', High Point/Low Point – 3,230'-5,500', End – 5,500 (Gunsight Pass)

Estimated Duration of Hike: 3 to 4 hours up, 2.5 to 3.5 hours down

Sweat Index: buckets of sweat (difficult)

Mountain Bike Sweat Index: no sweat (easy) the first 2 miles, then strenuous or not suitable after that

Best Features: beautiful forest hiking, mountain views

Availability of Water Along the Trail: There is good water along much of this trail, including two small springs high on the mountainside, one just below the final switchback and the last about 100 yards past the junction of the vista trail about 6 miles up.

Stream Crossings: The trail crosses the South Fork of Silver Creek twice in the first mile, then has another easy crossing about 2 miles up, plus several boggy spots.

Campsites: The trailhead has several primitive, though partially developed, campsites.

Precautions: This area is open range for cattle.

Alternate Hikes: Trails 123 and 119 share this trailhead. At the end of Trail 123, primitive trails head south toward Sherlock Peak and north up onto a ridgeline toward Abercrombie Mountain.

Sherlock Peak Trail No. 139

This is a Family Fun Hike

Destination: Sherlock Peak, 6,365 feet. *Map, page 50.*

Best Suited For: hiking, horseback riding, mountain biking

How Much Use: A Little * **A LITTLE MORE** * A Lot * A Lot More * Excessive

What's it like? Miners did some extensive exploration up here at one time, and so old roads crisscross the mountainsides near the trailhead. In fact, the trail follows an old mining road for 2.3 miles to the single-track trail, which then climbs steadily upslope through lodgepole pine. Interestingly, the forest floor here is carpeted with more thimbleberry bushes than I have ever seen. But higher up, the forest thins out and the views are dramatic. On the ridge top a trail to the right ascends a steep slope to a bench that affords a breathtaking view of Sherlock Peak with Abercrombie and Hooknose in the background. On this bench is a camp where I found the remains of a wooden cross with the inscription, "Year of our Lord 2000 I Mark Arbia buried my fingertip on this spot." The

Sherlock Peak

splintered cross is now in the woodpile. The trail to the peak branches off to the left at the fork and meanders gradually up a pleasant ridge to a final, stiff scramble to the top. The 360-degree view is magnificent. Mountain bikers would enjoy the first couple miles along the old road at the start of this trail, but the single-track is increasingly steep and less suitable.

USGS Map: Deep Lake, Metaline

Trailhead: In downtown Colville, Washington, turn east on Third Avenue (also Highway 20) and go just over a mile. Turn north on Aladdin Road (County Road No. 9435) and go approximately 23 miles to Deep Lake-Boundary Road No. 9445 and go northeast about 7 miles to Silver Creek. Turn east and travel 1.9 miles to a fork. Bear right on Road 070 for one-half mile, then go right again on Road 075. It is 4.7 miles on this steep, narrow, rough road to the trailhead. A small parking area accommodates 4 to 6 vehicles.

Trail Length: 3.5 miles to official end of trail, 4 miles to the peak

Trail Condition: excellent

Elevation: Trailhead – 4,500', High Point/Low Point – 4,500'-6,365', End – 6,365'

Estimated Duration of Hike: 2 to 3 hours up, 1.5 to 2.5 hours down

Sweat Index: break a sweat (moderate)

Mountain Bike Sweat Index: no sweat (easy) at first, then perhaps not suitable the last mile

Best Features: mountaintop vistas

Availability of Water Along the Trail: none

Stream Crossings: none

Campsites: none with water, but there is a hunters' camp at the end of the trail on a ridgeline bench

Alternate Hikes: The Forest Service-maintained trail ends on the ridge top where the trail forks three ways. The left fork goes one-half mile up the ridge to the summit; the right fork goes a hundred feet steeply up a hill to a hunters' camp, and the middle fork is a rough trail most often used by horsemen that cuts maybe 3 miles across the east side of Sherlock to Gunsight Pass and connects to South Fork Silver Creek Trail No. 123.

Wild Notes: Thimbleberry (*Rubus parviflora*) is in the Rose family. It is a low shrub that grows in thick patches, and when it flowers all at once the forest can look as though it is arrayed in blankets of white. The fruit is a red achene resembling a thimble. It is very tasty and sweet, though it goes to seed quickly.

Trails: Meadow Creek Trail No. 125, Big Meadow Lake Trail No. 120

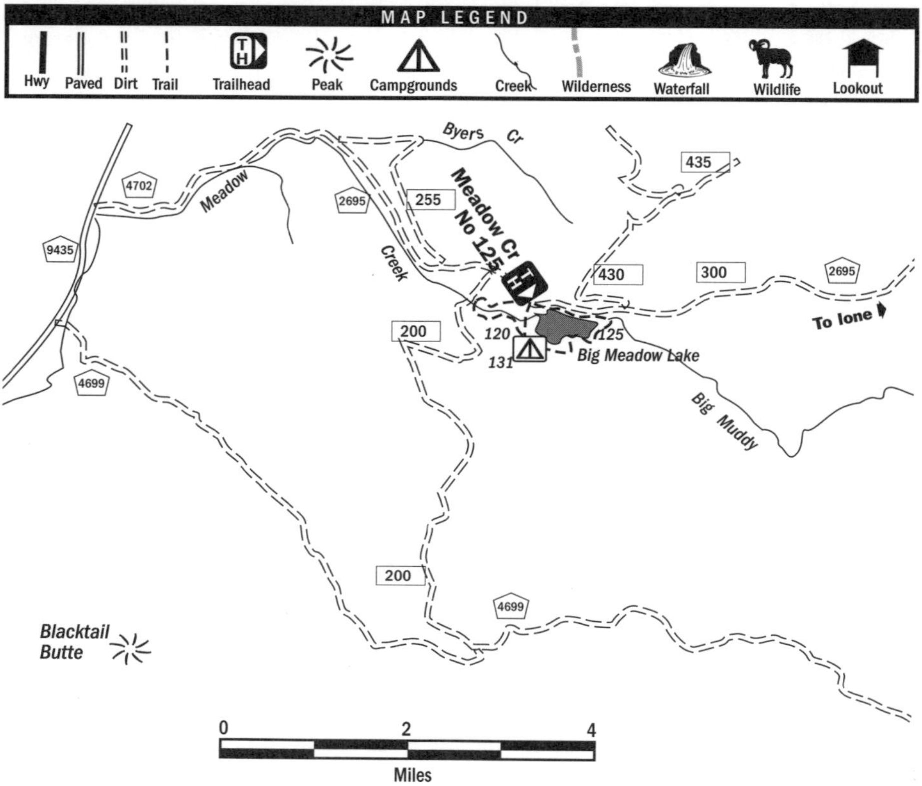

Big Meadow Lake

Meadow Creek Trail No. 125 and Big Meadow Lake Trail No. 120

ACCESSIBLE: A paved loop trail nicely accommodates wheelchairs, and the campground is largely barrier-free.

This is a Family Fun Hike

Destination: Meadow Creek and Big Meadow Lake. *Map, page 56.*

Best Suited For: hiking, mountain biking

How Much Use: A Little * A Little More * A Lot * **A LOT MORE** * Excessive

What's it like? The wild surroundings of low, forested hills and a nicely designed recreation area make Big Meadow Lake a pleasant place to visit. A dike across the west end of a large meadow is what actually created the shallow lake, a 71-acre impoundment which has fish and is a good body of water for rafts, canoes and kayaks. The area is fenced to keep range cattle out, but it is not wholly effective. Nonetheless, the campsites are comfortable and the opportunity for short or longer hikes and bike rides are excellent. Trail 125 explores both sides of Meadow Creek and includes interpretive signs about wildlife in the area. It has several benches for relaxation and contemplation, and connects to a paved, handicapped-accessible trail. At the south end of the handicapped trail, below the lake and situated on the edge of a marshy meadow, is an elevated wildlife viewing platform. It is not unusual to see moose, deer, eagles, osprey and blue herons from here. Also connecting to 125 is a spur trail that goes to the Hess Homestead. A replica of early homesteaders' cabins has been erected on the site and is open to the public for use. It fronts the main road into the recreation area just a short distance from its entrance. Trail 120 explores the shoreline of the lake and also includes interpretive signs about wildlife, plus one about leeches in the lake. In 2003 this was a free use area, but posters indicated shrinking funding meant Big Meadow Lake would likely become a fee area in 2004. (Note: The forest map and Colville Ranger District trails booklet identifies these two trails as Nos. 120 and 125, but at the lake a sign indicates one of them is Trail 126.)

USGS Map: Aladdin Mountain

Trailhead: In downtown Colville, Washington turn east on 3rd Avenue (also Highway 20) and go just over a mile. Turn north on Aladdin Road (County Road No. 9435) and go approximately 17.5 miles to Meadow Creek Road. Travel 6.1 miles to the well-signed recreation area. In Ione, Washington, turn west off Highway 31 and follow Roads 2714 and 2695 approximately 7 miles to the recreation area.

Trail Length: There are about 3.5 miles of trails in this recreation area. Trail 125 is a 1.5-mile loop along Meadow Creek, and Trail 120 is a 1.5-mile loop around the lake. There is also a paved, fully accessible loop trail about one-quarter mile in length and a one-quarter mile spur trail to the old Hess Homestead from Trail 125.

Trail Condition: good

Elevation: Trailhead – 3,430' (at campground), High Point/Low Point – 3,390' (crossing of Meadow Creek), 3,450' (along road 2695) End – 3,430'

Estimated Duration of Hike: 30 minutes to 2 hours on any of these loops

Sweat Index: no sweat (easy)

Mountain Bike Sweat Index: no sweat

Best Features: lake, wildlife, historic cabin (replica)

Availability of Water Along the Trail: Because of the presence of livestock around this lake, it is recommended that you bring your own water.

Stream Crossings: A footbridge crosses Meadow Creek on Trail 125.

Campsites: There are 16 developed campsites at the recreation area with picnic tables and fire rings. Several vault toilets are available.

Precautions: Swimming in the lake should be carefully considered, as there are leeches and, despite fencing designed to keep them out, cows often breech the fence and utilize much of the shoreline.

Alternate Hikes: Each loop trail can be done individually or the whole system can be enjoyed in 2 to 3 hours.

Wild Notes: The Hess family homesteaded this area in the early 1900s. All that is left now of their efforts to establish a life along Meadow Creek are the rotting ruins of their home, some scattered fruit trees and the clearing they struggled to create, which is now growing back thickly into lodgepole pine. A replica of what their cabin, and the homes of other settlers of the era, looked like is located near the ruins about one-quarter mile west of Big Meadow Lake.

Trails: Gillette Ridge Trail No. 131, Mount Rogers Loop No. 130

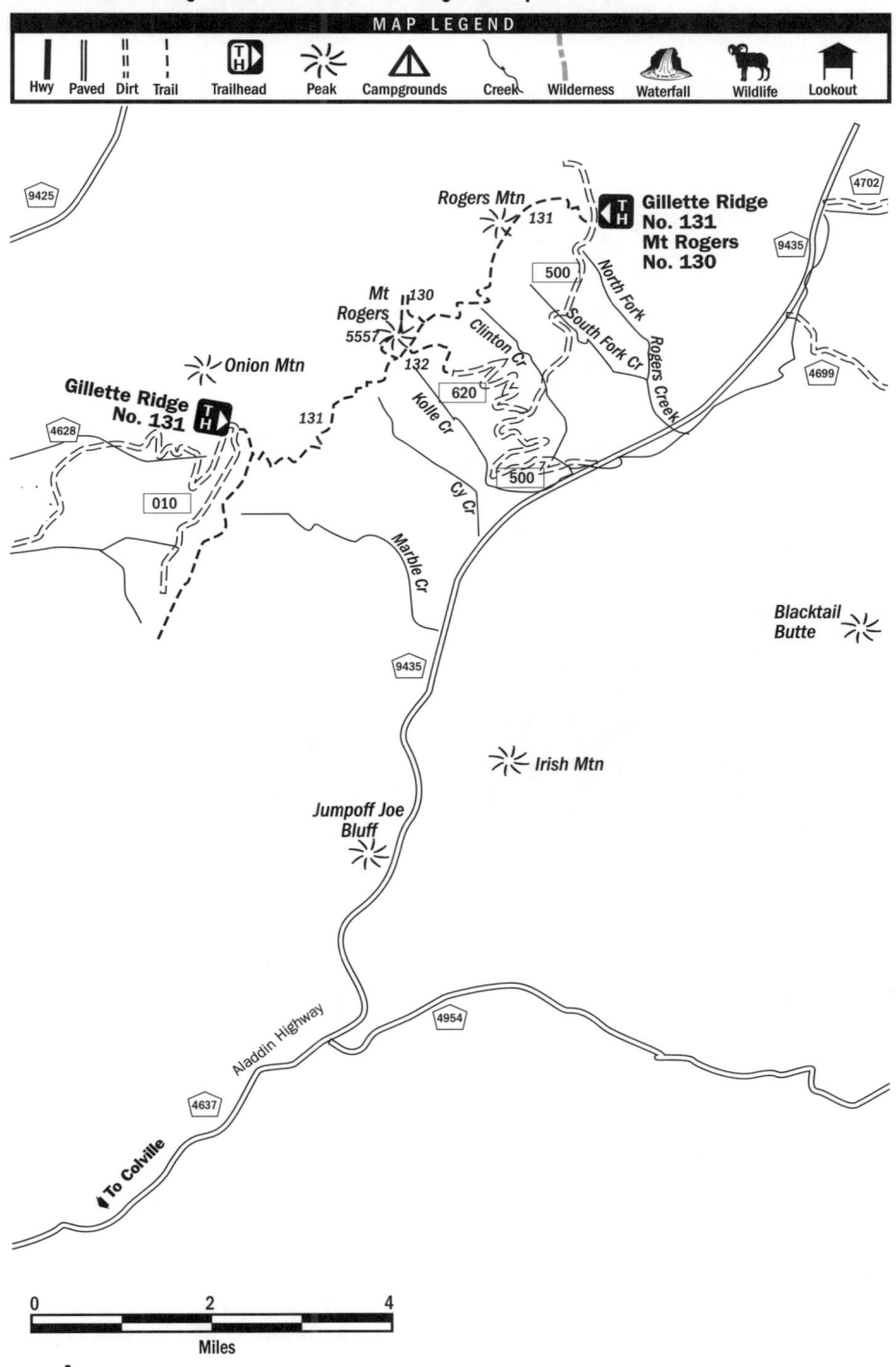

Gillette Ridge Trail No. 131 and Mount Rogers Loop Trail No. 130

Destination: Rogers Mountain, 5,775 feet, Mount Rogers, 5,557 feet and Gillette Ridge. *Map, page 59.*

Best Suited For: hiking, horseback riding, mountain biking

How Much Use: A Little * A Little More * **A LOT** * A Lot More * Excessive

What's it like? Using the best trailhead at the end of Road 500 as the starting point, this trail makes a steady climb to the top of Rogers Mountain. The forest is fairly dense at first, with some big, brushy openings interspersed along the way for terrific views to the east. Once near the ridgeline, stunted lodgepole pine takes over as the dominant tree. About one-half mile from the top, the trail crosses an old jeep track that once accessed the lookout that used to be at the summit. The

An old barn in the Aladdin Valley north of Gillette Ridge

view from on top is stupendous, especially down Onion Creek toward the Columbia River and across the valley to the Kettle Crest. A hundred yards down the jeep track from the top is an old sign indicating Kohley Creek Road (now spelled "Kolle" on the Colville Forest map) is 3 miles away and Clugston Creek is 8 miles. But the trail continues right over the summit and down the ridge into a deep saddle, past a dry meadow and on to the junction with the trail coming off Road 620 (Kolle Creek Road). From here for several miles are fine old-growth specimens of larch, Douglas fir, spruce and cedar in the fabulous forest draped over Mount Rogers and Gillette Ridge. Mount Rogers Loop Trail No. 130 cuts across the east and north sides of the peak on its way to the top, then drops back to Trail 131 just above another saddle. Another climb into a forest of skinny lodgepole pine finally comes to the junction with the trail from road 010 (about 0.6 miles from the fork in the trail). But Trail 131 continues another 3 miles out along Gillette Ridge to a dead end. These trails would be challenging on a mountain bike, but for the most part they appear to be suitable for experienced riders. By the way, note that there are two peaks here with the name Rogers – Rogers Mountain (5,775 feet), where the lookout used to stand, and Mount Rogers (5,557 feet), accessed by the loop trail.

USGS Map: Gillette Mountain, Spirit

Trailhead: In downtown Colville, Washington, turn east on Third Avenue (also Highway 20) and go just over a mile. Turn north on Aladdin Road (County Road No. 9435) and go approximately 14 miles and turn west onto Road 500. It is 6.4 miles to the end of the road and the trailhead for the northeast end of Trail 131. There is a big turnaround and room for eight to 10 vehicles in the parking area. About 3.5 miles along Road 500 is a junction with Road 620, which can be taken 2.7 miles to a trailhead access to Trail 132. This is a steep, narrow road with a small turnaround and room for only two or three vehicles. The southwest end of Trail 131 can be accessed by taking Highway 395 northwest of Colville about 2 miles to the Williams Lake Road. Go north on it approximately 6 miles then bear right onto Road 9425. Follow it almost 4 miles to Road 4628, which, after about 3 miles, becomes Forest Road 010, and about 2 miles farther accesses a trailhead. The road is narrow and brushy and there is room near the trailhead for only a couple of vehicles.

Trail Length: Trail 131 is 12.1 miles end to end. From the main trailhead on Road 500, it is 2.5 miles to the site of the old lookout on Rogers Mountain, 5.2 miles to the start of Mount Rogers Loop Trail No. 130 (which is 1.4 miles long), 6.3 miles to the trailhead at the end of Road 620, and 9.7 miles to the trailhead on Road 010.

Trail Condition: excellent

Elevation: Trailhead – 4,720' (north end at Road 500), 5,200' (south end at Road 010), High Point/Low Point – 5,775' (Rogers Mountain), End – 5,700' (south end on Gillette Ridge)

Estimated Duration of Hike: 1.5 to 5 hours one-way, depending on destination

Sweat Index: break a sweat (moderate)

Mountain Bike Sweat Index: bathed in sweat (strenuous)

Best Features: mountaintops, panoramic vistas, old-growth forest

Availability of Water Along the Trail: virtually none. There is one tiny spring on Trail 131 a few yards southwest of its junction with Trail 132 coming from Road 620.

Stream Crossings: none

Campsites: The Clinton Creek Forest Camp is a primitive campground with several good sites and water about 4 miles up Road 500.

Alternate Hikes: Trail 131, with its three access points, and Trail 130 offer several good loops ranging from 5 to 20 miles in length.

Crawford State Park and Gardner Cave

There is a remarkable surprise just waiting to be discovered in the far northwest corner of the American Selkirks, a surprise tucked away in the extreme northeastern corner of Washington. It was first discovered more than one hundred years ago by a man named Ed Gardner, but since 1921 thousands of others have rediscovered Gardner Cave at Crawford State Park near Metaline, Washington.

Just try to imagine what the region now known as the Selkirk Mountains looked like 500 million years ago. The high peaks and lush forests we see today did not exist. Geologists say this landscape was covered by a vast ocean full of primitive sea life. As these organisms died, their shells settled to the bottom in certain places and formed limestone ooze. As the millennia passed, this layer of ooze was buried under tremendous amounts of sediment. The pressure from the weight of the overlying sediments finally caused the ooze to metamorphose into rock, creating a layer known today as the Metaline Limestone.

Rumblings from deep in the earth as the crust began to move caused the bottom of this great sea to rise and buckle. The water drained away, exposing the sediments to the forces of nature. Much of the soft primitive rock eroded, bringing the limestone close to the surface. Limestone is also highly erodable. It dissolves easily in the acidic solution created when rainwater absorbs carbon dioxide, which comes primarily from the soil. Over time this weak acidic solution seeped into the limestone, slowly eating it away.

North of the small town of Metaline and barely one-quarter mile south of the Canadian border, the product of this geologic process formed what is now known to be the second-longest limestone cave in the state of Washington. Ed Gardner, who lived many years in the area and was known as a bootlegger, discovered the cave in 1899. A couple of decades later, in 1921, a man named William Crawford acquired the land around the cave, but, seeing the unique value of the cavern, he deeded 40 acres to the state to be preserved as a state park.

Since that time the cave has been thoroughly explored and developed into a major attraction. Almost half of the cave's 1,055 feet is open to the public. From the main entrance to a viewing platform, visitors wind their way along 494 feet of flowstone, rimstone pools, stalactites and stalagmites. The well-lighted path passes by remarkable formations such as the Christmas Tree, Fried Eggs and the Queen's Throne. But some of the most interesting things to see may be hidden away in dark corners, so bring a flashlight to probe the secrets of the cave. Cameras are welcomed, but remember you will likely need a flash. The temperature remains rather constant in this underground wonderland at 41 to 43 degrees. A jacket even in the height of summer is recommended.

Most important of all is that you resist the urge to touch the colorful walls. The oils in our skin will interfere with the age-long processes that have created the marvelous formations we find so dazzling, and taint their brilliance. Smoking is also not allowed in the cave, and pets must be left outside.

Crawford State Park and Gardner Cave is located 11 miles north of Metaline, which is about 60 miles north of Newport, Washington, via State Highways 20 and 31. To get to the park, go one-half mile north of Metaline and turn onto Boundary Dam Road. Follow that to the "Y" and bear left to the park. There are picnic tables and a comfort station near the parking area. A short, paved trail leads to the cave entrance. Access to the cave is with tour guides only. Tours begin at 10 a.m., 12 p.m., 2 p.m. and 4 p.m. during the summer months. The cave is closed on Tuesdays and Wednesdays. For more information call the park at (509) 446-4065 or visit www.parks.wa.gov/parks/.

Gardner Cave and the beauty of Crawford State Park is an experience suitable for people of all ages. It may truly be one of the most surprising secrets in the American Selkirks.

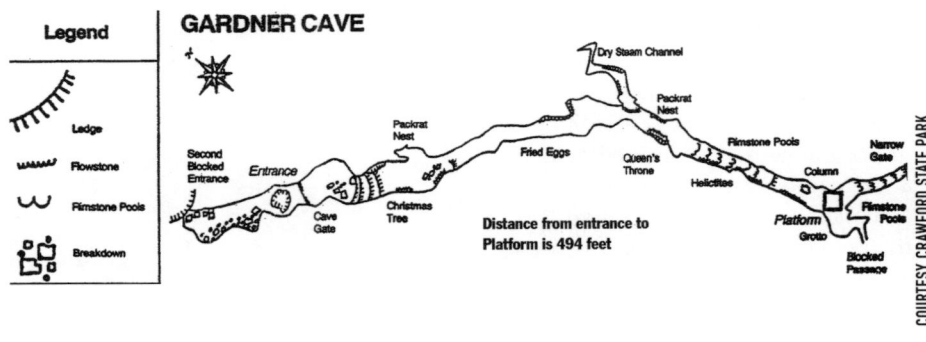

Little Pend Oreille Lakes to Newport

As the Selkirk Mountains spread south into undulating foothills, National Forest lands become less prevalent. However, between state-owned lands, a National Wildlife Refuge and what parcels of the Colville National Forest there are, you will find a vast expanse of terrain wide open for exploration. This terrain is bounded by the Pend Oreille River on the east and the Colville River on the west, both of which flow northward. The heart of this country is drained by two primary watersheds – the Little Pend Oreille River, which oddly enough flows into the Colville, and Calispell Creek, which flows into the Pend Oreille.

At the north end of this subsection is one of the biggest outdoor playgrounds in the range, the Little Pend Oreille Lakes Basin. On either side of a string of beautiful mountain lakes surrounded by forested hills rising to 5,000 feet or more is a network of trails and campgrounds for all kinds of recreationists. From Lake Sherry to Nile Lake and from Green Mountain to Granite Peak, this area offers limitless opportunities for outdoor enjoyment. South of here is the Little Pend Oreille National Wildlife Refuge. Set aside for the benefit of wildlife, it also serves as a great place to explore and discover fascinating tidbits about the natural world around us. The hills continue to roll south past 49 Degrees North Ski Resort on Chewelah Mountain and the small network of ORV trails in the Middle Fork of Calispell Creek. From there the Little Spokane River meanders southwesterly toward the southern limit of the range. Access is plentiful and easy with Washington State Highway 20 following the Little Pend Oreille River from Colville to Tiger. From this ribbon of asphalt and from Flowery Trail between Usk and Chewelah, all parts of this well-developed section of the Selkirks between the Columbia and the Pend Oreille are accessible to anyone needing a break in the great outdoors.

Coyote Rock above Frater Lake; recreation in winter is as big as in summer in the Little Pend Oreille Lakes Recreation Area

West of Calispell Lake is a small series of trails I did not get a chance to hike. It's the Middle Fork Calispell ORV Trail Nos. 313, 314 and 315. Designed primarily for motorized recreation, they are also open for hiking, mountain biking and horseback riding.

Little Pend Oreille National Wildlife Refuge

About 13 miles east of Colville, Washington, is a unique gem of outdoor recreational opportunities – or at least, it is unique within the National Wildlife Refuge system. The Little Pend Oreille National Wildlife Refuge is the only mountainous, mixed-conifer forest refuge in the United States outside Alaska. It sprawls across 40,198 acres of meadows, wetlands, old farm fields and forest habitats along the south side of the river for which it is named. Most refuges encompass wetlands, ponds and streams primarily for the rehabilitation and protection of waterfowl habitat. This refuge was established not only to enhance waterfowl populations but to recover the white-tailed deer population in the Little Pend Oreille Valley as well. It is hard to believe white-tailed deer were threatened at one time when you see how prolific they are now.

This refuge was designated in the early years of the creation of the refuge system that was conceived in 1935. In 1939 President Franklin D. Roosevelt established Little Pend Oreille NWR by Executive Order. Lands within the refuge were acquired through the Resettlement Administration, which retired marginal farmlands and moved families to more productive areas, through the purchase of properties from willing sellers and land exchanges with the Washington Department of Natural Resources. Today there is still about 9,400 acres of private property within the refuge, most of which is owned by Stimson Lumber Co. and Boise (formerly Boise Cascade).

Fur trappers were likely the first Europeans to come to this area. In fact, the name Pend Oreille was given to local Indians by French Canadian trappers because of the pendants they wore in their ears. Pend Oreille literally means "hanging ears." This area was settled from the 1890s through about 1925. More than a hundred homesteaders moved in along with several lumber companies. A railroad for the purpose of transporting logs was built into the valley in 1909 by Winslow Logging Company. The old grade, scattered railroad ties and decaying trestles can still be seen along the west side of the refuge over a distance of about 16 miles. The giant ponderosa pines that used to cover the valley were all sawn down and taken to a mill, either by rail or by log drives down the Little Pend Oreille River. There were once two schools on what is now the refuge, plus the Biarly Post Office.

Those homesteading days came to an end with the Depression of the 1930s, and with the resettlement of many farm families, some 27,000 acres were acquired and became the fledgling wildlife refuge. From 1,800 feet near the river at the refuge's west end to 5,610 feet atop Olson Peak on the east end, the refuge transcends half a dozen forest zones. Within these various habitats 196 species of birds have been documented, along with 58 mammals, six amphibians and eight reptiles. There are several lakes and ponds and more than 80 miles of streams harboring native and non-native fish alike. Native fish species include redband rainbow and cutthroat trout, red-sided shiner and sculpin. Other trout introduced to the area's waters include Eastern brook, coastal rainbow and German browns.

A network of roads, improved and primitive, provide access to the refuge, which has nine entry points. This access affords all kinds of recreational activities, such as viewing wildlife, photography, hiking, mountain biking, hunting and fishing. From Trilbey Falls on the Little Pend Oreille River to Bayley Lake to the subalpine forests of Olson Peak and McDonald Mountain, there is a lot to see and do in the Little Pend Oreille National Wildlife Refuge. The U.S. Fish and Wildlife Service manages the refuge, taking over in 1994 after the Washington Department of Natural Resources had controlled it for 30 years. A comprehensive plan for management of the refuge was completed in 2000. The Little Pend Oreille National Wildlife Refuge is one of 535 refuges in the nation, together making up the world's largest network of lands and waters devoted specifically to the protection of wildlife and the enhancement of wildlife habitat.

To get to the refuge headquarters from Colville, take Highway 20 east about 5.5 miles. Near milepost 360 turn south on Artman-Gibson Road and go 1.6 miles to a left hand turn on Kitt-Narcisse Road. Follow that for 2 miles to Bear Creek Road where you take a right and go 3.5 miles to the visitors' center. For more information you can write to Little Pend Oreille NWR, 1310 Bear Creek Road, Colville, WA 99114; call (509) 684-8384; or visit the refuge's website at http://littlependoreille.fws.gov.

MAP OF LITTLE PEND OREILLE NWR

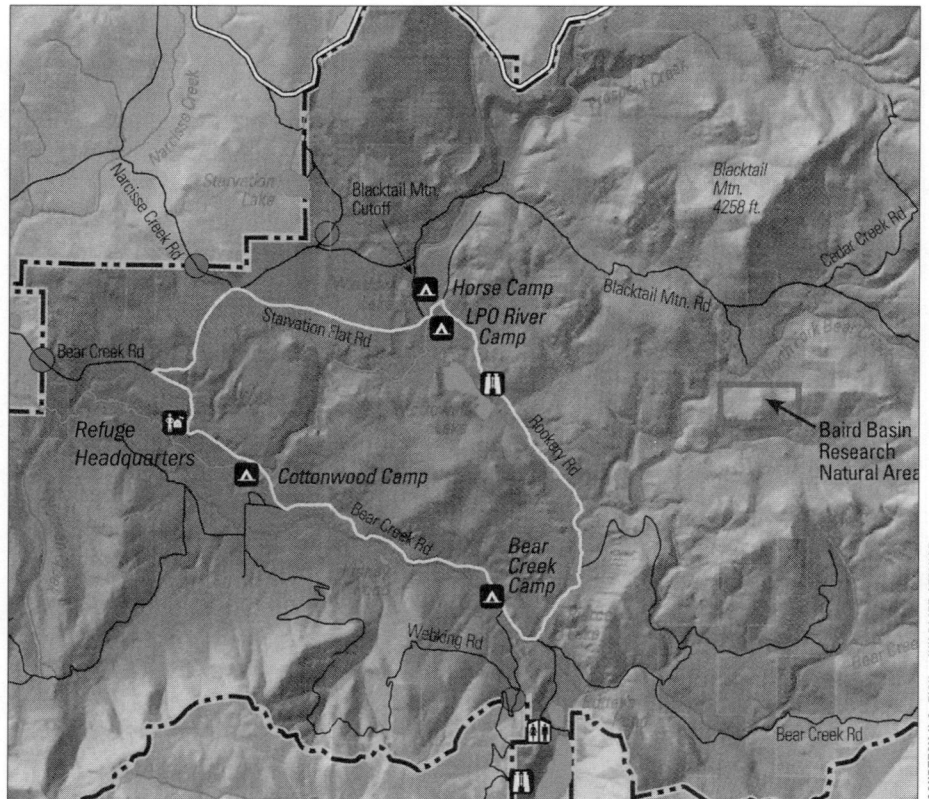

Trails: Little Pend Oreille Lakes Nos. 140, 142-146, 148, Frater Lake No. 150, Lake Leo No. 155, Granite Peak No. 145, Springboard No. 149, Rufus No. 148, Sherry No. 147

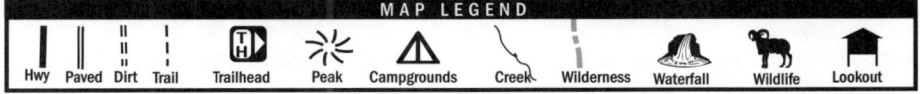

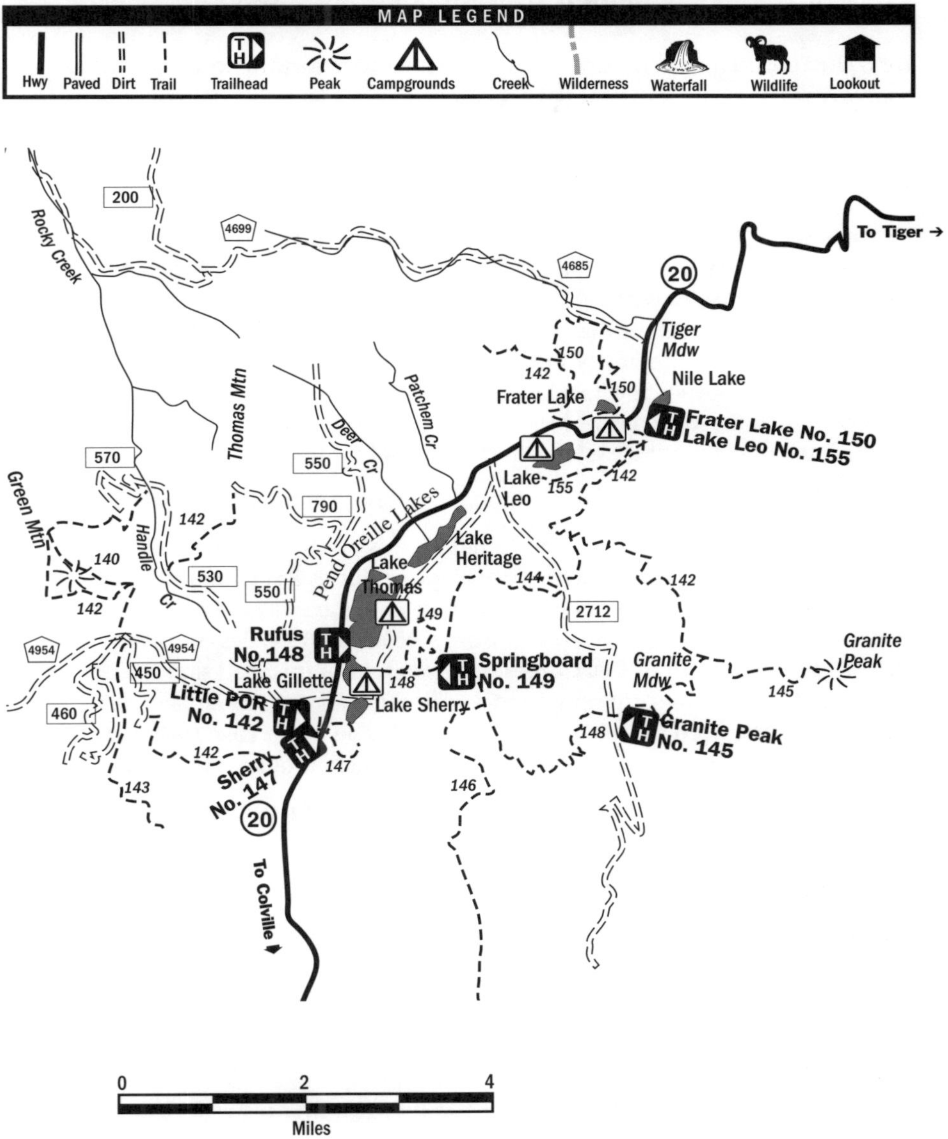

Little Pend Oreille Lakes Trails System Trail Nos. 140, 142-146, 148 and Thomas Mountain Trail No. 151

Destination: Little Pend Oreille Lakes Basin and surrounding terrain. *Map, page 67.*

Best Suited For: hiking, horseback riding mountain biking

How Much Use: A Little * A Little More * A Lot * **A LOT MORE** * Excessive

What's it like? From the heights of Thomas Mountain, Green Mountain and Granite Peak to the shores of Frater Lake and the brushy banks of the Little Pend Oreille River and everywhere in between, this trail system offers a huge variety of routes to explore. Much of this region is heavily timbered, but the trails often come out on rocky outcrops or open mountain slopes and provide wonderful views of the landscape. Spectacular displays of summer wildflowers and glimpses of wild animals like deer, elk or moose add to the enjoyment. This is one of the largest interconnected trail systems in the Selkirk Mountains.

USGS Map: Lake Gillette, Aladdin Mountain, Ione, Timber Mountain

Trailhead: There are several ways to get on this trail system. For Mill Creek, take Highway 20 east from Colville, Washington, about 25 miles and turn west onto County Road 4954. Go one-quarter mile to the trailhead. For Clark Creek (or Flodelle Creek), take Highway 20 east from Colville for 19 miles or so to County Road 2389. Turn north to Clark Creek and watch for a trailhead sign or turn south and go to Flodelle Creek Campground and a trailhead. For Frater Lake, take Highway 20 east from Colville almost 30 miles to the Frater Lake trailhead. There is ample parking at each of these access points, which require a fee for parking.

Trail Length: 67.5 miles total (refer to detailed forest maps to determine loops of various distances).

Trail Condition: variable from fair to excellent

Elevation: varies from 3,000 feet to more than 5,200 feet

Estimated Duration of Hike: an hour or two, a day hike, an overnighter or for a week, depending on how much ground you want to cover

Sweat Index: primarily break a sweat (moderate) to buckets of sweat (difficult)

Mountain Bike Sweat Index: runs the gamut from no sweat (easy) to bathed in sweat (strenuous)

Best Features: forest trails, views, wildlife

Availability of Water Along the Trail: Throughout the system there are numerous sources of water.

Stream Crossings: From boggy mud patches to rock hops, bridges and boardwalks, there are numerous wet areas to navigate, but all in all there is nothing too significant.

Campsites: There are primitive backcountry sites along the trails and several developed fee area campgrounds near all the trailheads.

Precautions: This entire system is open to motorized use, so hikers, mountain bikers and horsemen should be alert for dirt bikes and ATVs.

Alternate Hikes: 67.5 miles of trail in a variety of loops to choose from

Frater Lake Trail No. 150 and Lake Leo Trail No. 155

ACCESSIBLE: A large parking area is located near the shores of Frater Lake and there is a handicapped-accessible vault toilet available. The trails are rather narrow and rough surfaced, but immediately around the lake they may meet the most difficult accessibility standards.

These are Family Fun Hikes

Destination: Coyote Rock and other loops in the upper Little Pend Oreille Lakes basin. *Map, page 67.*

Best Suited For: hiking, mountain biking

How Much Use: A Little * A Little More * A Lot * **A LOT MORE** * Excessive

What's it like? These trails offer some beautiful forest hiking with great views of Frater Lake and Lake Leo. A cabin on the northwest shoreline of Frater Lake is open to the public. It is especially popular in the winter when these trails are occasionally groomed for cross-country skiing. The idea of this marvelously constructed warming hut was dreamed of and designed by Curt Heidlebaugh. A woodshed in the back, called The Guide Wood Shed, is dedicated to the memory

View of Frater Lake and its warming cabin after the lake has frozen over

of Guy McKee, a Forest Service employee from 1940 to 1992. Granite outcrops dot the forest terrain, the largest of which is Coyote Rock. There is a nice view looking down the Little Pend Oreille River valley from its pinnacle. These trails are largely suitable for people of all ages and offer some fine exploring among the pines, firs and larch.

USGS Map: Lake Gillette, Aladdin Mountain, Ione, Timber Mountain

Trailhead: From Colville, Washington, follow Highway 20 east almost 30 miles to the well-signed trailhead. A large parking area will handle more than 20 vehicles. A fee is required to park here.

Trail Length: The various loops of these two trails total 10 miles.

Trail Condition: excellent

Elevation: Frater Lake Trailhead – 3,210', High Point/Low Point – 3,483' (Coyote Rock), End – 3,210'

Elevation: Lake Leo Trailhead – 3,210', High Point/Low Point – 3,170' (by Lake Leo), End – 3,210'

Estimated Duration of Hike: 30 minutes to 2 hours depending on the loop

Sweat Index: break a sweat (moderate) for the most part

Mountain Bike Sweat Index: no sweat (easy) to buckets of sweat (difficult)

Best Features: lake views, wildlife

Availability of Water Along the Trail: Water can be taken from either lake, but it is best to bring your own.

Stream Crossings: nothing significant

Campsites: Lake Leo Campground, a developed fee area facility, is nearby.

Precautions: A portion of these trails, for about 2.25 miles, is shared by Trail 142, which is open to motorized use. Be watchful for dirt bikes.

Alternate Hikes: There are a variety of loops to explore here, plus these trails connect to Trail 142, which provides access to Thomas Mountain to the west or Granite Peak to the south.

Granite Peak Trail No. 145

Destination: Granite Peak, 5,238 feet. *Map, page 67.*

Best Suited For: hiking, horseback riding, mountain biking

How Much Use: A Little * A Little More * **A LOT** * A Lot More * Excessive

What's it like? The trail to Granite Peak branches off Trail 142 about 2.5 miles below the summit of the mountain. To get to it can be a long distance if starting on Trail 142/148 from Gillette Campground, but it is a nice hike through the forest all the way to road 2712. A wooden sign on Trail 148 indicates it is 9 miles to Granite Peak. At the road Trail 148 ends and Trail 142 crosses the road and goes a little over 2 miles to the fork. The terrain is broken and uneven, making for some interesting landscapes and views, but mostly the timber is thick until near the top of the mountain. The south flank of the mountain is dominated by open meadows, and the views south along the Pend Oreille River are excellent.

USGS Map: Ione, Timber Mountain

Trailhead: From Colville, Washington, follow Highway 20 east for almost 25 miles. Watch for the sign for Gillette Campground and turn right. Go one-half mile and enter the campground. The trailhead is on the north side. This trail is accessed via Trails 142 and 148. You can also get on this trail by staying on Highway 20 another 3.5 miles and take Lakeside Road to Road 2712, then follow 2712 approximately 3 miles or so to where Trail 142 crosses the road. This provides a shorter route to 145.

Trail Length: 9 miles one-way from Gillette Campground or 4.5 miles one-way from Road 2712.

Glacier lilies are ubiquitous throughout the Selkirks

Trail Condition: good

Elevation: Trailhead – 4,500' (Trail 142 at Road 2712), High Point/Low Point – 4,450' (junction of Trails 142 and 145), End – 5,238'

Estimated Duration of Hike: 3 to 4 hours each way from Gillette Campground or 1.5 to 2.5 hours each way from Road 2712.

Sweat Index: buckets of sweat (difficult)

Mountain Bike Sweat Index: bathed in sweat (strenuous)

Best Features: great views of the Pend Oreille River valley and surrounding mountainous landscapes

Availability of Water Along the Trail: Some water can be found along Trail 148 between the campground and Road 2712, but don't expect any above the road.

Stream Crossings: nothing significant

Campsites: dispersed primitive sites on Road 2712 or a developed fee area campground at Gillette Lake

Precautions: This trail is part of the Little Pend Oreille ORV trails system and is open to motorized use.

Alternate Hikes: Trail 145 branches from Trail 142 which nearly encircles the entire Little Pend Oreille Lakes basin and ties into numerous other trails.

Springboard Trail No. 149 and Rufus Trail No. 148

This is a Family Fun Hike

Destination: Thomas Mountain Overlook. *Map, page 67.*

Best Suited For: hiking only on Trail 149; horseback riding and mountain biking on Trail 148.

How Much Use: A Little * A Little More * **A LOT** * A Lot More * Excessive

What's it like? At Gillette Campground grab an interpretive brochure and follow the trail as it passes through a wooden fence, then forks. Pulling out straight ahead is Trail 142, slicing through the forest to a junction with Trail 148. This accesses miles and miles of trails in the Little Pend Oreille lakes trails system. It is a moderately easy climb through timber and undulating terrain to Road 2712 and the end of 148, but 142 continues. The left fork is Springboard Trail No. 149. It drops down a short slope and crosses Gillette Creek, then forks itself. You can go either way, as it makes a loop, but the brochure follows interpretive sites that have been laid out by going clockwise. The trail intersects Trail 148 and just a few steps beyond is the first historic site. It is an old stump cut by using springboards, and hence the name of the trail. Just up the slope there is a sign about early settlers Charles and Dora Kaufman and their son, Elmer. They came from Indiana to the Little Pend Oreille Lakes area in 1908 and homesteaded 160 acres. This trail passes through much of the original homestead. You can see old stumps throughout the area, but it has

This is how the loggers of old did it. Notice the notches for the springboards

grown back into a dense stand of small Douglas fir and lodgepole pine. The trail meanders gently uphill through this forest to a rocky outcrop that provides a good view of Thomas Mountain. There is a viewing platform at this location about a mile from the trailhead. Lake Thomas below is largely screened from sight by trees. The loop continues over a low hill and through the forest, coming out in some granite openings with views of Gillette Creek before dropping back down to the old homestead. Some timber harvest units have been marked along this trail, but as of December 2003 there had been no cutting. A great loop for mountain bikers might include starting at Gillette Campground, then riding on Highway 20 to Road 2712, following that to where Trail 142 crosses that road, then taking Trail 142/148 back to the campground. That would cover a distance of maybe 10 to 12 miles.

USGS Map: Lake Gillette, Aladdin Mountain, Ione, Timber Mountain

Trailhead: From Colville, Washington, follow Highway 20 east for almost 25 miles. Watch for the sign for Gillette Campground and turn right. Go one-half mile and enter the campground. The trailhead for 149 is on the north side. Parking is scarce and limited to 2 hours. A fee is required for parking. For Rufus Trail No. 148, go about one-third of a mile past the entrance to Gillette Campground. The trailhead is on the right with a vault toilet and parking for one or two vehicles.

Trail Length: Trail 149 is a 2.4-mile loop; Trail 148 is 3.4 miles one-way to Road 2712.

Trail Condition: good

Elevation: Springboard Trailhead – 3,190' (Gillette Campground), High Point/Low Point – 3,607', End – 3,190'

Elevation: Rufus Trailhead – 3,190', High Point/Low Point – 4,500' (at Road 2712), End – 4,450' (junction with Trail 145)

Estimated Duration of Hike: 1 to 2 hours for Trail 149, 1.5 to 2.5 hours each way for Trail 148

Sweat Index: break a sweat (moderate) for both trails

Mountain Bike Sweat Index: break a sweat (moderate) on Trail 148 (bikes are not allowed on 149)

Best Features: historic values, pleasant forest walks

Availability of Water Along the Trail: From Gillette Campground the trails cross Gillette Creek, and there is water in the campground.

Stream Crossings: There is a sturdy wooden bridge over Gillette Creek.

Campsites: Gillette, Gillette Lake and Lake Thomas are fee areas with developed campgrounds near the trailhead.

Precautions: Trail 148 is part of the motorized Little Pend Oreille ORV trails system. Be alert for dirt bikes and ATVs.

Alternate Hikes: Trail 149 is a self-contained loop trail with a self-guiding interpretive brochure. It crosses Rufus Trail No. 148, which in turn connects to Trail 142 at Road 2712. You may also notice a sign for Trail 142 at the campground trailhead for Trail 149. Trail 142 is a gargantuan trail practically encircling the entire Little Pend Oreille Lakes basin.

Wildlife Sighting: This area is important winter range for many animals, especially white-tailed deer. More than a dozen of them at different points along the trail watched me go by as I watched the cold December air breathed from their nostrils gather in great steamy clouds about their heads.

Wild Notes: Dalmatian toadflax, a noxious weed, has a beautiful snapdragon-like flower, but is an aggressive invader of disturbed sites, like this old homestead. Notice the infested area near the fork of Trail 149.

Sherry Trail No. 147

ACCESSIBLE: A system of flat, narrow trails leaves from a small parking area with a handicapped-accessible vault toilet. It may be difficult getting a wheelchair on these trails but some ambulatory folks might be able to enjoy the easy walk through this open forest.

This is a Family Fun Hike

Destination: Little Pend Oreille River. Map, page 67.

Best Suited For: hiking only

How Much Use: A Little * A Little More * A LOT * A Lot More * Excessive

The Little Pend Oreille River has its beginnings at the string of lakes in its upper basin

What's it like? The nearly flat river bottom west of the Little Pend Oreille River is easy terrain to walk over. Timber management has removed many trees but left others. The increased sunlight to the forest floor will stimulate forage species for big game animals, and it is possible you'll see deer and maybe a moose here. The trail comes close to the river, which at this point so near its origins is a small stream barely the size of a modest creek. The riparian zone is full of brush and lush vegetation and so harbors lots of birds in the spring and summer. This trail is occasionally groomed for cross-country skiing in the winter.

USGS Map: Lake Gillette

Trailhead: From Colville, Washington, follow Highway 20 east about 24 miles or so to the well-signed trailhead on the right side of the road. The parking area will accommodate about six vehicles. There are picnic tables and a vault toilet.

Trail Length: 3.8 miles in various loops

Trail Condition: good

Elevation: Trailhead – 3,160 feet

Estimated Duration of Hike: 30 minutes to 2 hours depending on the loop

Sweat Index: no sweat (easy)

Mountain Bike Sweat Index: prohibited

Best Features: pleasant forest walk and views of the Little Pend Oreille River

Availability of Water Along the Trail: Water can be taken from the river, but it is best to bring your own.

Stream Crossings: none

Campsites: Developed fee area campgrounds are nearby at Gillette, Gillette Lake and Lake Thomas.

Alternate Hikes: Loops of 1 to 4 miles are possible here, but this trail does not connect to any others.

Wild Notes: Much of the area traversed by this trail has been partially logged. Of the trees that were left, many are lodgepole pine, but a lot of those will not survive. An outbreak of bark beetles attacked these trees and have killed many. Look for the pitch tubes on the trunks, and where the bark has fallen away notice the intricate designs of the larval galleries eaten into the outer layer of wood.

Crystal Falls Viewpoint

This is a Family Fun Hike

Destination: Crystal Falls

Best Suited For: hiking only

How Much Use: A Little * A Little More * A Lot * A Lot More * **EXCESSIVE**

What's it like? This roadside viewpoint provides a great look at a magnificent waterfall. The walk to the overlook is less than 100 feet on a gravel surface that slopes rather steeply from the shoulder of the road to a flat area strewn with granite boulders. Beware of the sudden drop into the gorge below. The cliffs are vertical for close to 100 feet down to the churning waters.

USGS Map: Park Rapids

Trailhead: Take Highway 20 east from Colville, Washington, about 15 miles to Crystal Falls viewpoint. There's a picnic table and parking for three to five vehicles.

Trail Length: less than 100 feet

Trail Condition: good

Elevation: 2,840 feet

Estimated Duration of Hike: 2 minutes, but stay and enjoy the view awhile

Sweat Index: no sweat (easy)

Mountain Bike Sweat Index: no need for a bike

Best Features: spectacular waterfall on the Little Pend Oreille River

Availability of Water Along the Trail: none

Stream Crossings: none

Campsites: none

Precautions: The drop-off into the gorge is steep, rocky and dangerous. There are no barricades to prevent little children from getting too close.

Trails: Batey-Bould Nos. 306-312, Tacoma Peak No. 309

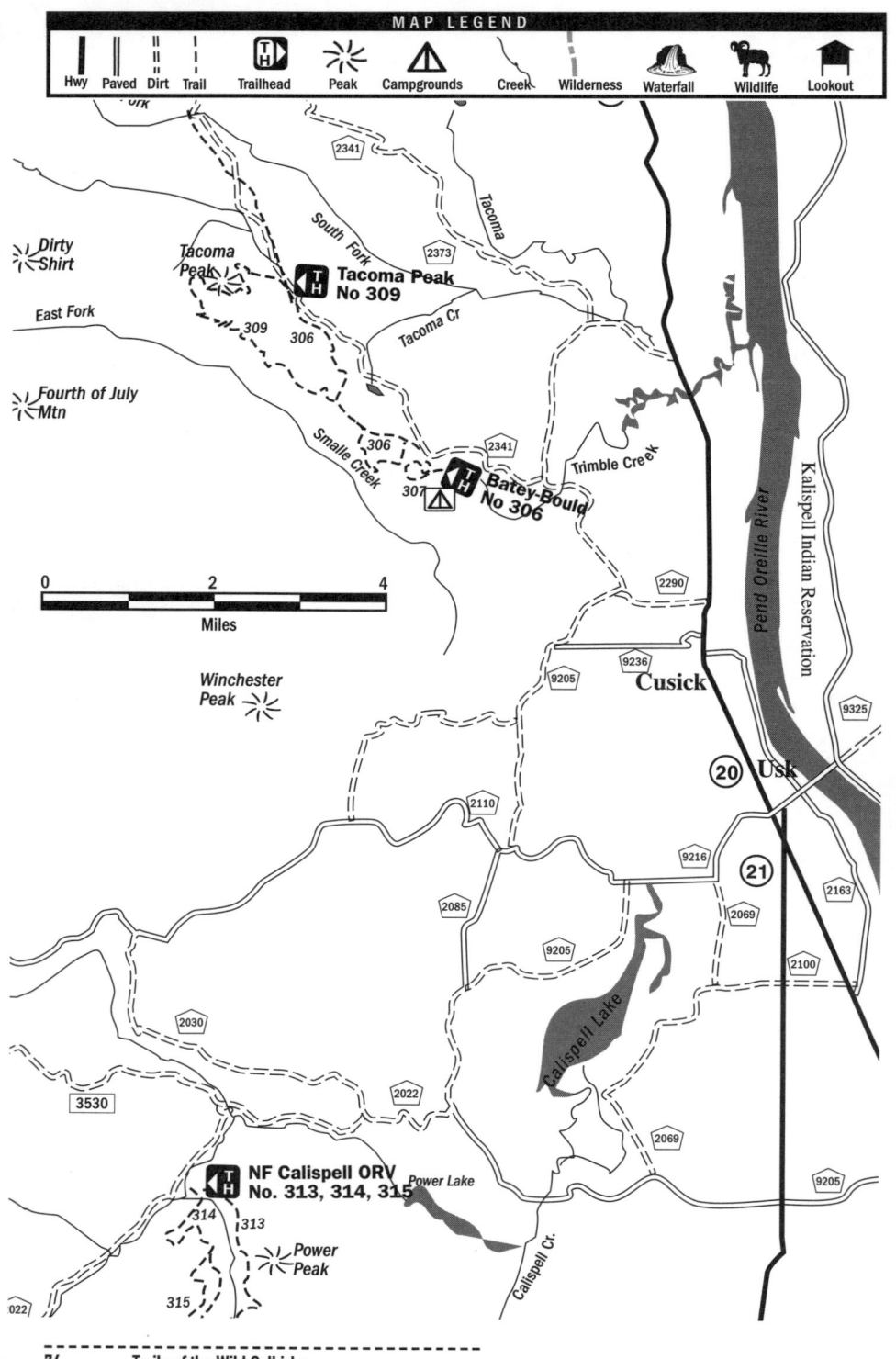

Batey-Bould Trails System Trail Nos. 306-312

Destination: Tacoma Peak, Boulder Mountain, Lost Meadows. *Map, page 76.*

Best Suited For: hiking, horseback riding, mountain biking

How Much Use: A Little * A Little More * **A LOT** * A Lot More * Excessive

What's it like? The Batey-Bould trails offer a variety of habitats and terrain for all kinds of recreationists. From dirt bikes to mountain bikes to horses and those on foot, these trails provide a treasure chest of excitement in the Great Outdoors. Much of the landscape here is heavily forested and intensely managed for the production of timber. The trails will often pass through areas that have been harvested at one time or another, but this has allowed for the growth of forage plants for wildlife. It is not unusual to see deer, moose or maybe even elk and bear while exploring these trails. From some vantage points the views are terrific, especially out across the Pend Oreille Valley. The trails visit meadows, mountaintops, streams and rocky openings. Wildflowers are plentiful in the spring and summer, and listen for the myriads of songbirds. Various loops can be explored for almost any distance ranging from 1 mile to more than 20 miles.

USGS Map: Tacoma Peak, Timber Mountain

Trailhead: On-half mile north of Cusick, Washington, on Highway 20 turn west onto Kapps Lane. Go about 4 miles to the trailhead, which requires a fee for parking. There is a lot of room and the trailhead offers a vault toilet, picnic tables, fire pits and water. Other parts of the trail can also be accessed from other roads in the area. Refer to forest maps for details.

Trail Length: 38.2 miles for the whole system; individual trails are 20.6 miles for 306, 1 mile for 307, 1.4 miles for 308, 6 miles for 309, 3.9 miles for 310, 5.3 miles for 311, and 0.3 mile for 312. Distances are all one-way.

Trail Condition: fair to excellent

Elevation: ranges from around 2,500 feet to more than 5,000 feet

Estimated Duration of Hike: 30 minutes to several days depending on the route.

Sweat Index: no sweat (easy) to buckets of sweat (difficult)

Mountain Bike Sweat Index: no sweat to bathed in sweat (strenuous)

Best Features: views, wildlife, mountaintops

Availability of Water Along the Trail: This trail crosses the Tacoma Creek drainage and its many tributaries multiple times, and water is abundant in numerous locations.

Stream Crossings: some bridges and boardwalk, some seeps that are boggy and some open stream crossings

Campsites: Primitive sites can be found along the way.

Precautions: This trail system, built from 1984 to 1986 with the use of Washington Off Road Vehicle Funds, is particularly designed for motorized use, but non-motorized users are welcome, too.

Alternate Hikes: Hikers might especially enjoy Tacoma Peak Trail No. 309 (see separate write-up) and Boulder Mountain Trail No. 311. This system connects to the Little Pend Oreille Trails System, making for more than 105 miles of trails connected by Trail 306 via Lost Meadows.

Tacoma Peak Trail No. 309

Destination: Tacoma Peak

Best Suited For: hiking, horseback riding

How Much Use: A Little * **A LITTLE MORE** * A Lot * A Lot More * Excessive

What's it like? The best way to hike the Tacoma Peak trail is to begin at the east end of the trail, go up and over the peak and come down a long ridge to the south where it ties in with Trail 306. The climb from the east is steady as the path switchbacks through heavy timber. It crosses logging roads on four occasions and skirts a couple of clear-cuts higher up the slope. But these openings provide terrific views of the Pend Oreille River and the Pend Oreille-Priest Divide to the east. The peak is a small, bald knob growing over with young Douglas fir trees. The ski area on Chewelah Mountain, 49 Degrees North, can be seen to the southwest, and Calispell Peak, the highest point in the area at over 6,800 feet, is visible through the trees to the northwest. The real treat along this trail, however, is the descent along rocky ledges and through brushy meadows on the way down. The shrub ocean spray is abundant and in places really resembles the surf breaking on a rocky beach when it is in full bloom. Spring and early summer wildflowers are prolific, including the not-so-common yellow coralroot. To complete the loop, follow Trail

Ocean spray blooms prolifically on Tacoma Peak

306 for a couple miles or so, some of which climbs steeply back uphill. The last mile parallels the road, so the temptation is to simply cut through the woods to the road, but you would miss an old cabin and a pleasant walk through a shady forest.

USGS Map: Tacoma Peak

Trailhead: Drive north from Newport, Washington, to Cusick on Highway 20. Continue past Cusick about one-half mile and turn west onto Kapps Lane. After a mile it intersects with West Calispell Road. Turn north and follow it 2 miles to Sicely Road (Road No. 2341) and turn west again. Go approximately 1.5 miles and you will come to the parking area and trailhead for the Batey-Bould ORV trail system (a fee area). Continue about 3 miles farther on road 2341. A quarter-mile or so beyond where Trail 306 crosses the road, there is an old clear-cut and the junction of Road No. 215. This is the best place to park. There is room for six to 10 vehicles. Just beyond the clearcut Trail 309 takes off into the timber.

Trail Length: 6 miles end-to-end (about an 8.5-mile loop with a portion of trail 306)

Trail Condition: fair

Elevation: Trailhead – 3,240', High Point/Low Point – 5,000', End – 3,190' (junction with Trail 306)

Estimated Duration of Hike: 3 to 5 hours for the loop

Sweat Index: buckets of sweat (difficult)

Mountain Bike Sweat Index: not suitable

Best Features: mountaintop, views of 49 Degrees North Ski Area and Calispell Peak

Availability of Water Along the Trail: none other than a small brackish spring near the junction of Trails 309 and 306

Stream Crossings: none

Campsites: There is a primitive campsite near the parking area adjacent to the clear-cut and a fee area campground at the Batey-Bould ORV trailhead.

Precautions: Tacoma Peak Trail No. 309 is part of the Batey-Bould ORV trails system so hikers need to be watchful for motorized recreation vehicles.

Alternate Hikes: The Batey-Bould trails system is comprised of more than 38 miles of trails extending north to the Little Pend Oreille Lakes trails system.

Trails: Wolf Trails Nos. 304 and 305

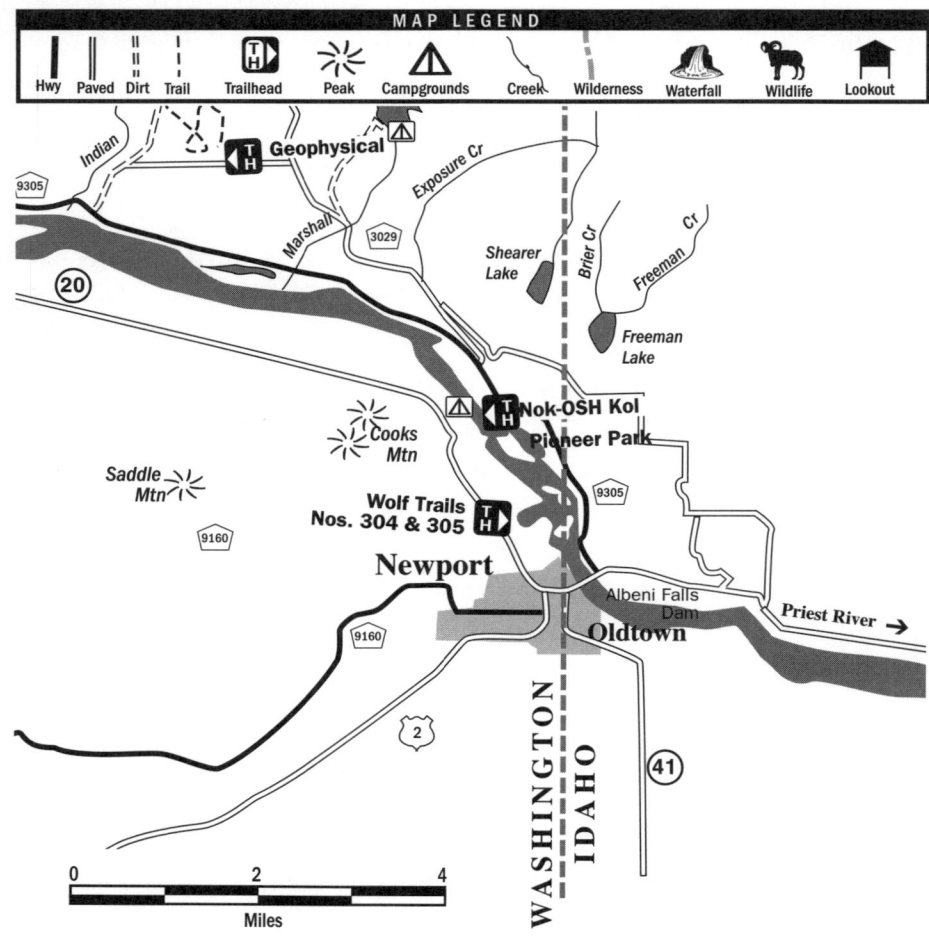

Upper Wolf Trails and Lower Wolf Trail Nos. 304 and 305

ACCESSIBLE: The Lower Wolf Trails are described in the Newport Ranger District's trails booklet as meeting Challenge Level II of Accessibility Standards. That means they are useable by disabled people, but they may not be wholly accessible. The trails probably rate as most difficult for disabled access. The upper trails may actually be more accessible with a large parking area and easy, wide trails that undulate across the gentle terrain.

This is a Family Fun Hike

Best Suited For: hiking, mountain biking

How Much Use: A Little * A Little More * **A LOT** * A Lot More * Excessive

What's it like? On the north edge of Newport, Washington, there is a block of

Forest Service land called the Wolf Donation. A series of hiking, biking and Nordic trails have been developed, making for a variety of easy to moderate loops totaling close to 5 miles. The Upper Wolf trails lie on both sides of Laurelhurst Drive. On the west side is the Alpha loop and below the road are Scapegoat, Howler, Lone Wolf and Arctic loops. From the Scapegoat loop a trail crosses Highway 20 to the Lower Wolf trail system. They all traverse an open forest comprised mostly of Douglas fir with some ponderosa pine, Grand fir and larch. Thick saplings and brush make up the understory. Nearly a mile of the Lower Wolf trails is accessible to wheelchairs. Scenic viewpoints along the lower trails overlook Ashenfelter Bay on the Pend Oreille River. These easy trails are perfect for beginning mountain bikers and for families with children of all ages.

Trailhead: To access the Upper Wolf trails, take Highway 20 to the edge of Newport, Washington, and just as the highway leaves town turn west onto Larch Street. Go about one block and turn north on Laurelhurst Drive, then proceed less than one-half mile to the parking area. The Lower Wolf trailhead is accessed by turning onto Warren Road off Highway 20 across from the Newport Ranger Station. Go about 0.6-mile to the parking area on the west side of the road.

Trail Length: several loops total about 5 miles

Trail Condition: excellent

Elevation: Trailhead – 2,160', High/Low Point – 2,280', End – 2,200'

Estimated Duration of Hike: 1 to 2 hours

Sweat Index: no sweat (easy)

Mountain Bike Sweat Index: no sweat (with a few steep pitches for a bit of a challenge)

Best Features: shady forest walks close to town

Availability of Water Along the Trail: none

Stream Crossings: none

Campsites: A Forest Service campground is located nearby at Pioneer Park.

Precautions: A connecting trail between Upper and Lower Wolf crosses Highway 20. Use extreme caution when crossing the highway.

Alternate Hikes: Upper Wolf and Lower Wolf can be enjoyed all at once by carefully crossing Highway 20, allowing for longer hikes and bike rides.

The Pend Oreille River from Lower Wolf Trail

Spokane Area

On the far southern edge of the landmass called the Selkirk Mountains, the Spokane River flows from Lake Coeur d'Alene in Idaho for a distance of some 70 miles to its confluence with the mighty Columbia. About halfway between the river's beginning and its end is the city of Spokane, Washington, the largest city between the Cascades and the Continental Divide in America's Inland Northwest. Home to more than 175,000 people, it is situated in the middle of Spokane County, which straddles the river, and harbors another quarter million people north and south of its rushing waters.

This region is steeped in history, going back thousands of years with Native Americans and almost 200 years since David Thompson first explored the area for the North West Company. The broad valley filled with wildlife, the fabulous lakes of the region, the rivers rich in furs and fish and the expansive forests of ponderosa pine and Douglas fir lured early mountain men, explorers and then settlers to this paradise. The city grew quickly and came to dominate the region's commerce, becoming the economic hub of an area covering thousands of square miles.

Nonetheless, despite the decidedly urban character of much of Spokane County, some exquisite jewels of wild nature have been preserved and numerous parks and historic sites have been established that provide a variety of recreational opportunities. From the site where David Thompson established a highly successful trading post at the confluence of the Little Spokane and Spokane rivers to the 37-mile-long Spokane River Centennial Trail to the heights of Mount Spokane northeast of the city, there is some fine hiking and fascinating history to be enjoyed on the outskirts of the area's metropolitan center.

Aside from the river itself, the area's major cities are connected by Interstate 90. North from there Highways 2 and 395 provide the primary thoroughfares into the southern foothills of the Selkirks. Highway 25 offers a magnificent route of travel along the east side of the Columbia River, connecting Davenport to Kettle Falls and on to Northport and the Canadian border. Between Highway 25 and Highway 395, tucked into the wedge of land separating the Columbia River from the Spokane River is the Spokane Indian Reservation with its tribal headquarters at Wellpinit. Numerous public campsites are located along the Spokane River on the reservation. For more information about tribal lands and the people who lived here for countless generations before European explorers came to this region, go online to www.spokanetribe.com. Look in Appendix 2 for additional contact information regarding other Indian tribes who have lived in or near the Selkirks for millennia.

Riverside State Park and the Spokane River Centennial Trail

For those who like their recreation close to home and a little tamer than, say, the wilds of the Salmo-Priest Wilderness, there is a magnificent park on the fringes and in the heart of eastern Washington's greatest city, Spokane. Riverside State Park sprawls across nearly 10,000 acres along the Spokane River. For the most part, it is indeed an urban park, but you would hardly think so at times when down by the river above Nine Mile Falls among ancient basaltic formations or when astride a horse on the more than 25 miles of equestrian trails set aside exclusively for horseback riding. It is an area of amazing diversity and even for those who love it most, it always harbors new surprises and discoveries.

Thanks to the generosity of concerned citizens and Avista Corp. (formerly Washington Water Power), 30 miles of shoreline are encompassed by this spectacular park, including portions of the Spokane River, the Little Spokane and Lake Spokane behind Nine Mile Falls Dam. Through the years numerous facilities have been built to better serve park visitors, but many of them came to be in the 1930s when the Civilian Conservation Corp was at its peak. Recreational opportunities offered today include hiking and mountain biking, horseback riding, motorized use for ATVs and dirt bikes in the special Off Road Vehicle Area, picnicking, camping, viewing wildlife and educational programs for all ages. But the fun doesn't stop there. You can also try boating and canoeing and experience whitewater rafting, go rock-climbing, running or just go out for a Sunday drive through the countryside. The possibilities are limited only by your imagination and energy.

An area of the park referred to as the Bowl and Pitcher harbors the park's headquarters as well as one of the most scenic attractions in the park. Vast lava flows once inundated this region and the resultant rock formations, called basalt, are truly wondrous. Interestingly, the "Pitcher" has been identified, but there is uncertainty as to just what the "Bowl" might be, according to the website, www.riversidestatepark.org. At this location a suspension bridge crosses the river. The views are magnificent. Also, the facility is barrier-free and accessible to the disabled. This bridge connects to miles of trails going north and south along the river, the greatest of them all being the Spokane River Centennial Trail. In all, the park offers 55 miles of hiking trails, 55 miles of bike trails and 25 miles of horse trails. Plus there is a 600-acre area for ATVs

One way to get to Riverside State Park is to turn off Interstate 90 at Exit No. 280, go north across the Maple Street Bridge and at the second stoplight, about a mile after the exit, turn left at Maxwell. Follow that road westward and then northward as Pettit Drive, then drive past Downriver Golf Course to the park. The Bowl and Pitcher are about two miles north of the park entrance along Aubrey L. White Parkway.

Spokane River Centennial Trail

Life has always been centered on rivers in the Inland Northwest, and the Spokane River is no different. Archaeological evidence indicates the presence of humans along this river more than 11,000 years ago. That wasn't long after the Ice Age glaciers choking the Selkirk Mountains to the north receded to the Arctic. It was where David Thompson established one of his most successful trading posts at Spokane House, and it is where the city of Spokane prospers today. But though the river has almost always been recognized as a life-giving force, it was abused and its beauty degraded during the middle part of the 20th century. Then came Expo 74 to Spokane and with it a wave of change.

A concerted effort to restore the river corridor to a more natural condition was sparked by preparation for Expo, and here 30 years later the fruit of those efforts is epitomized in a spectacular trail that meanders for 60 miles along its banks. The Spokane River Centennial Trail (also called the Spokane Centennial Trail) is a masterpiece of collaboration and perseverance. Conceived in 1979 as a bicycle/pedestrian pathway, it evolved into a two-state coordinated project that is a model for communities throughout the nation.

While Washington was preparing for its centennial celebration in 1989, Idaho was doing the same for that state's 100th birthday in 1990. As visionaries on both sides of the state line dreamed of marking those occasions in special ways, the idea of coordinating a trail that would connect Spokane with Post Falls and Coeur d'Alene was born. The Spokane Centennial Trail and the North Idaho Centennial Trail (not to be confused with the Idaho Centennial Trail – see Appendix 5 for more on that one) are the result of those dreams.

For 37 miles in Washington and another 23 miles in Idaho, these two Centennial Trails follow the Spokane River from its birth at the outlet of Lake Coeur d'Alene to Spokane House and beyond to Nine Mile Falls. The entire distance is paved and accessible not only to vigorous joggers and bikers, roller bladders and hikers, but it is a barrier-free trail as well for the disabled. The trail can be accessed at numerous locations along its length and is patrolled frequently by park rangers and other officers who help ensure the safety of park visitors.

In Washington the trail is broken into four segments. The west segment begins at Nine Mile Falls and traverses some of the best scenery found along its entire corridor. It winds through pine forests and up and down the hills of Riverside State Park, often overlooking the Spokane River and providing panoramic views of the Spokane Valley. At times the trail must be shared with motorized vehicles, but that is mostly limited to local residents. As the trail approaches downtown, it crosses from the south (or west) side of the river to the north and continues into Riverfront Park in the heart of Spokane. Along this segment you will encounter the Miracle Mile Medallions. Once through the park the trail crosses the river on Howard Street Bridge from where the most fantastic views of Spokane Falls are found. The central segment of the trail leaves the city for open fields, meadows of wildflowers and pine woodlands north of the newer city of Spokane Valley. Here the trail closely hugs the banks of the river, which affords many opportunities for a cooling swim in the heat of summer. Into the eastern segment of the trail, which is back on the south side of the river, the terrain is flat and more open. It ends at the Idaho state line near the Visitors' Center. Here the trail continues east as the North Idaho Centennial Trail along the river, across the

Rathdrum Prairie and into Coeur d'Alene.

All along this visionary pathway are facilities to enhance visitors' experiences. There are camping sites, picnic areas, swimming, horseback riding, bicycling, benches for quiet reflection and a great deal more. In Washington, the trail is cared for by a consortium of interests, including Washington State Parks; the cities of Spokane, Spokane Valley and Liberty Lake; Spokane County; and a non-profit organization responsible for fundraising activities, Friends of the Centennial Trail. For more information about the trail, write to Friends of the Centennial Trail, P.O. Box 351, Spokane WA 99210-0351. You can also visit these websites: www.spokanecentennialtrail.org, www.riversidestatepark.org, www.spokaneoutdoors.com, and www.parks.wa.gov. In Idaho the trail is under the care of Idaho Parks and Recreation and the North Idaho Centennial Trail Foundation. For information about the Idaho portion of this magnificent trail, log onto www.northidahocentennialtrail.org and www.idahoparks.org.

Spokane House and Little Spokane River Natural Area

About six years from the release of this book, an anniversary will mark the passage of 200 years, a new bicentennial. This one will turn back the pages of time to when David Thompson established Spokane House in 1810 at the confluence of the Spokane and Little Spokane rivers. This fur trading post, along with a network of others he had built throughout the northern Rockies, was the beginning of monumental changes for the Inland Northwest. The way of life that indigenous peoples had passed from one generation to another through centuries untold would soon all but end.

Spokane House

The start of Westward expansion began in 1778 when the North West Company launched a fur-trading empire that spanned the North American continent, primarily in what is now Canada. But once over the Continental Divide, explorers and fur trappers followed tributaries of the mighty Columbia River into present-day Washington and adjacent Idaho. In 1810 David Thompson sent Finan McDonald and Jaco Finlay to the mouth of the Little Spokane River and instructed them to build a trading post. The crude cabin that was first erected was called Spokane House and became the first permanent white settlement in the state of Washington. The land was good, the waters pure, the furs abundant and Spokane House flourished for a decade.

This old barn is near the confluence of the Little Spokane River and the Spokane River where David Thompson built Spokane House

By 1826, though, the number of beaver had dwindled, and the rambunctious Spokane River continuously made navigation tricky at best and disastrous at its worst. And so the post was moved to Fort Colville farther north near Kettle Falls on the Columbia. Another decade later little remained of Spokane House.

Today a historic site and interpretive center reside at the site where David Thompson expanded the territory of the North West Company into Spokane country. The year 2010 will mark the 200th anniversary of that site. Efforts are under way to recreate the stockade and fur trading post erected by McDonald and Finlay.

To get to Spokane House, take the Division Street exit off Interstate 90 in downtown Spokane and go north to Francis Street (State Route 291). Turn left (west) and follow that out of town about 6 miles. Spokane House will be on the west side of the highway. It is open seasonally Memorial Day through Labor Day Thursday through Monday from 10 a.m. until 6 p.m. The Little Spokane River Natural Area is nearby.

Little Spokane River Natural Area

Nearly 2,000 acres and more than 7 miles of river were protected with the designation of the Little Spokane River Natural Area. A serpentine stream meandering through meadows and marshes, among giant cottonwoods and past steep-sided hills dotted with pines and firs, this little piece of wildness is nearly the way it was 200 years ago when trappers plied its waters in birch bark canoes. When under the influence of this magical landscape, it is hard to believe a bustling city of 200,000 people is just a few miles away.

Not only can the natural area be experienced on foot along its trails, waterlovers can take to canoes and kayaks and float the river. That may, in fact, be the best way to get a genuine feel for what it must have been like in the early 1800s when the land seemed young and wild. The trick, of course, is that anyone floating the river should be accomplished at handling their craft in a narrow stream fraught with sharp bends, logs and brushy banks.

Little Spokane River is a paddler's paradise

A host of wildlife inhabits this area and demands the care and respect of people visiting for a day or even just a few hours. Remember the animals live here. It is not unlikely that you could see beaver, muskrat, porcupines, raccoons, whitetailed deer and maybe even a moose. Listen also for the abundant bird life and for choruses of frogs in the spring. Most interestingly, a great blue heron rookery is located among tall cottonwoods near the river. These great birds are sensitive to disturbance, and so it is best to view them and then leave them alone.

For paddlers, watercraft can be launched at the trailhead near St. George's School on School Road or at Painted Rocks. Each location requires a short walk and carry to the river. A good takeout is located near Highway 291.

Little Spokane River Natural Area Trail

Destination: along the Little Spokane River

Best Suited For: hiking

How Much Use: A Little * A Little More * A Lot * **A LOT MORE** * Excessive

What's it like? At pretty much any time of the year, a walk along the Little Spokane River is a joy, and this trail provides the perfect avenue for that enjoyment. The trail meanders through forests of ponderosa pine and Douglas fir on the rocky hillsides, while cottonwoods and birch and alders dominate the riparian zone next to the stream. From St. George's School Road to Painted Rocks, the trail follows along the south side of the river. At Rutter Parkway it crosses over to the middle trailhead. The Indian pictograph site is less than 100 feet from the parking area. A commemorative sign notes the land for this special area was given to the state parks commission by Professor and Mrs. H.M. Hart, Jr. Mrs. Hart was the daughter of Aubrey White, the founder of the Spokane park system. From the pictograph the trail is often quite close to the riverbank. This section of the trail also has 10 interpretive sites for which a self-guiding brochure can be obtained at the trailheads. From the meandering river to a heron rookery, the painted rocks to tranquil meadows, hiking this trail soothes the toil and stress induced by the city just over the hill.

Trailhead: There are three places to get on the Little Spokane Natural Area Trail: near St. George's School at the east end; at Indian Painted Rocks in the middle; and just off Highway 291 at the west end near Spokane House. To get to the Little Spokane Natural Area, take the Division Street exit off Interstate 90 in downtown Spokane and go north to Francis Street (State Route 291). Turn left (west) and follow that out of town. It is about 6 miles from downtown Spokane to this site. Where the highway crosses the river, a road to the right accesses the west end of the trail. Shortly before getting to the river, turn east onto Rutter Parkway and follow it to where it meets Indian Trail. Continue on the parkway and it will cross the river at the Painted Rocks Trailhead. A couple miles farther, it re-crosses the river. At St. George's School Road, turn right and go to the east trailhead.

Trail Length: 6 miles one-way

Trail Condition: good

Elevation: Trailhead – 1,520' (at Highway 291), High Point/Low Point – 1,540' (at the Indian Painted Rocks), End – 1,550' (near St. George's School)

Estimated Duration of Hike: 2 to 3 hours either way

Sweat Index: break a sweat (moderate)

Mountain Bike Sweat Index: prohibited

Best Features: wildlife, views of the Little Spokane River

Availability of Water Along the Trail: You can get it out of the river, but it is best to bring all you need.

Stream Crossings: the trail crosses the river on Rutter Parkway

Campsites: not allowed

Precautions: Be sure to read park rules posted at each of the trailheads.

Alternate Hikes: Stay on established trails so as not to unnecessarily disturb wildlife.

Wild Notes: It is unknown just how old the pictographs at Painted Rocks are, but standing there in wonder at whom created them, when and why can send tingles up your spine. The overhanging rock has protected the site through the years from the elements, but prying hands and fingers could quickly ruin it. A metal barricade similar to a wrought iron fence protects the artwork from potential damage by overzealous visitors. Please respect that protection. Admire, but don't touch.

Lake Roosevelt National Recreation Area and Fort Spokane

In the early days of settling the West, the Columbia River was an intimidating stream flowing fast and furious between range after range of towering mountains, especially the Selkirks. But once this country was opened to settlement, particularly with the coming of the railroads, the landscape and the river that nourished it were soon tamed almost beyond recognition.

One of the most massive projects intent on corralling this rambunctious river was the building of Grand Coulee Dam in 1941. For 40 miles below the juncture of the Spokane River with the Columbia and for 90 miles above it, this feisty river was transformed into a lake. It was named Franklin D. Roosevelt Lake, and that 130-mile stretch from Grand Coulee to China Bend came to be known as Lake Roosevelt National Recreation Area. Though the dam was primarily built for flood control, irrigation and the generation of electricity, an offshoot benefit was the creation of a gigantic playground.

Highway 25 bridge over the Spokane River near its confluence with the Columbia

The recreation area is managed by the National Park Service and over the past six decades numerous facilities and sites have been constructed that offer a wide variety of recreational experiences, including hiking trails. The trails are generally short and accessible to people of all ages and abilities. But most people use this area for watersports. Getting to Lake Roosevelt is easy, as well. Washington State Highway 25 parallels the east shore from Davenport to Northport, passing through small hamlets like Enterprise and Hunters and skirting the edge of the town of Kettle Falls. Along the way are access points to campgrounds, picnic sites, historic sites and boat launches. Just south of the Columbia, away from the Selkirks, Highway 2 provides access to the recreation area and its headquarters at Coulee Dam via routes 174 from Wilbur and 155 from Coulee City.

Kettle Falls and St. Paul's Mission

Catholic missionaries were making their way into the Inland Northwest as early as the late 1830s. Two priests, Father Blanchet and Father Demers, were the first to arrive at the Hudson Bay Company's Fort Colville, where it is reported they met with members of five Indian tribes and baptized 19 of them. It is said to have been the first Catholic Mass conducted between the Rocky Mountains and the Cascades. A few years later, in 1845, Father DeSmet returned to the area where the Colville River empties into the Columbia, and north of there, he and other priests built St. Paul's Mission. This became the center of Jesuit activity in the region for over 10 years.

With the outbreak of a smallpox epidemic and the increase of white settlers in the area in search of gold, once it was discovered near the mouth of the Colville River, the influence of the missionaries among the native peoples diminished. In 1858 the mission was abandoned and closed, but only temporarily. Through the 1860s and into the 1870s, the mission was active and other missions were built. Still, the final service held at St. Paul's took place on August 14, 1875. Its deterioration began, and over the course of 65 years it slowly fell apart.

Finally, though, in 1939 a group headed by Father Georgen undertook a project to restore the building and today, nearly 160 years after it was first erected, St. Paul's Mission still stands as a monument to westward expansion and the effects the settling of the region had on native tribes.

Today, as part of the Lake Roosevelt National Recreation Area, a one-quarter-mile-long barrier-free trail explores the site where the Mission still stands. Along the way, interpretive signs explain the history of the area. Nearby, a mile-long trail explores the Old Kettle Townsite. It meanders among foundations, sidewalks, fruit trees and other landmarks of the past, eventually leading to a beach and playground on the lakeshore.

Fort Spokane and Sentinel Trail

Gold. Just speaking the word raised goose bumps on the flesh of every dreamer flowing into the Inland Northwest. And in 1855 a new fever spread across the territory when gold was discovered in the Colville area. A rush of fortune seekers streamed up the Columbia, and tensions between the newcomers and native residents increased. In 1859 the U.S. military established Fort Colville in order to protect the growing cadre of settlers in the area, and 21 years later the construction of Camp Spokane began. It was a ramshackle collection of temporary buildings at first, but a year later, upon an inspection by Commanding Officer General Nelson A. Miles, the scene was set for the "camp" to grow into a military compound. In 1882 it was renamed Fort Spokane.

Spokane River meets the mighty Columbia at Fort Spokane

The fort was situated on the south bank of the Spokane River on a level plateau sparsely covered with majestic ponderosa pines, just upstream from its confluence with the Columbia. At its height it housed more than 300 soldiers plus their families and other civilians. In the course of 19 years more than 45 buildings were constructed, including a brick guardhouse. However, in 1898 the Spanish-American War erupted, and the entire garrison at Fort Spokane was withdrawn to another fort near the growing city of Spokane.

Fort Spokane remained active, but as an Indian boarding school. The enrollment peaked at 229 students in 1902, but by 1914 the number of students had dwindled to a couple dozen and the school closed. Fifteen years later the fort closed up for good and was abandoned. In 1960 the site, still in federal ownership, was transferred to the National Park Service and restoration projects were initiated. The guardhouse now serves as the visitor center and museum.

The Sentinel Trail is a 2-mile-long, barrier-free path that takes the wanderer back in time to when the fort was an active military post. Interpretive signs are located along the way, imparting information about life at the fort and even further back in time. For the more adventurous, the trail climbs 300 feet to the top of a bluff overlooking the plateau where the fort was built, offering spectacular views of the confluence of the two rivers.

To get to Fort Spokane take Highway 2 west from Spokane to Davenport, then turn north on Highway 25 and go 22 miles to the entrance. There is camping, a visitors' center, a boat launch and picnicking with amenities such as water, vault toilets and RV dump stations. For more information about Lake Roosevelt and Fort Spokane, call (509) 633-9441 or go online to www.nps.gov/laro.

Mount Spokane State Park

When someone says, "Let's go hiking in the Selkirks," most people would think they mean somewhere up by Sandpoint or Bonners Ferry in Idaho, or way up in the Upper Priest River Country, or near Ione, Washington, around the Little Pend Oreille Lakes, or in the remote backcountry of the Salmo-Priest Wilderness. But they might mean hiking within a half hour's drive of downtown Spokane; if that's the case, they mean, "Let's go hiking on Mount Spokane."

At 5,883 feet, Mount Spokane is the highest summit in the southern end of the Selkirks. You have to go clear to Usk, 60 or 70 miles north to find taller peaks. And so, because of that fact, Mount Spokane stands out like a sentinel above the river, the valley and the city of the same name. It has a long history of development, but despite all the years of growth and construction much of this mammoth chunk of forested granite is still relatively wild and inviting to all kinds of adventurers who want to explore its hulking bulk. Considering there are 100 miles of hiking trails, 90 miles of biking trails, 100 miles of horse trails, 50 miles of groomed snowmobile trails and another 15 miles of groomed cross-country ski trails – not to mention 1,250 acres of alpine skiing terrain – you get the idea that Mount Spokane is a recreation mecca.

In the early settlement days of the Spokane Valley, this mountain was variously called Mount Carlton or Mount Baldy. From 1909 to 1912 Francis H. Cook built a road, for which he charged a toll, to within three miles of the summit. This access preceded the official designation of 1,500 acres on the mountain as the first version of Mount Spokane State Park in 1927. Over the course of the next 35 years the acquisition of properties and the outright donation of land expanded the park boundaries to more than 13,000 acres. Today, the park covers 13,919 acres and encompasses not only Mount Spokane, but Mount Kit Carson, Beauty Mountain and Quartz Mountain as well. In 2002 the community celebrated the park's 75th anniversary.

Vista House atop Mt. Spokane, 5,883 feet, was renovated in 2003

This state park, the first one in Washington east of the Cascades, is a year-round destination. Between alpine skiing, Nordic skiing, snowshoeing, dog sledding and snowmobiling, it is as much fun in the winter as it is in the summer. The world's first double chair lift opened on Mount Spokane in 1946.

A variety of facilities are located in the park, from the Selkirk Lodge and Vista House to the CCC Cabin and Bald Knob Overlook picnic shelter. There are plenty of parking areas, rest rooms and access to the myriads of trails laced across the mountainous terrain. The trail system is fantastic, and though you can drive to the summit in summer time, you can also hike to it. A plethora of trailheads along the primary access road allows for hikes from just a couple miles to loops of more than 20 miles.

To get to Mount Spokane State Park, follow Highway 2 north of Spokane to Mead and turn east onto State Road 206. That leads to the park entrance over a distance of 15 miles. There is a fee to utilize the park, though motorists can drive to the top without being charged. For more information call the park headquarters at 509-238-4258, or contact the Friends of Mount Spokane by visiting its website at www.mtspokane.org.

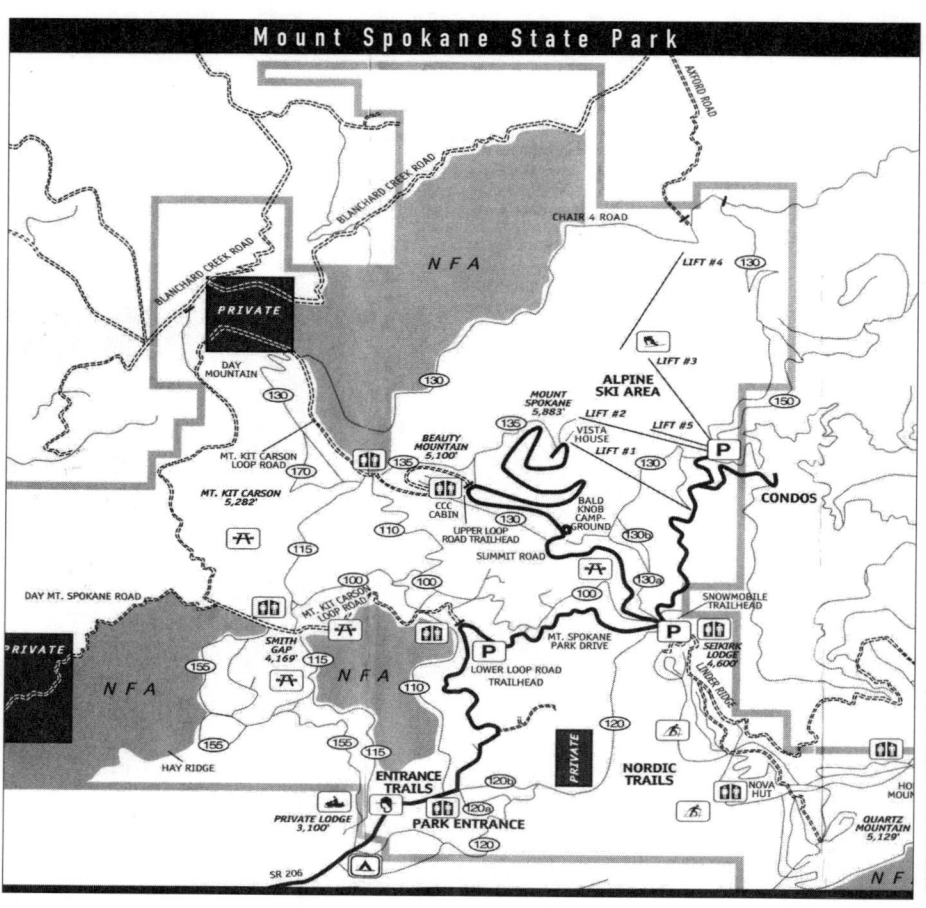

Essay:

Aladdin

Could I have been any luckier if I had been a kid who, upon finding a magic lamp, rubbed it and a genie appeared? With a genie at my command, what would I wish for?

Riches? I felt as rich as the richest man on earth with the treasures of the Selkirk Mountains falling away in every direction and rising again in distant grays and blues and greens. The vastness and beauty of the landscape were riches enough for me.

Glory? The glorious sunshine warming my head, the gentle breeze cooling my brow, the magnificent peak on which I stood was all the glory I wanted. On the wind through the trees and in the murmur of waters deep in the valley below I could hear angels singing the Hallelujah Chorus. The glory of the moment filled my soul, and I needed no personal sense of grandeur the wilderness did not bestow.

A beautiful woman by my side?

Well, now, that might've been something I could've wished for.

But as it was I stood alone on the summit of Abercrombie Mountain, more than 6,000 feet above the Columbia plains, its rocky ramparts towering over the deep canyon of the Pend Oreille. The Salmo-Priest Wilderness loomed ragged and tattered to the east, the Columbia River surged southwest toward the Kettle River Range, and straight south rolled forested hills and shadowed valleys into the dim distance fading from sight at the edge of the visible world.

I couldn't think of anything to wish for, unless maybe it was a good soaking rain, though I hated the thought of a storm clouding my perfectly lovely day. Elsewhere, though, the day was not quite so perfect. Canada lay practically at my feet and north across the border in half a dozen directions columns of smoke rose into the sky. British Columbia was on fire that summer afternoon, and tens of thousands of people were not so peaceful and content in themselves as I that day. The fury of the fires belched black, boiling soot into the atmosphere until high-level winds grabbed it and carried it across the mountains to the plains. Due east another eruption seemed to be occurring, and I later learned that Myrtle Creek, near Bonners Ferry, Idaho, where I had just been hiking a few days before, had caught fire.

Smoke obscured every horizon, but there in the middle of it all I sat perched in a patch of crystal blue sky on the highest peak between the Columbia and Pend Oreille rivers, wrapped in the warmth of the afternoon sun. For me the week had been fabulous. The long drive from Noxon, Montana, to Colville, Washington, culminated when I saw the street sign at the corner of a narrow paved road and Highway 20. Aladdin Road was stenciled white on green, and I turned north. This was my first time in the Aladdin Valley and I wondered what discoveries awaited me.

The road enters a narrow canyon squeezed tight by Jumpoff Joe Bluff and Little Roundtop where the North Fork of Mill Creek tumbles among rocks and alder. Beyond Cy Creek, but just before Kolle Creek, County Road 9435 crests an imperceptible divide in the shadow of Rabbit Mountain, then crosses a pair of streams that come together and flow north as the South Fork of Deep Creek.

Inky black shade lie thick on the asphalt, and dew moistened every blade of grass along the shoulder of the road, as the sun had not cleared the ridgeline. But the treetops rising in stair-step fashion up the mountainside to the northwest were aglow with early morning rays of luminous gold. I kept an eye out for the turn I wanted to make and nearly drove past Road No. 500 slinking off into a cow pasture behind a wall of alders. A sign proclaimed it was 6 miles to the Gillette Ridge trailhead.

My Dakota pickup eased along the two-track dirt road, past the Clinton Creek Forest Camp and up a steeply ascending grade to the trailhead. Eager to hit the trail, I hopped out of the truck, grabbed my pack and disappeared into the timber. Douglas fir gave way to lodgepole pine on the climb to the top of Rogers Mountain where a lookout tower once resided. From there the trail led me to Mount Rogers a couple of miles farther along the ridge. Striding three feet or more to a step with my gaze fixed on the rocky tread, I surprised a mule deer buck that surprised me and we both froze for an instant, wondering who would make the first move. He did, and in a flash he was gone. Just the momentary noise of his giant, gray body crashing through the undergrowth convinced me that he really had been standing 30 feet from me seconds ago.

The descent from Mount Rogers passed through a brushfield and into a saddle where the forest had been corrupted by root rot. Dying trees leaned against each other, and skeletons already littering the ground lay tangled in ninebark, vine maple and other twisting stems creeping like the fingers of death and decay around the rotting corpses. And in the middle of the thicket an unseen animal went, "Woof!" There was no confusing that grunt with a chattering squirrel or a startled deer. A bear was clearly expressing its displeasure that I had stumbled into its bedding area. I stopped long enough to glimpse a large black shape lifting itself from the ground then began walking again, now talking loudly to the bruin who was surely contemplating whether to attack, kill and bury me for later consumption, or whether to allow me to pass unharmed.

Out along Gillette Ridge, having been allowed to pass the sleepy-eyed bear, the skinny lodgepole pine was so thick it was impossible to see out over the valley spreading west toward the Columbia. But the shade was nice and the sunlight refracting amongst the gently swaying pine needles added a peaceful feel to the mountain. After awhile I turned around and went back the way I had come, tiptoeing through the saddle where a bear had slept. I camped that night down by

Clinton Creek and laid my bag upon the ground beneath a sky so full of stars you wondered how the Maker found room for them all. The creek sang a lullaby and the sounds of forest critters coming out at night brought on a deep sleep. I dreamed about bears.

Dawn was announced by the scolding of a squirrel and an unmistakable stench. Cows. There were four or five of them just on the other side of the creek. I exclaimed, "Good morning!" to the blank stares of several long bovine faces, then rose, stretched and clambered into the truck. No sense in having breakfast in a barnyard, I figured, so off I went to my next point of interest, Big Meadow Lake.

En route to the lake I drove past the spot on the map marked "Aladdin." Rocky Creek splashes from a steep-walled basin surrounded by forested ridges and peaks with names like Blacktail Butte, Seldom Seen Mountain and Aladdin Mountain. It merges with the South Fork of Deep Creek a long stone's throw south of a driveway with a small metal sign humbly announcing the fields and buildings on either side of the road as the Aladdin Hereford Ranch. I figured if I were that boy with the magic lamp I would've wished for a place as serene and beautiful as that for my very own.

About a mile and a half farther, I turned east on Meadow Creek Road and drove a few miles to the old Hess Homestead and Big Meadow Lake. A replica of the typical homesteaders' cabins built around the turn of the 20th century piqued my curiosity and once at the lake, I hiked a trail back to it. Ruins of the original Hess cabin, long ago fallen in and overrun with wild lilacs, made a mound of black rotting wood out in front of the newer log structure. I stood quietly in the meadow and tried to imagine what it must have been like right there in that spot more than a hundred years ago.

Voices whispered on the wind. Shouts of laughter from kids at play sounded over the bellowing of a cow. The crow of a rooster greeted a century-old sunrise. I could see in my mind's eye the toil and labor it took this family to carve a home and life out of the wilderness. I could see the anxiety on the old farmer's face when the snow piled higher and the wind blew colder. I imagine if he'd had a magic lamp he might've wished for more fertile soil, or for winters less harsh, or for fewer biting insects swarming his head. He might have wished for a lot of things, but in the end all the wishes in the world could not plow the ground or feed the children. Whenever they left, the Hess family left a legacy shared by thousands of others when this land was yet wild and free and had not been subdued by man.

I stayed two days and a night at Big Meadow Lake and on the morning of the second day a bull moose with antlers reaching beyond his shoulders on either side paid a visit to my camp. The splashing of his hooves in the shallow water at the lake's edge woke me that morning. What would old man Hess have done? Seen meat for the table and grabbed his rifle? No doubt, but well fed and with a grocery store in every town, I saw a wild animal and grabbed my camera. Such are the times we live in now, without the fear of a long winter or the failure of a crop.

That afternoon I drove farther north, past a fork in the road with a couple of houses in a community called Spirit and on past Deep Lake to Silver Creek. I hiked first to Sherlock Peak and found a campsite on a high, flat bench overlooking the Pend Oreille Valley. In front of the pole frame for a wall tent was a pile of wood, including a splintered cross. I picked up the pieces and read the inscription, "The Year of Our Lord 2000 I Mark Arbia buried my fingertip on this spot." Poor Mark. Perhaps he cut it off while chopping wood or field dressing an elk. But then he took the time and effort to bury the severed extremity and mark its final resting place with a cross, only to have someone come along and yank it from the ground and add it to the woodpile.

From the summit of Sherlock Peak an hour later I gazed longingly at the higher slopes to the north where Abercrombie pierced the sky with its own rocky summit. Two days later that's where I sat wishing for rain, hoping the sky would remain blue. Had I found a magic lamp tucked behind a rock or hidden in the beargrass up on that glorious peak and was successful in summoning a genie, what really would I have wished for?

That a buck as nice as the one I had surprised on Mount Rogers would step into the crosshairs of my 30.06 next hunting season; that bears would always have a place to roam wild and free; that the Aladdin Hereford Ranch would always be there in the heart of that magical valley; that the Hesses found fertile farmland and lived happily ever after; that Mark Arbia's finger doesn't hurt anymore; and that it would rain for days on end bringing relief to the tortured forests and the people fleeing in the face of infernos sweeping the north. And I would wish for riches and glory so I could share it all with friends, neighbors, family and even with perfect strangers. But then, that wish came true in the heart of the Selkirks. A richer, more glorious place I can hardly dream of and those spectacular mountains await you to go in search of your own magical lamp, and when you find it, make a wish.

Section II:

Pend Oreille-Priest Divide

The Lay of the Land

A state line runs through it. That is part of what characterizes the Pend Oreille-Priest Divide straddling the Washington-Idaho border from Canada all the way to the Pend Oreille River where it separates Newport, Washington, from Oldtown, Idaho. This section of the American Selkirks is 56 miles long from north to south and averages more than 20 miles wide, and down the center of it is a crest stretching from Snowy Top to Stone Johnny and Newport Hill. On the west is the Pend Oreille River and paralleling it on the east is the Priest River, but they flow in opposite directions and the Priest actually flows into the Pend Oreille at a place called "The Mudhole" just outside the city of Priest River, Idaho.

Nearly 80 percent of this landscape is managed by the U.S. Forest Service. The divide is the border between the Colville National Forest and the Idaho Panhandle National Forests, though at one time it was all part of the Kaniksu National Forest. Sections of corporate timberlands and state lands and parcels of private property are scattered across the middle and southern parts of this area.

At the apex of this 1,100-square-mile expanse of country is the Salmo-Priest Wilderness. It is tucked tightly into the extreme northeast corner of Washington adjacent to the unspoiled reaches of Idaho's Upper Priest River. Some of the best stands of temperate rainforest in the nation are found in the deep river bottoms just south of the Canadian line. Other wildlands extend south from Pass Creek Pass at the southern tip of the wilderness, including both sides of Grassy Top Mountain from Hall Mountain to the Roosevelt Grove of Ancient Cedars on Granite Creek and the Upper West Branch Priest River from Hungry Mountain to Pyramid Pass. There are some 95,000 acres here that some day could join the Salmo-Priest in the wilderness preservation system.

Only a few lakes dot this region, but the largest lake in the range lies on its eastern fringe. For 20 miles north to south Priest Lake glimmers from The Thorofare, which connects it to Upper Priest Lake to the north, to Outlet Bay. Almost due west of the upper lake on the other side of the divide is Sullivan Lake, a deep, narrow glacial trough 3.5 miles long by a mile wide and 332 feet deep. It covers 1,380 surface acres. The wilderness harbors four small lakes: the two Gypsy Lakes, Watch Lake and Crater Lake. Farther south lakes are more plentiful, especially close to the Pend Oreille River. The biggest of those are Bead Lake and nearby Marshall Lake.

At the far north end of this section, its highest peak rises to 7,572 feet. Snowy Top is the fifth highest named summit in the American Selkirks and is one of only two named peaks in this section that top the 7,000-foot mark. The other is Gypsy Peak at 7,309 feet (or 7,318 according to some sources of information) on the west side of the wilderness. A nameless mountain flanking Watch Lake on the south has an elevation of 7,177 feet, and another peak north of Gypsy Lake simply labeled "South Fork" on the 1993 wilderness map is 7,152 feet. South of the wilderness the mountains generally become lower and more rounded with only four summits exceeding 6,000 feet.

The west side of this divide is drained by two major watersheds and numerous other small streams. Sullivan Creek and Harvey Creek come together a quarter mile north of Sullivan Lake and flow westward into the Pend Oreille River as Sullivan Creek at Metaline Falls. LeClerc Creek encompasses an area of nearly 100 square miles south of Molybdenite Mountain. South of there, more than 20 streams descend the narrowing hills all the way to Albeni Falls. On the east side everything goes into the Priest River.

This is the heart of the American Selkirks, and several towns and cities have sprung up over the years. In Washington, following the northward flow of the Pend Oreille are Newport, Usk, Cusick, Ione, Metaline and Metaline Falls. In Idaho, Priest River is situated at the confluence of the river from which the town derives its name and the Pend Oreille. North of there the small hamlet of Coolin resides at the south end of Priest Lake, and the even smaller hamlet of Nordman nestles in a valley dominated by Bismark Meadows.

From these communities access into the Pend Oreille-Priest Divide portion of the Selkirks is ample. U.S. Highway 2 connects Newport to Priest River and, in turn, Sandpoint, Idaho, farther east. Less than 50 miles southwest of Newport, Highway 2 enters Spokane, Washington. At Priest River, Highway 57 meanders through the Priest River valley to Nordman and connects to a huge network of forest roads all along the way. At Newport, Washington, State Highway 20 bends north and follows the Pend Oreille River to Tiger where Highway 31 continues as a two-lane road all the way to the Canadian border. There are four bridges across the river connecting these highways to roads accessing the west side of the divide. They are at Newport/Oldtown, Usk, Ione and Metaline Falls.

Most of the maintained trails in this section are in the north half. The wilderness has a fine system that connects to more trails in the Upper Priest River and southward to Grassy Top and Hall Mountain. Between the crest of the divide and the Priest lakes there are dozens of trails accessing mountaintops, stream bottoms and points of varying interest, such as ancient cedar groves, forest fire lookouts and peat bogs known as fens. These trails are often shared by many different users, including motorized and non-motorized, and in all seasons of the year.

From Pioneer Park Heritage Trail to Hanna Flats Nature Trail to the rugged heights of the Shedroof Divide, the central portion of the American Selkirks offers an incredible array of recreational opportunities. It is time well spent exploring this remarkable landscape.

Salmo-Priest Wilderness and Upper Priest River

Are the world's oldest Western red cedars in the South Salmo and Upper Priest river bottoms? I don't know, but some information I picked up while hiking in this remarkable environment suggested some of those trees may actually be up to 3,000 years old! It doesn't really matter how old they are anyway because, regardless of age, the forests draped over the mountains and across the river valleys of the far north end of the Pend Oreille-Priest Divide are magnificent. And then there is the subalpine country of the highest peaks and ridges in stark contrast to the dark bottomlands. From Snowy Top to Helmer Mountain and from Gypsy Peak out along Crowell Ridge, there is some amazing high-elevation terrain in the Salmo-Priest Wilderness, a wilderness marking its 20th anniversary in 2004. Established in 1984, almost 40,000 acres along the Canadian border and the Washington-Idaho state line joined the wilderness preservation system. It is mostly high-elevation ridge tops and peaks, but the exception is along the South Salmo River and Watch Creek. A short way upstream of Crutch Creek is the dilapidated Salmo Cabin, a popular place to visit and camp along the Salmo Basin loop, an 18-mile hike through the wilderness.

Just over the state line in Idaho the country is just as wild but not officially protected as wilderness. Here the Upper Priest and Hughes Fork converge from either side of Hughes Ridge. The Priest flows out of Canada over a spectacular waterfall that is relatively easy to visit via Continental Trail No. 28. At Hughes Meadows an old smokechaser cabin is still used by the Forest Service. This undisturbed haven is the home of grizzly bears and woodland caribou, plus deer, elk, moose and black bears. It is easy to get to by following roads along Slate Creek or Sullivan Creek from Metaline Falls, Washington, and cruising Highway 57 and forest roads in the Upper Priest from Priest River and Nordman, Idaho.

Several of the trails that still show up on maps are no longer in service, especially on the Priest River side of the wilderness. Those to be wary of include Helmer Creek 303, Jackson Mountain 309, North Gold 320 and South Jackson Mountain 321. There might be faint traces of these trails through the forest, but none of them have been cleared in 10 years or more according to information I received from the Priest Lake Ranger District.

The smokechasers' cabin at Hughes Meadows

Trails: Continental No. 28, Upper Priest River No. 308, Little Snowy Lookout No. 14, Little Snowy Top No. 349

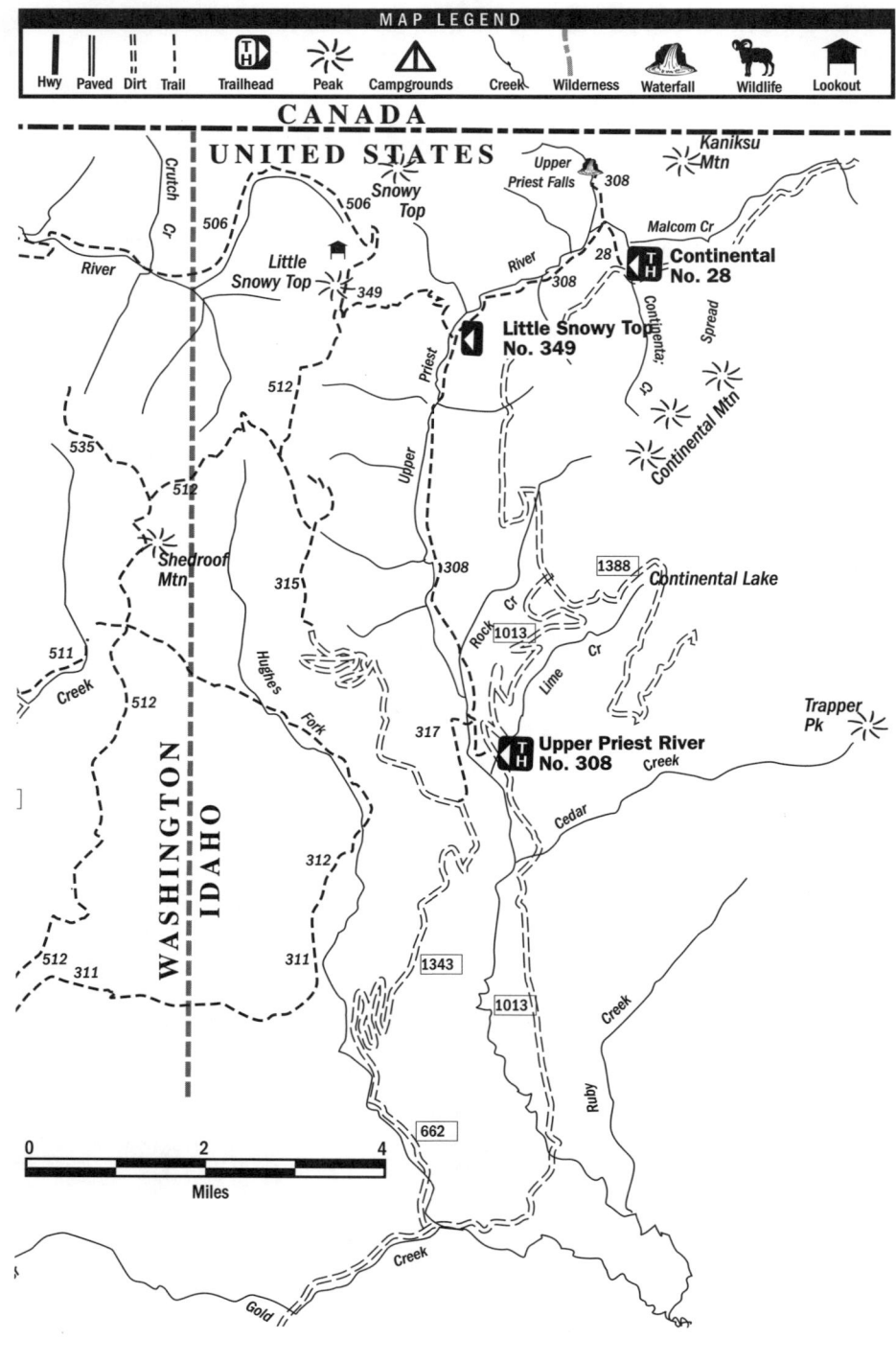

Continental Trail No. 28

Destination: Upper Priest Falls (also called American Falls). *Map, page 100.*

Best Suited For: hiking, horseback riding, mountain biking

How Much Use: A Little * A Little More * A Lot * **A LOT MORE** * Excessive

What's it like? Near the crossing of Continental Creek on Road 1013, this trail begins its descent through the old growth that occupies the entire Upper Priest River valley. In fact, take note of the quadruplets about one-quarter mile from the trailhead on the downhill side of the trail. They are magnificent specimens! The trail drops gradually down the mountainside through a series of 10 switchbacks. Ancient cedars and hemlocks are

Upper Priest Falls

all around, while Pacific yew chokes the understory. The trail joins Trail 308 just above Malcolm Creek, which is spanned by a bridge as the trail turns north toward the falls. There is one brief, but steep, climb on the way to the falls. Interestingly, the old-growth forest abuts abruptly up against Kaniksu Mountain that was burned over during the extreme fire season of 1967 and is now mostly a bald, granite dome. The trail comes to its end at a large pool below the falls gushing from a narrow crevice in the gorge up above. The fishing is actually quite good in this pool, but remember this stream is catch and release only. At this point Canada lies less than one-half mile to the north.

USGS Map: Continental Mountain

Trailhead: From Priest River, Idaho, drive Highway 57 north to Nordman, approximately 36.5 miles. From there follow Road 302 for almost 14 miles to Granite Pass and the junction of Road 1013. Travel Road 1013 nearly to where it is gated, or about 24 miles. The trailhead is on the left. There is a large turn-around area and parking for six to eight vehicles.

Trail Length: approximately 1.5 miles one-way to its junction with Trail 308; it is almost another mile to the falls on 308

Trail Condition: good

Elevation: Trailhead – 4,220', High/Low Point – 4,220'-3,180', End – 3,180' (junction with Trail 308)

Estimated Duration of Hike: 1.5 to 2 hours to the falls

Sweat Index: break a sweat (moderate)

Mountain Bike Sweat Index: buckets of sweat (difficult)

Best Features: old-growth forest, waterfall

Availability of Water Along the Trail: There is good water at the campsite on Upper Priest River where this trail joins 308.

Stream Crossings: nothing significant; Malcolm Creek is spanned by a bridge.

Campsites: There is a large, well-used primitive site at the junction of Trails 28 and 308 and another site at the falls.

Precautions: The falls emerge from a steep, rocky gorge. Beware of climbing around on the surrounding cliffs.

Alternate Hikes: Trail 308 follows the Upper Priest River southward for more than 7 miles from its junction with this trail.

Wild Notes: Beneath the spectacular ancient trees of the old-growth forest, this trail passes through another smaller forest. The "understory," as it is called by foresters, in this case is comprised primarily of sapling-sized hemlocks and a shrub that can easily be confused with these saplings, Pacific yew. One way to tell them apart is yew, for the most part in this area, really is a shrub, emanating from multiple stems. Hemlocks, even the young ones, grow from a single stem. The needles on yew are a much darker green than those on hemlock, and they have a sharp pointy tip. Hemlock needles are blunter. And always look for the "droopy" leader at the top of hemlock trees. It makes you wonder how they grow straight up. Yew is a source of an effective cancer treatment drug known as taxol. Just a few years in the past, yew bark was collected by the ton from many forests within the Inland Northwest, but now it largely comes from cultivated plants.

Upper Priest River Trail No. 308

This is a Family Fun Hike

This trail is part of the 1,200-mile-long Idaho Centennial Trail

Destination: Upper Priest River and Upper Priest Falls. *Map, page 100.*

Best Suited For: hiking, horseback riding, mountain biking

How Much Use: A Little * A Little More * **A LOT** * A Lot More * Excessive

What's it like? There is no question that one of the premier destinations in the Upper Priest River is Upper Priest Falls, also called American Falls. Those falls are pretty easy to get to via Trail 28, but this trail allows one to enjoy the extensive old-growth forest of the Upper Priest River before reaching the falls. From the moment you step from the roadside into this cathedral forest, it envelopes you in its magic mile after mile. The sheer immensity of the trees is awesome enough, but the fact they go on for unbroken miles is astonishing. This is one of the largest tracts of intact, old-growth forest in the Pacific Northwest. The trail gently undulates along the river bottom, sometimes close to the river but often several hundred yards away from it, winding among trees that occasionally push

10 feet in diameter. This forest is comprised almost entirely of cedar and hemlock, though there are also whitepine, spruce and larch scattered about. The vegetation is sometimes sparse because of the dense overstory, but don't miss the maidenhair ferns among all the other ferns and Pacific Coast plants that are found in this inland rainforest. The Upper Priest is one of the wettest, low-elevation valleys in the Northern Rockies. Though the trail is 8 miles long, this magnificent forest can be enjoyed for any distance, making it suitable

One of the largest, intact remnants of old-growth forest in the northern Rockies is along the Upper Priest River

for smaller children and the elderly who like to hike. See Trail 28 for a description of the falls.

USGS Map: Continental Mountain

Trailhead: From Priest River, Idaho, drive Highway 57 north to Nordman, approximately 36.5 miles. From there follow Road 302 for almost 14 miles to Granite Pass and the junction of Road 1013. Travel Road 1013 11.3 miles to the signed trailhead on the west side of the road. A small parking area will accommodate four to six vehicles.

Trail Length: 8.1 miles one-way to the falls

Trail Condition: excellent

Elevation: Trailhead – 2,760', High/Low Point – 2,760'-3,400', End – 3,400' (Upper Priest Falls)

Estimated Duration of Hike: 4 to 5 hours each way

Sweat Index: break a sweat (moderate)

Mountain Bike Sweat Index: break a sweat

Best Features: old-growth forest, waterfall

Availability of Water Along the Trail: There is a lot of water along this trail.

Stream Crossings: Most water along this trail is crossed via footbridges or boardwalk. There are two easy rock hops over small streams.

Campsites: There is a primitive site where Rock Creek crosses the trail a mile or so from the trailhead; there is a big site at the junction of Trails 308 and 28 less than a mile from the falls; and there is also a primitive site at the falls.

Alternate Hikes: Continental Trail No. 28 joins this trail less than a mile from the falls and offers a shortcut to Upper Priest Falls. About 2.5 miles south of that junction, Little Snowy Top Trail No. 349 takes off from Trail 308, crosses the Upper Priest River and begins one of the steepest climbs in the region. However, an avalanche in early 2003 wiped out long sections of the trail about 2 miles up. A mile or so from the trailhead, Trail 317 crosses the river and soon joins with Trail 315, which connects to the Shedroof Divide.

Wild Notes: A couple of miles perhaps from the trailhead, a large Western hemlock fell across the trail. Sawyers cleared away the tree, which was about 3 feet in diameter, by sawing off thin sections of the trunk (about 6 to 10 inches thick). Perhaps the reason for this was because the trunk was hollow. A rind of wood about 2 or 3 inches thick was all that was left of this tree. Hemlocks, and cedars too, for that matter, are notorious for rotting from the inside out. The culprit is often one fungus or another, or even several all at once. Still, even though these trees are prone to internal rot, they can withstand the decay for centuries and grow to gigantic size, attesting to the resiliency of those thin outer layers of wood which keep the tree upright year after year.

Little Snowy Lookout Trail No. 14 and Little Snowy Top Trail No. 349

Destination: Little Snowy Top, 6,829 feet. *Map, page 100.*

Best Suited For: hiking, horseback riding

How Much Use: A Little * A Little More * **A LOT** * A Lot More * Excessive

What's it like? The Shedroof Divide is a fabulous, long ridge along the western side of the Salmo-Priest Wilderness. See the description for Trail 512 for more about that hike, but you have to take that trail at some point in order to get to Little Snowy Trail No. 14. A couple of hundred yards north of where Trail 349 joins 512, this short trail takes off upslope on its rather steep ascent to the summit. The views of Upper Priest River and the north end of the Selkirk Crest are outstanding, but wait until you get on top. The old lookout is still intact and sits on a narrow, rocky pinnacle and boasts a 360-degree view that is hardly matched anywhere else. Just below the lookout is a small, flat area that hikers have used as a campsite. There is a fire ring and the earth has been compacted by repeated use. The Forest Service is considering renovating Little Snowy Lookout and making it available as an overnight rental.

USGS Map: Continental Mountain, Salmo Mountain

Trailhead: To get to Trail 14, follow Trails 535 and 512 from the Salmo Pass trailhead. Trail 349 is accessed from Upper Priest River Trail No. 308.

Trail Length: Trail 14 is 0.7 miles long one-way; Trail 349 is 4.7 miles long one-way (from the Salmo Pass trailhead, it is almost 9 miles one-way to Little Snowy Lookout via Trails 535, 512 and 14).

Trail Condition: Trail 14 is good, Trail 349 is not (a large portion of it was wiped out in avalanches during the winter of 2002/03 and it is no longer passable due to exceedingly steep terrain).

Elevation: Start – 6,530' (junction with Trail 512), High/Low Point – 6,530'-6,829', End – 6,829' (Little Snowy Top)

Estimated Duration of Hike: 15 to 30 minutes on Trail 14 from its junction with Trail 512. From the Salmo Pass trailhead, it takes 3.5 to 4.5 hours to reach Little Snowy Lookout via Trails 535, 512 and 14.

Sweat Index: buckets of sweat (difficult)

Mountain Bike Sweat Index: prohibited in the wilderness and not suitable otherwise

Little Snowy Top Lookout

Best Features: historic lookout structure, fantastic views of the Upper Priest River and surrounding mountainous terrain

Availability of Water Along the Trail: A short way north of the junction of Trails 535 and 512 on Trail 512 is a series of tiny springs that may have enough water to fill a canteen. There is also a spring and small stream on Trail 512 about 5.5 miles from the Salmo Pass trailhead, or nearly 2.5 miles from the junction of Trails 535 and 512.

Stream Crossings: one small brook easy to step across and several little springs

Campsites: There are a couple of primitive campsites at the Salmo Pass trailhead good for campers and trailers and a primitive site at the water source on Trail 512. There is also a campfire ring on top of Little Snowy Top just below the lookout.

Alternate Hikes: Trail 14 is a connecting trail from Trail 512 to Little Snowy Lookout. The only way to get there is to get on Trail 512 from any one of five access points. The closest trailhead is at Salmo Pass. Trail 349 was obliterated about 2 miles up the mountain from its junction with Trail 308 in the Upper Priest River by an avalanche. The Forest Service indicated early in the summer that the trail might be abandoned. However, the Pacific Northwest Trail Association reported that a massive trail reconstruction project will be undertaken on Trail 349 in the summer of 2004. Originally, Trail 349 was famous for its 72 switchbacks up a steep-sided mountain to Shedroof Divide Trail No. 512.

Trails: Salmo Basin No. 506, Salmo Divide No. 535, Shedroof Divide No. 512, Shedroof Cuttoff No. 511, Thunder Creek No. 526

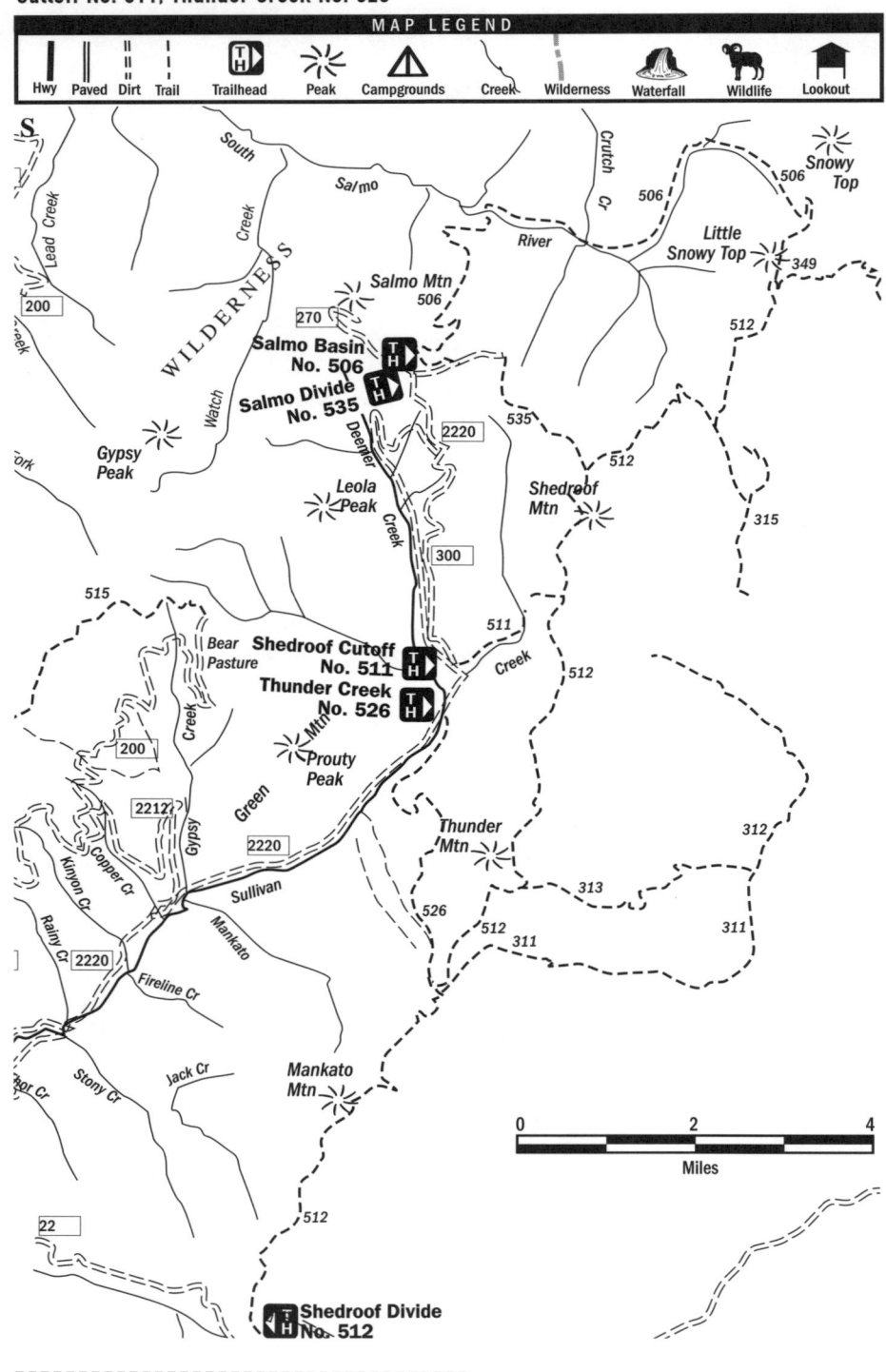

Salmo Basin Trail No. 506 and Salmo Cabin Trail No. 531

Destination: South Salmo River and Salmo Cabin. *Map, page 106.*

Best Suited For: hiking, horseback riding

How Much Use: A Little * A Little More * A Lot * **A LOT MORE** * Excessive

What's it like? This is the most heavily used trail in the Salmo-Priest Wilderness, and it is easy to see why. From the road the trail almost immediately crosses the wilderness boundary and enters that magical world of old-growth cedar and hemlock so prevalent in this region. Up high, like at the start of the trail, there is also spruce and subalpine fir. But as the trail descends towards the river, a drop in elevation of about 2,000 feet, the typical, temperate rainforest habitat takes over. The trail takes its time going down at an easy grade along a small stream that it crosses after a mile and a half. From time to time you can catch glimpses of the

Salmo Cabin, about ready to fall down, is deep within the Salmo-Priest Wilderness

north side of the South Salmo River and even detect the Canadian border cut through the forest high on the opposite mountainsides. Some 450 feet from the river, a spur trail accesses a new campsite. The Forest Service is trying to rehabilitate campsites next to the river that have been heavily impacted over the years. Once across the river you might notice an old trail junction and a trail heading into the forest to the northwest. That used to be Trail 530, but it has been abandoned and is no longer maintained. At the Crutch Creek crossing there is a good campsite and less than a half mile farther is Trail 531 to the cabin. It is situated amongst giant cedars and spruce, though many of the spruce have died, presumably from bark beetles, and are falling down. One has fallen across a corner of the cabin, making it unstable and unsafe for entry. Only a couple hundred yards east of the junction with Trail 531 is the Idaho state line and the wilderness boundary, but the countryside is as wild as what you just left. The trail climbs steadily into a basin full of spruce and rhododendron, then switchbacks a few times to the ridge top and a campsite. Here the trail merges with Trail 512. Due north of this spot is the looming presence of Snowy Top, beckoning the adventurous to climb to its lofty summit.

USGS Map: Salmo Mountain, Continental Mountain

Trailhead: At milepost 3 on Highway 31 a mile south of Ione, Washington, turn east onto Sullivan Lake Road 9345. At milepost 13, just past the Sullivan Lake Ranger Station, turn east onto Road No. 22. Go 6 miles to the junction of Road 2220 and follow that road about 12 miles, then go right one-half mile to the Salmo Pass trailhead. There is a large parking area good for more than a dozen vehicles. This also serves as the trailhead for Trail 535.

Trail Length: 506 is 8.8 miles one-way, 531 is about one-quarter mile. It is about 5.25 miles to Salmo Cabin from the trailhead.

Trail Condition: good

Elevation: Trailhead – 5,880', High/Low Point – 4,160' (Salmo River crossing), End – 6,280' (junction with Trail 512)

Estimated Duration of Hike: 2.5 to 3.5 hours to the cabin each way

Sweat Index: buckets of sweat (difficult)

Mountain Bike Sweat Index: prohibited

Best Features: access to wilderness and the South Salmo River, historic cabin, old-growth

Availability of Water Along the Trail: There is a strong, perennial stream about 1.5 miles from the trailhead, and there is good water all along the South Salmo River, even up to within one-quarter mile of the ridgeline below Snowy Top at the end of this trail.

Stream Crossings: The most significant crossings are of the South Salmo River. The first is about 3 miles from the trailhead. At low water it is an easy rock hop, but it could be tricky during spring runoff. Trail 531 into Salmo Cabin also crosses the river.

Campsites: There are numerous campsites along this trail, the first of which is at the stream crossing a mile and a half below the trailhead. A new campsite has been cleared on the south side of the river where old campsites adjacent to the river are being revegetated. The cabin, which is falling apart, is the site of a large camp, and you will find other primitive sites dispersed along the trail all the way to where it meets Trail 512 at the north end of the Shedroof Divide. Camping is also allowed at the trailhead where there is a vault toilet.

Precautions: The river crossings can be dangerous during high water, and Salmo Cabin is deteriorated to the point where it is not safe to enter.

Alternate Hikes: A fine 18-mile loop is possible with this trail and Trails 512 and 535. On Trail 512 a spur trail (Trail 14) ascends to the summit of Little Snowy Top where there is an old lookout. Snowy Top, the highest mountain in the area at 7,572 feet, is climbable from the saddle where Trails 506 and 512 meet. It is a steep 1,200-foot climb.

Salmo Divide Trail No. 535

ACCESSIBLE: This trail begins as a wide, boulder-lined path that has been converted from a road. The surface is gravel, but the incline is gentle and may be accessible for some disabled people. The roadbed goes on for 2 miles.

Destination: Shedroof Divide and Trail 512. *Map, page 106.*

Best Suited For: hiking, horseback riding

How Much Use: A Little * A Little More * **A LOT** * A Lot More * Excessive

What's it like? The trail follows a roadbed for 2 miles, and a good road it is. But the first hundred yards have been lined with giant boulders, so its width has been narrowed down to allow hikers and horses to pass. Where the single track begins, there seems to be a spur trail off to the right, but if you follow it a mere 50 feet you will see that it must be the top end of an old logging road coming up out of Sullivan Creek. It is now overgrown, though there seems to be a path heading off through the thickly growing small trees. Here the trail crosses onto the south side of the ridge, the wilderness boundary, and offers nice views out over Sullivan Creek and of Crowell Ridge and Gypsy Peak to the west. It passes through some beautiful, open meadows on its way to joining Trail 512 just north of Shedroof Mountain.

In spring bears love to claw tree trunks as the sap begins to flow

USGS Map: Salmo Mountain, Continental Mountain

Trailhead: From Highway 31 at the south end of Ione, Washington, turn east onto Sullivan Lake Road 9345. At milepost 13, just past the Sullivan Lake Ranger Station, turn east onto Road No. 22. Go 6 miles to the junction of Road 2220 and follow that road about 12 miles, then go right one-half mile to the Salmo Pass trailhead. There is a large parking area good for more than a dozen vehicles. This also serves as the trailhead for Trail 506.

Trail Length: 3 miles one-way

Trail Condition: excellent

Elevation: Trailhead – 5,880', High/Low Point – 6,390', End – 6,360' (junction

with Trail 512)

Estimated Duration of Hike: 1 to 2 hours to the junction with Trail 512

Sweat Index: no sweat (easy)

Mountain Bike Sweat Index: prohibited

Best Features: access to wilderness, views

Availability of Water Along the Trail: none

Stream Crossings: none

Campsites: There is camping available at the trailhead, where there is a vault toilet.

Alternate Hikes: This trail forms part of an 18-mile loop with Trails 506 and 512.

Wildlife Sighting: A nice bull moose stepped onto the trail not 30 feet in front of me about 2 miles from the trailhead.

Shedroof Divide Trail No. 512

Destination: Shedroof Divide in the Salmo-Priest Wilderness. *Map, page 106.*

Best Suited For: hiking, horseback riding

How Much Use: A Little * A Little More * **A LOT** * A Lot More * Excessive

What's it like? Shedroof Divide Trail No. 512 is probably the longest continuously running trail in the American Selkirks. But the beauty of it is that it can be accessed from numerous points, making it possible to do a variety of day hikes or overnighters. And I swear every step of the way along this trail is absolutely beautiful. Since it spends a great deal of its time on or near ridge tops, panoramic views are frequent and found in every direction. The trail also traverses a wide variety of habitats, from old-growth spruce, cedar and hemlock to alpine meadows to talus rock. The high points on the trail are at about 6,600 feet, just below the summits of Helmer Mountain, Shedroof Mountain and Little Snowy Top. The low points are at its beginning at Pass Creek Pass and at its junction with Trails 511 and 312, both near 5,400 feet. The allure of hiking this trail increases with the realization that it is quite easy to attain the tops of several peaks along this divide. Old trails still climb to Round Top, Thunder Mountain and Shedroof Mountain, and it is

Mankato Mountain on the Shedroof Divide seen from Round Top Mountain; Helmer Mountain is in the background

an easy scramble to the summits of Mankato and Helmer mountains. At the north end of the trail, Little Snowy Top has a maintained trail going up to its lookout, and from the end of the trail it is a tough but very doable ascent to the lofty peak of Snowy Top. My favorite part of the trail was the far south end, from the pass to Helmer Mountain. But the whole thing offers wonderful excursions into the high country of the Salmo-Priest Wilderness.

USGS Map: Helmer Mountain, Salmo Mountain

Trailhead: At milepost 3 on Highway 31 a mile south of the Ione, Washington, turn east on Sullivan Lake Road and go 13 miles to Road 22 just past the Sullivan Lake Ranger Station. Take Road 22 for 6 miles to its junction with Road 2220, but stay on Road 22 for another 6.5 miles to Pass Creek Pass. The trail is about one-quarter mile east of the pass. There is a turnout near the trail that will accommodate one vehicle, or park on the pass where three or four vehicles will fit. The road is narrow and winding for about 5 miles.

Trail Length: approximately 22 miles end to end. There are many destinations and landmarks along the way. Here are one-way distances to some of them. Round Top Mountain, 1.5 miles; a spring and campsite between Mankato and Helmer mountains, 3.9 miles; junction with Trails 311 and 526, 6.6 miles; a spring and campsite on the south side of Thunder Mountain, 8.3 miles; junction with Trails 511 and 312, 13 miles; junction with Trail 535, 15.7 miles; a campsite with water near the junction of Trail 315, 18.1 miles; junction of Trail 14 to Little Snowy Top, 20.2 miles; end of trail where it merges with Trail 506, approximately 22 miles.

Trail Condition: good the whole way

Elevation: Trailhead – 5,360', High – 6,600' (Shedroof Mountain)/Low Point – 5,480' (junction with Trail 511), End – 6,280' (junction with Trail 506)

Estimated Duration of Hike: Depending on the destination, it can range from 1 hour to several days.

Sweat Index: buckets of sweat (difficult)

Mountain Bike Sweat Index: prohibited

Best Features: magnificent views, the heart of the wilderness, wildlife

Availability of Water Along the Trail: Springs and small streams are frequent enough to make the availability of water little or no problem along the entire length of this trail. The best water sources are at mileposts 3.9, 8.3, 15.8 and 18.2. Other water may be available depending on the time of year by following a connecting trail anywhere from one-quarter to 1 mile down from the Shedroof Divide.

Stream Crossings: nothing significant

Campsites: Primitive campsites are often found at trail junctions or near water sources.

Alternate Hikes: A slew of loops and open loops abound along this trail. The best way to plan alternate hikes is to refer to a wilderness map. Keep in mind that some trails that appear on the 1993 wilderness map, such as Trails 309, 313 and 320, are no longer maintained and may be difficult, if not impossible, to follow.

Wildlife Sighting: I sat near the spring at the 8.3 mile point and quietly watched a snowshoe hare hop by. Then not far from the Shedroof Divide Cutoff trail junction I was resting at the exact right time to see a fabulous mule deer buck making his way through the brush below the trail. Ironically, this was only 30 minutes after encountering a couple of hunters who had seen nothing all day. The buck was a trophy for sure with at least five or six points on each side of a massive rack. But the real treat while on this trail was stumbling upon a Cooper's hawk feeding on some poor little critter that comprised its lunch. It sat in the beargrass among several small subalpine firs, tearing at the carcass when I came walking along. Then as silent as a light breeze it lifted itself off the ground and glided down the trail and out of sight, its impressive wingspan clipping the twigs of the trees lining the trail.

Shedroof Cutoff Trail No. 511

Destination: Shedroof Divide in the Salmo-Priest Wilderness. *Map, page 106.*

Best Suited For: hiking, horseback riding

How Much Use: A Little * A Little More * **A LOT** * A Lot More * Excessive

What's it like? Two-thirds of this trail follows an old roadbed that heads up Sullivan Creek to old logging units. After about 1.2 miles, the trail crosses the creek, parallels it for a hundred yards, then strikes off uphill into the dark timber. All along the road and single track is old-growth cedar and hemlock, with spruce and subalpine fir showing up higher on the slope. At the junction with Trail 512 you can go north or south for some fine hiking.

USGS Map: Salmo Mountain, Helmer Mountain

Trailhead: At milepost 3 on Highway 31 a mile south of the Ione, Washington, turn east on Sullivan Lake Road and go 13 miles to Road 22 just past the Sullivan Lake Ranger Station. Take road 22 for 6 miles to its junction with Road 2220 and

Gypsy Peak seen from Shedroof Divide

take that road 6.5 miles to the trailhead. There is parking for three or four vehicles.

Trail Length: 1.7 miles one-way

Trail Condition: good

Elevation: Trailhead – 4,340', High/Low Point – 4,340'-5,480', End – 5,480' (junction with Trail 512)

Estimated Duration of Hike: 1 hour each way to Trail 512

Sweat Index: break a sweat (moderate)

Mountain Bike Sweat Index: prohibited

Best Features: old-growth forest, access to the Salmo-Priest Wilderness

Availability of Water Along the Trail: Sullivan Creek is a perennial stream about a mile up the trail, and there is a nice spring near the ridge top.

Stream Crossings: easy rock hop across Sullivan Creek

Campsites: There are numerous dispersed sites along Road 2220 and only one-half mile before the trailhead is a semi-primitive campground at Gypsy Meadows where there is a vault toilet.

Alternate Hikes: This trail makes a good loop of about 13 miles with Trails 512 and 526. It connects to Trail 512 at the same spot where Trail 312 comes out of the Hughes Fork.

Wildlife Sighting: A nice mule deer buck showed his face the day I hiked this trail, which happened to be during Washington's big game hunting season. Two other vehicles were parked at the trailhead, presumably hunters, and I suppose they would have loved to see the 4x4 rack this buck was sporting.

Thunder Creek Trail No. 526

Destination: Shedroof Divide in the Salmo-Priest Wilderness. *Map, page 106.*

Best Suited For: hiking, horseback riding

How Much Use: A Little * A Little More * **A LOT** * A Lot More * Excessive

What's it like? For a little over 2 miles, the trail follows an old road that was built into Thunder Creek, apparently for the purpose of putting in a single clearcut. That was probably more than 20 years ago, and now that clear-cut has regenerated with young trees of various species. Before reaching that harvested area, the road slices through some nice old growth, but nothing like what you will go through once the single-track trail takes off from the end of the road and enters the wilderness. At the wilderness boundary there is a large, hollow cedar tree. You know it is hollow because flames evidently burned it out, but also someone took a chainsaw and cut a rectangle out of one side of it. This may have been used as a way to trap fur-bearing animals like the pine marten I saw

An old marten trap in a cedar snag along Thunder Creek

on this trail. The trail climbs over a ridge and crosses a tributary to Thunder Creek, climbs over another ridge, then drops into a basin full of exquisite, old-growth cedar and hemlock. For the next mile and a half this temperate rainforest works its magic like so much of the other old growth to be found in the Salmo-Priest Wilderness and surrounding area. Close to the top, evidence of a wildfire that singed Helmer Mountain in 1994 is right along the trail. Lightning caused the fire and flames to burn right over the summit and down into the Thunder-Jackson saddle. It is in that saddle where this trail joins Trail 512, just 100 feet from the junction of Trail 311.

USGS Map: Salmo Mountain, Helmer Mountain

Trailhead: At milepost 3 on Highway 31 a mile south of the Ione, Washington, turn east on Sullivan Lake Road and go 13 miles to Road 22 just past the Sullivan Lake Ranger Station. Take road 22 for 6 miles to its junction with Road 2220 and take that road 6.1 miles to the trailhead. There is parking for three or four vehicles.

Trail Length: 5 miles one-way

Trail Condition: good

Elevation: Trailhead – 4,180', High/Low Point – 4,180'-5,550', End – 5,550' (junction with Trail 512)

Estimated Duration of Hike: 2 to 3 hours each way

Sweat Index: buckets of sweat (difficult)

Mountain Bike Sweat Index: prohibited

Best Features: old-growth forest and access to the Salmo-Priest Wilderness

Availability of Water Along the Trail: There is plenty of water in several locations along the way, including Thunder Creek within one-half mile of the junction with Trail 512.

Stream Crossings: There are bridges and boardwalks, plus an easy step across Thunder Creek up high.

Campsites: There are numerous dispersed sites along Road 2220, and only a couple hundred yards before the trailhead is a semi-primitive campground at Gypsy Meadows where there is a vault toilet.

Alternate Hikes: This trail is part of a good loop with Trails 512 and 511. Also, it connects to Trail 512 in the same saddle where Trail 311 comes up out of Jackson Creek from Hughes Meadows.

Wildlife Sighting: About 15 feet up in a small spruce about 2 miles up the trail, a motion and noise caught my attention. I stopped and peered into the prickly foliage and there, perched on a limb, hissing and snarling at me, was a pine marten. It is only the third one I have ever seen and the first in 11 years. This secretive creature of the deep woods is a member of the weasel family.

Trails: Jackson Creek No. 311, Hughes Fork No. 312, Hughes Ridge Lookout No. 314, Upper Hughes No. 315 and Cabinet Pass No. 317

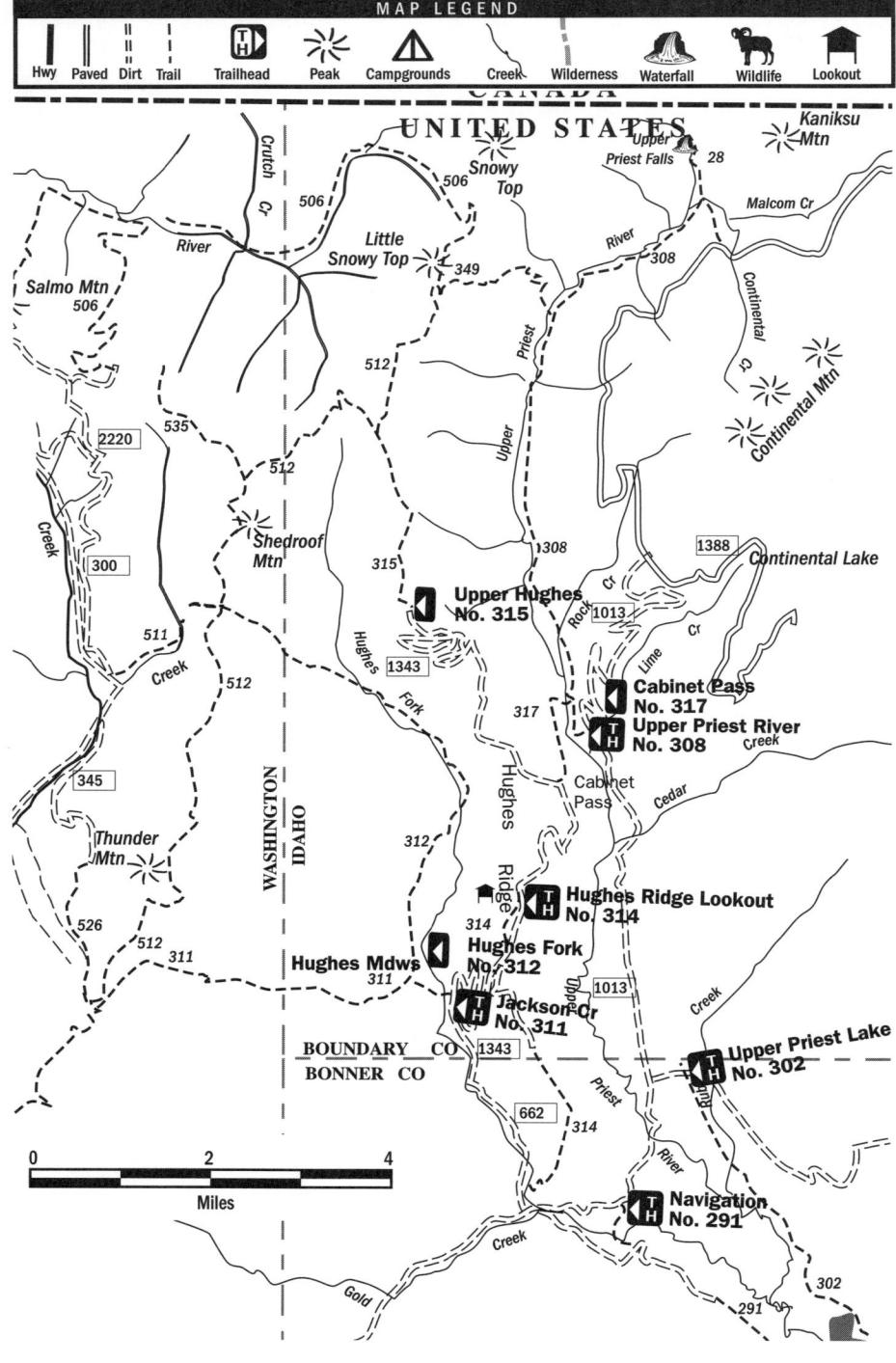

Jackson Creek Trail No. 311

Destination: Shedroof Divide in the Salmo-Priest Wilderness. *Map, page 116.*

Best Suited For: hiking, horseback riding

How Much Use: A Little * A **LITTLE MORE** * A Lot * A Lot More * Excessive

Looking down Jackson Creek toward Upper Priest Lake

What's it like? A good sign and a beautiful, rock-lined path mark the start of this trail, but it only takes a few steps to realize you will have to wade the Hughes Fork of the Priest River to continue. It is not too wide, but depending on the season, the water may well be 3 feet deep. And then on the other side there is the head-high grass to contend with, stinging nettles and a broken bridge that is crossable but tricky. Once through all that, though, an old boardwalk ushers the hiker into an absolutely gorgeous grove of giant cedars, hemlocks, spruce and whitepine sidling up to the south end of the expanse of reeds, grasses and willows that occupy Hughes Meadows. This is a tremendously beautiful place, and the anxiety of getting across the river and through the marsh is soon forgotten in the overwhelming presence of this ancient forest. The trail meanders amongst ferns and devils club to a junction perhaps one-half mile from the trailhead. Go left to continue up Jackson Creek to the Shedroof Divide some 5 miles away. The climb is fairly steady but never too steep. The trail mostly traverses the mountainside through heavy timber, but some views open up of Jackson Creek and the dark forest on the other side. Up high the trail is pretty brushy and more nettles show up in some small, boggy brushfields. It could be difficult to follow when the vegetation is fully leafed out. Be aware, if you are referring to the 1993 Salmo-Priest Wilderness map, that Trail 311 joins Trail 512 in a deep notch on the ridgeline more than a mile southwest of where the map shows the junction. In the same notch Trail 526 comes out of Thunder Creek and joins 512.

USGS Map: Helmer Mountain, Upper Priest Lake

Trailhead: From Priest River, Idaho, drive Highway 57 north to Nordman, approximately 36.5 miles. From there follow Road 302 to Granite Pass and the junction of Road 1013. Go 4.2 miles on 1013 to the junction of Hughes Meadows Road No. 662. Turn north and go 2.1 miles, then bear left. It is 1.1 miles from there to the trailhead and another 0.4 mile to Hughes Meadows Cabin.

Trail Length: 5.6 miles one-way

Trail Condition: fair

Elevation: Trailhead – 2,900', High/Low Point – 2,900'-5,540', End – 5,540' (junction with Trail 512)

Estimated Duration of Hike: 2.5 to 3.5 hours up, 2 to 3 hours down

Sweat Index: buckets of sweat (difficult)

Mountain Bike Sweat Index: not suitable

Best Features: old-growth, access to wilderness, historic cabin near the trailhead

Availability of Water Along the Trail: Water is located in several places, including a decent source within 200 yards of the end of the trail on the Shedroof Divide.

Stream Crossings: The most difficult one is right at the beginning where the Hughes Fork of the Priest River must be waded, and it is up to 3 feet deep. Other crossings are either easy rock hops or boggy areas where springs seep to the surface.

Campsites: A couple of primitive campsites are near the junction of Trail 311 with Trail 512. You can also camp by the Forest Service smokejumper cabin at the meadows, but the cabin is off limits to public use.

Alternate Hikes: Hughes Fork Trail No. 312 branches from this trail about a half-mile from the trailhead and accesses the wilderness and Trail 512 farther north. This trail joins Trail 512 in a saddle north of Helmer Mountain.

Wildlife Sighting: A magnificent grizzly bear sporting the distinctive "silver-tip" markings was on the road near the trailhead and again on the trail just across the Hughes Fork the day I struck off on this hike. I was as close as 40 feet twice, but the big bruin let me pass in peace. The meadows just north of the trail are full of waterfowl and wildlife, including beaver.

Hughes Fork Trail No. 312, Thunder Mountain Trail No. 313 and Bench Creek Trail No. 319

Destination: Shedroof Divide in the Salmo-Priest Wilderness. *Map, page 116.*

Best Suited For: hiking, horseback riding

How Much Use: A LITTLE * A Little More * A Lot * A Lot More * Excessive

What's it like? Put your wading shoes on because at the very start of this trail, which is actually on Trail 311, be prepared for about 3 feet of water when crossing the Hughes Fork of Priest River. Notice that there was once a footbridge across the river, but it fell into the stream long ago. On the other side is head-high grass, some boardwalk across a short portion of a much larger area of marsh and a broken bridge that gets you over Jackson Creek, barely. From there the trail enters a magical forest of giant cedars and hemlock with ferns and devils club carpeting the forest floor. It is a truly majestic place. Then comes the junction with Trail 312 and off it goes along the west side of Hughes Meadows. There is a screen of trees all the way, but it is possible to step out into the meadows' edge from time to time for a wonderful view of this tranquil setting. Beyond the north end of the meadows, the trail enters a forest that was burned in 1926. Notice the blackened cedar snags that still stand more than 75 years later. You probably will not notice the junction with Trail 313 (I didn't), but there is a sign that indicates Trail 319 near Bench Creek. About 100 feet of that trail

The trail from Hughes Fork offers great views of Snowy Top, a high peak a mile south of Canada

was cleared recently, but that is all. After that it is a nightmare to follow. By staying on Trail 312 you cross the Hughes Fork for a second time, but it is dry much of the summer. Then comes the third crossing, a bit trickier, and wet feet are probable. Regular maintenance seems to end here but the trail is still pretty easy to find as it climbs up the mountainside toward the Shedroof Divide. You may find yourself fighting brush and blowdown all the way over the ridge until the trail connects to Trail 512 on the east side.

USGS Map: Upper Priest Lake, Helmer Mountain

Trailhead: From Priest River, Idaho, drive Highway 57 north to Nordman, approximately 36.5 miles. From there follow Road 302 for almost 14 miles to Granite Pass and the junction of Road 1013. Go 4.2 miles on 1013 to the junction of Hughes Meadows Road No. 662. Turn north and go 2.1 miles, then bear left. It is 1.1 miles from there to the trailhead and another 0.4 mile to Hughes Meadows Cabin.

Trail Length: approximately 7.5 miles one-way

Trail Condition: good to the third crossing of the Hughes Fork, but poor after that due to infrequent maintenance

Elevation: Start – 2,980' (junction with Trail 311), High/Low Point – 2,980'-5,480', End – 5,480' (junction with Trail 512)

Estimated Duration of Hike: 3 to 4 hours up, 2.5 to 3.5 hours down

Sweat Index: bathed in sweat (strenuous)

Mountain Bike Sweat Index: prohibited because these trails enter the wilderness

Best Features: historic cabin near trailhead, access to wilderness, wildlife

Availability of Water Along the Trail: There is good water at the third crossing of the Hughes Fork and another stream just after that.

Stream Crossings: Right at the start of the hike, the Hughes Fork must be waded (it may be up to 3 feet deep). The second crossing of the Hughes Fork is dry later in the year but could pose a problem during spring runoff. The third crossing is a rock hop, but the stream is wide enough and might be deep enough to get boots wet. There is a small stream just after that to step across.

Campsites: There are no campsites along this trail, though there is plenty of water for makeshift camping when using "Leave No Trace" techniques. You can camp by the Forest Service smokejumper cabin at the meadows, but the cabin is off limits to public use.

Alternate Hikes: This trail is reached by starting out on Trail 311. About one-half mile from the trailhead, Trail 312 strikes off northward along the west side of Hughes Meadows. It joins Shedroof Divide Trail No. 512 at the same location where Shedroof Cutoff Trail No. 511 comes up out of Gypsy Meadows. With Trails 512 and 311, this trail makes an excellent loop hike of about 19.5 miles. Two other trails branch off Trail 312 – Trails 313 and 319. There is still a sign for 319 near Bench Creek, but both trails have been abandoned for all practical purposes and are next to impossible to follow.

Hughes Ridge Lookout Trail No. 314

This is a Family Fun Hike

Destination: Hughes Ridge Lookout. *Map, page 116.*

Best Suited For: hiking

How Much Use: A Little * A Little More * A Lot * **A LOT MORE** * Excessive

What's it like? This short hike takes you to a lookout active during fire season with incredible views of Hughes Meadows, the east side of the Salmo-Priest Wilderness and the Upper Priest River. It begins in heavy timber, climbs steadily but not too steeply, then breaks out into open meadows cloaking the top of the ridge. Your head will swivel as you debate which view to take in first. Hughes Ridge is not very high – at well under 5,000 feet – but the way it is situated in the Upper Priest valley gives it a unique perspective of the area. The lookout tower rises perhaps 30 feet. You can ascend the stairs, but in the off-season the upper deck is inaccessible through the locked trap door. Past personnel at the lookout have taken good care of the site as painted rocks line walkways and highlight the depiction of a giant flower laid out with rocks on the south side of the tower.

USGS Map: Upper Priest Lake

Trailhead: From Priest River, Idaho, drive Highway 57 north to Nordman, approximately 36.5 miles. From there follow Road 302 for almost 14 miles to Granite Pass and the junction of Road 1013. Go 4.2 miles to the junction of Hughes Meadows Road No. 662. Turn north and go 2.1 miles and bear right on Road 1343. Go 5 miles to where the road forks. Just before that fork is the trailhead. There is parking for four to six vehicles.

Trail Length: three-quarters of a mile one-way

Trail Condition: good

Elevation: Trailhead – 3,960', High/Low Point – 3,960'-4,248', End – 4,248' (Hughes Ridge Lookout)

Estimated Duration of Hike: 15 to 30 minutes each way

Sweat Index: no sweat (easy)

Mountain Bike Sweat Index: buckets of sweat (difficult)

Best Features: forest fire lookout tower and tremendous views

Availability of Water Along the Trail: none

Stream Crossings: none

Campsites: none

Precautions: This is a working lookout during fire season, and it may be restricted to public access during times of high fire danger.

Upper Hughes Trail No. 315 and Cabinet Pass Trail No. 317

Destination: Shedroof Divide Trail No. 512. *Map, page 116.*

Best Suited For: hiking, horseback riding

How Much Use: A LITTLE * A Little More * A Lot * A Lot More * Excessive

What's it like? If you only go as far as Cabinet Pass, this is a fine hike. The trail starts out on 308 along the Upper Priest River through some of the most stunning old-growth forest in the region. The cedars and hemlocks are magnificent. Strolling among them can take you back in time a thousand years. The obscure junction with trail 317 is only marked with a pink ribbon, so keep an eye out for the narrow path striking off towards the river. At a gravel bar lined with big logs and brush, the trail crosses to the other side. Depending on the time of year, the stream could be as much as 3 feet deep. Trail 317 continues across the Upper Priest River bottomlands, then turns south and crosses a dilapidated bridge. It is easier to just go around the collapsed structure. From there it climbs steadily to a final, very steep ascent to Cabinet Pass where it joins Trail 315. At this point Trail 315 is an old logging road, and it continues that way for miles. Only the final 2 or 3 miles are single track up onto a ridgeline to the Shedroof Divide. But while on that road acting as a trail, the views are fabulous and wildlife is abundant.

USGS Map: Continental Mountain, Salmo Mountain

Thunder Mountain between aspens

Trailhead: From Priest River, Idaho, drive Highway 57 north to Nordman, approximately 36.5 miles. From there follow Road 302 for almost 14 miles to Granite Pass and the junction of Road 1013. Travel road 1013 for 11.3 miles to the signed trailhead on the west side of the road. A small parking area will accommodate four to six vehicles.

Trail Length: Trail 308 to the junction with Trail 317 is about one-half mile; Trail 317 is 1.3 mile and Trail 315 is 9.1 miles. So to reach Shedroof Divide Trail No. 512 via these three trails is a distance of about 11 miles one-way.

Trail Condition: fair

Elevation: Trail 317, Start – 2,770' (junction with Trail 308), High/Low Point – 2,740' (Upper Priest River crossing), End – 3,520' (junction with Trail 315)

Elevation: Trail 315, Start – 3,520' (junction with Trail 317), High/Low Point – 6,000', End – 5,930' (junction with Trail 512)

Estimated Duration of Hike: 1 to 2 hours to Cabinet Pass and 4 to 6 hours to the Shedroof Divide

Sweat Index: buckets of sweat (difficult)

Mountain Bike Sweat Index: not suitable

Best Features: superb, old-growth forest along the lower stretches of Trail 317, terrific views of the surrounding mountainous terrain along 315

Availability of Water Along the Trail: After crossing the Upper Priest River, there are a few small springs and streams along Trail 317. Don't expect to find any more after that.

Stream Crossings: Upper Priest River must be waded, and there is a large boggy area on Trail 317.

Campsites: none

Precautions: Be cautious crossing the Upper Priest, especially at high water. The current can be dangerously strong.

Alternate Hikes: Trails 315 and 317 are connecting trails between Trail 308 and Trail 512. Where 317 joins 315 at Cabinet Pass, it is possible to follow the old road south toward Hughes Ridge Lookout, but the road is exceedingly brushy.

Wild Notes: It is not unusual to see white-tailed deer practically everywhere in rural northern Idaho and northeastern Washington. But nonetheless, they are always a delight to see, especially out on the trail. In this case, I surprised a doe while hiking Cabinet Pass Trail No. 317. She was just below the trail in a tangle of blowdown but chose to step up on the trail and bound for the pass. In typical fashion, that big, white tail shot straight up as she ran off. Instead of the white flag of surrender or truce, it is a warning sign to other deer in the area that danger lurks nearby.

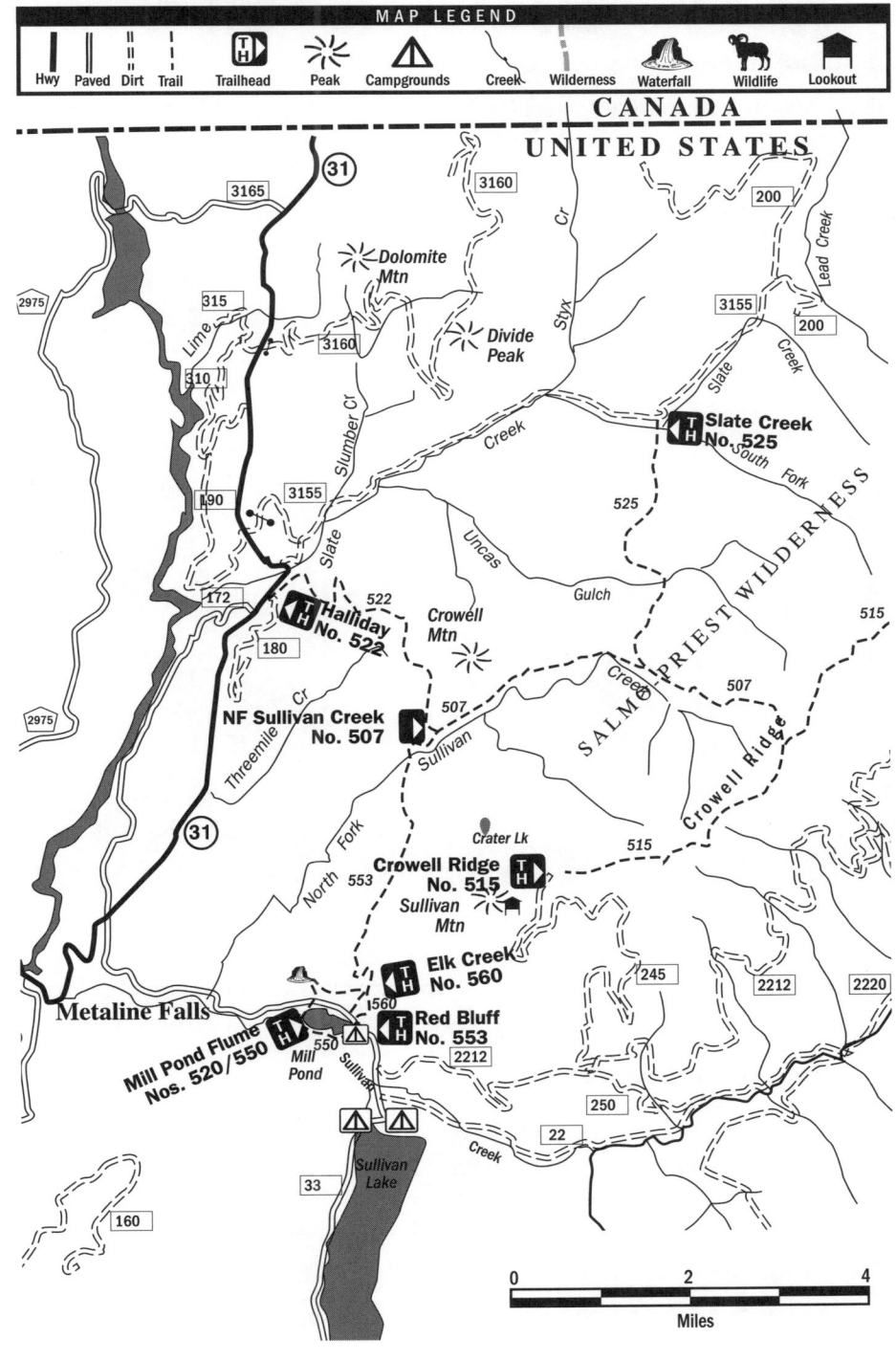

Crowell Ridge Trail No. 515

Destination: Crowell Ridge, 6,885 feet. *Map, page 123.*

Best Suited For: hiking, horseback riding

How Much Use: A Little * **A LITTLE MORE** * A Lot * A Lot More * Excessive

What's it like? Trail 515 is the major route through the west side of the Salmo-Priest Wilderness. It is entirely a high-elevation path, spending almost all its time above 6,000 feet. That makes for some magnificent views both east and west. The south end of the trail from Sullivan Mountain is mostly through timber, though it is sparse enough for numerous vistas. As is typical of mountain

The rugged high country of Crowell Ridge and Gypsy Peak

ridges, the terrain goes up and down and the trail with it. About 3 miles along the trail, you might notice a trail junction that doesn't show on the maps. An old wooden sign indicates that mystery trail is no longer maintained. Another mile or so brings you to the junction with Trail 507 in a notch on the ridge at about 6,600 feet. Trees are scarce and stunted, and the views are tremendous. From here the trail cuts across side-hill, but a brief, easy scramble up the shoulder of the mountain will take you to the highest point on Crowell Ridge and the site of an old lookout. Only the platform remains. Off in the distance you can see the trail snaking through the alpine meadows toward Bear Pasture and the barren ridge tops of the rugged high country surrounding Gypsy Peak.

USGS Map: Metaline Falls, Gypsy Peak

Trailhead: At milepost 3 on Highway 31 just south of Ione, Washington, turn east on Sullivan Lake Road and go 13.3 miles to Highline Road, about three-quarters of a mile north of the Sullivan Lake Ranger Station. Follow Highline Road No. 2212 for 3.4 miles to the junction of Road 245. Travel 245 approximately 7.5 miles to a switchback on a ridgetop and a gate. Sullivan Mountain Lookout is one-half mile behind that gate. The trailhead is at the switchback where parking will accommodate three to five vehicles. Road 245 is narrow, rough and rocky and is recommended for high-clearance vehicles. The northeast end of the trail can be reached by taking Road 22 from Sullivan Lake Road 0.4 miles north of the ranger station. Go 6 miles to Road 2220 then follow that road approximately 1.5 miles to Road 2212. Go about 3.5 miles to Road 200 and go to the end of the road and the trailhead at Bear Pasture. The last couple miles of 200 are rough and should not be attempted with a regular passenger car. This road is closed after August 15.

Trail Length: 7.8 miles end to end (Sullivan Mountain to Bear Pasture); 4.1 miles to the junction with Trail 507 (from Sullivan Mountain)

Trail Condition: fair

Elevation: Trailhead – 6,260' (near Sullivan Mountain Lookout), High Point/Low Point – 6,530' (junction with Trail 507), End – 5,660' (Bear Pasture)

Estimated Duration of Hike: 3.5 to 4.5 hours either way, about 2 hours to Trail 507 from either direction

Sweat Index: buckets of sweat (difficult)

Mountain Bike Sweat Index: prohibited

Best Features: access to Salmo-Priest Wilderness, high-elevation ridge top hiking, fantastic views, remains of old lookout

Availability of Water Along the Trail: no dependable source

Stream Crossings: none

Campsites: none on the trail

Alternate Hikes: Trail 507 comes out of the North Fork of Sullivan Creek and connects with this trail about midway. It provides for a couple of nice open loop options with Slate Creek, Halliday and Red Bluff trails. The north end of Trail 515 also provides off trail access to Gypsy Peak, the highest mountain in the Salmo-Priest Wilderness.

Wildlife Sighting: While hiking this trail following a dusting of about an inch of snow in early November, I came upon a set of cat tracks. Maybe a half-mile later I came upon the cat itself, still padding silently along the ridge. It was a bobcat and in one instant it was on the trail looking over its shoulder at me, and in the next instant it was gone. These elusive creatures are seldom seen in the wild, and it was a real treat stumbling upon this fellow.

Slate Creek Trail No. 525

Destination: Crowell Ridge in the Salmo-Priest Wilderness. *Map, page 123.*

Best Suited For: hiking, horseback riding

How Much Use: A Little * **A LITTLE MORE** * A Lot * A Lot More * Excessive

What's it like? The value of this trail is that it can be used for a good, open-loop hike of about 16 miles with Trails 507 and 522. It spends most of its time in heavy timber, which is at times incredibly dense doghair cedar and hemlock saplings beneath scattered larch, Douglas fir and other species. The trail drops down to Slate Creek, then climbs about 500 feet to an area of broken, uneven topography. Because of the density of the forest cover, there are almost no views. But the forest is interesting and wildlife might be encountered on the trail. About a mile and a half from the trailhead, the trail skirts a small meadow. Undulating up and down for several miles, the trail finally curves around a ridge and descends to its junction with Trail 507 in a dark cedar hollow.

Wooden footbridges are common in the Selkirks for crossing streams and marshy areas

USGS Map: Gypsy Peak

Trailhead: At milepost 21.8 on Highway 31, about 7.5 miles north of Metaline Falls, Washington, turn east onto Slate Creek Road. Go 6 miles to the trailhead, which is just below a switchback where two or three vehicles can be parked.

Trail Length: 4.3 miles one-way

Trail Condition: good

Elevation: Trailhead – 3,790', High Point/Low Point – 3,590' (crossing Slate Creek), End – 4,550' (junction with Trail 507)

Estimated Duration of Hike: 2 to 3 hours each way

Sweat Index: break a sweat (moderate)

Mountain Bike Sweat Index: prohibited

Best Features: access to the wilderness

Availability of Water Along the Trail: Slate Creek has good water just one-quarter mile from the trailhead, and Uncas Gulch offers a good water source about 3 miles up the trail.

Stream Crossings: Slate Creek and Uncas Gulch, the two largest streams along this trail, must be stepped across, but other small draws and boggy areas have footbridges or boardwalk.

Campsites: There is a primitive site at Uncas Gulch.

Alternate Hikes: This trail connects to Trail 507 in the Salmo-Priest Wilderness, which makes for a great open loop with Trail 522.

Halliday Trail No. 522

Destination: North Fork of Sullivan Creek. *Map, page 123.*

Best Suited For: hiking, horseback riding, mountain biking

How Much Use: A Little * **A LITTLE MORE** * A Lot * A Lot More * Excessive

What's it like? For a quarter mile or more, this trail parallels Highway 31 before turning into the forest and up a moderately steep slope. As it goes over a bald knob, you will notice a sign for a Research Natural Area. These are parts of the National Forest System that have been set aside for study because of the special qualities they contain. This RNA is called Halliday Fen, which you will see from the trail as it winds into a nifty little basin holding a beaver pond and wetland meadow and continues meandering toward Crowell Mountain. Along the way there are occasional views to the west of Abercrombie and Hooknose mountains. In a saddle 600 feet below the summit, the trail begins a descent toward the North Fork of Sullivan Creek. Straight out in front of you are Sullivan Mountain and the lookout on its summit. Two hundred vertical feet above the creek this trail joins Trail 553 coming in from the south and Trail 507 heading westward into the wilderness.

USGS Map: Gypsy Peak, Boundary Dam

Trailhead: At milepost 20.6 on Highway 31 about 6.5 miles north of Metaline Falls, Washington, turn east on Road 180 and immediately turn left and go 0.1 mile to the trailhead. There is a highly visible sign on the highway. An unloading ramp for horses is located just off the highway. There is a large turnaround area and plenty of parking.

Trail Length: 4.2 miles one-way

Trail Condition: good

Elevation: Trailhead – 2,520', High Point/Low Point – 4,080', End – 3,610' (junction with Trail 507)

Estimated Duration of Hike: 1.5 to 2.5 hours each way

Sweat Index: break a sweat (moderate)

Mountain Bike Sweat Index: buckets of sweat (difficult)

Best Features: access to the Salmo-Priest Wilderness via Trail 507, good views of Abercrombie and Hooknose mountains, Research Natural Area

Availability of Water Along the Trail: none

Stream Crossings: there is a footbridge over the outlet of Halliday Fen about a mile up the trail.

Campsites: none

Alternate Hikes: This trail comes to a 3-way junction with Trails 553 and 507. A great open loop of about 16 miles can be had with Trails 507 and 525 or another open loop with Trail 553.

Wild Notes: A common and beautiful plant in the Selkirk Mountains is one that often goes overlooked. It is a creeping, vine-like, little woody plant called northern twinflower. It has roundish evergreen leaves that are toothed on the edges and produces a pair of bell-shaped pink flowers that stick up 3 or 4 inches. Trail 522 and other trails in this area are full of this plant, whose scientific name is Linnaea borealis. Borealis means "north" and the genus name, Linnaea, is in honor of the man credited with devising the scientific naming system for plants and animals, Carlos Linnaeus.

Red Bluff Trail No. 553

Destination: North Fork of Sullivan Creek. *Map, page 123.*

Best Suited For: hiking, horseback riding, mountain biking

How Much Use: A Little * **A LITTLE MORE** * A Lot * A Lot More * Excessive

What's it like? A mixed forest of conifers interspersed with birch and aspen makes this a wonderful hike through the woods. In the first mile there are glimpses of Sullivan Lake and Mill Pond, but once the trail wraps around a ridge tumbling off Sullivan Mountain, it slowly descends toward the North Fork of Sullivan Creek. The trail undulates for a while with the terrain, sometimes dropping into deep cedar bottoms that are as quiet as a nursery at naptime. At the creek crossing there are several giant cedars lining the stream and surrounding a primitive campsite. The site has not been treated very well as there was a lot of trash in the fire pit. It is a brief, easy climb out of the creek bottom to a terrace where the trail joins Trails 507 and 522.

USGS Map: Metaline Falls, Boundary Dam

Trailhead: At milepost 16.4 on Highway 31 about 2.3 miles north of Metaline Falls, Washington, turn east onto the north end of Sullivan Lake Road (the south end is at Ione,

Sullivan Lake is glimpsed through the trees along Red Bluff Trail

Washington) and travel 4 miles to the signed trailhead. There is parking for two to three vehicles.

Trail Length: 5.2 miles one-way

Trail Condition: good

Elevation: Trailhead – 2,590', High Point/Low Point – 3,760', End – 3,610' (junction with Trail 507)

Estimated Duration of Hike: 2 to 3 hours each way to the junction with Trails 507 and 522

Sweat Index: break a sweat (moderate)

Mountain Bike Sweat Index: buckets of sweat (difficult)

Best Features: a nice forest hike

Availability of Water Along the Trail: Water can be found at Elk Creek about a mile or so up the trail and at the North Fork of Sullivan Creek, just one-half mile from the junction with Trails 507 and 522. There is also a small brook between North Fork Sullivan Creek and the trail juncture.

Stream Crossings: Both Elk Creek and North Fork Sullivan Creek are easy rock hops.

Campsites: There is a developed campground at Mill Pond near the trailhead and a primitive campsite at the crossing of the North Fork of Sullivan Creek.

Alternate Hikes: This trail connects to Trail 507, which accesses Crowell Ridge in the Salmo-Priest Wilderness. It also connects to Trail 522 providing for an open loop to Highway 31.

Wildlife Sighting: The wind was calm, the forest all but silent when a warbling call followed by a single clear note echoed through the trees. An answering call rang out a short distance away. For several moments two pygmy owls talked back and forth as I sauntered along this trail. I didn't actually see the birds, but they were close and listening to their song was a highlight of this fine hike.

North Fork Sullivan Creek Trail No. 507

Destination: Crowell Ridge and the Salmo-Priest Wilderness. *Map, page 123.*

Best Suited For: hiking, horseback riding

How Much Use: A Little * **A LITTLE MORE** * A Lot * A Lot More * Excessive

What's it like? On a terrace above the North Fork of Sullivan Creek, Trail 507 emerges from a junction with two other trails. It follows that terrace for quite some ways, providing pretty good views of the lookout on Sullivan Mountain across the valley. The timber is generally pretty thick all the way to the wilderness boundary, 2 miles from the start of the trail. Just inside the wilderness there is a campsite near the creek, and not far beyond that is the junction with Trail

525. From there this trail begins a steady climb toward Crowell Ridge, switchbacking half a dozen times on the way. The forest changes to almost pure lodgepole pine, which allows for long sight distances up and down the mountainside. Huckleberry bushes carpet the forest floor. It is a stunningly beautiful forest. On the high slopes the trees become stunted and scarcer, and spectacular views begin to show up, especially to the west. The trail wraps around a shoulder of the ridge and then joins Trail 515 right on top.

USGS Map: Gypsy Peak

Trailhead: This is a connecting trail that is accessed from Trails 522, 525 or 515.

Trail Length: 5.3 miles one-way from its junction with Trails 553 and 522 to its junction with Trail 515.

The junction of Trail 507 with Crowell Ridge Trail No. 515 is marked by a weathered sign

Trail Condition: good

Elevation: Start – 3,610' (junction with Trail 522), High Point/Low Point – 4,550' (junction with Trail 525), End – 6,530' (junction with Trail 515)

Estimated Duration of Hike: 2.5 to 3.5 hours up, 2 to 3 hours down

Sweat Index: buckets of sweat (difficult)

Mountain Bike Sweat Index: prohibited

Best Features: access to the wilderness, excellent views to the west on the higher slopes

Availability of Water Along the Trail: About 2 miles or so from the junction with 553 and 522 and only about one-quarter mile from Trail 525, the trail is within 100 feet of the North Fork of Sullivan Creek. That is the only place for water along this trail.

Stream Crossings: none

Campsites: A primitive site is located at the water source near Trail 525.

Alternate Hikes: Trail 507 forms a connecting link between Trails 522, 525, 553 and 515.

Wildlife Sighting: I met two young mule deer wandering on the trail not far from the top of the ridge. They looked like the previous year's fawns, which were probably driven away by mom when she had new fawns in the spring of 2003.

Essay:
Longevity

The sky was clear and the sun shone bright in a turquoise sea, but they were both nearly hidden from me in the deep shade of the Upper Priest River. Deep is right. From ground level, where Malcom Creek spills noisily into the river, the shade rises 200 feet into the interlaced branches of cedars that have survived more than 30 generations of man. One fine day in September I walked among these ancient trees and wondered what it's like to be old, truly old.

Road No. 1013 slices through the forest of the Upper Priest valley, but about five and a half miles from where the road crosses to the east side of the river, it pulls away from the river bottom and climbs up a mountainside. From there, for a stretch of more than 8 miles, the forest is unbroken but for the river itself and a foot trail, both winding casually among the trees.

I stepped into the dark forest from the trailhead that glorious autumn day, high-stepping it and humming a lighthearted tune until overcome with the sense I was entering Fangorn, that malevolent wood older than time in J.R.R. Tolkien's *Lord of the Rings*. My pace slowed and my voice grew silent. On either side were trees 5, 6, 8 and ten feet in diameter, and who knows how many centuries they had stood there. Their massive trunks towered into the sky beyond sight, lost in the tangled canopy hundreds of feet overhead. Gnarly roots curled into the soft soil, gripping the earth with long, woody fingers. I was suddenly aware of how small and frail I am.

A soft breeze murmured in the treetops, and the whispering of the river drifted in and out of shadows. It was as though they held a conversation, the wind and the stream, speaking to the trees, to each other, and I was an eavesdropper, uninvited and unwelcome in this place of long-lived secrets.

The trail led me farther into the forest and I walked with reverence, as though I had entered a cathedral. In the dim light of midday, a day awash in sunshine beyond the over-arching boughs crowning cedar and hemlock, the forest floor was veiled in twilight. But the ground was a living thing decorated with shimmering iridescent green fronds of lady ferns, the leathery olive-green of sword ferns, the dagger-studded stems of devils club. Here and there, where a stray beam of sunlight penetrated the gloom, a crimson huckleberry bush, adorned in its autumn raiment, boasted of its colorful garb. Moss lay in thick piles like carpet draped over logs, wrapped around stumps, clinging to boulders. Its aquamarine aura gave the impression of waters gently lapping at a wooded shore.

Time moves with imperceptible slowness in this forest. I was in too big of a hurry, even by just standing still trying to listen to the sounds it made, for in moments I was off again, one foot in front of the other. I wanted to pry into their secrets, discover a nugget of wisdom that only old age endears. But maybe I was too young, too impatient. To a cedar a decade is like a minute, a hundred years like a blink of the eye. Motionless through centuries, except for the caress of the wind on their ragged heads, the cedars stood there transfixed from one year to another. I wanted to feel sorry for the trees in their immobility, but instead I felt their pity for my frenzied rushing through their great forest.

My walk through the forest of the Upper Priest valley took me to a waterfall spilling from the lip of a canyon gouged into the earth's surface where Canada sits heavy on top of Idaho. To the east, glistening silver and white in the radiant sunshine, rose the granite dome of Kaniksu Mountain. Made naked by fire in 1967, it conveyed an impression of youthfulness. With the forest cover stripped from its skin by flames, the mountain looked young and restless beneath the larger dome of the blue sky. The sun, free of the interference of tall trees and leafy stems, bathed the mountain in glorious warmth. Even I felt younger, more energetic on the exposed rocks.

But a closer look revealed the wrinkles and pock marks, the lines and shadows, the breaks and fractures that come with longevity. I knelt and listened to the rocks, listened for some small voice to bring clarification to my thoughts, to impart some ancient wisdom hinted at in the calloused face of the mountain. Standing on stone older than the forest below, older than the river rushing off its rugged flanks, I knew the secrets locked in its ancient vaults would not be unveiled for me. Behind my persistent yearning for knowledge of things grown old was the urge to move on to the next sight, the next sound, the next moment in time with hopes a discovery would set me free from the need to always be in motion.

I would be a cedar in the forest, my roots gripping the earth, drinking from the everlasting stream coursing from the mountains.

In a matter of seven or eight hours, I strode 17 miles up and down the length of the Upper Priest. The mountains, the trees were silent. Perhaps about the time one of them was prepared to speak to me I was out of earshot.

Imagine the stories they could tell, if mountains and trees and animals could speak! And who's to say they don't? John Denver once sang, "Who knows? Perhaps they do. How do you know they don't just because they've never spoken to you?"

Someday I hope to hear them speak.

Sullivan Lake to Blacktail Mountain

One of the most beautiful mountains in all the Selkirks towers more than 4,000 feet above Sullivan Lake. Crowned with golden meadows and flanked by evergreen forests, Hall Mountain (6,323 feet) is a breathtaking monument on the Pend Oreille-Priest Divide. And at its base is the magnificent lake itself, the deep glacial waters from Harvey Creek pooled as Sullivan Lake. History, and not just wild beauty, lives here, as exhibited at Mill Pond Historical Site. A great system of trails not only accesses the lake and the mountain, but also historical sites, and the Salmo-Priest Wilderness is only a mile from its northern shore. On that shore sits the the Sullivan Lake Ranger Station. East of this fine country is the crest of the divide at Grassy Top and then the sprawling hills and valleys of Granite Creek.

There are two National Recreation Trails in this subsection, one along the Sullivan lakeshore and the other connecting Pass Creek Pass to the Middle Fork of Harvey Creek via Grassy Top Mountain. Other trails summit Blacktail Mountain, where one of the finest views of Priest Lake is found; another explores among the survivors of a 1926 wildfire at the Roosevelt Grove of Ancient Cedars; and one of the most fascinating interpretive sites south of the border is located at Huff Lake.

Getting into this area is easy from both sides of the divide. Ione and Metaline Falls provide routes to Sullivan Lake, and Nordman is the gateway to Granite Pass, the most unusual "Shoe Tree," and a host of trails surrounding the infamous Stagger Inn.

This area also harbors a lot of trails that have not seen a trail crew in a decade or longer. Among the trails I explored but found to be next to impassable was North Fork-Grassy Top Trail No. 379. It has a well-signed trailhead just south of the Roosevelt Grove, and for a mile it seemed to be a promising adventure. But the trail abruptly hit a wall of blowdown that had not seen a saw since the early 90s at least. At the top, the trail, visible among brush, beargrass and dead lodgepole lying across its tread, was extremely difficult to follow. Another system of trails that proved to be disappointing begins at the Tillicum Creek trailhead. Trails 261, 264, 284 and 373 have all fallen into disrepair and disuse. But the trailhead is worth a stop just to see a remarkable cedar 5 feet in diameter and perhaps 150 feet tall – not because of its dimensions but because of the thousands of pairs of shoes adorning its trunk and lower limbs! I also sought to explore Sema Creek Trail No. 241 and Trails 262 and 378 all on South Fork Mountain, but the Forest Service is not maintaining them. Trail 241 has received some attention, perhaps from hunters, but because it passes through a section of Stimson Lumber Co. land, which they hope to log as soon as possible, it is not included in the trail descriptions found in this book. Boulder Creek Trail No. 296 and North Blacktail Trail No. 324 are two trails that may be in good enough shape to hike, but I didn't find the trailhead for either.

Trails: Mill Pond Flume No. 520, Mill Pond No. 550, Elk Creek No. 560

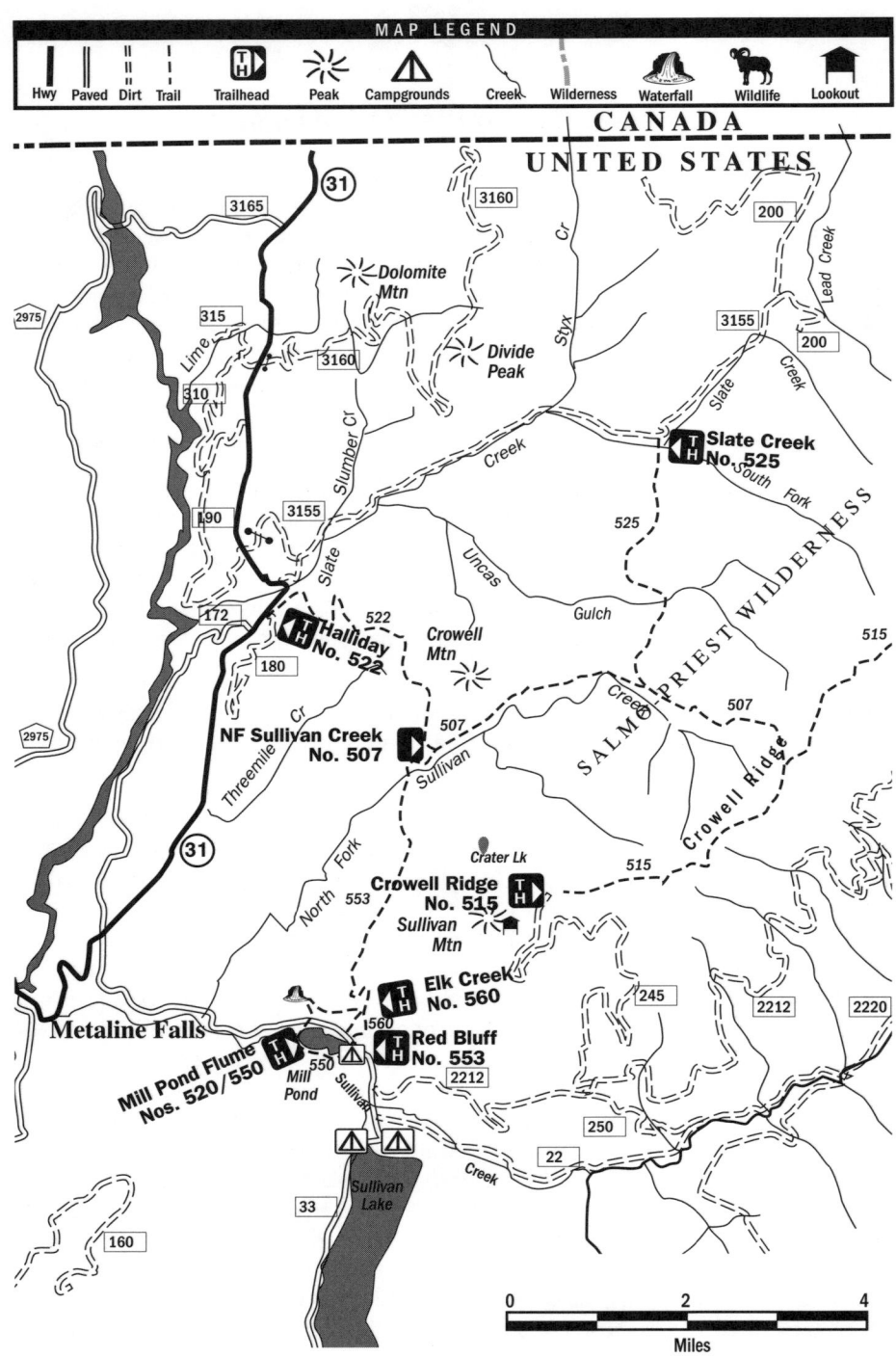

Mill Pond Flume Trail No. 520 and Mill Pond Trail No. 550

ACCESSIBLE: A wide, level trail crosses a sturdy steel bridge to a gravel pathway that explores some of the old remains of the flume.

This is a Family Fun Hike

Destination: Mill Pond Flume and Mill Pond. *Map, page 134.*

Best Suited For: hiking only

How Much Use: A Little * A Little More * **A LOT** * A Lot More * Excessive

What's it like? There is a lot of history in the Selkirk Mountains, but the story to be told at Mill Pond was almost forgotten. Then the Forest Service stepped forward with other partners and created the Mill Pond Historical Site. It is truly fascinating and well worth a journey into this part of the range. An interpretive trail suitable for wheelchair access tells the story of Lewis P. Larsen's vision for a hydroelectric facility in the Sullivan Creek canyon to power a mining operation that developed a limestone deposit near Metaline Falls, before there was even a town of that name. It also tells of the changes that took place for Enoch Carr, the only resident at that site in 1909. A year later the railroad was extended from Newport, and the town was flourishing. The flume that provided the water for the power plant was severely damaged by avalanches in the 1950s and was never repaired.

Mill Pond with Sullivan Mountain in the background

That ended an era that lasted more than 40 years. But there is still evidence of the work camps and the flume itself, which can be seen from Trail 520, a wide paved trail with virtually no slope. Trail 550 goes along the south edge of Mill Pond to where Sullivan Creek empties into the impoundment.

USGS Map: Metaline Falls

Trailhead: At milepost 16.4 on Highway 31 about 2.3 miles north of Metaline Falls, Washington, turn east onto the north end of Sullivan Lake Road (the south end is at Ione, Washington). Go 3.3 miles to the Mill Pond Historical Site and the trailheads. There is parking for six to eight vehicles at Trail 550 and for another eight to 10 vehicles at Trail 520.

Trail Length: Trail 520 forms a loop of about 0.6 mile; 550 follows the south shore of Mill Pond for three-quarters mile.

Trail Condition: Trail 520 is excellent, Trail 550 is good.

Elevation: Trailhead – 2,520', High Point/Low Point – 2,600', End – 2,520'

Estimated Duration of Hike: 15 minutes to 1 hour

Sweat Index: no sweat (easy)

Mountain Bike Sweat Index: prohibited

Best Features: historical

Availability of Water Along the Trail: There is potable water at Mill Pond Campground one-half mile east of the trailheads.

Stream Crossings: Trail 520 crosses the outlet of Mill Pond over a sturdy metal bridge; Trail 550 requires wading Sullivan Creek above Mill Pond to reach the campground (not recommended) or simply returning the way you came.

Campsites: There is a developed campground at the east end of Mill Pond.

Alternate Hikes: Trail 560 to Elk Creek Falls shares the parking area for Trails 520 and 550.

Elk Creek Trail No. 560

This is a Family Fun Hike

Destination: Elk Creek Falls. *Map, page 134.*

Best Suited For: hiking only

How Much Use: A Little * A Little More * **A LOT** * A Lot More * Excessive

What's it like? From the upper parking area at the Mill Pond Historical Site, the trail crosses Sullivan Lake Road and immediately begins to climb through scattered trees and brush. This is a south-facing slope, so if you are hiking this on a hot summer's day it is best to go in the early morning or evening. The trail snakes into a draw that is pleasantly cool with cedar trees shading the ground, but it curves back out into the brush fields on the slopes above Mill Pond. From this vantage point the views of Mill Pond and Sullivan Lake are fantastic. Shortly, the trail enters the steep canyon framing the falls and it drops down to the creek. A bridge crosses the stream

Elk Falls

below the main falls, which are beautiful and about 20 to 30 feet high. The cascade continues well below the bridge, too. The spray from the falls will be soothing on a hot day. The trail winds down the hill, crossing the creek once more, then coming back to the road. Cross it and follow the trail to its junction with a spur trail. Go left to the Mill Pond Campground or go right back to the parking area.

USGS Map: Metaline Falls

Trailhead: At milepost 16.4 on Highway 31 about 2.3 miles north of Metaline Falls, Washington, turn east onto the north end of Sullivan Lake Road (the south end is at Ione, Washington). Go 3.3 miles to the Mill Pond Historical Site and the trailhead. There is parking for six to eight vehicles.

Trail Length: 2.1-mile loop with a spur trail of 0.3 miles to the campground

Trail Condition: good

Elevation: Trailhead – 2,520', High Point/Low Point – 2,820' (Elk Creek Falls), End – 2,600' (junction with Trail 550)

Estimated Duration of Hike: 1 to 2 hours around the loop

Sweat Index: break a sweat (moderate)

Mountain Bike Sweat Index: prohibited

Best Features: fabulous views of Mill Pond and Sullivan Lake, a nice waterfall

Availability of Water Along the Trail: Elk Creek is a perennial stream.

Stream Crossings: The trail crosses Elk Creek twice, but both times are via sturdy wooden footbridges.

Campsites: There is a developed campground next to the Mill Pond Historical Site.

Precautions: The trail crosses Sullivan Lake Road twice, so be careful and watch for oncoming traffic.

Alternate Hikes: This trail shares the parking area for Trails 520 and 550.

Trails: Sullivan Lakeshore National Recreation No. 504, Noisy Creek No. 588

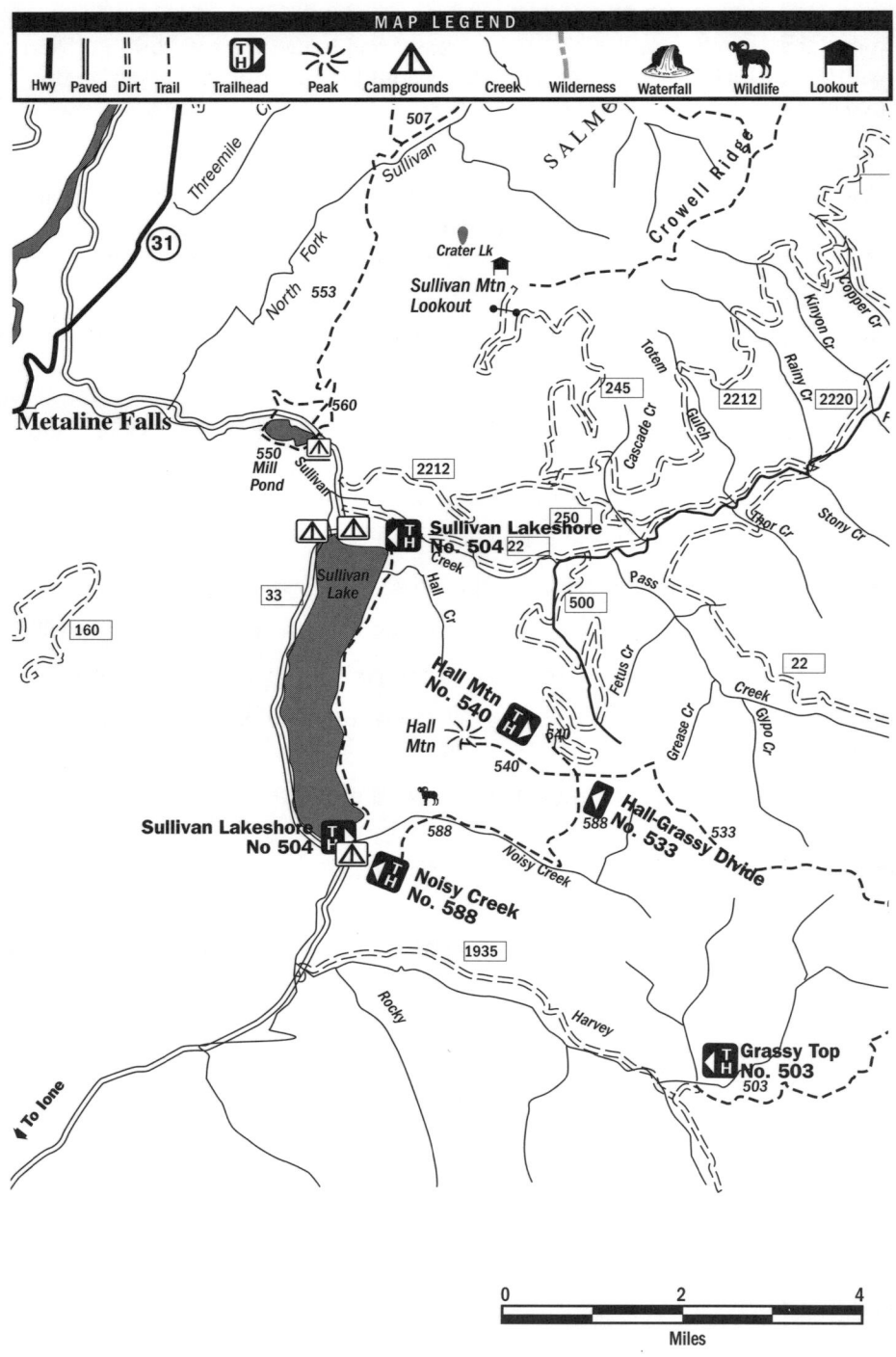

Sullivan Lakeshore National Recreation Trail No. 504 and Sullivan Nature Trail No. 509

This is a Family Fun Hike

Destination: Sullivan Lake. *Map, page 138.*

Best Suited For: hiking only

How Much Use: A Little * A Little More * **A LOT** * A Lot More * Excessive

A squirrel perches on a rock above the placid waters of Sullivan Lake

What's it like? A party of hikers can take advantage of this trail the most by parking vehicles at either end, then enjoying a leisurely stroll along the east side of Sullivan Lake from one end to the other. But lone hikers will enjoy this trail and its magnificent scenery, too. From the south end the trail wraps around the southeast corner of the lake and climbs slightly to the site of an old mine shaft. It has been barricaded to prevent entry into a potentially dangerous area. I don't know how far back the shaft goes into the mountainside, but a sign warns of unstable ladders, deep pools of water, no oxygen and possible poisonous gases, among other things. A couple hundred feet farther and the trail reaches a wooden bench on a high point overlooking the lake. The mountainside rises steeply but the trail remains relatively gentle across areas of talus rock. Notice the scattered, giant Douglas firs and Western larch along the trail. Virtually all of Hall Mountain and the east side of the lake burned in 1926, but some trees survived the flames. At the third spring there is a small grove of particularly impressive firs, some of them perhaps over 4 feet in diameter. They all have singed bark still evident from the fire more than 75 years ago. Beyond this stand of giants, the trail enters a magical grove of birch trees with scattered aspens and cottonwoods. It is truly a beautiful spot and nearby is a campsite on the shore of the lake. At the north end the trail enters a dense forest, which has suffered considerable damage from root rot, bark beetles, mistletoe and high winds. About 0.1 miles from the north trailhead is the nature trail. Grab a self-guiding brochure at the junction. By the time you read this, that trail has probably been cleaned up, but in November 2003 there was a lot of blowdown and uprooted trees all along it. The interpretive sites explain natural processes at work in the forest. Beyond the nature trail the main trail climbs well above the lake to a wooden bench on a high bluff with a great view looking south.

USGS Map: Metaline Falls

Trailhead: At milepost 3 on Highway 31 just south of Ione, Washington, turn east onto Sullivan Lake Road. Go 8.4 miles to Noisy Creek Campground. Inside the campground go left to the trailhead, which is by the boat launch. A paved parking area will accommodate six or more vehicles. The north end of the trail is accessed by continuing on Sullivan Lake Road another 4.5 miles to Road 22, about 0.4 miles past the Sullivan Lake Ranger Station. Turn east and go 0.4 miles to the entrance of East Sullivan Campground. Go about one-third mile to the trailhead. A graveled parking area accommodates six or more vehicles. This trailhead also accesses Sullivan Nature Trail No. 509.

Trail Length: 4.1 miles end to end; the nature trail is a 0.6-mile loop.

Trail Condition: good

Elevation: Trailhead – 2,590' (East Sullivan Campground), High Point/Low Point – 2,840', End – 2,600' (Noisy Creek Campground)

Estimated Duration of Hike: 1.5 to 2.5 hours either way on 504; about one-half hour on the nature loop

Sweat Index: break a sweat (moderate)

Mountain Bike Sweat Index: prohibited

Best Features: beautiful views of the lake along 504 and interpretive sites on the nature trail

Availability of Water Along the Trail: Five small springs are located along Trail 504 within the first mile or so of the south end, and there is a seasonal stream about one-half mile from the north end. The trail also passes close to the lakeshore in several places.

Stream Crossings: The springs are easy to step across, though some could be boggy during wet times of the year. The stream has a wooden footbridge over it.

Campsites: Developed campgrounds are at either end, and a primitive site is located about halfway next to the lake.

Alternate Hikes: The trailhead for Noisy Creek Trail No. 588 is located near Trail 504 in the Noisy Creek Campground.

Noisy Creek Trail No. 588

Destination: Hall Mountain, 6,323 feet. *Map, page 138.*

Best Suited For: hiking, horseback riding, mountain biking

How Much Use: A Little * A Little More * **A LOT** * A Lot More * Excessive

What's it like? About as soon as you strike off on this trail, it joins an old roadbed but only for 100 yards before it leaves the road and climbs the mountainside. The timber is interspersed with some brushy openings, and a little higher up there are some nice views of the south end of Sullivan Lake. From there the trail drops into Noisy Creek, crosses the stream where the old roadbed meets

Early morning fog dissipates over Sullivan Lake

the creek, then hugs the stream for more than a mile. The coolness of the shade can be refreshing on a hot summer day, but late in the year this narrow gorge can be a funnel for frigid air sinking to the lowlands from the high country. The trail finally pulls away from the creek and starts up the south slope of Hall Mountain. The path follows an easy grade slicing through the dense forest of young larch and lodgepole pine. On the ridge top it joins Trail 540, which continues 1.8 miles out to the summit of Hall Mountain.

USGS Map: Metaline Falls, Pass Creek

Trailhead: At milepost 3 on Highway 31 just south of Ione, Washington, turn east onto Sullivan Lake Road. Go 8.4 miles to Noisy Creek Campground. Inside the campground, go right to the trailhead, which is by the group camping area. A paved parking area will accommodate five or more vehicles.

Trail Length: 5.3 miles to junction with Trail 540, 7.1 miles to Hall Mountain, one-way

Trail Condition: good

Elevation: Trailhead – 2,600', High Point/Low Point – 3,410' (crossing Noisy Creek), End – 5,540' (junction with Trail 540)

Estimated Duration of Hike: 3.5 to 4.5 hours up, 3 to 4 hours down

Sweat Index: bathed in sweat (strenuous)

Mountain Bike Sweat Index: bathed in sweat

Best Features: some views of Sullivan Lake and alpine meadows, spectacular views and wildlife (bighorn sheep and mule deer, maybe elk) on Hall Mountain

Availability of Water Along the Trail: There is a good stream about 1.5 miles up the trail, then the trail closely follows Noisy Creek for over a mile. The last chance for water is from a small stream perhaps 3 miles from the trailhead.

Stream Crossings: The smaller streams are easy to step across, but Noisy Creek is a tedious rock hop, and during spring runoff it could be challenging to get across.

Campsites: Noisy Creek Campground is located near the trailhead.

Alternate Hikes: This trail connects to Trail 540, which begins in Johns Creek on the north side of the Hall-Grassy Divide. And just 150 feet from that junction, Trail 533 to Grassy Top branches off Trail 540.

Wild Notes: A forest fire roared across Noisy Creek and Hall Mountain in 1926, burning thousands of acres. Most trees were killed in the inferno, but along the trail you might notice some that survived. For instance, take a close look at a Western larch a short ways past the crossing of Noisy Creek. You can't miss it. It is right along the trail and is enormous. Notice how thick the bark is on this tree – up to 6, 7 or even 8 inches of fire resistant "clothing" that protects this species from the ravages of fire. They don't all survive, of course, but the protective bark of trees like larch, ponderosa pine and Douglas fir gives them an advantage over other species in the face of fire.

Wildlife Sighting: Noisy Creek and Hall Mountain are famous for the herd of bighorn sheep that live here. I confess I did not actually see any sheep while hiking this trail, dang it, but a wintertime feeding station is located at the north end of the campground. Sheep by the dozens come here for handouts that help them survive the brutal winters common to this valley.

Trails: Hall Mountain No. 540, Hall-Grassy Divide No. 533, Grassy Top National Recreation No. 503

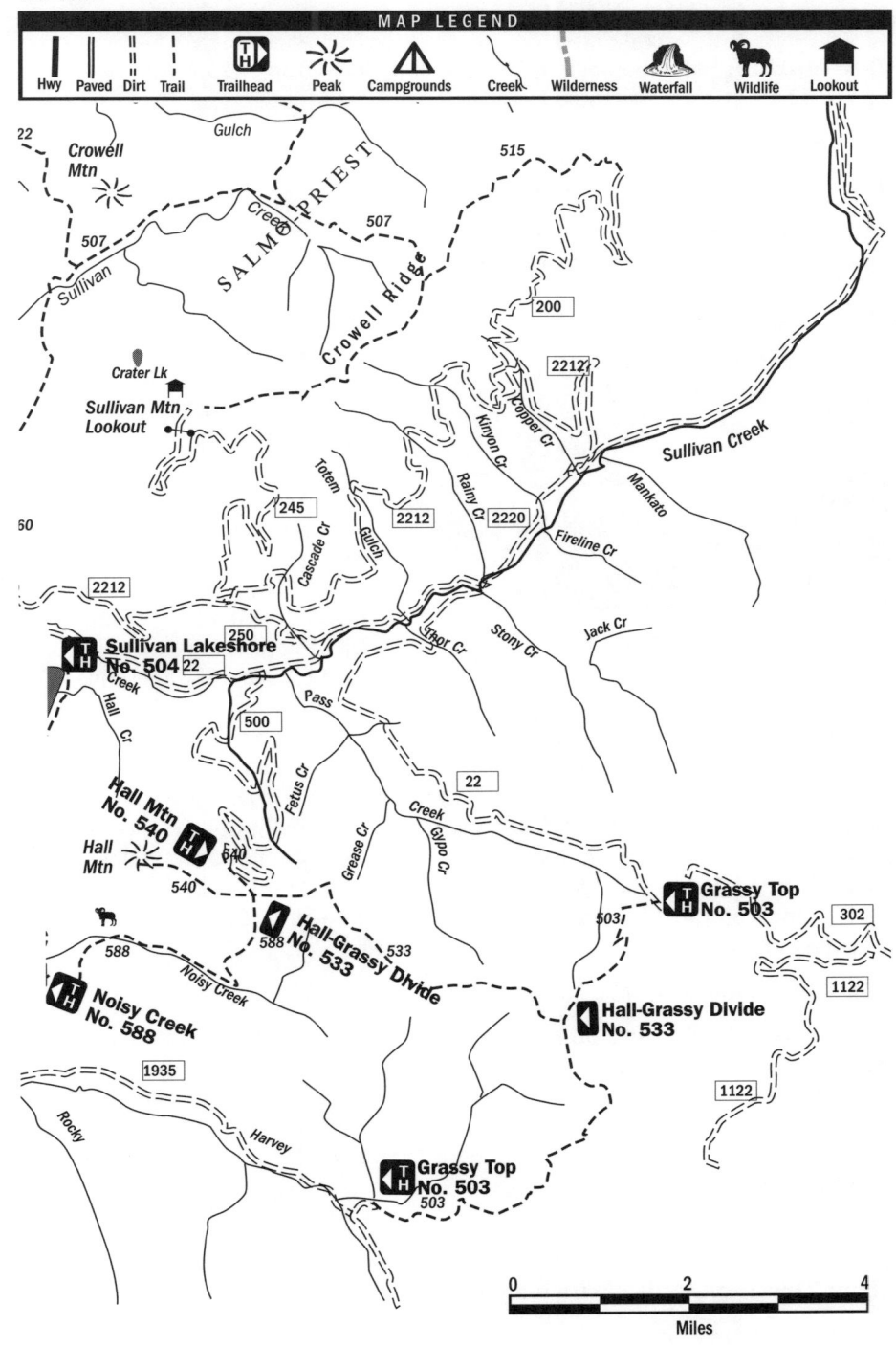

Pend Oreille-Priest Divide 143

Hall Mountain Trail No. 540 and Hall-Grassy Divide Trail No. 533

This is a Family Fun Hike (to Hall Mountain)

Destination: Hall Mountain, 6,323 feet, and Grassy Top, 6,253 feet. *Map, page 143.*

Best Suited For: hiking, horseback riding, mountain biking

How Much Use: A Little * A Little More * **A LOT** * A Lot More * Excessive

What's it like? Near the end of Road 500 is a gate and small parking area for Trail 540 in an old overgrown clear-cut. The trail stays on the roadbed for three-quarters of a mile to the ridge top where Trail 533 branches off to the east. West up the ridge for just 150 feet is the junction with Trail 588. From there Trail 540 switchbacks a couple times through the forest, then enters the first of many increasingly larger meadows. This is one of the more spectacular hikes in the Selkirks. The views are stunning and the south and west slopes of Hall Mountain are strikingly beautiful. Note the presence of sagebrush in some of the first small meadows. It seems incongruous that a dry-land shrub like that would be present with spruce and subalpine fir not far above a cedar and hemlock forest. A short way farther and the sagebrush gives way to vast expanses of grassy meadows dominated by Idaho fescue. It is a truly serene setting. The far southern tip of Sullivan Lake is visible briefly, but the mountain falls away so steeply for so far that the lake is lost to sight 4,000 feet below. A lookout once sat atop Hall Mountain, but not much is left now. Bighorn sheep are common on Hall Mountain, so keep your eyes open for these nimble creatures feeding in the high country during summer.

Remains of the lookout on Hall Mountain

USGS Map: Metaline Falls, Pass Creek

Trailhead: At milepost 3 on Highway 31 just south of Ione, Washington, turn east onto Sullivan Lake Road. Go 13 miles to Road 22, 0.4 miles past the Sullivan Lake Ranger Station. Turn east and go about 3 miles to Johns Creek Road 500. Travel it 7 miles to the end of the road and the trailhead. This road is open July 1 through August 14 only. The turnaround is fairly tight, but there is room for parking four or five vehicles.

Trail Length: Trail 540 is 2.5 miles one-way to Hall Mountain; Trail 533 is 5.1 miles from its junction with Trail 540 to its junction with Trail 503 (a total of about 7 miles to Grassy Top from the trailhead at Johns Creek).

Trail Condition: good

Elevation: Trail 540, Trailhead – 4,840', High Point/Low Point – 5,520' (junction with Trail 533), End – 6,323'

Elevation: Trail 533, Start – 5,520' (junction with Trail 540), High Point/Low Point – 5,520'-6,380', End – 6,380' (junction with Trail 503)

Estimated Duration of Hike: 1 to 2 hours to Hall Mountain, 2.5 to 3.5 hours to Grassy Top via Trails 540, 533 and 503

Sweat Index: break a sweat (moderate) for 540 to Hall Mountain, buckets of sweat (difficult) for Trails 540, 533 and 503 to Grassy Top

Mountain Bike Sweat Index: buckets of sweat

Best Features: fantastic views of the surrounding countryside

Availability of Water Along the Trail: There is a small spring dribbling from a pipe about one-quarter mile from the trailhead; otherwise there is no water along either trail.

Stream Crossings: none

Campsites: Developed campgrounds are at the north and south ends of Sullivan Lake.

Alternate Hikes: Trail 540 provides access to Trail 533, which follows along the Hall-Grassy Divide out to Trail 503, a National Recreation Trail over Grassy Top. Trail 533 mostly meanders through timber with limited views, but there are some nice, open meadows within a mile of its junction at Trail 503. Trail 540 also connects to Trail 588 coming out of Noisy Creek.

Grassy Top National Recreation Trail No. 503

Destination: Grassy Top, 6,253 feet. *Map, page 143.*

Best Suited For: hiking, horseback, riding mountain biking

How Much Use: A Little * A Little More * **A LOT** * A Lot More * Excessive

What's it like? From the south end, the trail follows an old roadbed for 3.3 miles. Actually, the first 2 miles or so are really on a gated road, some of which is a bit brushy, but beyond a marshy area full of alder it becomes more like a dozer trail. There are some nice views of the Middle Fork of Harvey Creek and the three summits of Grassy Top (each with their own fabulous grassy meadows) along the road. Once past the alder the dozer trail turns sharply uphill. Watch for spur trails so you are sure to stay on the right path, but it is pretty obvious which way to go. After encountering a large old deck of rotting cedar logs on the left hand side of the trail in a patch of old growth cedar, you will encounter three forks. Go right-left-left, always taking the steeper route up the mountain. And steep it gets. The dozer operator from years ago did not mind pushing his machine straight up the slope. Soon, however, the trail reaches the bottom edge of a beautiful meadow and views of the Selkirk Crest to the east and south to Tillicum Peak and North Baldy are impressive. The dozer trail comes to an end

Beautiful meadows dotted with clumps of subalpine fir decorate Grassy Top Mountain

on top of a knob south of Grassy Top in an opening becoming less and less open. It is quickly being crowded out by sapling-sized subalpine firs. A primitive campsite with a fire ring is located here. Perhaps a half-mile farther is a spur trail that follows the ridge to the summit of Grassy Top. It only takes 10 minutes to get to the helispot on top. From Pass Creek Pass, the trail climbs steadily through heavy timber, though there are views of Round Top Mountain and the southeast end of the Salmo-Priest Wilderness as you gain elevation. After 2.7 miles it comes to the junction with Trail 533. Another mile farther is that spur trail to the summit of Grassy Top.

USGS Map: Pass Creek

Trailhead: At milepost 3 on Highway 31 just south of Ione, Washington, turn east onto Sullivan Lake Road. Go about 7 miles to Harvey Creek Road 1935 and turn east. Go 5.2 miles to just after the third bridge over Harvey Creek, and turn onto Road 030. Go a half-mile or so to a fork in the road. Both forks are gated within a couple hundred feet of this fork. The right fork is the start of the south end of Trail 503. Parking at the fork will accommodate three or four vehicles. The north end of the trail can be reached by following Sullivan Lake Road to Road 22 near the Sullivan Lake Ranger Station and traveling it 12.5 miles to Pass Creek Pass. The trail begins about one-quarter mile west of the pass but the only parking available is at the pass for three or four vehicles.

Trail Length: 7.8 miles end to end, 4 miles from Harvey Creek to Grassy Top and 3.8 miles from Pass Creek Pass to Grassy Top

Trail Condition: good

Elevation: Trailhead – 5,360' (Pass Creek Pass), High Point/Low Point – 6,380' (junction with Trail 533), End – 4,150' (at Road 030)

Estimated Duration of Hike: 2 to 3 hours one-way to Grassy Top from either trailhead

Sweat Index: buckets of sweat (difficult)

Mountain Bike Sweat Index: bathed in sweat (strenuous)

Best Features: alpine meadows, terrific views

Availability of Water Along the Trail: Don't count on any water at all along this trail, though there may be some spring runoff lingering into mid-summer in a draw a mile up the south end and in a brushfield of alder about 2 miles or so from the south end.

Stream Crossings: none, but a marshy area in that patch of alder

Campsites: Primitive sites are located at Pass Creek Pass and on a knob a mile south of Grassy Top.

Alternate Hikes: Trail 533 connects to this trail 2.7 miles from the pass, making for a nice open loop with Trails 503, 533, 540 and 588.

Wildlife Sighting: The new snow on the trail when I hiked it in November was littered with tracks, mostly deer tracks. And then high on the ridge near Grassy Top itself, I startled a magnificent mule deer buck bedded down in the timber. Can you say trophy? He was truly a gigantic specimen with a rear end as wide as a boxcar and antlers branching out like tree limbs.

Trails: Muskegon Lake, Huff Lake

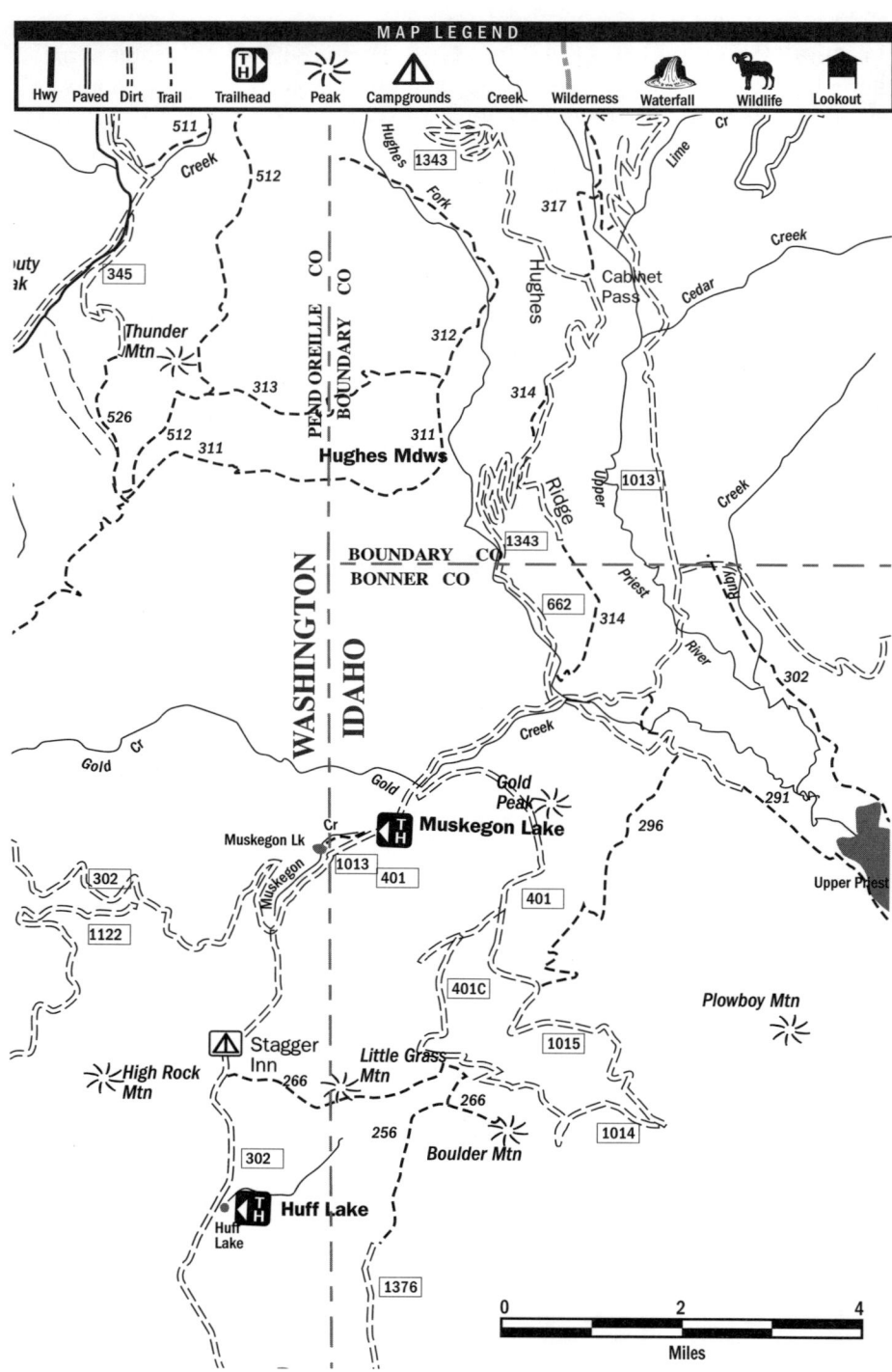

Muskegon Lake Trail

ACCESSIBLE: The short distance to this nice forest lake may not be suitable for wheelchairs, but the trail is easy enough that perhaps ambulatory people with minor disabilities could make it to the water's edge.

This is a Family Fun Hike

Destination: Muskegon Lake. *Map, page 148.*

Best Suited For: hiking

How Much Use: A Little * A Little More * **A LOT** * A Lot More * Excessive

What's it like? Fishermen are who mostly access this small lake, but you don't have to fish in order to enjoy this beautiful setting. The short walk takes

A pair of wood ducks cuts a "V" across the still water of Muskegon Lake

you to the side of a lake surrounded by heavy forest, but it is not unusual to see waterfowl on its placid surface or a moose feeding on its far edge. And there are actually two lakes here. A brief bushwhack north of the first lake takes you to the second. The serenity of the surrounding forest makes this a good place to sit and enjoy the peace and quiet of the north woods.

USGS Map: Helmer Mountain, Upper Priest Lake

Trailhead: From Priest River, Idaho, go north on Highway 57 past Nordman to Road 302, a distance of about 37 miles. Continue on Road 302 about 14 miles to Granite Pass and the junction of Road 1013. Take Road 1013 for 1.2 miles to Muskegon Campsite on the south side of the road. The trail to the lake is across the road.

Trail Length: approximately 150 yards

Trail Condition: excellent

Elevation: Trailhead – 3,430', High/Low Point – 3,420' (Muskegon Creek crossing), End – 3,441'

Estimated Duration of Hike: 5 minutes

Sweat Index: no sweat (easy)

Mountain Bike Sweat Index: no sweat

Best Features: small forest lake, fish, wildlife

Availability of Water Along the Trail: Muskegon Creek is a perennial stream.

Stream Crossings: There is a footbridge over Muskegon Creek.

Campsites: Several primitive campsites are located on both sides of Rd. 1013.

Huff Lake Trail

ACCESSIBLE: A nice parking area and a wide, short, flat trail makes this site easy to enjoy by everyone.

This is a Family Fun Hike

Destination: Huff Lake. *Map, page 148.*

Best Suited For: hiking, wheelchairs

How Much Use: A Little * A Little More * **A LOT** * A Lot More * Excessive

What's it like? Road 302, the major access route into the Upper Priest River valley, passes by a small, unassuming lake by the name of Huff. Other than glancing for a feeding moose, most passersby probably ignored this little lake until the Forest Service developed an interpretive site. Turns out this is a pretty special lake, as it exhibits beautifully how a small shallow body of water like this slowly becomes solid ground. Aside from the encroachment of grasses and sedges, shrubs and trees, the south end of this lake is being overrun by a floating mat of peat moss. It is a rare and unusual habitat called a fen. Enjoy the signs that explain what is going on at Huff Lake, and keep an eye out for moose, or even for the small trout that rise to the surface for insects, but stay on the trail. This is a highly sensitive and fragile environment.

USGS Map: Orwig Hump

Trailhead: From Priest River, Idaho, drive Highway 57 north to Nordman, approximately 36.5 miles. From the end of 57 follow Road 302 for 10.5 miles to Huff Lake. There is parking for four to six vehicles.

Trail Length: 150 feet

Trail Condition: excellent gravel trail and wooden dock to viewing platform

Elevation: 3,185'

Estimated Duration of Hike: as long as you want to admire this beautiful, small lake

Sweat Index: no sweat (easy)

Mountain Bike Sweat Index: no need for a bike

Best Features: natural history interpretive site, wildlife

Availability of Water Along the Trail: none (it is best not to take it from the lake)

Stream Crossings: none

Campsites: Muskegon Campsite, a semi-primitive campground, is about 5 miles away.

Precautions: Please don't step off the trail, as this is a fragile area comprised, in part, of floating sphagnum peat moss.

Huff Lake Interpretive Site

Huff Lake is a fen. This unique habitat, left over from the days when huge blocks of ice lay scattered across the landscape, remnants of the great glaciers that once covered the entire region, is a specialized kind of wetland. These glacial depressions collect debris, sediment and runoff from slow groundwater seepage and over the course of thousands of years a deep, moist organic layer of soil forms. The organic matter in a fen may be dozens of feet thick and growing across the surface is primarily peat moss (sphagnum). These tiny plants might only look to be a few inches tall but when pulled apart it quickly becomes evident that there are millions of individual plants tangled together, forming a thick, spongy mat. Within this mat, as other organic debris accumulates and decays, other plants take root.

The Priest Lake Ranger District, in conjunction with the Northeastern Chapter of the Washington Native Plant Society, recognized the value of this site and in recent years erected interpretive signs and constructed a short path to the viewing platform from which I watched the fish feeding. In the case of Huff Lake, the fen partially encircles the southwest end of open water. At the water's edge it is fascinating to observe the floating mat of peat moss and the deep black sediments on the shallow lake's bottom.

Within this unique habitat are plants that are seldom found anywhere else, including two species of the carnivorous sundews, *Drosera anglica* and *Drosera rotundifolia*. Bog laurel, also called swamp laurel (*Kalmia microphylla*), is a small shrub associated with fens and other wet sites in the mountains. It has narrow, dark green leathery leaves that are whitish or gray velvet on their bottom sides and it contains poisonous alkaloids. An interesting plant from which Scandinavians made a type of bread, bog bean (*Menyanthes trifoliata*), is found here. It is reported that Finns and Lapps took the rhizomes of this plant and made "missen" or "famine" bread. In July or August you might notice dark reddish-purple to maroon colored flowers dotting the fen. This is swamp cinquefoil (*Potentilla palustris*). If you can get close, you might also notice a foul odor emitted by this otherwise beautiful native. The smell attracts insects ordinarily found on carrion, which then pollinate the flower. It may be a defense mechanism against would-be predators.

There are at least four species of rare plants found at Huff Lake: bog cranberry, creeping snowberry, northern starflower and podgrass. These plants are known to grow only in peatland habitats, and because this kind of habitat is rare across the landscape these areas are protected. More than half of the rare plants found in the Priest River Valley occur in peatland communities like that found at Huff Lake.

For more information about Huff Lake and other sensitive habitats, stop by the Priest Lake Ranger District and pick up a brochure or contact members of the Northeastern Chapter of the Washington Native Plant Society by writing to 22508 S. Carman, Cheney, WA 99004. Visit the society's website at www.wnps.org.

Trails: Roosevelt No. 266, Granite-Roosevelt Nos. 301 & 301A

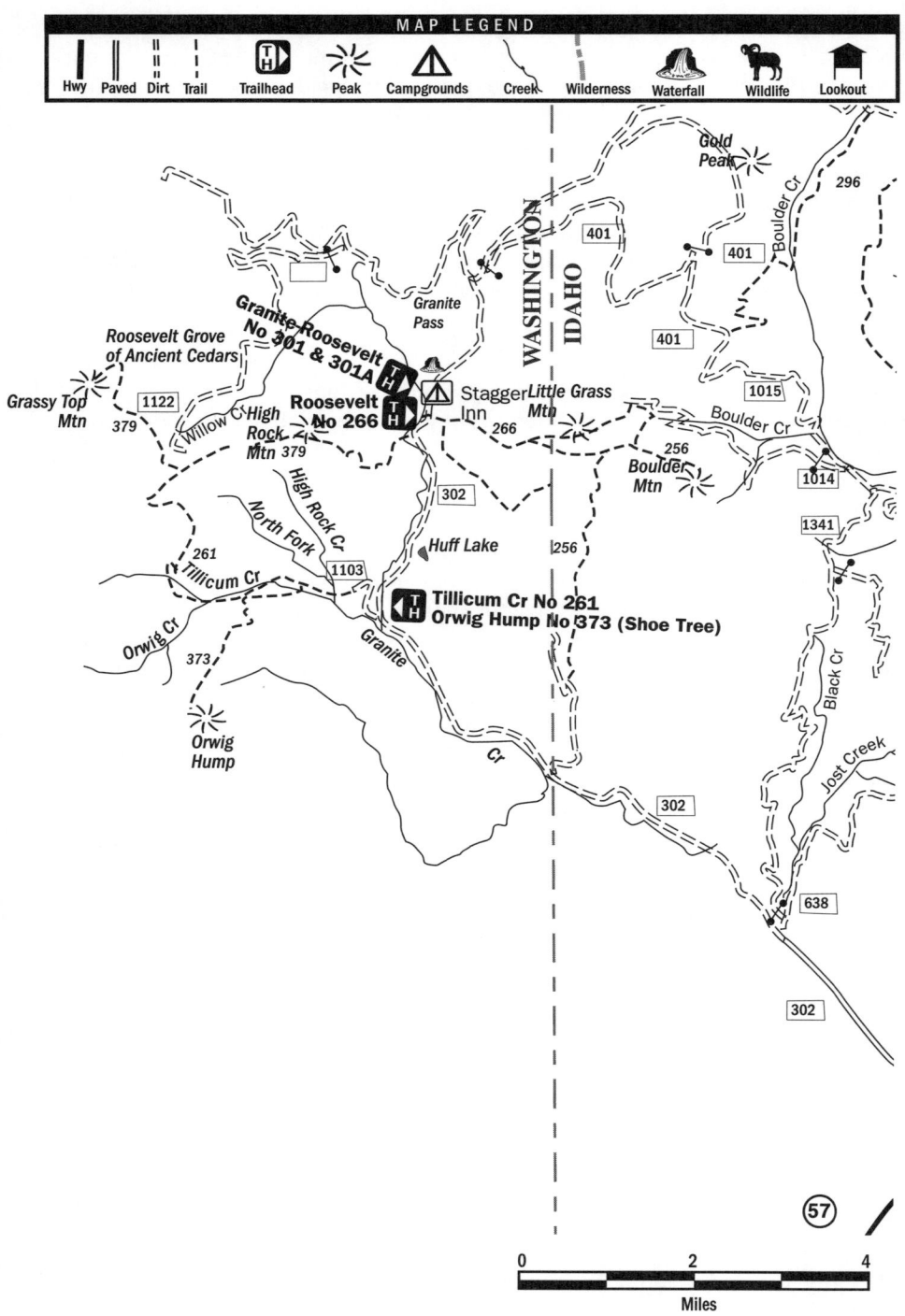

Roosevelt Trail No. 266, Zero Creek Trail No. 256, Little Grass Mountain Trail No. 265 and Boulder Mountain Trail No. 293

Destination: Little Grass Mountain, 5,696 feet, and Boulder Mountain, 5,654 feet. *Map, page 152.*

Best Suited For: hiking, horseback riding

How Much Use: A LITTLE * A Little More * A Lot * A Lot More * Excessive

What's it like? This little-used trail is a treat that not many people seem to enjoy. From its beginning on Road 302, it climbs up a harrowingly steep mountainside and the tread is sometimes narrow. But the ascent is only moderate. At first there is dense timber all around, but at a switchback on the edge of an area of talus rock, there is a good view up the North Fork of Granite Creek and of some of the giant cedars and larch sprawling across the mountains framing it. Soon the trail hits a fairly level spot and crosses the hillside into a fabulous basin at the headwaters of the stream that feeds Huff Lake. The fire that burned across this mountain years ago, creating the doghair forest of small trees competing for sunlight, missed this basin and old-growth cedar and hemlock still survive here. It is a fabulously beautiful spot. In this same area is an old wooden sign marking the line between Washington and Idaho. After some gentle ups and downs, the trail starts to descend through a stand of young larch averaging about 10 inches in diameter, then at the edge of a brushfield is the junction with Zero Creek Trail No. 256. Trail 266 continues into this brushfield and across some soft seepy spots, then meanders upward into a broad saddle. The obscure junction with Trail 293 is here and though it is only a mile to the top of Boulder Mountain, the condition of the trail makes it very difficult to follow. Staying on 266, it traverses near a small meadow as it curves around a ridge to its junction with Trail 265. From the saddle, the trail condition deteriorates, but it is still easy enough to follow. Trail 265 begins at the end of an old logging road only 200 feet from its junction with Trail 266, but the road is closed during the entire summer some 4 miles from the trailhead. The hike to Little Grass Mountain is a bit annoying because of the brush and blowdown, but as you proceed the reason for the mountain's name becomes evident – the upper slopes are vast meadows of grasses, sedges and beargrass, and the views become extraordinary. A lookout tower once rested on top, but all that is left now are some concrete footings and wire.

Little Grass Mountain looking toward Boulder Mountain

USGS Map: Upper Priest Lake

Trailhead: From Priest River, Idaho, take Highway 57 past Nordman to the junction of Road 302, a distance of about 37 miles. Follow Road 302 for 12 miles to the turnoff for Stagger Inn Campground. The trail is about 100 yards past the turnoff, but it is best to park at the campground. Go 0.3 mile to the campground and trailhead. There is room for up to a dozen vehicles.

Trail Length: Trail 266 is 4.5 miles one-way; it is 5.5 miles to the summit of Little Grass Mountain via Trails 266 and 265 and also 5.5 miles to Boulder Mountain via Trails 266 and 293. Zero Creek Trail No. 256 is 3.7 miles one-way.

Trail Condition: 266 is fair and 265, 293 and 256 are all poor due to no maintenance for several years.

Elevation: Trail 266 Trailhead – 3,500', High/Low Point – 3,500'-5,696', End – 5,696' (Little Grass Mountain)

Estimated Duration of Hike: 2.5 to 3.5 hours each way to Little Grass Mountain or Boulder Mountain

Sweat Index: buckets of sweat (difficult)

Mountain Bike Sweat Index: not suitable

Best Features: old-growth forest and views of Priest Lake and surrounding mountains

Availability of Water Along the Trail: There are two places for water, one about 2.5 miles along Trail 266 where it crosses the stream that flows eventually into Huff Lake. The other is in Zero Creek about 4 miles out on Trail 266.

Stream Crossings: two you can just step across and lots of seeps with soft, boggy areas to tiptoe through

Campsites: Stagger Inn Campground is at the Roosevelt Grove of Ancient Cedars and has four primitive sites with a vault toilet, picnic tables and fire pits.

Alternate Hikes: Trail 266 connects to Trail 256, which descends Zero Creek; it also connects to Trail 293 to Boulder Mountain and to Trail 265 to Little Grass Mountain. Each of those three trails is overgrown and crisscrossed with blowdown. It has been up to 10 years since they were last maintained.

Wildlife Sighting: Three young bull elk crossed the trail in front of me about 30 yards away right where an old sign indicates the location of the Idaho/Washington state line.

Wild Notes: Keep your eyes open for a big, old larch maybe 2 miles up the trail. It is on the downhill side but right next to the path. It has an obvious lightning scar spiraling down its 4-foot thick trunk. Western larch can be among the tallest trees in the forest in the "montane" zone (generally mid-slope), and because of that they are targets for bolts of lightning during thunderstorms. But because their bark is so thick, these trees often resist the ignition of a fire. However, the result of that electrical jolt will be visible for the rest of the life of that tree as a splintered scar curling down its trunk.

Granite-Roosevelt Trail No. 301 and Cedar Grove Trail No. 301A

ACCESSIBLE: A short, though rugged, path accesses the plunge pool of Granite Falls from the parking area. Trail 301A is a gentle, wide trail that may be useable for those in wheelchairs with a little help.

This is a Family Fun Hike

Destination: Roosevelt Grove of Ancient Cedars, Granite Falls, La Sota Falls. Map, page 152.

Best Suited For: hiking only

How Much Use: A Little * A Little More * A Lot * **A LOT MORE** * Excessive

What's it like? The story goes something like this: When crews were battling a wildfire in the Upper Priest drainage years ago they would come staggering in to the fire camp at Granite Falls at the end of the day. Hence, the name of the Stagger Inn Campground that now occupies that site. This is one of the most visited attractions in the Selkirks because of the magnificent grove of ancient cedars and because of the two dramatic waterfalls issuing from the gorges cut by the North Fork of Granite Creek over tens of thousands of years. The Roosevelt Grove of Ancient Cedars was named for President Theodore Roosevelt. A short loop trail explores the lower grove by

La Sota Falls empties into a refreshing, deep pool

the campground, while a longer trail climbs via a steep single track or via an old logging road to the upper grove. By taking the single track, you not only come to awesome views of Granite and La Sota falls, but also to a memorial for Arthur W. Carothers, a USFS Civil Engineer from 1959 to 1993. The plaque dedicating a viewing platform to his memory reads, "Beauty at the End of the Trail." And beautiful it is; but beware if you suffer from vertigo. The platform, though strong and perfectly safe, seems to hang right out over a deep gorge into which pour the waters of Granite Falls. A little way farther is a view of the stunning La Sota Falls. Actually, it is difficult to see the entire falls because of the narrowness of the gorge. Both the lower grove and the viewpoint at the bottom of Granite Falls are accessible to wheelchairs. The trails are wide, graveled paths and are quite short.

USGS Map: Helmer Mountain, Upper Priest Lake

Trailhead: From Priest River, Idaho, take Highway 57 past Nordman to the junction of Road 302, a distance of about 37 miles. Follow Road 302 12 miles to the turnoff for Stagger Inn Campground. Go 0.3 mile to the campground and trailhead. There is room for up to a dozen vehicles.

Trail Length: 301A is a one-quarter mile loop, less than 100 yards to view the lower falls from the bottom, approximately one-half mile to the viewing platform at the top of the falls and 1.5 miles one-way to the upper grove.

Trail Condition: good

Elevation: Trailhead – 3,280', High/Low Point – 3,280'-3,560', End – 3,560'

Estimated Duration of Hike: from 5 minutes to 2 or 3 hours

Sweat Index: break a sweat (moderate)

Mountain Bike Sweat Index: prohibited

Best Features: old-growth forest, waterfalls

Availability of Water Along the Trail: There is good water in the North Fork of Granite Creek at the campground.

Stream Crossings: none

Campsites: Stagger Inn Campground has four or five semi-primitive sites with a vault toilet, fire pits and picnic tables.

Precautions: Use the utmost caution when viewing the falls from above. The gorge has cliffs with straight drop offs into the churning waters below.

Alternate Hikes: The lower cedar grove right next to the campground can be enjoyed on a short loop of perhaps one-eighth mile, and Granite Falls can be viewed from the bottom by hiking a mere 200 feet on a spur trail from the trailhead. For the more adventurous, the trail climbs rather steeply for spectacular views of both Granite and La Sota Falls and then continues up an old logging road to the upper grove. Just past the entrance to Stagger Inn on Road 302 is the trailhead for Trail 266 to Little Grass and Boulder mountains.

Trail: Blacktail Mountain No. 292

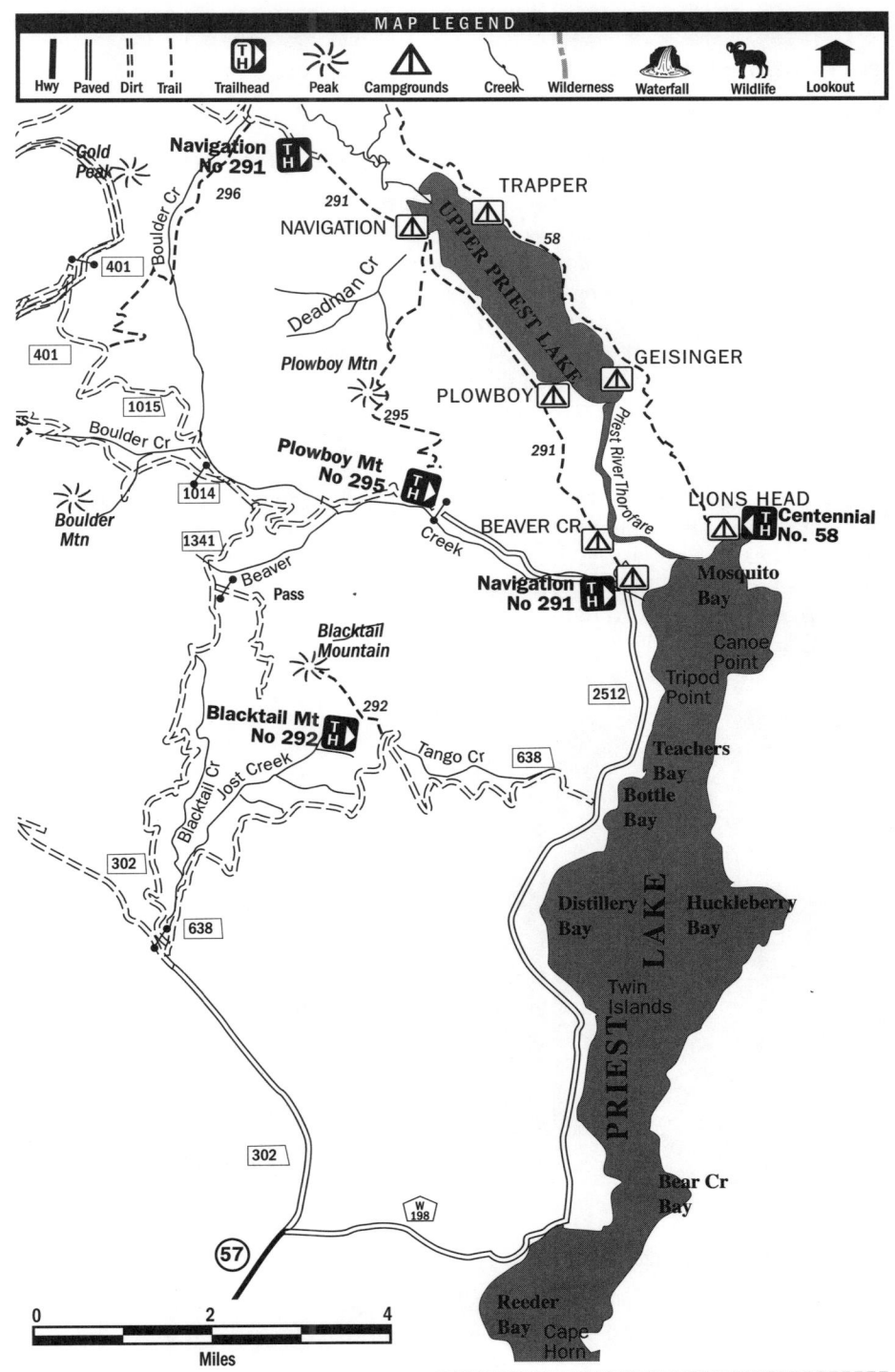

Blacktail Mountain Trail No. 292

This is a Family Fun Hike

Destination: Blacktail Mountain, 5,495 feet. *Map, page 157.*

Best Suited For: hiking, horseback riding

How Much Use: A Little * **A LITTLE MORE** * A Lot * A Lot More * Excessive

What's it like? Right from the get-go, this trail climbs rather steeply through heavy timber. The tread is narrow and huckleberry bushes crowd the path, but the trail is easy to follow. It finally gains the ridgeline but continues its steep ascent, though with a few respites now and then on a flat bench. The trees thin out higher up and grassy meadows become more common. Views to the south are terrific, but wait until you get to the top. The last 50 vertical feet require rock hopping among big boulders and then you are on the summit. And what a magnificent place! In every direction there are superb views of mountains and valleys, and the view of Priest Lake is perhaps the best from any vantage point I was on all summer. You can even see the southwest corner of Upper Priest Lake. The Selkirk Crest to the east is glorious. An old lookout tower once sat up here, but all that is left is a mound of rocks with a map and compass pedestal, some concrete and wire and the rundown old outhouse. This is a wonderful destination, and though the hike is a bit difficult because of the steepness of the trail, it struck me as a great place to bring the family.

The map and compass pedestal from Blacktail Mountain Lookout still looks out over Priest Lake

USGS Map: Priest Lake NW, Upper Priest Lake

Trailhead: From Priest River, Idaho, take Highway 57 north past Nordman to where it merges into Road 302, a distance of approximately 37 miles. At milepost 3 on Road 302, right at the end of the pavement, turn north onto Tango Creek Road 638. Go 5 miles to a saddle where there is a parking area for two vehicles. The trail is about 0.1 mile past that saddle. There is also a wide spot in the road for one or two vehicles at the trailhead. The last mile of the road to the saddle is very rough and rocky.

Trail Length: approximately 2 miles to the top of Blacktail Mountain

Trail Condition: fair

Elevation: Trailhead – 4,200', High/Low Point – 4,200'-5,495', End – 5,495'

Estimated Duration of Hike: 1 to 2 hours up, 1 to 1.5 hours down

Sweat Index: buckets of sweat (difficult)

Mountain Bike Sweat Index: not suitable

Best Features: magnificent views, remains of old lookout

Availability of Water Along the Trail: none

Stream Crossings: none

Campsites: none

Alternate Hikes: This trail connects to North Blacktail Trail No. 324 on the north side of Blacktail Mountain. I did not hike Trail 324, but Forest Service information indicates it was maintained in 2002, so it should be in pretty good shape.

Kalispell Rock to Pioneer Park

The divide between the Pend Oreille and Priest rivers becomes narrower starting at Kalispell Rock, an impressive mountain with twin granite monoliths rising on either side of the decadent remains of a cabin. A large roadless area lies across the headwaters of Kalispell Creek and Lamb Creek south of these granite protrusions, encompassing nearly 20,000 acres of undeveloped lands all the way to North Baldy (6,173 feet), the highest summit in the south half of the Pend Oreille-Priest Divide. From the top of North Baldy, it is only 6 miles to the Pend Oreille River near the mouth of LeClerc Creek. South of that is a series of small lakes left over from the days when glaciers fed them with melting ice. Browns Lake, North and South Skookum lakes, Kings Lake and the biggest of the bunch, Bead Lake, among others, sit in pockets on the west slope of the divide a few hundred feet above the valley bottom and the meandering river. Some of them have trails along their shorelines.

    A great deal of this landscape on the east side of the crest burned in the great fires of 1926, but some notable stands of old-growth survived, such as the small grove of giant cedars, hemlocks and whitepine at Hanna Flats. Near there the Priest Lake Ranger Station is headquartered. Hiking trails become nonexistent south of Binarch Creek as the forest, more and more in mixed ownership, has been heavily roaded and managed, which means utilized primarily for timber production. LeClerc Creek Road out of Newport/Oldtown and Highway 57 north from Priest River provide the main access to countless logging roads climbing up and over the divide from both directions. One of the prizes at the far south end of this section is the Nok-OSH-Kol Heritage Trail at Pioneer Park only a couple of miles from Newport. It is an easy trail with handicapped access and a self-guiding interpretive trail that overlooks the Pend Oreille River and takes the wanderer back in time to when Native Americans lived along the river.

A giant Douglas fir grows right out of the rock on the Pend Oreille-Priest Divide near Kalispell Rock

Trails: Kalispell Rock No. 37, Kalispell Rock-North Baldy No. 103, Stateline No. 162, Squaw Valley No. 164, Icy Springs No. 197

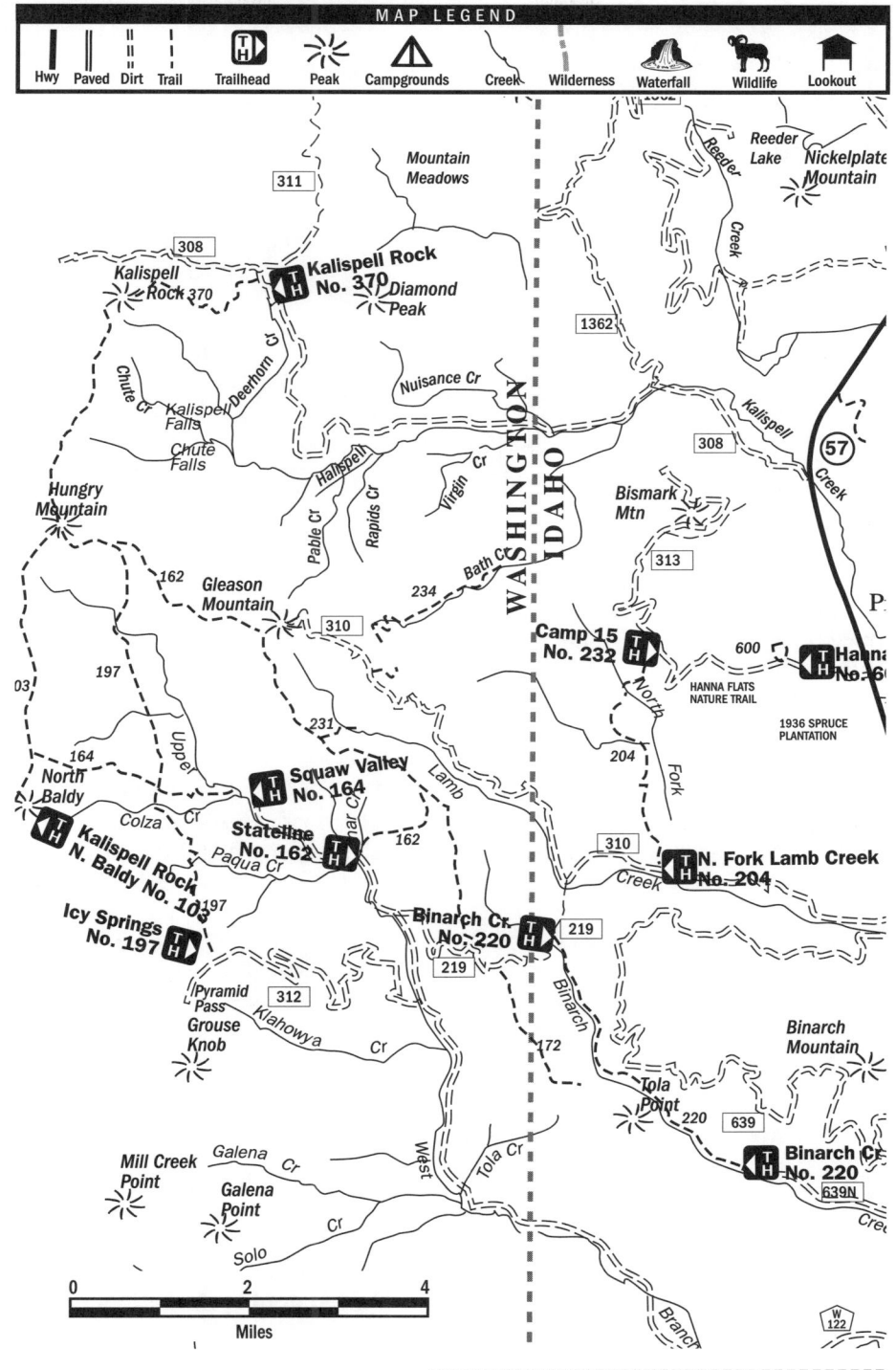

Pend Oreille-Priest Divide

Kalispell Rock Trail No. 370

This is a Family Fun Hike

Destination: Kalispell Rock, 5,278 feet. *Map, page 161.*

Best Suited For: hiking, horseback riding, mountain biking

How Much Use: A Little * **A LITTLE MORE** * A Lot * A Lot More * Excessive

What's it like? The trail follows an old roadbed through scattered timber, then joins a logging road, which in turn joins another logging road. Bear left at each junction. There are areas of timber harvest along the way, but don't let that and the roads keep you from hiking this route. You won't regret the views or the destination. After about a mile

The cabin at Kalispell Rock

the logging road veers around to the right while the old road (more like a dozer trail) continues straight up a modestly steep slope. This bends around the hillside and soon breaks out into brushy meadows. The climb is steady but not too steep. It is in these brushfields where deer and elk may very well be spotted feeding among giant granite boulders. And the views are extraordinary. Besides looking out over the unspoiled upper reaches of Kalispell Creek to Gleason and Hungry Mountains, notice the emerging views of Bismark Meadows and Lakeview Mountain to the east. You can even catch a glimpse of Priest Lake in the distance. On the main ridge, which is the Pend Oreille-Priest Divide, the old road continues south along the ridge as Trail 103, while a single-track trail branches north upslope. Take this trail a few hundred yards until it reaches a shoulder of the mountain amongst some big old Douglas firs. There seems to be a trail junction here, but the path going downhill soon disappears. The trail to the top turns sharply to the right, passes by some giant larch and attains the summit between two impressive granite outcrops between which is the remains of a cabin.

USGS Map: Gleason Mountain, Orwig Hump, Monumental Mountain

Trailhead: In Priest River, Idaho, turn north on Highway 57 and travel to milepost 34. Turn west on to Kalispell Creek Road 308 and go 9.25 miles to the trailhead (no sign) just before a saddle where there is a fork in the road (the intersection is a triangle). The right fork goes to Petit Lake. The trail goes behind a metal barricade on the left. Parking for only one vehicle is in front of the barricade, but several others can park along the roadside at the fork.

Trail Length: 2.5 miles one-way

Trail Condition: good

Elevation: Trailhead – 3,885', High Point/Low Point – 3,885'-5,278', End – 5,278'

Estimated Duration of Hike: 1 to 2 hours each way

Sweat Index: break a sweat (moderate)

Mountain Bike Sweat Index: break a sweat

Best Features: historic cabin on top, marvelous views, wildlife

Availability of Water Along the Trail: none

Stream Crossings: none

Campsites: none

Alternate Hikes: connects to Kalispell Rock-North Baldy Trail No. 103

Wild Notes: High on the ridge near the top of the mountain, the trail passes through a brushfield dominated by shiny-leaved ceanothus, also called evergreen ceanothus (*Ceanothus velutinus*). Thank goodness for the trail because you don't ever want to have to beat your way through this 3- to 6-foot high, stiff shrub. It grows thickly on dry sites. You may have noticed a lot of it cloaking the hillsides on the way up to this trailhead. Its close relative, redstem ceanothus (*Ceanothus sanguineus*), is a favorite browse species of deer and elk.

Wildlife Sighting: Speaking of deer and elk, the shallow layer of snow on this trail when I hiked it in mid-November was churned up by both deer and elk tracks – fresh tracks, at that. So fresh, in fact, I stumbled upon a small band of elk just on the edge of timber at the west end of the brushfield. There were 10 or 12 cows and calves and a couple of raghorn bulls.

Kalispell Rock-North Baldy Trail No. 103

Destination: North Baldy, 6,173 feet, Hungry Mountain, 5,552 feet and Kalispell Rock, 5,278 feet. *Map, page 161.*

Best Suited For: hiking, horseback riding, mountain biking

How Much Use: A Little * A Little More * **A LOT** * A Lot More * Excessive

What's it like? Being a ridge top trail, this path undulates with the terrain. It begins at North Baldy at an elevation of 6,173 feet and is essentially all downhill from there; that is, until the trail hits a saddle, then climbs again toward Hungry Mountain. Much of the ridge is heavily timbered, but there are enough openings and meadows for some terrific views east and west. Just north of North Baldy is the junction with Trail 164 and up on Hungry Mountain is the junction with Trail 162, which goes right over the summit on its way to Gleason Mountain. Hungry

An early snowfall accents granite boulders; Hungry Mountain is in the background

Mountain has a nice, grassy meadow on top that affords wonderful views of North Baldy and the Upper West Branch of Priest River. From the ridge just north of Hungry Mountain the trail drops sharply. It is a steep descent, or ascent, depending on your direction of travel, for about one-quarter mile. At the bottom of this pitch, the trail skirts a switchback on a logging road. It then meanders over another low summit before hooking up with an old dozer trail that serves as the hiking route the rest of the way to its junction with Kalispell Rock Trail No. 370.

USGS Map: North Baldy, Monumental Mountain

Trailhead: This trail can be reached from several directions. From Priest River, Idaho, go north on Highway 57 to milepost 21.5 and turn west on Squaw Valley Road. Go 7.25 miles to a T-junction. Solo Creek Road 659 goes left. Go right on Road 312 and follow it all the way to Pyramid Pass. Then take Road 306 to North Baldy Lookout and the trailhead. You can also get to North Baldy Lookout by crossing the Pend Oreille River at Usk, Washington, then turning north on County Road 9325. Take it approximately 14 miles to Mill Creek Road 12, which then goes to Pyramid Pass and the junction with Road 306 to the lookout. The north end of this trail can be accessed via Kalispell Rock Trail No. 370.

Trail Length: 8 miles from end to end (a Forest Service trails list provided by the Priest Lake District says this trail is 6.5 miles, but an old sign at the start of the single-track a mile or more south of Kalispell Rock says it is 7 miles from there to North Baldy – so the best estimate seems to be more like 8 miles).

Trail Condition: fair

Elevation: Trailhead – 5,950' (on Road 306), High Point/Low Point – 5,440' (junction with Trail 162), End – 4,960' (junction with Trail 370)

Estimated Duration of Hike: from North Baldy 1.5 to 2.5 hours one-way to Hungry Mountain, 3.5 to 4.5 hours one-way to Kalispell Rock.

Sweat Index: buckets of sweat (difficult)

Mountain Bike Sweat Index: bathed in sweat (strenuous)

Best Features: wonderful ridgeline hiking, excellent views, active lookout

Availability of Water Along the Trail: none

Stream Crossings: none

Campsites: none

Alternate Hikes: There is a good system of interconnecting trails on the east side of North Baldy coming out of the Upper West Branch of Priest River. Trails 162 and 164 connect to 103. Trail 197 is a connecting trail between 162 and 164. Trail 103 also connects to Trail 370 at its north end.

Stateline Trail No. 162

Destination: Gleason Mountain, 5,416 feet, and Hungry Mountain, 5,552 feet. *Map, page 161.*

Best Suited For: hiking, horseback riding, mountain biking

How Much Use: A Little * **A LITTLE MORE** * A Lot * A Lot More * Excessive

What's it like? From the nice, small meadow at the trailhead, an old jeep track parallels a small stream on its west side. After a mile or so, it swings across the draw and begins to climb toward the ridge top. Up on that ridge the jeep track connects to another jeep track coming from Road 219 near an old mine site called "Last Chance." On the ridge the trail follows it to the northwest, sometimes on the ridge and sometimes off to one side or the other, but always climbing. Along the way you might notice a short connecting trail, Trail 231, joining this trail from a spur road the other side of Lamb Creek All along the way there are views into Lamb Creek and of Bismark Mountain, and you might glimpse Bismark Meadows higher up. Near Gleason Mountain the trail swings across the southwest flank of the mountain, but a spur trail takes off into a saddle between its double peaks and connects to a road that gains the top of the mountain. From that spur trail junction, the main trail gains the ridge, then begins to slant down into the deep saddle between Gleason and Hungry mountains. The saddle is a nice broad flat area making for a pleasant walk through the forest. Once it begins to climb again, you will soon encounter the junction with Trail 197, which slices south right across the whole basin of the Upper West Branch Priest River. Trail 162 continues to head up, more steeply now, and finally enters the meadows draped just off the summit of Hungry Mountain. These are some beautiful, grassy openings with magnificent views to the south and east. The trail lunges over the top, then down a shoulder of the mountain to the north and joins Trail 103 on the main divide.

USGS Map: Gleason Mountain

Trailhead: In Priest River, Idaho, turn north on Highway 57 and go to milepost 21.5. Turn west on Squaw Valley Road and go 7.25 miles to a T-junction. Solo Creek Road 659 goes left. Go right on road 312 for 2.7 miles to a fork. Road 312 continues to the left and Road 1107 goes right. Take 1107 for 1.1 miles to another fork. Stay to the right for about one-eighth mile to the trailhead in a small meadow (just past the junction with Road 219). There is plenty of parking.

Trail Length: 9 miles one-way (approximately 5 miles to Gleason Mountain, 9

miles to Hungry Mountain)

Trail Condition: good

Elevation: Trailhead – 2,640', High Point/Low Point – 5,200' (near summit of Gleason Mountain), End – 5,440' (junction with Trail 103)

Estimated Duration of Hike: 2 to 3 hours to Gleason Mountain, 4 to 5 hours to Hungry Mountain.

Sweat Index: buckets of sweat (difficult)

Mountain Bike Sweat Index: bathed in sweat (strenuous)

Best Features: part of a great loop hike, excellent views higher up

Availability of Water Along the Trail: An intermittent stream parallels the trail at first, but after a mile the trail climbs toward the ridgeline. Don't expect any water the last 8 miles to Hungry Mountain.

Stream Crossings: nothing significant

Campsites: Several primitive campsites are located at the trailhead with fire rings and picnic tables.

Alternate Hikes: This trail is part of a popular loop of about 20 miles, especially for backcountry horsemen, with Trails 103 and 164. Trail 197 also connects this trail with trail 164 and to Pyramid Pass Road 312.

Squaw Valley Trail No. 164

Destination: North Baldy, 6,173 feet

Best Suited For: hiking, horseback riding, mountain biking. *Map, page 161.*

How Much Use: A Little * **A LITTLE MORE** * A Lot * A Lot More * Excessive

What's it like? From the end of the jeep track along the Upper West Branch Priest River, the trail wends through heavy timber close to the stream, crossing it and Colza Creek. From that second crossing the trail begins its long ascent up a ridge through broken terrain. The topography is fascinating, and the forest is dense. Much of this area burned in 1926, and most of the forest is relatively young. This trail enters a large roadless area encompassing the whole of the Upper West Branch basin. From time to time there are nice views across this unbroken expanse of forest. The path intersects Trail 197 and continues its westerly climb among flats and benches stair-stepping up the mountainside. It heaves over a knob at 4,769 feet, then angles sharply up a northeast slope to the main divide. Here the trail connects to Trail 103 less than a mile from North Baldy.

USGS Map: North Baldy, Gleason Mountain

Trailhead: In Priest River, Idaho, turn north on Highway 57 and go to milepost 21.5. Turn west on Squaw Valley Road and go 7.25 miles to a T-junction. Solo Creek Road 659 goes left. Go right on Road 312 for 2.7 miles to a fork. Road

312 continues to the left and Road 1107 goes right. Take 1107 for 1.1 miles to another fork and stay to the left on 1107. The road from here becomes very rough and narrow. It is approximately 2 miles to the trailhead, but you might be better off parking in the meadow at the Trail 162 trailhead and hiking or riding from there.

Trail Length: 5.5 miles one-way to the junction with Trail 103 (or about 8 miles from the meadow at Trail 162). It is another three-quarters of a mile to the summit of North Baldy.

Trail Condition: good

Elevation: Trailhead – 3,000', High Point/Low Point – 3,000'-5,410', End – 5,410' (junction with Trail 103)

Estimated Duration of Hike: 2 to 4 hours each way

Sweat Index: buckets of sweat (difficult)

Mountain Bike Sweat Index: bathed in sweat (strenuous)

Best Features: access to North Baldy Lookout, part of an excellent loop hike

Availability of Water Along the Trail: The Upper West Branch Priest River and Colza Creek offer plenty of water at first, but don't expect any in the last 3 miles or so.

Stream Crossings: The West Branch and Colza Creek must be crossed, and at high water they might be tricky.

Campsites: There are several primitive campsites in the meadow at the trailhead for Trail 162 only a few hundred yards from Road 1107 leading up to the trailhead for this trail.

Alternate Hikes: This trail is part of a popular loop of about 20 miles, especially for backcountry horsemen, with Trails 103 and 162. Trail 197 also connects this trail with Trail 162 and to Pyramid Pass Road 312.

Icy Springs Trail No. 197

Destination: North Baldy via trail 164 and Hungry Mountain via Trail 162. *Map, page 161.*

Best Suited For: hiking, horseback riding, mountain biking

How Much Use: A Little * **A LITTLE MORE** * A Lot * A Lot More * Excessive

What's it like? This is an excellent adventure through the heart of the Upper West Branch Priest River. This trail is most often used as a connecting trail between Trails 162 and 164 and utilized in a loop hike that also involves Trail 103. Pretty much this entire basin was burned in 1926, so the forest is dense and relatively young, but there are pockets of old-growth as the trail oscillates from ridge top to creek bottom several times. From its beginning at Road 312, the trail slants downhill into Paqua Creek just below Grouse Spring. After crossing that, it climbs over a low ridge and crosses two forks of Colza Creek, then climbs another ridge between there and a fork of the Upper West Branch. There are at least two crossings of streams along that stretch before the trail begins its sustained ascent to the east side of Hungry Mountain and its rendezvous with Trail 162.

USGS Map: North Baldy, Gleason Mountain

Trailhead: In Priest River, Idaho, turn north on Highway 57 and go to milepost 21.5. Turn west on Squaw Valley Road and go 7.25 miles to a T-junction. Solo Creek Road 659 goes left. Go right on Road 312 for 2.7 miles to a fork. Road 312 continues to the left and Road 1107 goes right. Stay on Road 312 toward Pyramid Pass. Just over half a mile before the pass the trail is on the right. Parking is limited to one or two vehicles.

Trail Length: approximately 2.5 miles to the junction with Trail 164 (and about 4.5 miles to North Baldy), 7.3 miles one-way to the junction with Trail 162 (and about 10 miles to Hungry Mountain)

Trail Condition: fair

Elevation: Trailhead – 4,560' (at Road 312), High Point/Low Point – 3,990' (junction with Trail 164), End – 4,760' (junction with Trail 162)

Estimated Duration of Hike: 1.5 to 2.5 hours each way to North Baldy, 3.5 to 4.5 hours each way to Hungry Mountain, or the loop with Trail 103 may take 6 to 8 hours.

Sweat Index: buckets of sweat (difficult)

Mountain Bike Sweat Index: may not be suitable

Best Features: access into large roadless area, fabulous forest hiking, nice streams

Availability of Water Along the Trail: plenty

Stream Crossings: lots of boggy spots and several major crossings that might be interesting at high water but should be no problem after spring runoff

Campsites: Primitive sites might be found along the way.

Alternate Hikes: Four trails in the Upper West Branch Priest River combine for a variety of great loop hikes. Check out a map to see how you want to explore this basin on Trails 103, 162, 164 and 197.

Trails: Hannah Flats No. 600, North Fork Lamb Cr. No. 204, Camp 15 No. 232, Binarch Creek No. 220

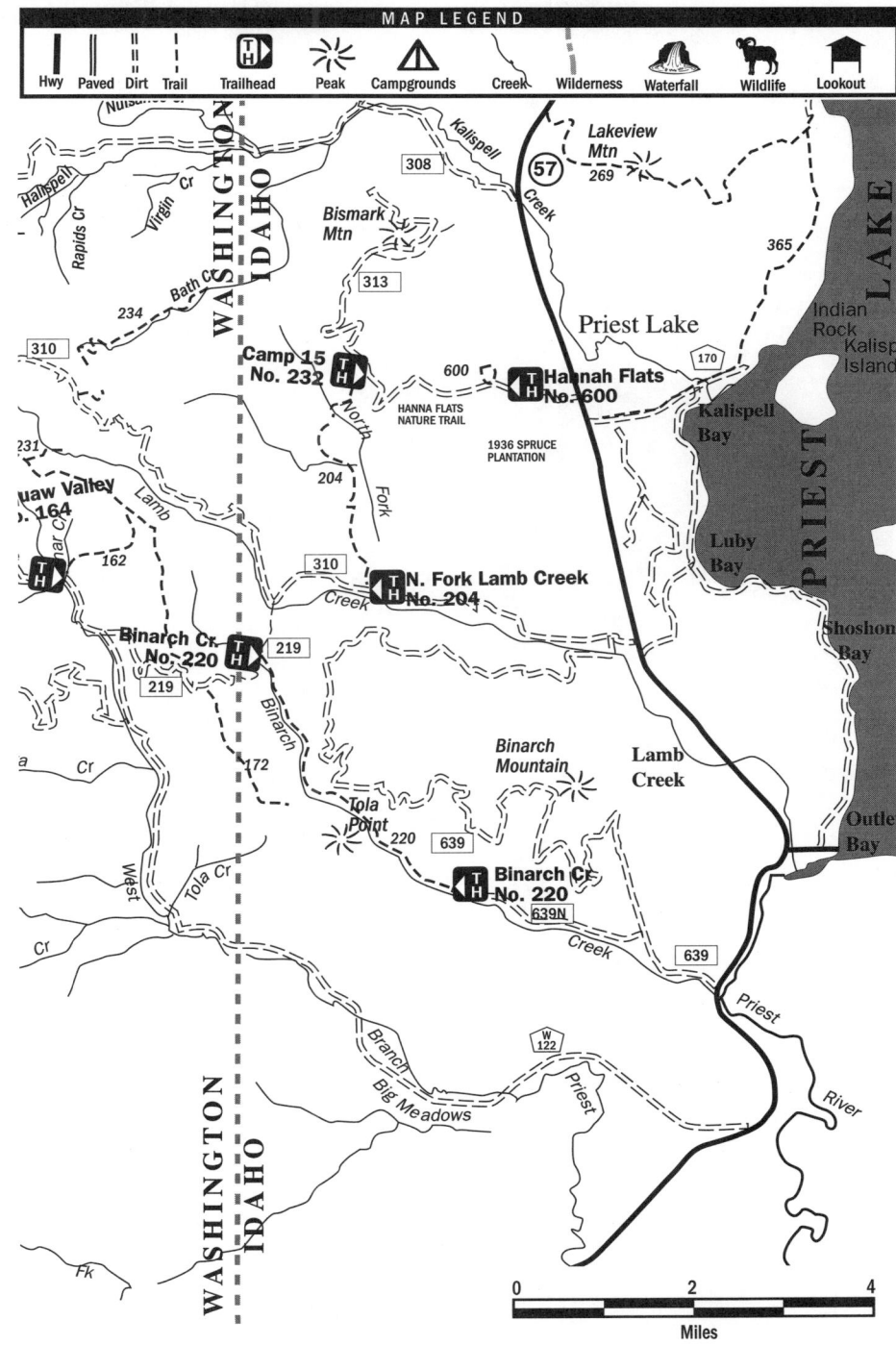

Pend Oreille–Priest Divide

Hanna Flats National Recreation Trail No. 600

ACCESSIBLE: This is an easy, level trail with a surface of some gravel and forest duff.

This is a Family Fun Hike

Destination: Hanna Flats Cedar Grove. *Map, page 169.*

Best Suited For: hiking

How Much Use: A Little * A Little More * **A LOT** * A Lot More * Excessive

What's it like? A 19-acre block of old-growth cedar, hemlock, whitepine and spruce survived a forest fire that burned along the west side of Priest Lake in 1926. It ripped across 80,000 acres but left this grove relatively unscathed. In 1955 the Forest Service preserved this site as a Natural Area and constructed a self-guiding nature trail through this remarkable grove of ancient trees. The area is named for a family of homesteaders who lived near here. Jim Hanna brought his family to Priest Lake in 1921 and survived the fire that was sparked by lightning on July 11, 1926. Though trees like what are found here were highly sought after by loggers in those days, this grove escaped the saw because it was so distant from a stream down which the logs could easily be floated to the lake and on to a mill. Many of these monarchs are 4 or 5 feet in diameter, 400 years old and pushing 200 feet tall. The trail is a wide, flat path winding through this cathedral forest, and though it is not at the highest standard of accessibility for the handicapped, it should be possible to help the elderly, the very young and even those in wheelchairs along this trail.

Interpretive sign at Hanna Flats

USGS Map: Priest Lake SW

Trailhead: From Priest River, Idaho, travel Highway 57 north 31.7 miles to Hanna Flats Road 313. Turn west and go 1 mile to the trailhead. There is a good parking area and a vault toilet. This trail is about 2 miles southwest of the Priest Lake Ranger Station.

Trail Length: one-quarter mile graveled loop

Trail Condition: excellent

Elevation: 2,600'

Estimated Duration of Hike: 10 minutes to as long as you want to enjoy this old-growth forest

Sweat Index: no sweat (easy)

Mountain Bike Sweat Index: Easy, though this trail is not really conducive to bikes because it is so short, but it could be a good beginner trail for young children just learning to ride.

Best Features: old-growth forest, interpretive nature trail

Availability of Water Along the Trail: none

Stream Crossings: none

Campsites: none

Alternate Hikes: Trail 232 connects to Hanna Flats Road a couple miles beyond the Hanna Flats trailhead.

North Fork Lamb Creek Trail No. 204 and Camp 15 Trail No. 232 (also called Hanna Cutoff trail)

This is a Family Fun Hike

Destination: North Fork Lamb Creek. *Map, page 169.*

Best Suited For: hiking, horseback riding, mountain biking

How Much Use: A LITTLE * A Little More * A Lot * A Lot More * Excessive

What's it like? From Road 310 Trail 204 follows an old roadbed for about a mile, then the trail carries on through a variety of forest types, from thick cedar and hemlock saplings to more open lodgepole pine and Douglas fir ridges. Along the way you will notice occasional ancient Douglas fir and larch that survived the fire of 1926. About 2 miles up Trail 204, there is a junction where an old metal sign proclaims "Camp 15 Trail No. 232, Priest River Highway 6, 3 mi." That trail crosses the North Fork of Lamb Creek and climbs over a low ridge to Road 301 about a mile away. From there it is 2.9 miles to the highway. A half-mile of bushwhacking above that crossing, the stream emerges from Bath Creek Gorge, a remarkable geologic feature. At a stream crossing on Trail 204 not far past the junction, a fellow named Gunnar Newquist (maybe a Forest Service trail crewman) left his name carved into a log with a chainsaw. The trail peters out 2 miles beyond the Camp 15 trail junction where it enters private property. There are really no vistas along these trails, but it is a nice stroll through the forest, and lots of deer and moose inhabit this area.

USGS Map: Priest Lake SW

Trailhead: At milepost 28.9 on Highway 57 north of Priest River, Idaho, turn west on Lamb Creek Road 310 and go 3.3 miles. Trail 204, marked by a couple of signposts but no sign, is adjacent to private property where the North Fork of Lamb Creek crosses the road in a small meadow. Two or three vehicles can park alongside the road. Trail 232 is accessed on Hanna Flats Road 301 at milepost 31.7 on Highway 57. Go 2.9 miles and look for an obscure sign attached to a tree above the road. Parking for two or three vehicles is available at a switchback a short way past the trail.

Trail Length: Trail 204 is approximately 3 miles long; Trail 232 approximately 1 mile.

Trail Condition: good

Elevation: Trailhead – 2,650' (Trail 204 at Road 310), High/Low Point – 2,910' (junction Trail 204 and 232), End – 2,930' (Trail 232 junction with Road 313)

Estimated Duration of Hike: 2 to 3 hours either way

Sweat Index: break a sweat (moderate)

Mountain Bike Sweat Index: buckets of sweat (difficult)

Best Features: forest silence, possibility of seeing wildlife

Availability of Water Along the Trail: Trail 204 has a couple of places for water and trail 232 crosses the North Fork of Lamb Creek.

Stream Crossings: The second stream crossing on 204 is a bit tricky on an old wooden bridge.

Campsites: none

Alternate Hikes: An off-trail hike into Bath Creek Gorge is quite an exciting adventure, but use extreme caution – the terrain is rugged.

Binarch Creek Trail No. 220

This is a Family Fun Hike

Destination: Binarch Creek. *Map, page 169.*

Best Suited For: hiking, horseback riding

How Much Use: A LITTLE * A Little More * A Lot * A Lot More * Excessive

What's it like? If the gate is open on Road 639N, this hike is shortened by 2 miles. At the end of this road the trail, which still follows the roadbed for another one-quarter mile before narrowing down to a single track, meanders along the edge of the riparian zone that typifies much of Binarch Creek. There is a lot of brush along the stream, and sometimes the vegetation is lush. Watch out for stinging nettles along the trail. As the steep slopes on either side draw closer together a mile or so from the trailhead, the trail crosses areas of talus rock. Several small meadows and ponds are encountered; there is sign of beaver activity and moose frequent this place. At the third meadow, the trail begins to climb upslope from a beaver pond. From the north end, beginning at Road 219, the trail enters a nice stand of old-growth hemlock, and the trail stays high on the ridges above the creek. It crosses several draws and skirts a couple of small hillside openings from which the beaver ponds and meadows in the creek valley below can be seen. It then drops into a draw and descends the hillside into the creek bottom.

Beaver ponds on Binarch Creek make for good moose habitat

USGS Map: Priest Lake SW

Trailhead: At milepost 24.2 on Highway 57 north of Priest River, Idaho, turn west on Binarch Creek Road 639. Go about 1.2 miles and turn left on road 639N. There is a gate one-third of a mile up the road, but it may well be open and allow you to drive another 1.7 miles to an old log deck landing, which is a good place to turn around and park. It will accommodate more than six vehicles. The trail starts about 200 yards farther. The north end of the trail is reached by taking Lamb Creek Road 310 at milepost 28.9 on Highway 57. Go 4.4 miles on 310, then turn south on 219 and go 0.6 mile to the trailhead. A sign marks the trail and there is parking for only one vehicle.

Trail Length: 3.5 miles one-way (5.5 miles if the gate is closed on 639N)

Trail Condition: good

Elevation: Trailhead – 2,680', High/Low Point – 2,680'-3,000', End – 3,000' (junction with Road 219)

Estimated Duration of Hike: 2 to 3 hours either way

Sweat Index: break a sweat (moderate)

Mountain Bike Sweat Index: buckets of sweat (difficult)

Best Features: riparian habitat, possible encounters with moose

Availability of Water Along the Trail: Water could be taken from Binarch Creek, but it is a slow-moving stream apparently with beaver. A small stream crosses the trail about a mile from the lower trailhead, and several draws from the upper trailhead have some water.

Stream Crossings: several brooks easy to step across

Campsites: The end of road 639N is in a large clearing suitable for a primitive campsite.

Trails: Browns Lake No. 320, South Skookum Lake No. 138

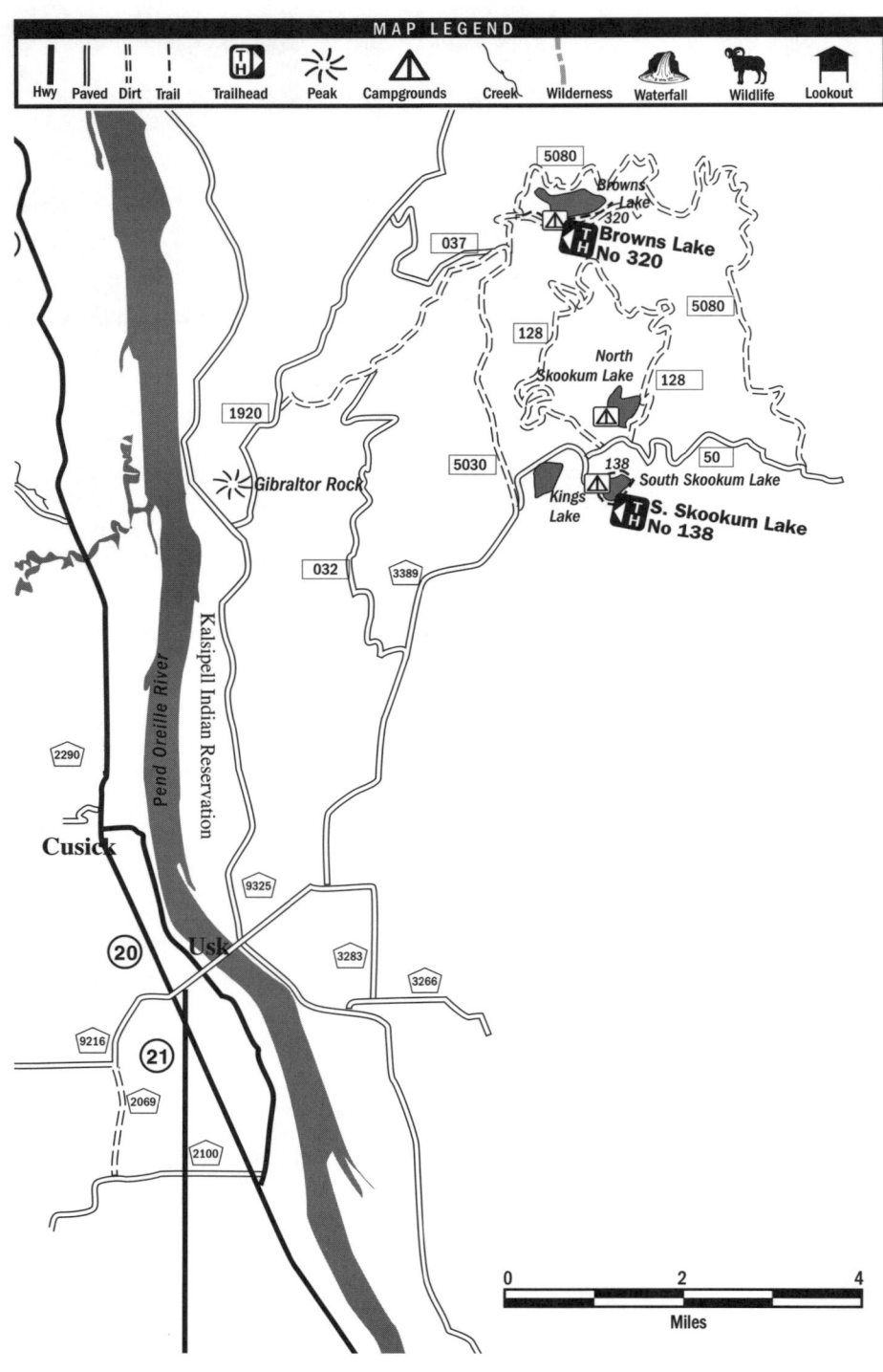

Browns Lake Trail No. 320

ACCESSIBLE: A fish-spawning viewing platform at the east end of the trail is suitable for wheelchairs, and a wide graveled path leads gently down to the grove of old-growth cedars at the lake's east edge.

This is a Family Fun Hike

Destination: Browns Lake. *Map, page 174.*

Best Suited For: hiking, mountain biking

How Much Use: A Little * A Little More * **A LOT** * A Lot More * Excessive

What's it like? The trail along the southern shore of Browns Lake was built in 1991 in memory of Jerry Rowland, a fly fisherman and long-time campground host. In fact, the lake and creek are dedicated to fly-fishing only, and the lake can only be accessed using non-motorized craft. The trail gently undulates along a steep, north-facing slope and has several wooden benches situated along the way for rest and contemplation. The east end of the trail descends to the creek and passes through a small grove of beautiful, old-growth cedar, then climbs up to the road, crosses it and proceeds to a fish-viewing platform. In early spring cutthroat trout can be watched spawning in the small stream at your feet. The viewing platform was erected as a joint venture of several agencies and organizations and is dedicated to the memory of Jordan Wheat "Joe" Lambert (1924-1995). The viewing platform and the east end of the trail to the old-growth cedar grove are handicapped accessible.

Browns Lake is open only to fly fishers and non-motorized boats

USGS Map: Browns Lake

Trailhead: On Highway 20 approximately 15 miles north of Newport, Washington, turn northeast toward the community of Usk. Follow this road through Usk and over the Pend Oreille River and continue straight on County Road No. 3389. Go about 4 miles to a "Y" in the road and go left on Road No. 5030 for another 4 miles. You will come to a Forest Service campground and fee area with plenty of parking. You can also bear right just before the campground on a narrow dirt road to a fish-viewing platform on Browns Creek and more primitive, but free, parking about a mile from the campground. Here you will also find a trailhead.

Trail Length: 1 mile

Trail Condition: excellent

Elevation: 3,411 feet at the lake

Estimated Duration of Hike: an hour or less each way

Sweat Index: no sweat (easy)

Mountain Bike Sweat Index: no sweat

Best Features: lake views, old-growth cedar forest

Availability of Water Along the Trail: The trail crosses Browns Creek near where it empties into the lake.

Stream Crossings: A footbridge spans Browns Creek in the grove of old cedars.

Campsites: There is a primitive campsite in the grove of old cedars at the east end of the lake; several Forest Service campgrounds are located in this area at Browns Lake, Skookum Creek and South Skookum Lake.

South Skookum Lake Trail No. 138

This is a Family Fun Hike

Destination: a loop around South Skookum Lake. *Map, page 174.*

Best Suited For: hiking, mountain biking

How Much Use: A Little * A Little More * A Lot * **A LOT MORE** * Excessive

What's it like? This trail offers an easy walk or bike ride through a nice forest on or near the shores of South Skookum Lake. There are some great picnic sites along the trail, especially on the north side of the lake where views of the lake and mountains are quite nice. It is not unusual to see moose feeding on the more remote edges of the lake or to see deer getting a cool drink late in the evenings. In the fall you might be lucky to view fish spawning in the creek between South and North Skookum lakes. This is a wonderful trail for families with small children and for more elderly, yet active folks.

USGS Map: Skookum Creek, Browns Lake

Trailhead: On Highway 20 approximately 15 miles north of Newport, Washington, turn northeast toward the community of Usk. Follow this road through Usk and over the Pend Oreille River and continue straight on County Road No. 3389. Go about 4 miles to a "Y" in the road and bear right on Kings Lake Road. There are signs all along the way for South Skookum Lake. You will go around Kings Lake, and after about 2.5 miles the entrance to South Skookum Lake will be on the left. The trailhead is down by the boat launch. This is a Forest Service fee area for camping and day use.

Trail Length: 1.3 miles

Trail Condition: excellent

Elevation: 3,529 feet at the lake

Estimated Duration of Hike: 1 hour on foot

Sweat Index: no sweat (easy)

Mountain Bike Sweat Index: no sweat

Best Features: beautiful mountain lake, wildlife

Availability of Water Along the Trail: Several small streams feed into the lake.

Stream Crossings: a number of easy crossings

Campsites: The trail begins and ends in a Forest Service fee area campground.

Alternate Hikes: There is a spur-trail loop called the Dragonfly Trail about 0.3 miles long on the east side of the lake.

Lush forests surround many of the lower-elevation lakes in the Selkirk Mountains

Trails: Bead Lake No. 127, Newport Geophysical Trails, Nok-Osh-Kol Heritage Trail at Pioneer Park

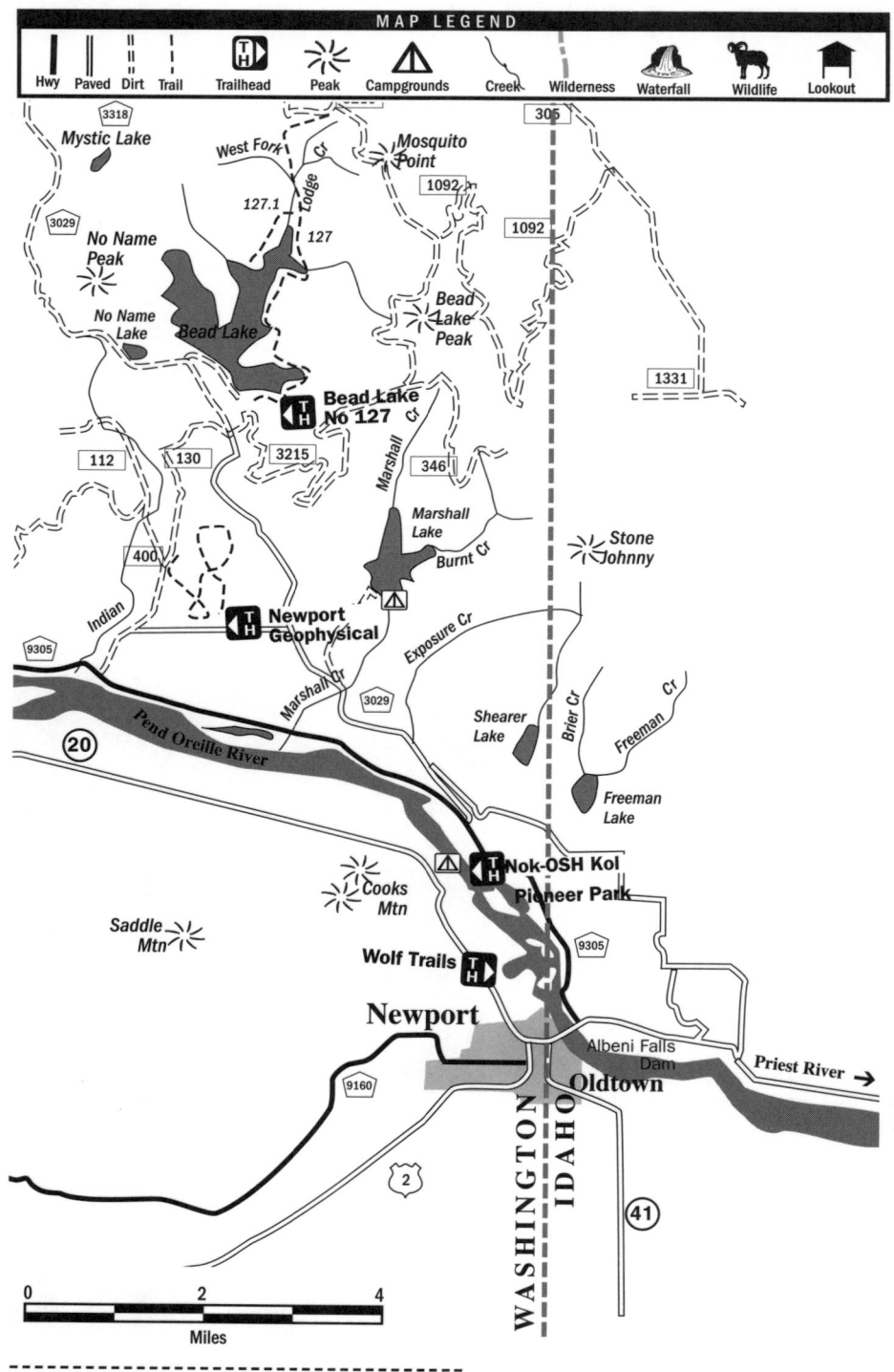

Bead Lake Trail No. 127

ACCESSIBLE: For about one-half mile from the day use parking area, an old roadbed cuts through the forest. It is flat and wide with a firm surface.

This is a Family Fun Hike

Destination: Bead Lake. *Map, page 178.*

Best Suited For: hiking, horseback riding, mountain biking

How Much Use: A Little * A Little More * **A LOT** * A Lot More * Excessive

What's it like? From the trailhead on Road No. 3215, the trail descends through a shady forest a couple hundred yards to the Forest Service day use area on the southeast shore of Bead Lake. From there it follows an old roadbed for perhaps a quarter mile to the first campsite below the trail on the lake's edge. At that point the trail begins again and meanders sometimes through heavy cedar forest and at other times through open ponderosa pine, usually 30 to 50 feet above the lake. At the southeast corner of the lake is Enchantment Camp, a beautiful primitive campsite among big cedars frequently used by Boy Scouts. After this the trail leaves the lakeside and climbs rather stiffly over a timbered ridge, then drops back down to the lake. Near the north end, about 4 miles from the trailhead, note the giant Western whitepine close to the trail. It is over 5 feet in diameter and may be approaching 200 feet in height. Few of these monarchs remain in the forests of the Selkirk Mountains. The trail goes beyond the lake and climbs through half a dozen switchbacks to the ridgeline and eventually ties in with Road No. 3215 again. Along this upper portion of the trail, be on the lookout for tiger lilies in season. Though most of the trail is narrow and often rocky, it offers a great mountain biking opportunity for riders of modest skill. A good loop might be to take Road 3215 west of the lake to the ridge top then follow the trail back down to the trailhead.

Bead Lake

USGS Map: Bead Lake

Trailhead: In Oldtown, Idaho, turn north off Highway 2 next to the Pend Oreille River onto LeClerc Road and go 2.7 miles. Turn east onto Bead Lake Road and go 6.2 miles to Bead Lake Ridge Road No. 3215, a gravel road that takes you about 0.5 mile to the trailhead. A large parking area is located here. Bead Lake Drive is a paved road right next to Road No. 3215 that accesses a subdivision on the southwest end of the lake, but before reaching the subdivision there is a paved road that enters a Forest Service day use area with a boat launch facility and a parking area adjacent to the Bead Lake trail. This facility is a Forest Service fee area. In 2003 it was open from 6 a.m. to 8 p.m. and was closed Mondays and Tuesdays.

Trail Length: 6.4 miles one-way

Trail Condition: excellent

Elevation: Trailhead – 3,220' (at Road 3215), High/Low Point – 2,830' (lakeside), End – 3,580' (junction with Road 3215)

Estimated Duration of Hike: 3 to 4 hours each way

Sweat Index: break a sweat (moderate)

Mountain Bike Sweat Index: break a sweat

Best Features: a beautiful lakeside hike with scattered, old-growth trees

Availability of Water Along the Trail: Three small streams cross the trail that may contain a trickle of water.

Stream Crossings: There are several boggy areas and streams, but boardwalks and footbridges cross most of them.

Campsites: A local Boy Scout troop has worked on this trail and established at least one campsite about a mile or so from the trailhead called the Enchantment Camp. Another campsite is located at the end of the old road, which marks the start of the trail, and a campsite is located at the north end of the lake next to the creek. Marshall Lake and Pioneer Park are Forest Service campgrounds nearby.

Alternate Hikes: A spur labeled Trail No. 127.1 takes off from the main trail just north of the lake at the campsite located there and proceeds about 1.5 miles along the northeast shore to several rocky outcroppings overlooking the lake. A cabin is tucked into heavy timber a little below this spur trail. It is privately owned and not open to public use.

Newport Geophysical Trails

This is a Family Fun Hike (suitable for mountain bikes especially)

Destination: loop trails through the forest. *Map, page 178.*

Best Suited For: hiking, mountain biking, horseback riding, Nordic skiing

How Much Use: A Little * A Little More * **A LOT** * A Lot More * Excessive

What's it like? The trails system at the Newport Geophysical Observatory was developed primarily for wintertime Nordic skiing, but it makes for some fine mountain biking and horseback riding opportunities in the summer as well. Hikers might enjoy the easy strolls through a mixed forest of ponderosa pines and Douglas fir, but the trails don't actually have a distinguishable tread. They are swaths through the forest cleared of brush and downfall, which happen to be full of goatweed and knapweed. Beginning and novice mountain bikers will find these trails valuable for honing their fat tire skills. Some of the best use, however, is in the winter on skis or snowshoes on groomed trails. This area is known as an important wildlife winter range, so the chances of seeing deer or elk are high. Just remember not to harass the animals, as wintertime stress is high enough as it is.

USGS Map: Bead Lake

Trailhead: In Oldtown, Idaho, turn north off Highway 2 at the east end of the bridge over the Pend Oreille River onto LeClerc Road. Travel about 7.5 miles to its junction with Indian Creek Road and turn right. This junction has a large sign for the Geophysical trails. Go about 1.5 miles to the trailhead on the left.

Trail Length: a variety of loops ranging from 1 to 7 miles (or more if you choose)

Trail Condition: good

Elevation: 2,480 feet to 2,633 feet

Estimated Duration of Hike: up to 4 hours on foot depending on the loops that are hiked

Sweat Index: no sweat (easy)

Mountain Bike Sweat Index: no sweat (with a few moderate loops and pitches)

Best Features: great trails for beginning mountain bikers through a shady, mixed-conifer forest and terrific Nordic skiing in winter

Availability of Water Along the Trail: none

Stream Crossings: none

Campsites: Pioneer Park, Marshall Lake and Bead Lake campgrounds are nearby and are all Forest Service fee areas. Check for dates they are open as they may be closed in winter.

Alternate Hikes: The Geophysical trails system has a variety of named segments – Chipmunk, Whitetail, Little Sweat, Perspiration, Rough Ridge, Flatlander and Cougar. They each vary from one-half mile to almost 2 miles in length.

Nok-OSH-Kol Heritage Trail at Pioneer Park

ACCESSIBLE: A paved parking lot affords good parking and access to toilet facilities and the trail.

This is a Family Fun Hike

Destination: a loop hike near the Pend Oreille River (this is a Forest Service camping and day use fee area). *Map, page 178.*

Best Suited For: hiking

How Much Use: A Little * A Little More * A Lot * **A LOT MORE** * Excessive

What's it like? This trail, suitable for wheelchair access, was developed with the inspiration and assistance of the Kalispel Tribe and provides a glimpse into the history of this proud people along the beautiful Pend Oreille River. A dozen interpretive sites tell the story of these Native Americans – how they lived and what they ate. Views of the river are excellent. Nok-OSH-Kol in the Kalispel language means "The Ancient Ones." A picnic area is located nearby for your enjoyment, following an illuminating walk through history on this excellent trail.

USGS Map: Bead Lake

Trailhead: In Oldtown, Idaho, turn north off Highway 2 at the east end of the bridge over the Pend Oreille River onto LeClerc Road. Go 2.4 miles to the entrance of Pioneer Park.

Trail Length: 0.3 miles

Trail Condition: excellent (wheelchair accessible)

Elevation: 2,040 feet

Estimated Duration of Hike: less than 1 hour

Sweat Index: no sweat (easy)

Mountain Bike Sweat Index: not suitable

Best Features: historical and interpretive displays about Native American culture

Availability of Water Along the Trail: Look for water in the campground nearby.

Stream Crossings: none

Campsites: Pioneer Park campground is located here.

The Priest Lakes and Lower Priest River

When you ask about "the most beautiful lake in Idaho," a lot of people will point to Lake Pend Oreille near Sandpoint and reply, "That's it." And of course, it truly is a marvelous body of water. But a case could be made for a different lake wearing that title and anyone asserting such could not be counted wrong. Priest Lake and its little sibling, Upper Priest Lake, are spectacular in their own right and rival any lake in the state and indeed the whole Inland Northwest for sheer grandeur and majesty. To the east rise the incomparable granite uplands of the Selkirk Crest and on the west are the rolling forested hills of the Pend Oreille-Priest Divide.

The lands immediately around these lakes are laced with numerous excellent trails. From Woodrat and Bulldog trails between Outlet Bay and Luby Bay to the Lakeshore National Recreation Trail and Plowboy Mountain, there is indeed a lot to see. Even one of the islands has a fine loop trail accessible only by boat. A trip to Kalispell Island is a fine adventure. And the river south of the big lake offers a couple of hiking opportunities at Chipmunk Rapids and Peewee-Steep Creek. From right by the water or at the top of a mountain, like Lakeview Mountain, the splendor of these glorious lakes and the mountains surrounding them can be enjoyed by everyone.

Access is easy on mostly paved roads. Highway 57 from Priest River, Idaho plies the dark forests of this heavily timbered valley to Nordman, and all along the way are side roads to special points of interest on the lake. Upper Priest Lake remains relatively wild with no direct motorized vehicle access other than boat, which makes for an especially exciting visit for those who love the more pristine setting of nature.

Trails: Upper Priest Lake No. 302, Centennial No. 58, Navigation No. 291, Plowboy No. 295

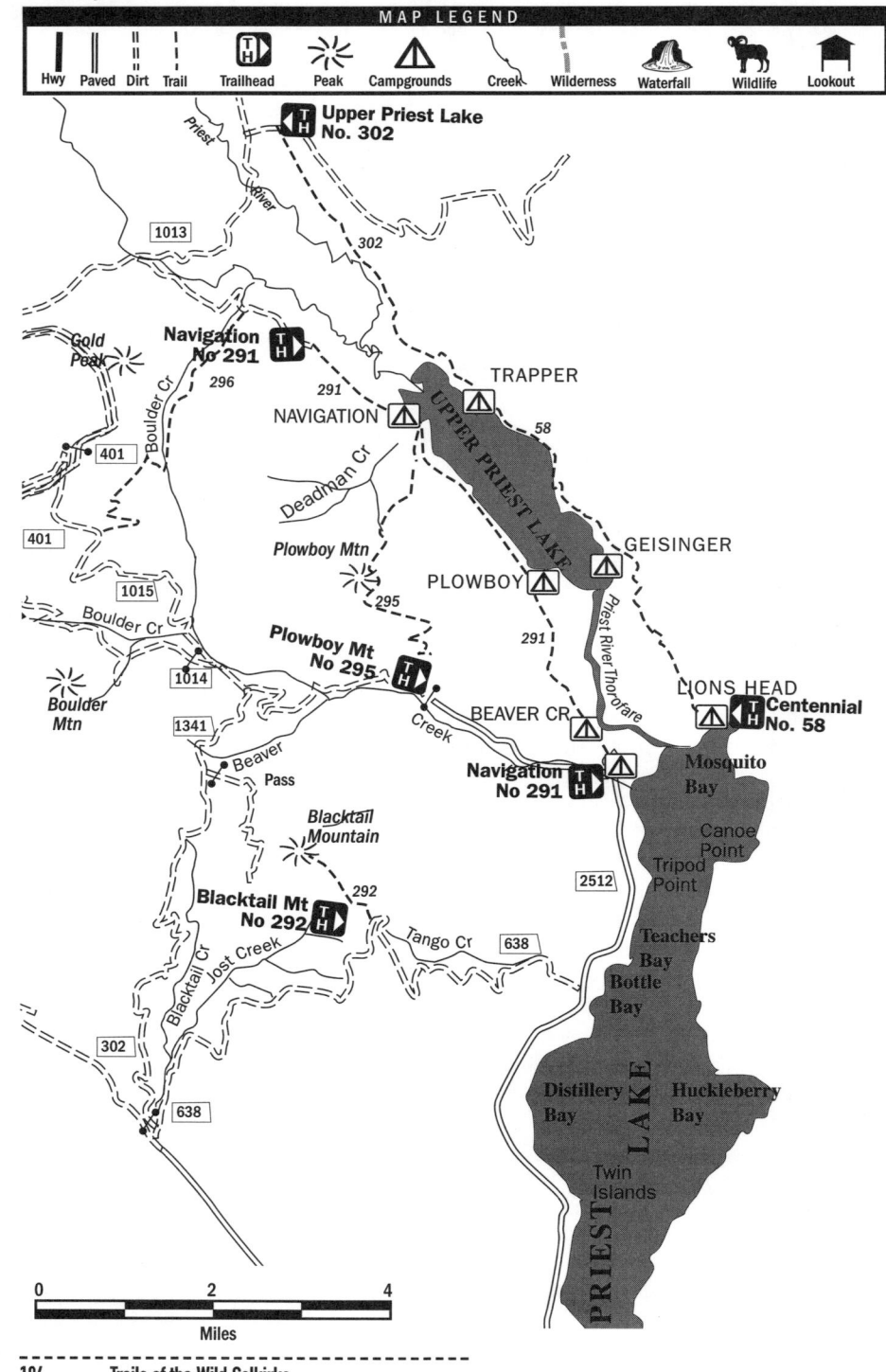

Upper Priest Lake Trail No. 302

This is a Family Fun Hike

This trail is part of the 1,200-mile long Idaho Centennial Trail

Destination: Upper Priest Lake, Trapper Campsite. *Map, page 184.*

Best Suited For: hiking, horseback riding, mountain biking

How Much Use: A Little * A Little More * **A LOT** * A Lot More * Excessive

What's it like? A nice stroll through old-growth cedar and hemlock gently descends toward Upper Priest Lake. Listen for the sound of the river not far away to the west. The timber is heavy, but the forest itself offers lots of interesting things to observe. About 3.75 miles along the trail, it passes by Coolin's Cabin, one of the original structures in the area from a hundred years ago. It has collapsed and is in an advanced stage of decay but it is not hard to imagine what it must have

Upper Priest Lake looking toward Shedroof Mountain

been like to live in this shelter near the north end of the lake, visible through the trees and alder. A short distance farther the trail emerges from the woods at the northeast corner of the lake in brilliant sunshine. It hugs the lakeshore for half a mile since a steep rocky slope rises sharply above. Watch for the old mine shaft near the Trapper campground. It is open because it is only about 20 feet deep. At the first campsites you come to at Trapper, there is a trail junction by a giant whitepine with a dead larch leaning into it. This trail carries on up Trapper Creek for a couple of miles. Campsites are scattered along the lakeshore for a couple of hundred yards from this point. There is a bear-proof food box, pit toilets and a nice bridge over Trapper Creek.

USGS Map: Upper Priest Lake

Trailhead: From Priest River, Idaho, follow Highway 57 north to Nordman, approximately 36.5 miles. Continue north until Highway 57 becomes Road 302 and go 14 miles to Granite Pass and the junction with Road 1013. At milepost 10.3 on Road 1013 turn west onto Road 655 and go 0.4 miles to the trailhead. Parking for three to five vehicles is on the left side of the road, and the trail begins on the right.

Trail Length: 4.3 miles one-way

Trail Condition: good

Elevation: Trailhead – 2,630', High/Low Point – 2,630'-2,450', End – 2,450' (Trapper Campground on Upper Priest Lake)

Estimated Duration of Hike: 1.5 to 2.5 hours each way

Sweat Index: break a sweat (moderate)

Mountain Bike Sweat Index: no sweat (easy)

Best Features: historic cabin, mine shaft, lake access, old-growth

Availability of Water Along the Trail: There are numerous springs and seeps along the way and a couple of streams, plus the lake itself.

Stream Crossings: Many marshy areas and springs are crossed with boardwalk and footbridges, but there is one stream you need to carefully step across. There is a nice wooden bridge over Trapper Creek.

Campsites: You will find numerous dispersed sites along Road 1013, and there is room for camping at the trailhead; also the semi-primitive campground at Trapper Creek has several sites with picnic tables, fire pits and pit toilets.

Alternate Hikes: This trail connects to Centennial Trail No. 58, which continues south along the west side of the lake on state lands, and also to Trapper Creek Trail, another state trail that has its beginnings on Priest Lake State Forest Road No. 1.

Centennial Trail No. 58

This is a Family Fun Hike

This trail is part of the 1,200-mile long Idaho Centennial Trail

Destination: Upper Priest Lake. *Map, page 184.*

Best Suited For: hiking, horseback riding, mountain biking

How Much Use: A Little * A Little More * **A LOT** * A Lot More * Excessive

What's it like? This is an excellent pathway not only for hiking but for mountain biking and horseback riding as well. It is also open to motorized use. The trail begins near the Lions Head Unit of Priest Lake State Park. It follows an old roadbed that enters a stand of young trees growing back in an old clear-cut. Several roads weave through this area, but it is pretty obvious which way to go. Keep heading toward Caribou Creek, and once you get to it the trail meanders adjacent to the stream for a short way before you are then faced with having to wade across it. During spring runoff that could be tricky, but later in the summer the water is not very deep. From here the trail is mostly in dense, dark timber but it is a beautiful stroll through the forest. After perhaps 2 miles there is a junction with a trail leading to Geisinger Campground on the south end of Upper Priest Lake. The main trail continues to the east side of the lake and undulates along its shoreline to Trapper Creek. The views of the lake and north to the Shedroof Divide in the Salmo-Priest Wilderness are magnificent.

USGS Map: Caribou Creek, Upper Priest Lake

Trailhead: This trail can be accessed from both ends. The south end is near the Lions Head Unit of Priest Lake State Park. Take Highway 57 north from Priest River, Idaho, approximately 23 miles and turn east toward Coolin. Go about 5.25 miles to Coolin Corners and turn east on Cavanaugh Bay Road. Travel another 3.3 miles to East Shore Road (Priest Lake State Forest Road No. 1). Take it approximately 22 miles to Lion Creek. Turn left on a road that will head into private residences by bearing right just after the turn. Take that right through a gate and park at a wide spot good for four to six vehicles. The trail is obvious leading into the forest pretty much straight ahead. This trail ends at Trapper Creek where it ties in with Upper Priest Lake Trail No. 302.

Trail Length: 5 miles one-way

Trail Condition: excellent

Elevation: Trailhead – 2,450', High/Low Point – 2,720', End – 2,450' (Trapper Campground on Upper Priest Lake)

Paddling from the Thorofare into Upper Priest Lake at Geisinger Campground

Estimated Duration of Hike: 2 to 3 hours each way to Trapper Creek, or about an hour each way to Geisinger Campground on Upper Priest Lake

Sweat Index: no sweat (easy)

Mountain Bike Sweat Index: no sweat (easy)

Best Features: Beautiful forested hike with access to the east side of Upper Priest Lake.

Availability of Water Along the Trail: The trail crosses Caribou Creek and closely follows much of the east side of Upper Priest Lake.

Stream Crossings: Caribou Creek must be waded.

Campsites: Semi-primitive sites are located at Geisinger and Trapper Creek, and a developed fee area campground is at Lions Head.

Alternate Hikes: At Trapper Creek this trail connects to Upper Priest Lake Trail No. 302 and to Trapper Creek Trail on state lands.

Navigation Trail No. 291 and Portage Trail

ACCESSIBLE: Portage Trail is an old roadbed that is wide and has a firm surface. It slants downhill at a decent grade, but it may be accessible to some with disabilities.

This is a Family Fun Hike

Destination: Upper Priest Lake, Navigation Campsite. *Map, page 184.*

Best Suited For: hiking, horseback riding, mountain biking

How Much Use: A Little * A Little More * **A LOT** * A Lot More * Excessive

What's it like? This spectacular trail meandering through old-growth hemlock and whitepine to the shores of Upper Priest Lake and beyond is dedicated to the memory of Gerald Lindquist, a Forest Service trail crew boss. A memorial plaque can be found at the south trailhead. For the most part this is a level trail through some beautiful woods. The trail is fairly wide and flat and might be accessible to wheelchairs with a helping hand. To the west you may catch glimpses of parts of Armstrong Meadows through the crowded hemlock, cedar and whitepine. For 3 miles this trail snakes through the forest, then comes to Plowboy Campground. A short spur trail accesses the campsites on the southwest shores of Upper Priest Lake. From this point the trail draws near to the lake's edge for about 2 miles, affording grandiose views of Lookout Mountain and up Trapper Creek. Near Navigation the trail pulls an uphill climb for a ways, then drops down to the spur trail to the Navigation campsites. The junction with Plowboy Mountain Trail No. 295 is also at this spot. From here the trail continues to the north end of the lake, leaving the Upper Priest Lake Scenic Area and joining an old roadbed. Keep an eye out for wildlife in the old clear-cuts. The trail leaves the logging road not far from its northern terminus and descends along an older roadbed to a spectacular crossing of the Hughes Fork of Priest River. A sturdy metal bridge spans the churning waters.

USGS Map: Upper Priest Lake

Trailhead: In Priest River, Idaho, turn north on Highway 57 and go 36.5 miles to Nordman. Take Reeder Bay Road east to the lake and then north as it becomes Road 2512. Go 11.8 miles from Nordman to Beaver Creek campground. The trailhead is on the north side. Follow the signs. There is parking for more than a dozen vehicles. The north end of the trail is reached by going north of Nordman on Highway 57 until it becomes Road 302, then follow it 14 miles to Granite Pass and the junction with Road 1013. Go 5.2 miles on 1013 to a side road (look for the trail sign) and go 0.4 miles along this narrow road to the trailhead. There is a good turnaround and parking for four to six vehicles.

Trail Length: 8.1 miles one-way (6 miles to Navigation Campsite from the south end).

Trail Condition: excellent

Elevation: Trailhead – 2,500' (at Beaver Creek Campground), High/Low Point

– 2,440' (Plowboy Campground on Upper Priest Lake), End – 2,600' (junction with road 655)

Estimated Duration of Hike: 2 to 3 hours to Navigation Campsite, 3 to 4 hours end to end.

Sweat Index: no sweat (easy)

Mountain Bike Sweat Index: no sweat

Best Features: old-growth forest, lakeshore access, great views

Availability of Water Along the Trail: There is a good stream near Plowboy Campground and at Deadman Creek near Navigation Campground.

Stream Crossings: Most wet sites are crossed with raised trail beds and wooden bridges.

Campsites: Semi-primitive campsites with picnic tables, fire pits and pit toilets are at Plowboy and Navigation campgrounds, and a developed fee area campground is at the Beaver Creek trailhead.

Alternate Hikes: Trail 295 connects to this trail and makes for a nice open loop of about 12 miles; the south end of the trail is close to the north end of Trail 294 at Beaver Creek Campground. Also at Beaver Creek next to the trailhead for Navigation is a trail of about one-third mile in length. This is the Portage Trail to The Thorofare for canoeists but it makes for a nice, short walk even if you are not boating. The trail is wide and gentle and could be considered accessible to wheelchairs. It passes through a nice stand of old-growth cedar and hemlock and descends gradually to the water's edge. Be careful at the end where the trail is a bit tricky just above the ribbon of placid water that connects Upper Priest Lake to Priest Lake.

Wildlife Sighting: As I crept up on the shoreline of Upper Priest Lake at Navigation, a cacophony of noise rose from out on the water. Dozens of tundra swans, along with Canada geese and numerous kinds of ducks, dotted the waves like bobbers on a pond during a kids' fishing tournament. The swans took flight and circled the upper end of the lake, landing directly across from where I had clumsily stumbled upon their quiet reverie.

Plowboy Mountain Trail No. 295

Destination: Plowboy Mountain, 5,119 feet. *Map, page 184.*

Best Suited For: hiking, horseback riding, mountain biking

How Much Use: A Little * **A LITTLE MORE** * A Lot * A Lot More * Excessive

What's it like? This nice, wide trail with the easy grade becomes narrower and steeper as it climbs up the south side of Plowboy Mountain. It is mostly in dense timber with limited views until higher up. That's when a few small meadows show up, first overlooking Beaver Creek to the south and west, then ultimately south and east to the lakes. And better yet are the views of the Selkirk

Crest to the east. Also you can pick out Round Top Mountain and Mankato Mountain along the eastern spine of the Salmo-Priest Wilderness. On top there is the remains of a rock foundation of an old lookout situated in a pretty little meadow. From the top the trail descends into heavy timber almost immediately. Being the north side of the mountain the forest here is dominated by cedar and hemlock with a few old larch scattered about. Near the bottom you can hear the rushing waters of Deadman Creek just above where it empties into Upper Priest Lake at Navigation Campground, where this trail joins Trail 291.

USGS Map: Upper Priest Lake

Trailhead: In Priest River, Idaho, turn north on Highway 57 and go 36.5 miles to Nordman. Take Reeder Bay Road east to the lake and then north as it becomes Road 2512. Go 11.8 miles from Nordman to Beaver Creek campground and the junction with Road 1341. Follow Road 1341 for 2.4 miles to a gate and the trailhead. There is parking for two or three vehicles.

Trail Length: 6 miles one-way (about 3 miles to the top of Plowboy Mountain)

Trail Condition: good

Elevation: Trailhead – 2,970', High/Low Point – 4,877' (site of old lookout on Plowboy Mountain), End – 2,500' (junction with Trail 291)

Estimated Duration of Hike: 2.5 to 3.5 hours each way (about 1.5 hours to the top of Plowboy Mountain)

Sweat Index: buckets of sweat (difficult)

Mountain Bike Sweat Index: bathed in sweat (strenuous)

Best Features: site of old lookout, good views of Upper Priest Lake, Priest Lake and the Salmo-Priest Wilderness

Availability of Water Along the Trail: There is a tiny spring about a mile from this trail's junction with Trail 291, but don't count on it as a good water source.

Stream Crossings: none

Campsites: Beaver Creek Campground is a developed Forest Service fee area and there are semi-primitive sites at Navigation Campground with picnic tables, fire pits and a pit toilet.

Alternate Hikes: This trail connects to Trail 291 and makes for a nice, open loop of about 12 miles.

A wintry view from the top of Plowboy Mountain

Trails: Priest Lakeshore No. 294, Kalispell-Reeder Bay No. 365

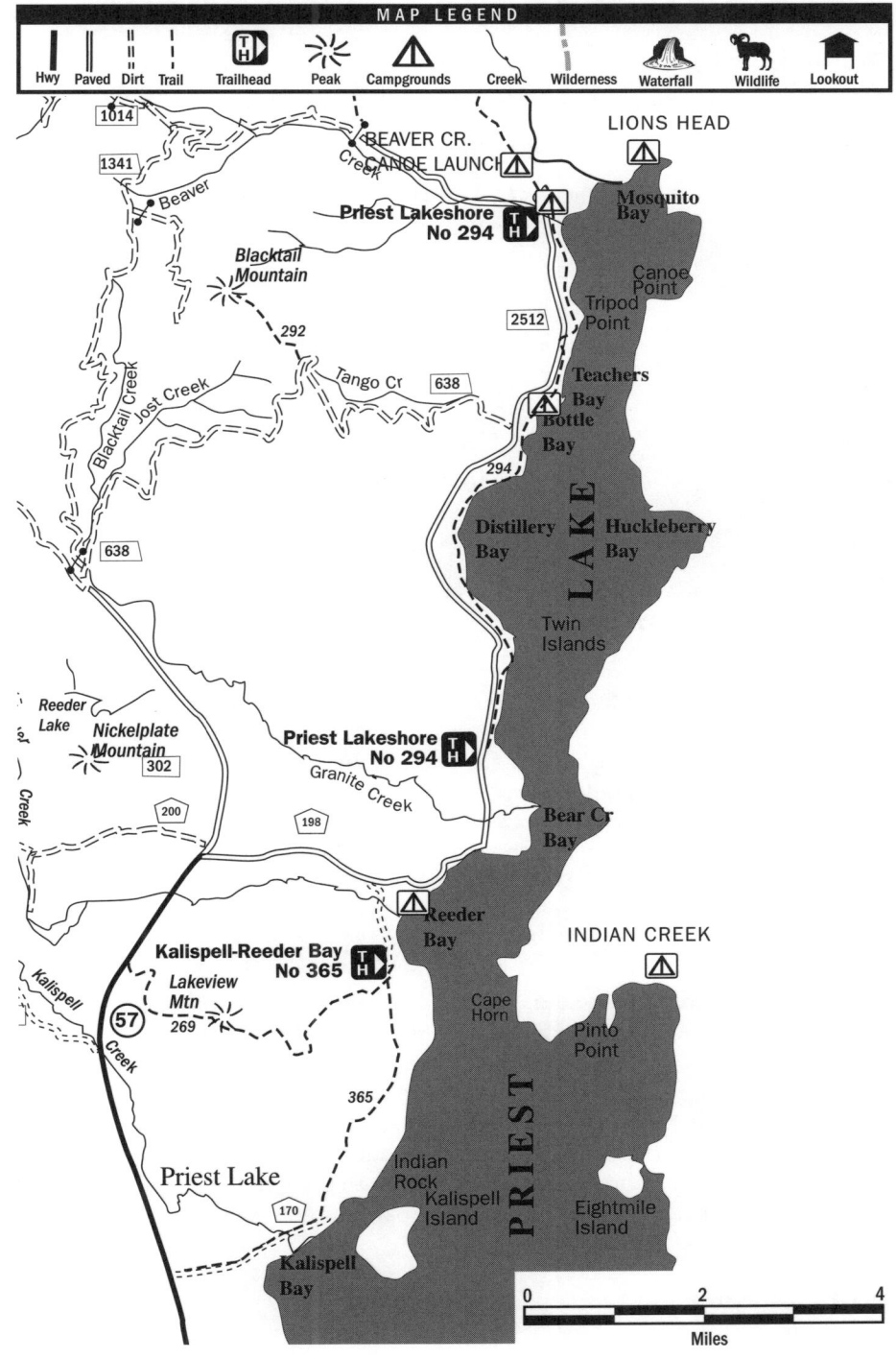

Priest Lakeshore National Recreation Trail No. 294

This is a Family Fun Hike

Destination: Priest Lake. *Map, page 191.*

Best Suited For: hiking, horseback riding, mountain biking

How Much Use: A Little * A Little More * A Lot * **A LOT MORE** * Excessive

What's it like? This spectacular trail is full of fantastic views. Priest Lake is truly one of the most beautiful lakes in the nation, and the background of this lake from this trail – the Selkirk Crest – is stunning. From Mount Roothaan and Chimney Rock northward to Lookout Mountain, the vistas are magnificent. No wonder this is a National Recreation Trail. The trail is often right at the water's edge, and at other times it passes through dense timber and heavy brush. Be sure to note some of the scattered big timber left over from fires of years gone by, and watch for waterfowl – the lake is alive with all kinds of ducks. You may get lucky and even see muskrats, beaver or even otters plying the waters. There are plenty of areas for swimming and fishing or just lazing out on a rock in the sun. A good way to enjoy the entire trail is to have vehicles at both ends, or maybe somewhere in between since there are three other points to access this trail. It gets a lot of use, so be sure to pick up after yourself. Don't leave trash behind. If everyone takes care of the trail, it will be enjoyed more by those who come after you.

Priest Lake in the glory of early autumn

USGS Map: Priest Lake NW, Priest Lake NE

Trailhead: In Priest River, Idaho, turn north on Highway 57 and go 36.5 miles to Nordman. Take Reeder Bay Road east to the lake and then north as it becomes Road 2512. Go 4.6 miles from Nordman to the south trailhead. Watch for the sign on the right hand side of the road. There is parking for five or six vehicles. The north end can be reached by going 11.8 miles from Nordman to Beaver Creek Campground. The trail is at the south end and there is plenty of parking. There are also three access points between the two trailheads, including a trail to Teacher's Bay and another to Bottle Bay, both of which have campsites.

Trail Length: 7.6 miles one-way

Trail Condition: excellent

Elevation: Trailhead – 2,600', High/Low Point – 2,640', End – 2,460' (Beaver Creek Campground)

Estimated Duration of Hike: The whole length of the trail takes 3 to 4 hours each way.

Sweat Index: no sweat (easy)

Mountain Bike Sweat Index: no sweat

Best Features: fantastic views of the lake and across the lake, great lake access to remote places otherwise accessible only by boat

Availability of Water Along the Trail: There are numerous streams along the way, and there is the lake itself.

Stream Crossings: A combination of wooden bridges and easy rock hops.

Campsites: Beaver Creek is a developed Forest Service fee area campground. There are also semi-primitive campsites at Bottle Bay and Teachers Bay, and other sites occur along the lakeshore.

Alternate Hikes: Three access trails connect the main trail to Road 2512 and allow for shorter hikes. At Beaver Creek this trail ends near where Trail 291 along Upper Priest Lake begins.

Kalispell-Reeder Bay Trail No. 365

Destination: Elkins Lodge at the north end and Kalispell Bay Road at the south end. *Map, page 191.*

Best Suited For: hiking, horseback riding, mountain biking

How Much Use: A Little * **A LITTLE MORE** * A Lot * A Lot More * Excessive

What's it like? From Reeder Bay this trail begins at Elkins Lodge, crosses Reeder Creek by the lakeside picnic area, then ascends easily through the forest above the west side of Priest Lake. The trail crosses two dirt roads on its way to the junction with Trail 269 in a grove of cedar. From Kalispell Bay Road this trail follows a gated road, sometimes rather steeply, for about 1.25 miles, then branches from the road to the right. Look for a small rock cairn and the path easing slightly downhill. The trail undulates through high brush and scattered timber

A bird's-eye view of Priest Lake from the north

for about another 2-plus miles to the signed junction with Trail 269. A good way to enjoy this trail is to have two vehicles available, one at either end of the trail. Mountain bikers might enjoy the challenge of this trail, which at times is a little brushy, though it is never very steep.

USGS Map: Priest Lake SW

Trailhead: From Priest River, Idaho, follow Highway 57 north about 31 miles to Kalispell Bay Road. Turn east and go about 2 miles. The south end of the trail starts out as a gated road just a hundred feet past the Kalispell Day Use Area. As there is hardly any room for parking at the gate, it is best to park at the day use area. The north end can be reached by traveling about 37 miles on Highway 57 to Nordman then taking Reeder Bay Road to Elkins Lodge. There is plenty of parking at the lodge by Trapper Creek Bar. Access the trail by crossing the bridge over Reeder Creek.

Trail Length: 4.5 miles; from Reeder Bay it is about a mile to the junction with Lakeview Mountain Trail No. 269.

Trail Condition: good

Elevation: Trailhead – 2,500' (at the gated road near the Kalispell Day Use Area), High/Low Point – 3,040', End – 2,438' (Reeder Creek at Elkins Lodge)

Estimated Duration of Hike: 2 to 3 hours either way

Sweat Index: break a sweat (moderate)

Mountain Bike Sweat Index: moderate to difficult (This could be a good trail for novice mountain bikers with some skill and experience to try single-track biking.)

Best Features: occasional views of the lake, nice forest trail

Availability of Water Along the Trail: Two small streams may have a trickle of water late in the summer. One is within a couple hundred yards of the junction of Trails 365 and 269.

Stream Crossings: both streams are easily crossed.

Campsites: Four Forest Service campgrounds are in the vicinity.

Alternate Hikes: Lakeview Mountain Trail No. 269 branches from this trail about a mile from Reeder Bay.

Trails: Lakeview Mountain No. 269, Beach No. 48, Kalispell Island No. 49, Woodrat No. 235, Bulldog Point No. 274, Chipmunk Rapids No. 192

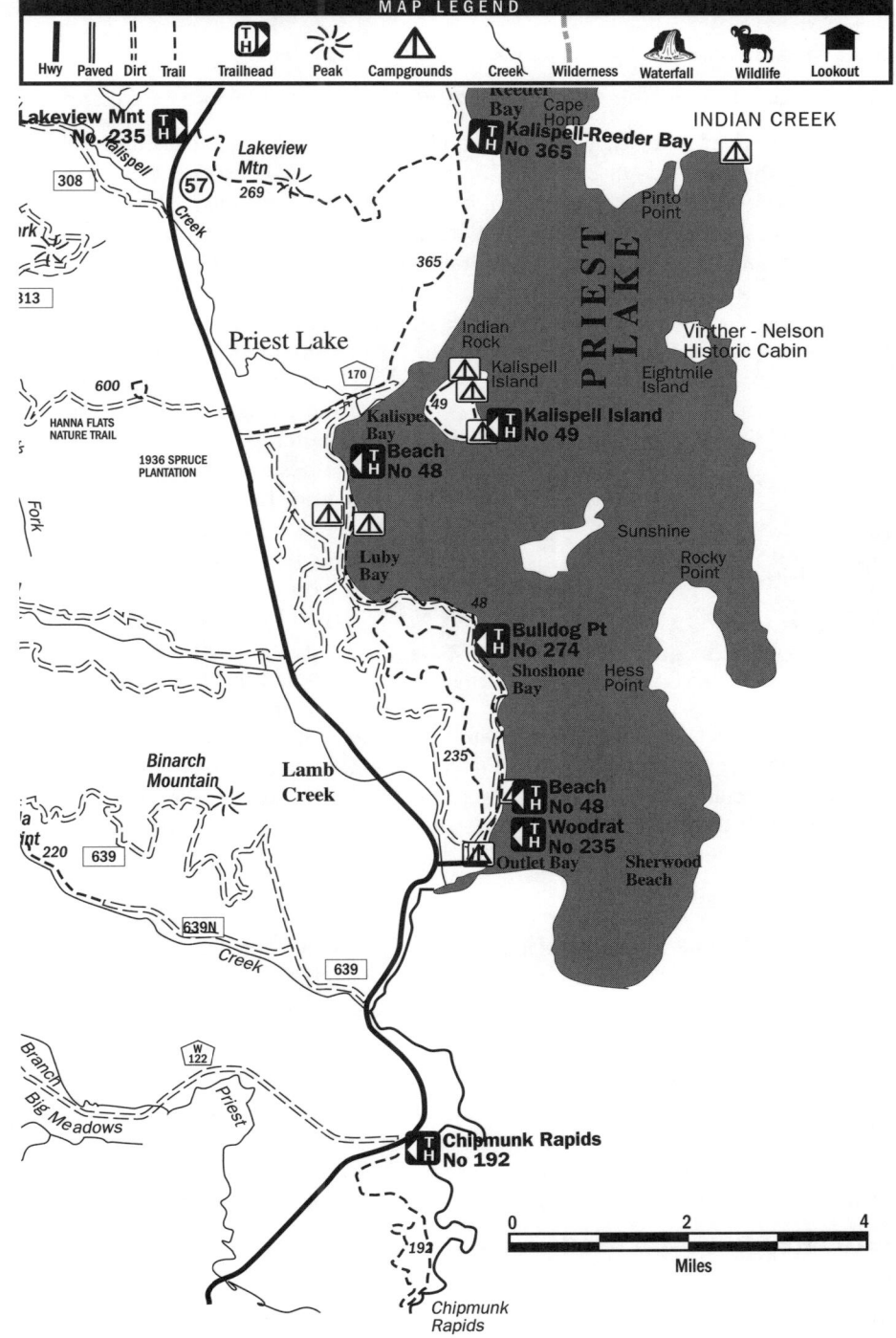

Lakeview Mountain Trail No. 269

Destination: Lakeview Mountain, 4,074 feet. *Map, page 195.*

Best Suited For: hiking, horseback riding, mountain biking

How Much Use: A Little * **A LITTLE MORE** * A Lot * A Lot More * Excessive

What's it like? A steady climb through heavy timber characterizes this trail ascending the west side of Lakeview Mountain. On the way up notice the creeping wintergreen (*Gaultheria ovatifolia*). It is not exactly a rare plant, but it seldom seems to be so abundant as what I noticed along this trail. Look along the uphill side of the trail. About 2 miles up, the trail comes to a saddle and forks. To the right a short spur trail goes to a rocky outcrop and a nice view of Priest Lake. The summit of Lakeview Mountain is a short way through heavy blowdown and brush just above this outcrop. There are open hillsides and brushfields too, and they might have feeding wildlife in early morning or late evening hours. But if you continue to follow the trail for another mile or so, you will see that it skirts some private property that has been partially logged over, and it carries on along a ridge with several small knobs to go over. The extra distance is well worth the effort once you reach another rock outcrop that affords spectacular views of the lake and the Selkirk Crest to the east. The trail then descends through a nice open forest of larch, Douglas fir and birch to its junction in the cedars with Trail 365.

Views of Priest Lake from Lakeview Mountain are terrific

USGS Map: Priest Lake SW

Trailhead: From Priest River, Idaho, follow Highway 57 north 35.7 miles to the trailhead on the east side of the highway across from Bismark Meadows. Look for the sign. The small parking area will accommodate two to four vehicles.

Trail Length: 5.3 miles to the junction with Trail 365; 2 miles to the summit of Lakeview Mountain from Highway 57

Trail Condition: good

Elevation: Trailhead – 2,613' (on Highway 57 at Bismark Meadows), High/Low Point – 4,050' (Lakeview Mountain), End – 2,600' (junction with Trail 365)

Estimated Duration of Hike: 1 to 2 hours to the summit of Lakeview Mountain

Sweat Index: buckets of sweat (difficult)

Mountain Bike Sweat Index: bathed in sweat (strenuous)

Best Features: views of Priest Lake

Availability of Water Along the Trail: About a mile from the trailhead on the highway there is a small spring that should have a strong enough flow for filling a water bottle; there are also several brooks that are likely dry late in the summer but might have a trickle earlier in the hiking season.

Stream Crossings: nothing significant

Campsites: none

Alternate Hikes: This trail connects to Kalispell-Reeder Bay Trail No. 365 on the east side of Lakeview Mountain. An open loop is possible with two vehicles by hiking over the mountain and out to either Elkins Lodge on the north end of trail 365 or to Kalispell Bay Road on the south end.

Wild Notes: When I hiked this trail from the east side, beginning on Trail 365 to its junction with Trail 269, it was late in the day. The forest was perfectly quiet as I followed the path up the slope. About halfway up the mountain, a faint noise to my right made me stop and peer into the thick woods and brush, and there, to my surprise, was a young black bear rambling away from me. The cub looked to be a 2-year old, perhaps, and maybe it had just been driven from its mother this summer as she prepares to give birth to another litter of cubs this winter. Bear cubs will typically spend a couple years by their mother's side before they are driven away to establish their home range and begin life on their own.

Beach Trail No. 48

ACCESSIBLE: Different parts of this trail, particularly close to campgrounds, may be accessible to wheelchairs, at least out to the lake's edge, but the surface is generally pretty rough.

This is a Family Fun Hike

Destination: Outlet Campground at the south end and Kalispell Bay at the north end. *Map, page 195.*

Best Suited For: hiking

How Much Use: A Little * A Little More * A Lot * **A LOT MORE** * Excessive

What's it like? For a close up and personal look at Priest Lake's southwest shoreline, this trail is it. For 9 miles it is seldom more than

On a sunny summer day, the cool waters of Priest Lake always offer a refreshing swim

50 feet from the water's edge, though twice it joins the road for a short way. This part of the lake's shoreline is lined with numerous summer homes, and near Luby Bay you can walk to the Priest Lake Museum from the trail. If you walk along the entire length of this route you pass between more than 100 summer homes and their docks, so for quietude summer might not be the best time to hike this trail (except those portions of it close to the public campgrounds). After Labor Day, when most folks are gone, and especially during the week, this trail is quiet and you might well have it all to yourself, as I did one day in mid-September. But remember to respect private property and stay on the trail. The views across the lake are gorgeous.

USGS Map: Priest Lake SW

Trailhead: To get to the south end take Highway 57 north from Priest River, Idaho, about 26 miles and turn on to Outlet Bay Road. Go one-quarter mile to West Lakeshore Road and turn north. Go three-quarters mile to Outlet Campground where the trail is accessed. The north end is reached via Kalispell Bay Road that branches from Highway 57 near milepost 31. Go about a mile, then turn south on West Lakeshore Road. Just past the Priest Lake Marina is the Kalispell Bay Boat Launch, a Forest Service facility that requires a fee for parking. The trail takes off from the south end of the parking lot.

Trail Length: 9 miles one-way, but short sections of this trail can be enjoyed from Outlet Campground, Osprey Campground, Luby Bay Campground and Kalispell Bay Boat Launch.

Trail Condition: fair

Elevation: 2,450 feet

Estimated Duration of Hike: from a few minutes to a full day

Sweat Index: no sweat (easy)

Mountain Bike Sweat Index: not allowed

Best Features: lakeshore hiking

Availability of Water Along the Trail: from the lake or from spigots at the campgrounds

Stream Crossings: none

Campsites: Three Forest Service campgrounds are along this trail.

Alternate Hikes: Woodrat Trail No. 235 and Bulldog Point Trail No. 274 can make for some nice loop hikes with this trail.

Kalispell Island Trail No. 49

This is a Family Fun Hike

Destination: Kalispell Island. Map, page 195.

Best Suited For: hiking

How Much Use: A Little * A Little More * A Lot * **A LOT MORE** * Excessive

Kalispell Island looks like a part of the mainland from this vantage point. Bartoo Island and tiny Papoose Island can be seen in the lake

What's it like? This is the largest island in Priest Lake, probably just barely eclipsing Bartoo Island in total area. It is a unique experience to boat or canoe to one of the many campsites and spend a night beneath the expansive starry sky stretched over the lake, and nothing compares to watching the moon rise above the Selkirk Crest to the east. The trail is an easy stroll through heavy timber, but views are good. It skirts all of the campsites, so if others are around it is important to respect their privacy so everyone enjoys their stay on Kalispell Island.

USGS Map: Priest Lake SW

Trailhead: You will need a boat to get to this trail that encircles Kalispell Island in Priest Lake. Take Highway 57 north from Priest River, Idaho, to Kalispell Bay Road that branches from Highway 57 near milepost 31. Go about a mile, then turn south on West Lakeshore Road. Just past the Priest Lake Marina is the Kalispell Bay Boat Launch, a Forest Service facility that requires a fee for parking. Boaters should land on the island at Sandy Point or Kalispell Vista Day Use Areas to access the trail.

Trail Length: 2.5-mile loop

Trail Condition: good

Elevation: Trailhead – 2,440', High/Low Point – 2,698' (top of the island), End – 2,440'

Estimated Duration of Hike: 1 to 2 hours

Sweat Index: no sweat (easy)

Mountain Bike Sweat Index: not allowed

Best Features: magnificent views of the countryside surrounding the lake

Availability of Water Along the Trail: none except for what comes from the lake itself

Stream Crossings: none

Campsites: Numerous campsites and toilet facilities are located on the island.

Woodrat Trail No. 235 and Bulldog Point Trail No. 274

Destination: Outlet Campground and Hills Resort. *Map, page 195.*

Best Suited For: hiking, horseback riding, mountain biking

How Much Use: A Little * **A LITTLE MORE** * A Lot * A Lot More * Excessive

What's it like? From Hills Resort's tennis courts, the trail slices through a dark cedar/hemlock forest, crosses Road 1048 after less than half a mile, then reenters that dark forest and climbs gently to a knoll. The thick timber inhibits any views, but maybe a mile along the trail there is a sign for the Lakeview Deck and Fire pit. A spur trail takes you to the top of an old, overgrown clear-cut and, sure enough, there is a view (though not a great one) to the northeast and a nice fire pit with lots of wood. This spur trail is part of a wintertime snowshoe route. Back on the main trail, a couple hundred yards farther on, Bulldog Point Trail No. 274 forks to the left. It goes 2 miles back to West Lakeshore Road, climbing a forested ridge to a couple of nice rock outcrops that offer tremendous views of the south end of Priest Lake. The descent from these viewpoints to the road is fairly steep. From that fork, Trail 235 continues another 3.5 miles or more through heavy timber to the road by Outlet Campground.

USGS Map: Priest Lake SW

Trailhead: From Priest River, Idaho, take Highway 57 north approximately 29 miles then turn onto Luby Bay Road. Go about 1.5 miles and turn south on West Lakeshore Road toward Hills Resort. A parking area for the resort's tennis courts also serves the trailhead for Trail 235. A fee is required to park here. This accesses the north end of the trail. The south end joins West Lakeshore Road across from the entrance to Outlet Campground, a Forest Service fee area.

Trail Length: Trail 235 is 5 miles one-way; Trail 274 is 2 miles one-way.

Trail Condition: good

Elevation: Trailhead – 2,520' (at Outlet Campground entrance), High/Low Point – 3,160', End – 2,470' (at Hills Resort tennis courts)

Elevation: Trail 274 Trail 235 Trailhead – 2,560' (on Road 35), High/Low Point – 3,030', End – 2,490' (junction with Trail 235)

Estimated Duration of Hike: 2 to 5 hours depending on the loop

Sweat Index: break a sweat (moderate)

Mountain Bike Sweat Index: buckets of sweat (difficult)

Best Features: pleasant forest trails with some views of the south end of Priest Lake (especially from Trail 274)

Availability of Water Along the Trail: Two small streams along Trail 235 may have a trickle late in the season.

Stream Crossings: one with a footbridge

Campsites: Outlet Campground and Osprey Campground are Forest Service fee areas nearby.

Alternate Hikes: Trail 274 branches from Trail 235 and connects to West Lakeshore Road about 2.5 miles east of Hills Resort. A good loop of nearly 12 miles could be hiked by utilizing Beach Trail No. 48 with Trail 235, or hike half that distance by starting off on 235 then taking Trail 274 to the road and cutting through the trees to Trail 48 and following it back to the parking area at the tennis courts.

Chipmunk Rapids National Recreation Trail No. 192

Destination: Kaniksu Marsh Research Natural Area, Priest River. *Map, page 195.*

Best Suited For: hiking, horseback riding, mountain biking

How Much Use: A Little * A Little More * **A LOT** * A Lot More * Excessive

What's it like? Several old logging roads wind through the woods between Highway 57 and Priest River just a short way south of the outlet of Priest Lake. From the information center, the trail follows one of these roadbeds slanting downhill through a gorgeous stand of ponderosa pines. On the flats the variety of trees includes lodgepole pine, larch, grand fir, Douglas fir and hemlock. The trail wanders along an elevated bench above Kaniksu Marsh maybe a couple of miles from the trailhead. It is a beautiful area full of waterfowl in the spring and early summer, and you might see a moose. The south loop bends close to the river at Chipmunk Rapids. This is a popular trail in winter for cross-country skiing.

USGS Map: Outlet Bay, Coolin

Trailhead: From Priest River, Idaho, follow Highway 57 north 22.3 miles to the Priest Lake Information Center. The trailhead is on the northeast side of a huge paved parking area.

Trail Length: 10.4 miles in a couple of connected loops

Trail Condition: excellent

Elevation: Trailhead – 2,500', High/Low Point – 2,500'-2,360', End – 2,360'

Estimated Duration of Hike: from 1 to 5 hours depending on how far along the loops you go

Sweat Index: no sweat (easy)

Mountain Bike Sweat Index: no sweat (easy)

Best Features: wildlife, natural marsh and wetland, views of Priest River

Availability of Water Along the Trail: none

Stream Crossings: none

Campsites: None, but a developed campground is only a few miles away at

Outlet Bay.

Alternate Hikes: none

Wild Notes: Created in 1981, Kaniksu Marsh Research Natural Area consists of an undisturbed, 90-acre, crescent-shaped marsh and wet meadow, and adjacent forested slopes totaling 195 acres altogether. Elevations in the RNA range from 2,420 feet to 2,525 feet. Open water, less than 6 feet deep, with submergent aquatic plants surrounds an island of emergent vegetation at the lower end of the marsh. The central portion of the marsh ranges from shallow water to saturated soil with sedges and rushes interspersed with beaver ponds. The habitat here partially consists of a spruce-hemlock bog and Sphagnum peat bog with margins supporting bog birch (*Betula glandulosa*). A number of rare plants are associated with the wetlands in the RNA, including *Eriophorum viridicarinatum, Gaultheria hispidula, Lycopodium inundatum, Trientalis arctica* and *Vaccinium oxycoccus*, for all you native plant lovers out there.

Swimming is one of the best ways to enjoy Priest Lake, but be on the lookout for those who skinny dip, or, as this small wood carving declares, for those who "chunky dunk"

Trails: Peewee-Steep Creek Nos. 175, 176, 177, 178, 179

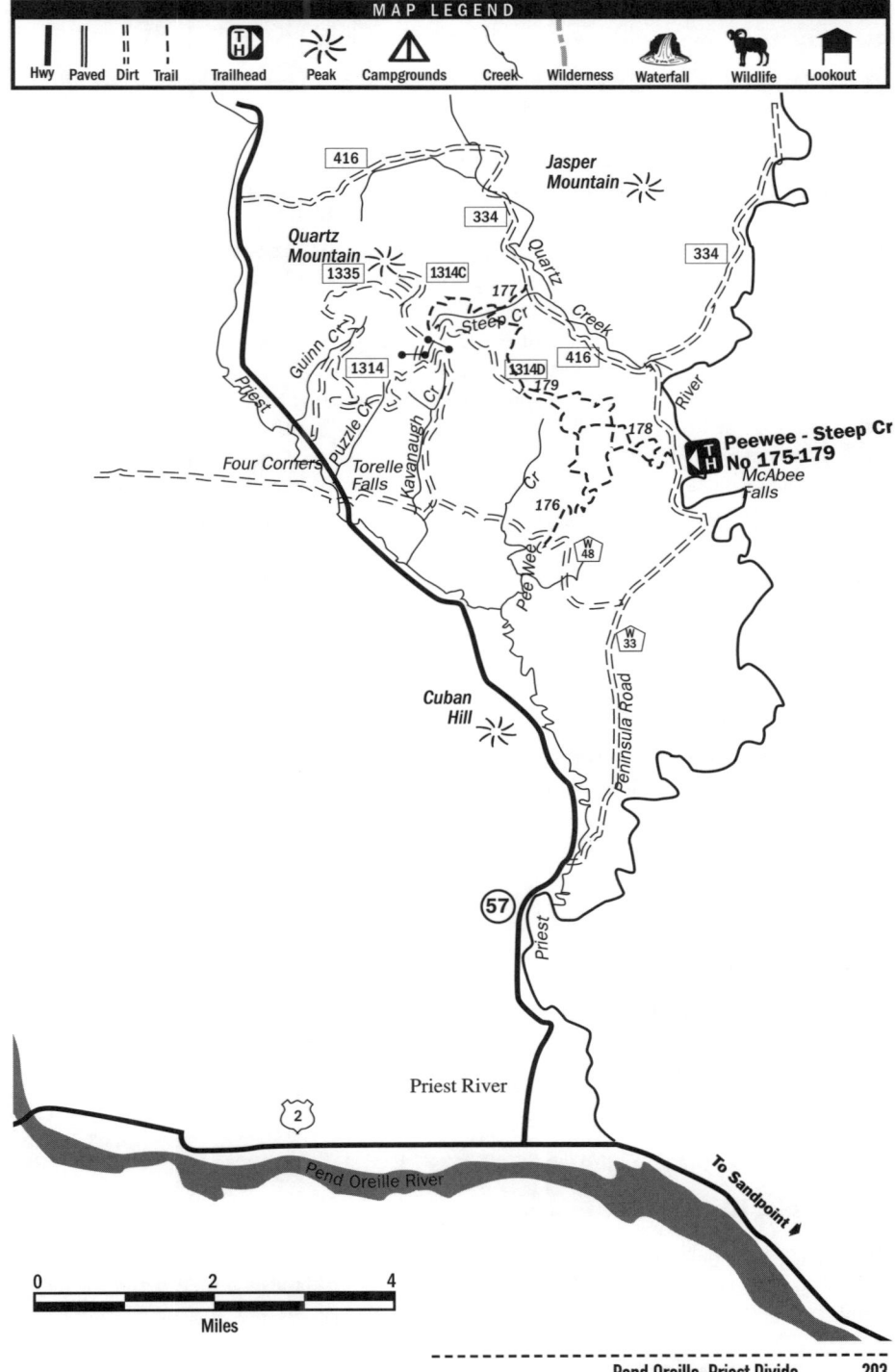

Pend Oreille-Priest Divide

Peewee-Steep Creek Trail Nos. 175, 176, 177, 178 and 179

Destination: ridges and hills southeast of Quartz Mountain. *Map, page 203.*

Best Suited For: hiking, horseback riding, mountain biking

How Much Use: A Little * A Little More * A Lot * **A LOT MORE** * Excessive

What's it like? The Priest River Valley Backcountry Horsemen, in association with the Forest Service, developed this wonderful system of trails primarily for the purpose of horseback riding. But other users are allowed, including motorized use by ATVs and dirt bikes. These trails also make for some fine hiking and some challenging mountain biking opportunities. The Peewee-Steep Creek trails are dedicated to Darold Ockert, a longtime member of this local backcountry horsemen's group. The two primary trails in this system are Peewee Trail 178 and Quartz View Trail 179, each about 6 miles long. They are connected at the northwest end by the 2.5 miles of Steep Creek Trail 177, which begins on Road 334 and ends on Road 1314. About one-half mile from Road 334 it connects to Trail 179 and at Road 1314 it joins Trail 178. At the southeast end John Wayne Trail 176 makes a nice 1.5-mile loop and has a spur that descends the ridge for a mile to Peterson Road. In the middle a short cutoff trail, No. 175, connects the two longer trails making a shorter loop possible. The ridges accessed by these trails do not exceed 4,000 feet in elevation, but the views are wonderful, especially from John Wayne and Peewee. The pastoral setting of lower Priest River and Blue Lake are visible many times, and from high on the ridges you can even see all the way to Scotchman Peak near Clark Fork, Idaho, to Packsaddle Mountain east of Lake Pend Oreille and even into Montana.

USGS Map: Quartz Mountain

Trailhead: From Priest River, Idaho, turn north onto Highway 57 and go about 3.5 miles to Peninsula Road. Turn east and travel approximately 4.5 miles. Turn west on a narrow gravel road on the south side of Priest River just before reaching the Green Owl Tavern. Go nearly a mile to a large parking and camping area at the trailhead next to a gravel pit.

Trail Length: approximately 18 miles altogether

Trail Condition: good

Elevation: Trailhead – 2,250' (at the gravel pit on Road 334), High/Low Point – 3,600', End – 2,400' (at the Steep Creek trailhead on Road 416)

Estimated Duration of Hike: Depending on the loop and the mode of travel, these trails can take from 2 to 8 hours.

Sweat Index: buckets of sweat (difficult)

Mountain Bike Sweat Index: bathed in sweat (strenuous)

Best Features: There are wonderful views of the lower Priest River valley, Blue Lake and the southern end of the Selkirk Crest. There is also a nice grove of old-growth forest along Steep Creek. Wildlife, including deer, elk and bear, may be seen in the vast brushfields above Peewee Creek.

Availability of Water Along the Trail: The John Wayne loop (Trail 176) has several small brooks that might have a trickle late in the summer. Quartz View Trail 179 crosses a small stream about a mile from its junction with Peewee Trail 178. Steep Creek Trail 177 joins Trail 179 where a footbridge crosses Steep Creek, which flows year-round. Several stock tanks are located along this trail system.

Stream Crossings: they all have footbridges

Campsites: Several primitive campsites are located at the trailhead along with a vault toilet.

Alternate Hikes: A variety of loops ranging from 5 to 15 miles are possible with these five interconnected trails.

Vinther-Nelson Cabin National Historic Site

It was not an easy task getting to Priest Lake at the turn of the 20th Century, but the arduous journey did not keep people from going there. The richness of the lands surrounding Priest Lake drew hearty folks who wanted to homestead, log or mine. By 1900 the Priest River Valley was rapidly being opened up to the outside world, and the pristine country among the most beautiful lakes in the young state of Idaho was being settled. The journey required various modes of travel; first by train, then by horse-drawn buckboard and then by boat.

Even the islands surfacing the crystalline waters of the big lake attracted adventurous settlers. In those early days it was an 8-mile row from Coolin to an island on the east side of the lake. The Crenshaw brothers built a cabin on Eightmile Island in 1897 and sold it a year later to W.J. Anders, who moved his family to the island and tried to farm the harsh ground. He cleared the top of the island and brought in cattle and planted crops, but he was quickly overwhelmed by the task. Two short years later he sold the homestead to cousins Sam Vinther and Nels Nelson. They had their eyes set on making their fortune at mining. Some prospecting had already taken place on the island, but ultimately no minerals of any value were found at the Deer Trail Lode. Nonetheless, they worked it 14 to 16 hours a day while working on what is now known as the Vinther-Nelson Historic Cabin.

Two families lived there for decades, but the land remained under U.S. Forest Service management because the unproductive mine site could never be patented. In 1967 the U.S. Department of Agriculture determined that all cabins on government-owned islands in Priest Lake must be demolished. This initiated a 15-year-long battle by the Vinther and Nelson families to preserve the site. In 1982 an agreement was reached when the homestead was placed on the National Register of Historic Places. The cabin was donated to the U.S. Government by the families who now serve as permanent caretakers and curators of the site.

Today, the island that is home to the Vinther-Nelson Historic Site is a major attraction for visitors to the area. The catch, however, is that the only way to get there is still by boat. The nearest launch facility is two miles to the north at Indian Creek. Visitors can moor to a dock and explore the island, hiking a trail to the clearing at the top and a trail to the old mine shaft, which collapsed long ago. The cabin and many relics have been well preserved in a fascinating display. Most of the items date back to the 1920s and '30s. Other visitors from the past have left their marks, carving their initials into logs and also into the original door to the outhouse. The name of steamboat Captain W.E. Slee can still be seen dated '08.

A trip to Eightmile Island is well worth the effort. The historic site and its short trails are suitable for people of all ages and is a great place for a picnic. On some sunny summer day, what could be better than enjoying a boat ride across Priest Lake and treasuring the history of this beautiful valley?

Section III:

Selkirk Crest

The Lay of the Land

Most people in the Inland Northwest know about the Selkirk Mountains. Many will tell you it is that range of beautiful peaks stretching north from Sandpoint, Idaho, to Bonners Ferry and the Canadian Border. You now know, however, that the Selkirks are much broader than that, extending west to the Columbia River and south to the Spokane River. Nonetheless, the most well-known and most-loved part of the Selkirks is what is called the Selkirk Crest – those beautiful peaks from Sandpoint to Canada.

Bounded by the Kootenai River and the Purcell Trench on the east and Priest River and Priest Lake on the west, the Selkirk Crest includes most of the highest peaks in the American portion of this fabulous mountain range and some of the most spectacular high country to be found anywhere. From the rental lookout on Shorty Peak to the ski resort at Schweitzer Mountain, this eastern edge of the Selkirks is awesomely rugged, breathtakingly beautiful and brimming with recreational opportunities.

The Idaho communities of Bonners Ferry, Naples and Sandpoint provide the primary access and supply points. There are six major routes into these mountains: Smith Creek Road 281, Trout Creek Road 634, Ball Creek Road 432, Myrtle Creek Road 633, Snow Creek Road 402 and Pack River Road 231. There are also ways to get to the crest from the towns of Priest River and Coolin through Priest Lake State Forest, but the roads there are not well signed and the trails are often not maintained at all.

Parker, Fisher and Smith peaks, three of the highest in the range, dominate the north end of the Selkirk Crest. South of them are scattered no less than 16 other peaks over 7,000 feet elevation. Characterizing all this high-mountain terrain are huge expanses of slab rock – exposed granite in the form of spires, domes, cliffs and talus.

The east side of these mountains is drained by more than a dozen streams, most of which flow into the Kootenai River or into Deep Creek, which then flows into the Kootenai River. The Pack River flows southeast into Lake Pend Oreille and itself has almost 20 tributaries upstream of Highway 95; the lower Pack River is then fed by numerous streams flowing out of the Cabinet Mountains. These creeks are often accentuated with sparkling blue lakes in glaciated basins. More than three-dozen lakes dot the high country along the Selkirk Crest.

Despite the rugged nature of this eastern rampart of the Selkirks, man has tamed a lot of this country in the last 125 years. Heavy snow and abundant rain coupled with a relatively long growing season means fast-growing and long-lived trees. The timber industry has taken full advantage of this over the years. Roads slice across virtually every mountainside and into almost every spruce and fir basin. A lot of lumber has been produced from the forests cloaking both sides of the crest.

Mixed ownership has been one cause for the extensive development of the timber resource in the Selkirks. The U.S. Forest Service manages most of the landscape on the east side, but there are about 50 sections of corporate timberlands (nearly 35,000 acres), some scattered sections of state-owned lands and quite a bit of privately held land, especially in the south end of this section of the Selkirks. The west side, between Priest Lake and the crest, lies almost entirely in the Priest Lake State Forest.

Some of the highest and remotest terrain remains in a wilderness condition, and there are two drainages that have escaped the incursion of roads and timber harvest: Long Canyon and Parker Creek. Pierced in its heart by the massif of 7,670-foot Parker Peak, this island of wilderness encompasses more than 30,000 acres of unspoiled lands.

About 30 trails totaling close to 150 miles wend through dark forests, along spiny ridges and among granite boulders on this side of the Selkirks. And literally hundreds of miles of roads provide access to these trails and other areas. Because of the beauty and wild features of these mountains, huge numbers of people are drawn to the Selkirk Crest. The impacts show. It is a wonderful thing that people want to get out and hike and pedal and ride horses and zip along on ATVs and dirt bikes, but it will take the cooperative efforts of everyone to save the Selkirk Crest and the animals that live here, the streams that are born here and forests that grow here.

A cryptic greeting awaits me on Red Top Trail No. 102

Forest Service officials have warned that fees and permits may soon define recreational use of this section of the Selkirks. People are simply loving it too much. We can all help alleviate the impacts by practicing Leave No Trace ethics, packing out everything we pack in and respecting the environment we so much want to enjoy.

The Selkirk Crest is an awesome area to explore. Tread lightly and leave it better than when you found it.

The North End
Shorty Peak to Myrtle Creek

The wildest landscape in the American Selkirks outside the Salmo-Priest Wilderness and the Upper Priest River can be found in the heart of the Selkirk Crest's northern end. Known as Long Canyon, it is the last un-roaded and undeveloped major drainage in the American portion of this range. When coupled with Parker Creek and the headwaters of other adjacent drainages converging on the rugged spine of the Crest, there is something like 110,000 acres of wildlands here. Long Canyon Trail No. 16 is the second longest trail in the Selkirks, and it ties in with others that make for unparalleled hiking adventure. This area is also home to the Kootenai National Wildlife Refuge where countless species of wildlife come for seclusion and food.

The greatest collection of alpine lakes in these mountains dot high-country basins and cirques from Joe Lake to Myrtle Lake on both sides of the Crest. Perhaps the most beautiful of all the lakes in the Selkirks nestles in a granite depression below Long Mountain and is known as Long Mountain Lake. From the lookout on Shorty Peak to the enormous cedars in the West Fork of Smith Creek, from the old cabin on Cutoff Peak to the hooked granitic spire on Harrison Peak, this part of the Selkirks epitomizes its isolated grandeur.

From U.S. Highway 2 from Sandpoint to Bonners Ferry and from State Highway 1 to Porthill on the Canadian border, access is excellent via a system of forest roads that climbs into just about every valley to numerous trailheads. Practically all the trails seen on the forest map in this region are well maintained. The exception to that is the south end of Trail 16 from its junction with Trail 7 to Long Canyon Pass. A wooden sign at that junction indicates the trail to the pass is not maintained. Also, Farnham Peak Trail No. 202 was one I didn't get to explore. It doesn't exactly connect to Fisher Peak Trail No. 27, though on a high switchback an old metal sign indicated Trail 202 was nearby. I couldn't find the tread. I searched for a trail from Two Mouth Lakes going down Two Mouth Creek into the Priest Lake State Forest but I didn't find it. However, Chris Bessler followed a trail up Two Mouth Creek for several miles and got quite high before losing it among the rocks.

Ann Wood and Jan Griffitts at Two Mouth Lakes

Trails: Italian Ridge No. 95, Red Top No. 102, Smith Creek-Red Top Ridge No. 21, West Fork Mountain No. 347, Smith Creek No. 17, Smith Ridge No. 18

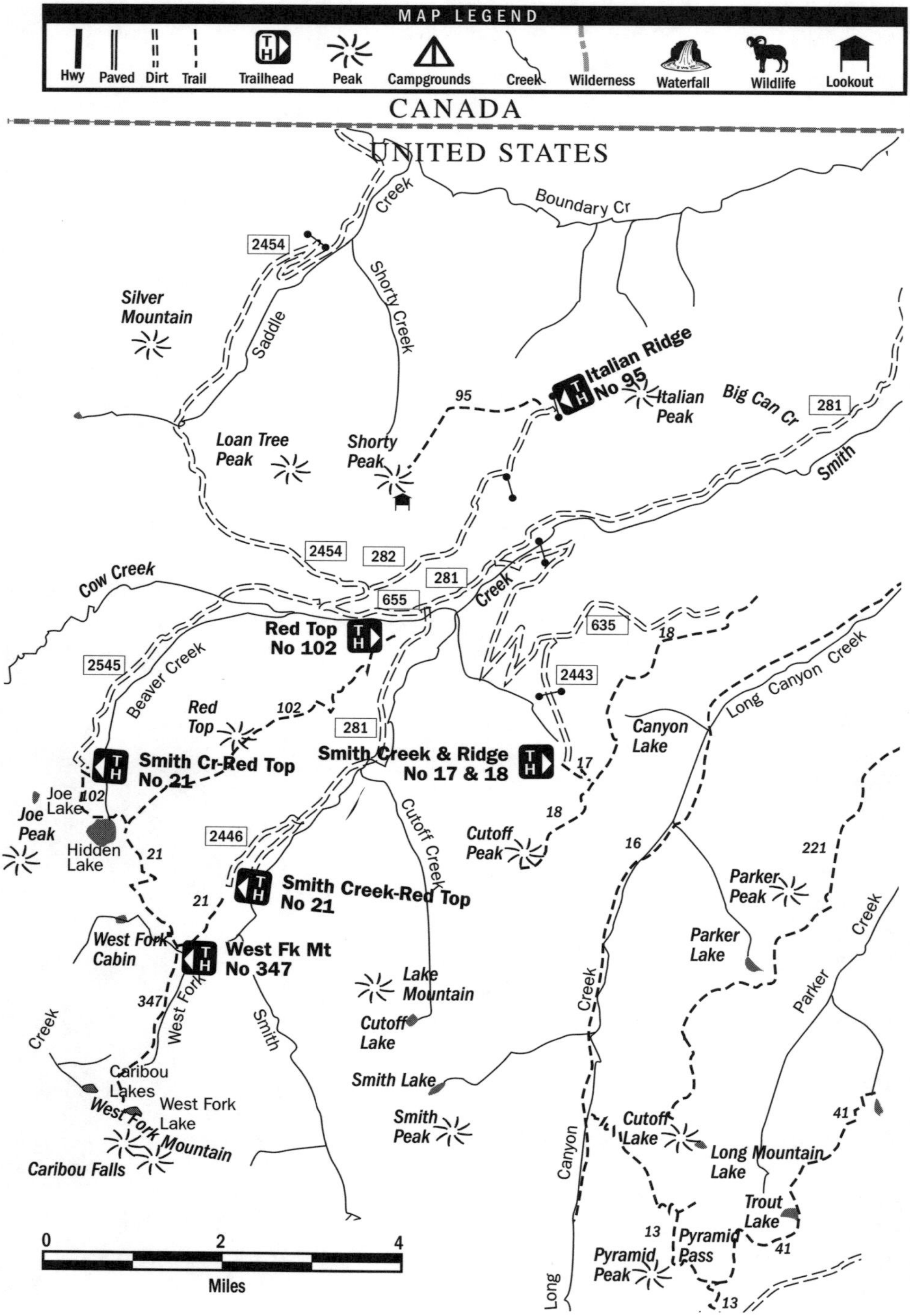

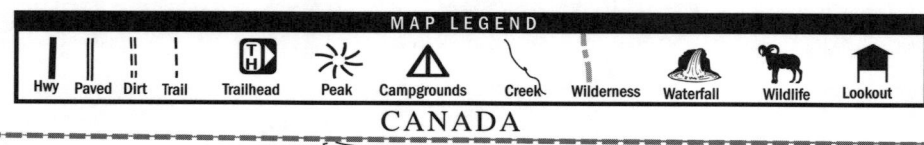

Italian Ridge Trail No. 95

This is a Family Fun Hike

Destination: Shorty Peak, 6,515 feet. *Map, page 210.*

Best Suited For: hiking, horseback riding, mountain biking

How Much Use: A Little * A Little More * A Lot * **A LOT MORE** * Excessive

What's it like? For about one-quarter mile the trail follows the edge of an old clear-cut, then enters the timber in a forest primarily of lodgepole pine and subalpine fir. It climbs gently through these trees until it gains a flat ridge, which the trail follows for at least a half mile. This pleasant stroll through shady woods is a joy on a hot, sunny day. Once the trail begins to climb again, a few whitebark pine

Dennis and his brother Archie at Shorty Peak Lookout

can be seen in the thinning forest. Higher on the slope the views begin to open up of the surrounding terrain, but the best views are right at the top of the mountain, after completing a rather steep, though brief, climb to the summit. There you will find a well-kept facility that was once used as a lookout for forest fires. The cabin is now rented to anyone interested in a night on the summit on a first-come, first-served basis. The view north into Canada is especially intriguing, and the city of Creston, British Columbia is easily visible to the northeast.

USGS Map: Shorty Peak

Trailhead: From Bonners Ferry, Idaho, travel 15 miles north on Highway 95 to the junction with State Highway 1. There was a major construction project going on at the old junction in 2003 that is likely continuing in 2004. Go 1 mile north on Highway 1 and turn west on Copeland Road (County Road No. 45). After 3 miles it crosses the Kootenai River on Copeland Bridge and 2 miles farther on it connects to West Side Road (still identified as County Road 45 on the 2003 Kaniksu Forest map, but it may be labeled as West Side Road No. 417 on signs). Travel northwest 9 or 10 miles to Smith Creek Road No. 281. This road is paved for the first 6 miles. Between mileposts 7 and 8 bear right on Road 655 for 1.5 miles then turn sharply right onto road 282. Follow it 2.8 miles to a saddle on the ridgetop. The trailhead is a short dirt road on the left. A tight turnaround area will accommodate three to five vehicles.

Trail Length: 2.6 miles one-way according to the Forest Service handout for this trail (3 miles according to the sign at the trailhead)

Trail Condition: good

Elevation: Trailhead – 5,250', High/Low Point – 5,250'-6,515', End – 6,515'

Estimated Duration of Hike: 1.5 to 2.5 hours up, 1 to 2 hours down

Sweat Index: break a sweat (moderate)

Mountain Bike Sweat Index: buckets of sweat (difficult) for about 2 miles, then not suitable

Best Features: Forest Service rental lookout, magnificent views

Availability of Water Along the Trail: There is a spur Trail No. 99 about one-half mile from the peak to a small stream emanating from beneath a slope of talus rock. Trail 99 is about one-half mile long. The stream may be all but dry in late summer.

Stream Crossings: none

Campsites: There is a primitive campsite at the trailhead. The lookout is available for overnight rental for a fee. Call the Bonners Ferry Ranger Station for details.

Alternate Hikes: It is possible to follow the ridge westward from Shorty Peak to Lone Tree Peak, 6,732 feet, and at one time the trail went in an easterly direction to Italian Peak, 6,083 feet.

Wild Notes: While hiking this trail in September 2003, my brother Archie and I ran into a Forest Service crew collecting pine cones – whitebark pine cones. Whitebark pine is a high-elevation tree that seldom grows under 6,000 feet. Up that high you'd hardly think it could be of much value, but the seeds, or nuts, produced by this species are among the largest of any conifer in North America. Because of that, and the excellent nutritional value of these nuts, they are a favorite of many birds, small mammals and rodents, and even bears, particularly grizzlies. The problem is that whitebark pine, like its close cousin the Western whitepine, is highly susceptible to a fungus called whitepine blister rust and to bark beetles. These two pathogens have nearly wiped out this species of tree over the past 50 years. The Forest Service has an ongoing program of collecting and propagating seeds from this species in an effort to replant it and keep it a part of the high country of the Selkirks and elsewhere.

Red Top Trail No. 102

This is a Family Fun Hike to Hidden Lake

Destination: Hidden Lake and Red Top, 6,265 feet. *Map, page 210.*

Best Suited For: hiking, horseback riding

How Much Use: A Little * A Little More * A Lot * A Lot More * **EXCESSIVE**

What's it like? In an old, overgrown clear-cut in Beaver Creek this trail climbs steadily but easily for nearly a mile into a cirque holding one of the larger high-mountain lakes in the Selkirks. The short duration of this hike and the beauty of the area lure lots of people to this destination. The lake has fish, is great for swimming and is in a magnificent setting at the base of Joe Peak, 6,748 feet. Fewer people continue up the steep slope east of the lake on the way to Red Top, but it really is a worthy destination itself. The rocky pinnacle has the remains of a lookout and the views are stupendous. The ridge to the northeast descends through subalpine fir and spruce, lodgepole pine and larch, then enters a forest of old-growth cedar and hemlock for a short way near the bottom.

Hidden Lake and Joe Peak

USGS Map: Grass Mountain, Shorty Peak

Trailhead: There are two ways to get on trail 102. The most popular starting point is at its west end. From Bonners Ferry, Idaho, travel 15 miles north on Highway 95 to the junction with State Highway 1. There was a major construction project going on at the old junction in 2003 that is likely continuing in 2004. Go 1 mile north on Highway 1 and turn west on Copeland Road (County Road No. 45). After 3 miles it crosses the Kootenai River on Copeland Bridge, and 2 miles farther on it connects to West Side Road (still identified as County Road 45 on the 2003 Kaniksu Forest map, but it may be labeled as West Side Road No. 417 on signs). Travel northwest 9 or 10 miles to Smith Creek Road No. 281. This road is paved for the first 6.5 miles. Between mileposts 7 and 8 bear right onto Road 655 for about 2.5 miles then take Road 2545 to its end, almost 3 miles. The parking area will accommodate four to six vehicles. To get to the east end of the trail stay on Road 281 at its junction with Road 655 and go about three-quarters of a mile to the trail sign. There is only a small wide spot in the road for one or two vehicles, but a parking area for stock vehicles is located a couple hundred yards from the trail.

Trail Length: The entire length is 8.5 miles; from the west end it is 1 mile to Hidden Lake and 3.5 miles to Red Top; from the east end it is 5 miles to Red Top and 7.5 miles to Hidden Lake.

Trail Condition: fair

Elevation: Trailhead – 4,990' (at Road 2545), High/Low Point – 6,265' (Red Top), End – 3,770' (at Road 281)

Estimated Duration of Hike: 30 minutes to the lake from the west end and 2 to 3 hours to Red Top

Sweat Index: no sweat (easy) to the lake; buckets of sweat (difficult) to Red Top

Mountain Bike Sweat Index: not suitable

Best Features: beautiful, large mountain lake and spectacular views from the mountaintop

Availability of Water Along the Trail: the outlet at Hidden Lake is the only water source along this trail.

Stream Crossings: a tricky log and rock hop across Hidden Lake's outlet

Campsites: There are numerous well-used campsites at the lake. It seems like some people don't like to haul their garbage out, which only makes it less enjoyable for others. Please inspect and clean up after yourselves. If you can pack in full cans and containers, surely you can pack them out empty.

Alternate Hikes: This trail connects with Trail 21 to West Fork Cabin about one-half mile beyond the lake on a ridge top. From Hidden Lake it is 2.5 miles to the cabin. Joe Peak can also be reached by taking the ridgeline from near the junction of these trails around the headwall of the Hidden Lake basin.

Smith Creek-Red Top Ridge Trail No. 21

This is a Family Fun Hike

Destination: West Fork Cabin. *Map, page 210.*

Best Suited For: hiking, horseback riding

How Much Use: A Little * A Little More * A Lot * **A LOT MORE** * Excessive

What's it like? West Fork Cabin is one of the finest destinations in the Selkirks. Nestled on the edge of a meadow looking out across a tributary valley to the West Fork of Smith Creek with Joe Peak and Bugle Ridge in the background, this setting is the perfect picture of serenity. The trail begins along an old logging road, then climbs easily through heavy timber, skirts the edge of another overgrown clear-cut with dramatic vistas of Smith Creek and the imposing presence of Smith Peak, second highest named peak in the American portion of the range, then connects to Trail 347 next to a beautiful stream. It is only one-quarter mile to the cabin from this trail junction and just walking up onto the backside of this 14-by-16-foot

Archie Nicholls in front of West Fork Cabin

log structure is in itself magical. The original cabin burned to the ground in 1998, but it was rebuilt. Coming round to the front of the cabin, the meadow opens up before you and the mountainous view is breathtaking. An outhouse can be found about 75 yards northeast of the cabin. Trail 21 continues beyond the cabin into a fabulous forest of old-growth Engelmann spruce, switchbacking up the mountainside. The tread is not in as good shape for the next 2 miles, but it remains easy to follow through brush and bracken fern. Note along the way some of the individual spruce up to 5 feet in diameter. On the ridge top the trail joins Trail 102 and it is one-half mile down to Hidden Lake or 2 miles up to Red Top Mountain.

USGS Map: Grass Mountain, Shorty Peak, Caribou Creek

Trailhead: From Bonners Ferry, Idaho, travel 15 miles north on Highway 95 to the junction with State Highway 1. There was a major construction project going on at the old junction in 2003 that is likely continuing in 2004. Go 1 mile north on Highway 1 and turn west on Copeland Road (County Road No. 45). After 3 miles it crosses the Kootenai River on Copeland Bridge, and 2 miles farther on it connects to West Side Road (still identified as County Road 45 on the 2003 Kaniksu Forest map, but it may be labeled as West Side Road No. 417 on signs). Travel northwest 9 or 10 miles to Smith Creek Road No. 281. This road is paved for the first 6.5 miles. Between mileposts 7 and 8 bear left at the junction with Road 655, continuing on Road 281 another 3 miles, then bear right on Road 2446 for 1.2 miles to the trailhead. A narrow turnaround area allows parking for four to six vehicles.

Trail Length: 1 mile to the junction with Trail 347, 1.25 miles to West Fork Cabin, 3.25 miles to the junction with Trail 102

Trail Condition: excellent to the cabin, fair beyond that point

Elevation: Trailhead – 4,100' (at Road 2448), High/Low Point – 4,760' (West Fork Cabin), End – 5,800' (junction with Trail 102)

Estimated Duration of Hike: 30 minutes to the cabin

Sweat Index: no sweat to the cabin (easy), buckets of sweat to Trail 102 and Hidden Lake (difficult)

Mountain Bike Sweat Index: break a sweat (moderate) to the cabin, not suitable after that

Best Features: rustic Forest Service cabin and fine mountain views

Availability of Water Along the Trail: There is a good stream within 100 yards of the cabin.

Stream Crossings: There are several boardwalks and footbridges along the way.

Campsites: West Fork Cabin is a first-come, first-served facility with two bunks. The meadow it is situated by affords good tent camping opportunities. Be courteous to other backcountry users, and always respect private property and gear. And most of all, respect the cabin, made available to the public for free. Don't write or carve on the walls or doors. There is a register in the cabin for recording the names and thoughts of visitors.

Alternate Hikes: This trail connects with Trail 347 that leads to West Fork Lake (about 3 miles from the cabin) and West Fork Mountain (about 4 miles from the cabin), and it continues to a junction with Trail 102 that winds past Hidden Lake and to the summit of Red Top Mountain. From the cabin it is about 2.5 miles to Hidden Lake and about 4 miles to Red Top.

West Fork Mountain Trail No. 347

Destination: West Fork Lake and West Fork Mountain, 6,416 feet. *Map, page 210.*

Best Suited For: hiking, horseback riding

How Much Use: A Little * A Little More * A Lot * **A LOT MORE** * Excessive

What's it like? Follow Trail 21 for a mile to its junction with this trail, which meanders mostly at a gentle grade up the West Fork of Smith Creek. Within the first half mile, Trail 347 passes through a magnificent forest of old-growth cedars, some of which are more than 8 feet in diameter. The trail crosses a corner of private land owned by a timber corporation that logged the property years ago, but some of the big trees were left behind. The trail then climbs steadily toward a granite ridge and switchbacks up the mountainside into the small basin cradling the lake. A spur trail goes left to the lake, while the main trail starts a rather grueling ascent to the peak. West Fork Mountain is actually two summits on a long

West Fork Lake

ridge stretching northwest to southeast. On this stony, barren, windswept rock is a metal lookout tower that must be 40 feet tall. The lower steps have been removed to prevent access to this rickety structure. The views in all directions are stunning.

USGS Map: Grass Mountain, Shorty Peak, Caribou Creek

Trailhead: This trail is reached by following Trail 21 for the first mile. See the directions to that trailhead (page 214).

Trail Length: From the trailhead for Trail 21 it is 1 mile to the junction with Trail 347, then approximately 2.5 miles to West Fork Lake and 3.5 miles to the summit of West Fork Mountain (so approximately 3.5 miles to the lake and 4.5 miles to the mountain from the parking area).

Trail Condition: fair

Elevation: Start – 4,740' (junction with Trail 21), High/Low Point – 5,770' (West Fork Lake), End – 6,416'

Estimated Duration of Hike: 1.5 to 2.5 hours to the lake, 2 to 3 hours to the peak

Sweat Index: buckets of sweat (difficult)

Mountain Bike Sweat Index: not suitable

Best Features: magnificent old-growth forest, a gorgeous high mountain lake, historic lookout, spectacular mountain vistas

Availability of Water Along the Trail: A good stream flows under the trail just 20 or 30 feet from its junction with Trail 21, and there are numerous other small brooks along the way that may have adequate water early in the hiking season.

Stream Crossings: There are boardwalks and footbridges and one easy rock hop.

Campsites: There is at least one well-used primitive site at the lake.

Alternate Hikes: At the beginning of this trail, Trail 21 can be followed another one-quarter mile to West Fork Cabin. There is some good off-trail ridge top hiking from West Fork Mountain that accesses Caribou Lakes to the west and it is possible to head for Abandon Mountain, 7,022 feet, to the southeast.

Wild Notes: It was late September when my brother Archie and I visited West Fork Lake and of all the adventures we were treated to, we most enjoyed spying a cow and calf moose from high on the mountain and then getting a close encounter with a bull moose that had one gigantic trophy antler and one deformed antler. He was most definitely in the rut and feeling just a bit lovesick, no doubt. For more than 10 minutes we watched and listened to this creature as he grunted his way around the lake in search of that cow bedded down in a meadow less than one-quarter mile away. Moose typically enter the rut about the same time as elk in the month of September, but they may carry on with the ritual of finding cows with whom to mate well into October.

Smith Creek Trail No. 17 and Smith Ridge Trail No. 18

Destination: Cutoff Peak, 6,844 feet, and Canyon Lake. *Map, page 210.*

Best Suited For: hiking, horseback riding

How Much Use: A LITTLE * A Little More * A Lot * A Lot More * Excessive

What's it like? These little-used trails offer access to a beautiful and interesting destination, namely Cutoff Peak. Trail 17 follows an old logging road for about one-half mile, then turns steeply uphill through old-growth spruce, subalpine fir, cedar and hemlock until it reaches the ridgeline after about a mile. A short ways over the ridge onto the south side is the obscure junction with Trail 18. To the right the trail descends slightly, then continues more or less side-hill. The northern flank of Cutoff Peak comes into view through the trees, and its rocky buttress looks a bit imposing. But the trail cuts across the slope and switchbacks up the south ridge until it gains the summit without too much trouble. At the top a surprise awaits – an old cabin still standing, though in a dilapidated condition. Plus, there is a magnificent view of Smith Creek from a rocky outcrop just a hundred feet from the cabin. To the south is the glorious wild country of Long Canyon, an area proposed for future wilderness designation and protection. Trail 18 meanders northeasterly along Smith Ridge, and though there is no trail to Canyon Lake, a shallow marshy body of water, it is only a mile or so from the junction with Trail 17 to a point where the ridge drops suddenly down a steep slope. A fine view of the lake is possible here.

USGS Map: Shorty Peak, Smith Peak

Trailhead: From Bonners Ferry, Idaho, travel 15 miles north on Highway 95 to the junction with State Highway 1. There was a major construction project going on at the old junction in 2003 and is likely continuing in 2004. Go 1 mile north on Highway 1 and turn west on Copeland Road (County Road No. 45). After 3 miles it crosses the Kootenai River on Copeland Bridge, and 2 miles farther on it connects to West Side Road (still identified as County Road 45 on the 2003 Kaniksu Forest map, but it may be labeled as West Side Road No. 417 on signs). Travel northwest 9 or 10 miles to Smith Creek Road No. 281. This road is paved for the first 6.5 miles. At about 6.5 miles turn left onto Road 2443 and follow it 6.6 miles to the end of the road and trailhead.

Trail Length: It is approximately 3 miles to Cutoff Peak via Trails 17 and 18, and approximately 2 miles to a point on the ridge above Canyon Lake via Trails 17 and 18 in the opposite direction from the peak. Trail 18 extends about 5 miles from its junction with Trail 17 to Triangulation Smith at the northeast end of Smith Ridge.

Trail Condition: fair

Elevation: Trailhead – 5,400', High/Low Point – 6,050' (junction with Trail 18), End – 6,844' (Cutoff Peak)

Elevation: Start – 6,050' (junction with Trail 17), High/Low Point – 6,360', End – 5,922' (Smith Triangulation)

Estimated Duration of Hike: 1 to 2 hours to the peak each way

Sweat Index: difficult (buckets of sweat)

Mountain Bike Sweat Index: not suitable

Best Features: mountaintop and historic old cabin at the summit of Cutoff Peak, or a nice view of Canyon Lake from the ridge top

Availability of Water Along the Trail: A tiny trickle may be found in a small draw on Trail 17.

Stream Crossings: none

Campsites: none

Alternate Hikes: Smith Ridge Trail No. 18 extends a total of about 7 miles along Smith Ridge. From Cutoff Peak it may be possible to continue on the ridgeline to Smith Peak, 7,653 feet, with some bushwhacking and rock hopping.

Inside West Fork Cabin, a first-come, first-served Forest Service cabin

Trail: Long Canyon Creek No. 16

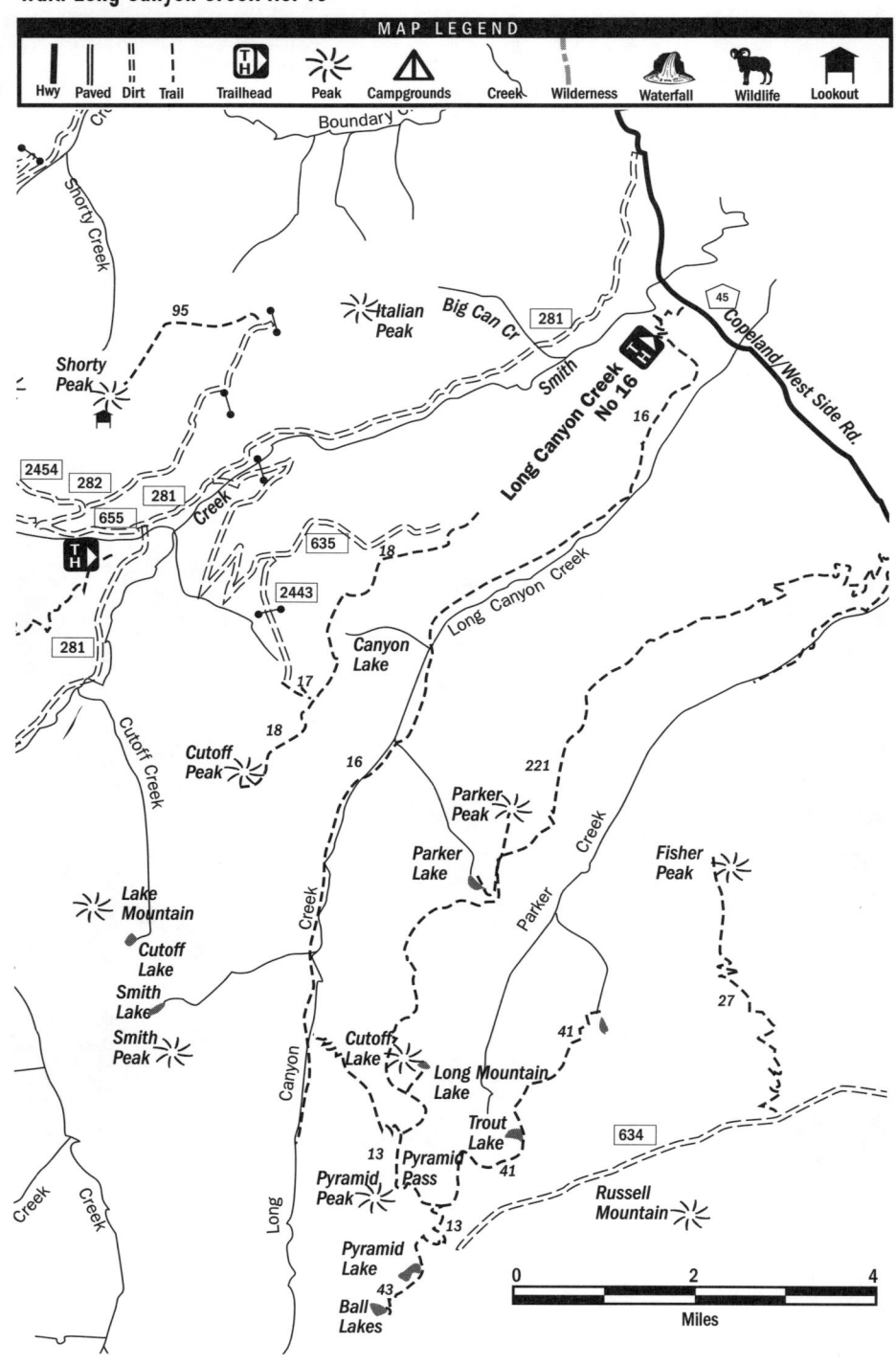

Long Canyon Creek Trail No. 16

Destination: Long Canyon, Pyramid Pass. *Map, page 220.*

Best Suited For: hiking, horseback riding, mountain biking

How Much Use: A Little * A Little More * **A LOT** * A Lot More * Excessive

What's it like? From the parking area next to the road, the trail cuts shortly through an area of weeds and brush and crosses a gated road at a switchback. It then gently climbs through a cedar forest to a narrow ravine that slices through the mountain in a southeasterly direction. The trail enters the Long Canyon valley at the end of this ravine high above the creek

Looking at Smith Peak from Parker Ridge, across Long Canyon

bottom nearly 2 miles from the trailhead. Angling across an open mountainside with scattered timber, the views of the lower canyon are terrific. At about 3 miles or so, the trail drops close to the creek, a campsite and a chance for water, then climbs back up the slope and continues up the drainage. The tree canopy is dense, so views are restricted to the surrounding forest. The first stream crossing is about 6 miles up at a logjam. A long, narrow log affords a way across the briskly flowing creek. It is here, where the creek flowing from Canyon Lake joins Long Canyon Creek, that the trail enters a vast forest of superb old-growth timber. Cedar and hemlock dominate the creek bottom, but there are big, old larch and Douglas fir as well. The real treat is the number of giant Western whitepine found along the trail. Many are dead from blister rust and bark beetles, but others are still alive, and they are often more than 4 feet in diameter and approaching 200 feet in height. Another treat, after the stream that flows from Parker Lake and the second crossing of Long Canyon Creek, is a peaceful grove of giant cedars with a forest floor carpeted with oak fern and devil's club. From there the trail enters a basin of old-growth spruce with a much denser understory of rhododendron and fool's huckleberry. Just after the third crossing of Long Canyon Creek, you may notice the decayed remains of an old cabin, probably utilized by a trapper many years ago. A campsite is nearby and the junction with Trail 7 on the east side of the creek is not far along. Lush vegetation crowds the trail for the last mile or so, but the tread is easy to follow. Trail 16 continues beyond the junction with Trail 7, but a sign lying across the path indicates it is not maintained.

USGS Map: Smith Peak, Shorty Peak, Smith Falls

Trailhead: From Bonners Ferry, Idaho, travel 15 miles north on Highway 95 to the junction with State Highway 1. There was a major construction project going on at the old junction in 2003 that is likely continuing in 2004. Go 1 mile north on Highway 1 and turn west on Copeland Road (County Road No. 45). After 3 miles it crosses the Kootenai River on Copeland Bridge, and 2 miles farther on it connects to West Side Road (still identified as County Road 45 on the 2003 Kaniksu Forest map, but it may be labeled as West Side Road No. 417 on signs). Stay on Road 45 for another 6 miles to the signed trailhead (it is called Canyon Creek Trail No. 16 on the wooden Forest Service sign). There is a large parking and turnaround area just off the main road.

Trail Length: A Forest Service handout for this trail says 21 miles, but from the trailhead to this trail's junction with Pyramid Mountain Trail No. 7 seems more like 12 miles. All the way to Pyramid Pass covers almost 17 miles.

Trail Condition: good (some upper stretches are fair or poor because of brush and obstacles in the trail like roots and holes and washouts)

Elevation: Trailhead – 1,800', High/Low Point – 4,520' (junction with Trail 7), End – 5,750' (Long Canyon Pass)

Estimated Duration of Hike: 8 to 10 hours or more the entire length of the trail

Sweat Index: buckets of sweat (difficult)

Mountain Bike Sweat Index: bathed in sweat (strenuous); I would've said unsuitable, but there was evidence of several hearty mountain bikers having come down this trail not long before I hiked it.

Best Features: old-growth forest, proposed wilderness

Availability of Water Along the Trail: Though much of the time the trail is high on the mountainside above Long Canyon Creek, it crosses the stream three times (about 6, 8 and 11 miles), and there are several small brooks and trickles scattered along the way. The first good water is not until the first major crossing.

Stream Crossings: The three crossings of Long Canyon Creek are tricky and require a balancing act on logs or rock hopping.

Campsites: There are primitive campsites and fire rings at each of the stream crossings.

Alternate Hikes: This trail connects to Pyramid Mountain Trail No. 7, which connects to Pyramid Pass Trail No. 13 and Parker Ridge Trail No. 221. A great loop hike of 50 to 60 miles can be enjoyed in this area.

Trails: Parker Ridge No. 221, Parker Creek No. 14

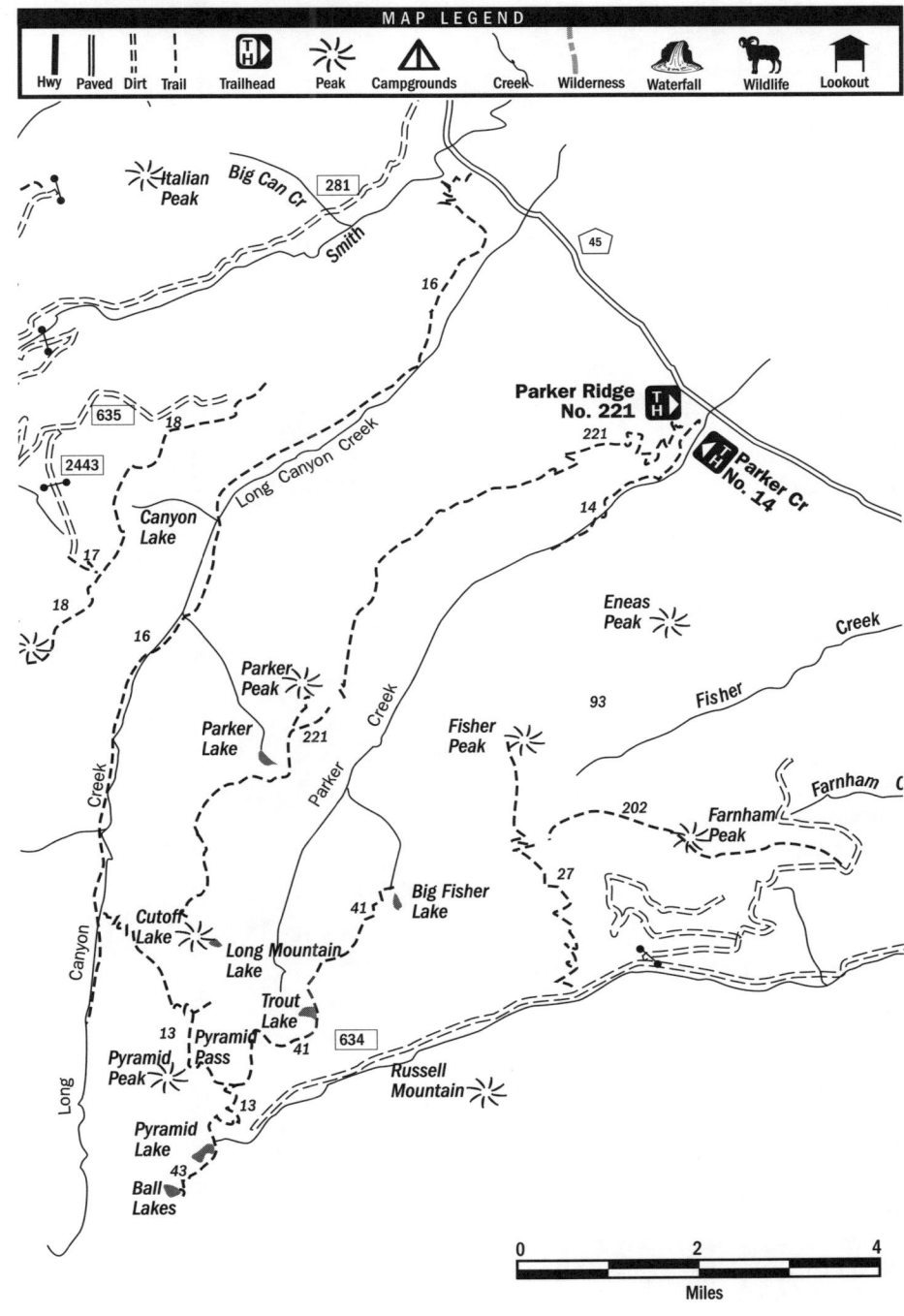

Parker Ridge Trail No. 221

Destination: Parker Peak, 7,670 feet, Long Mountain Lake, Parker Lake. *Map, page 223.*

Best Suited For: hiking, horseback riding

How Much Use: A Little * A Little More * **A LOT** * A Lot More * Excessive

What's it like? You should know right off the bat that one of the greatest things about Trail 221 is that it takes you to the top of the highest named peak in the American Selkirks. Parker Peak, at 7,670 feet, is higher than all others in this range south of the Canadian border; well, it is higher than any other named peak, that is. Two unnamed summits northeast of Big Fisher Lake are higher. A great deal of this trail is over 7,000 feet and so offers some of the most dramatic views of the surrounding countryside from anywhere. The best way to enjoy this trail is to begin at Pyramid Pass Trail No. 13. This trail will take you over Pyramid Pass to the junction with Trail 221 below Long Mountain. From there it is less than a mile to another junction on 221, this with the spur trail to Long Mountain Lake. A one-half mile walk and just a few hundred feet will take you down to this exquisite small lake. A ridge of granite on its east side looks like a landscaped retaining wall and offers some great diving spots into the cold waters. There is good camping available at this lake. Trail 221 continues over what the forest map identifies as Long Mountain (7,265 feet), though

Long Mountain Lake with Parker Peak in the background

just to the south of this are a couple of summits exceeding 7,500 feet connected by a long, high ridge. Another summit surpassing 7,500 feet is situated between Long Mountain and Parker Peak, but it has no name. The trail skirts its top by winding through chaotic granite boulders and out onto a beautiful ridge that bends around the headwall of a tiny, unnamed lake and a large, forested basin below. About 4 miles from the Long Mountain Lake junction is the spur trail to Parker Lake. A pretty lake from up on the ridge, it is less hospitable once down beside it. The lake is surrounded by heavy dark timber and thick brush. It is rather shallow with a silty bottom. There is one small campsite at its side. The junction for the spur trail to the top of Parker Peak is less than a mile away, and in a matter of 30 minutes you can be on top of the world. The remains of an old lookout continue to fall apart and deteriorate in the face of the harsh elements at this elevation. One of the most interesting views from on top is of the town of Creston, British Columbia. Consider that you are over 7,600 feet on Parker Peak and that the trailhead near the mouth of Parker Creek to the northeast is near 1,800 feet and the thought of descending nearly 6,000 feet becomes rather sobering. But it really is a beautiful hike with a fairly gentle grade. In the steep-sided basin below the peak, be sure to look up the rocky cliffs to the top for a view of the wooden remains of the lookout structure standing starkly against an azure summer sky. Even in the timber the hiking is pleasant. The forest of spruce and fir gives way to lodgepole pine, which is characterized by a unique environment of grouse whortleberry and pinegrass, a habitat seldom seen west of the Continental Divide. As the trail drops lower on the slopes of Parker Ridge, the lodgepole is replaced first by Douglas fir and ponderosa pine and open brushy meadows above the valley floor. There are several good rock outcrops on the ridgeline the trail skirts that offer great views of Fisher Peak and Parker Creek. Thank goodness there is one reliable water source along these 9 or so miles of trail at a spring just off a switchback about halfway between the peak and the trail's junction with Parker Creek Trail No. 14. During the descent, especially along the final 2 to 3 miles, the views of the Kootenai River are breathtaking.

USGS Map: Pyramid Peak, Smith Falls

Trailhead: The most popular access to Parker Ridge Trail No. 221 is from Pyramid Pass Trail No. 13. See directions to that trailhead, page 231, or travel about 15 miles north of Bonners Ferry, Idaho, to where Highway 1 forks to the northwest from Highway 95. Go another mile on Highway 1 to Copeland Road (County Road No. 45) and turn west. Follow this road over the Kootenai River and then about 2 miles or so to where it meets Road 18. Stay on Road 45 for another 2.5 miles to the signed trailhead for Parker Creek Trail No. 14. Parker Ridge Trail No. 221 is located about one-half mile up Trail 14. A small parking area is adjacent to a private road across from the trail.

Trail Length: It is 16.5 miles end to end; from the Pyramid Pass Trail No. 13 trailhead it is about 4 miles to Long Mountain Lake, about 7.5 miles to Parker Lake and almost 9 miles to Parker Peak. From the Parker Creek Trail No. 14 trailhead on Road 45 it is about 9 miles to Parker Peak.

Trail Condition: good

Elevation: Start – 2,120' (junction with Trail 14), High/Low Point – 7,670' (Parker Peak), End – 6,440' (junction with Trail 7 and Trail 13)

Estimated Duration of Hike: 2 to 3 hours to Long Mountain Lake, 3 to 4 hours to Parker Lake, 4 to 5 hours to Parker Peak from either direction

Sweat Index: buckets of sweat (difficult) to Long Mountain Lake or Parker Lake, bathed in sweat (strenuous) to Parker Peak

Mountain Bike Sweat Index: not suitable

Best Features: spectacular ridge top hiking, alpine lakes, unmatched mountain views

Availability of Water Along the Trail: The only places for water along Trail 221 is at Long Mountain Lake, Parker Lake and from a nice spring about 5.5 miles up the trail from Road 45 and the trailhead for Parker Creek Trail No. 14. There are several small streams along Trail 13 south of Pyramid Pass.

Stream Crossings: none

Campsites: Long Mountain Lake and Parker Lake each have primitive campsites and there are a couple of fire rings along the ridgetop trail.

Alternate Hikes: Trail 221 is essentially a connecting trail between Pyramid Pass Trail No. 13 and Parker Creek Trail No. 14. At the Trail 13 junction, it also joins Pyramid Mountain Trail No. 7 that connects to Long Canyon Trail No. 16. This means there is a fantastic loop hike of some 50 to 60 miles possible.

Parker Creek Trail No. 14

Destination: Parker Creek. *Map, page 223.*

Best Suited For: hiking, horseback riding

How Much Use: A LITTLE * A Little More * A Lot * A Lot More * Excessive

What's it like? The south-facing hillside on the north side of Parker Creek is steep and brushy, and the trail immediately starts switchbacking up this slope from West Side Road. It climbs high above the creek through a couple of nice draws with birch and cedar, then breaks out into an open meadow where the trail forks. Take a right to go up Parker Ridge and contin-

Sheepherder's cabin on Parker Creek

ue the 5,800-foot climb to Parker Peak, or stay straight to pass through expansive meadows and sparse ponderosa pine and Douglas fir on the way to an old sheepherder's cabin. The trail climbs steadily, switchbacking among several rocky cliffs before dropping back down close to the creek and to what's left of the 10-foot-square structure that once provided shelter for a shepherd. The trail is narrow but pretty easy to follow to this point, but once beyond the cabin its condition becomes poorer. It meanders another 2 miles up Parker Creek, though downfall and brush may cause you to turn back sooner, as it did for me. At one time this trail went all the way to Fisher Peak, but that has long been abandoned, and finding that trail now would be a challenge. The jaunt back down to the trailhead is rewarded with some marvelous views of the Kootenai River Valley.

USGS Map: Farnham Peak, Smith Falls

Trailhead: From Bonners Ferry, Idaho, travel 15 miles north on Highway 95 to the junction with State Highway 1. There was a major construction project going on at the old junction in 2003 that is likely continuing in 2004. Go 1 mile north on Highway 1 and turn west on Copeland Road (County Road No. 45). After 3 miles it crosses the Kootenai River on Copeland Bridge, and 2 miles farther on it connects to West Side Road (still identified as County Road 45 on the 2003 Kaniksu Forest map, but it may be labeled as West Side Road No. 417 on signs). Take it 3.4 miles northwest to the trailhead. The parking area is a small turnout next to a private road that will accommodate two to four vehicles.

Trail Length: 4 miles one-way (about 2 miles to the old sheepherder's cabin)

Trail Condition: fair to the cabin, poor beyond that

Elevation: Trailhead – 1,830', High/Low Point – 3,000' (approximate elevation of sheepherder's cabin), End – 3,800' (trail peters out)

Estimated Duration of Hike: 1 hour to the cabin each way

Sweat Index: break a sweat (moderate) to the cabin

Mountain Bike Sweat Index: not suitable

Best Features: historic old cabin, though now it is dilapidated and falling down

Availability of Water Along the Trail: none

Stream Crossings: none

Campsites: none

Alternate Hikes: Parker Ridge Trail 221 branches from this trail about one-half mile from the trailhead.

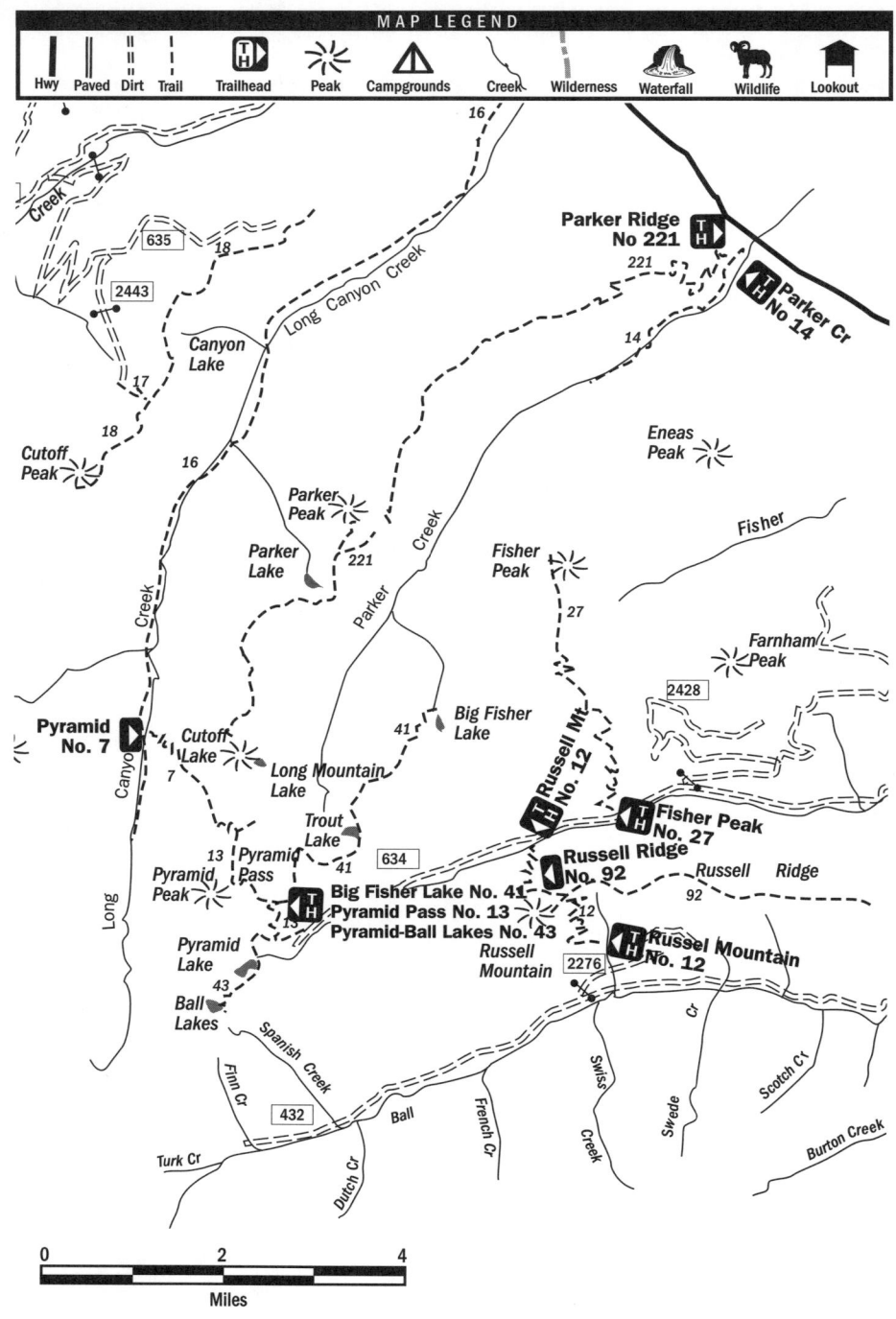

Fisher Peak Trail No. 27

Destination: Fisher Peak, 7,580 feet. *Map, page 228.*

Best Suited For: hiking, horseback riding

How Much Use: A LITTLE * A Little More * A Lot * A Lot More * Excessive

What's it like? This lengthy trail climbs through a variety of forest types, starting in an old clear-cut from perhaps 25 years ago. The young forest that has regenerated is thick and vigorous. The trail shortly enters a mature forest of mixed conifers beginning with cedar and hemlock, then larch and spruce and Douglas fir add to the variety. Some 2 to 3 miles up the trail crosses a closed logging road and enters an area where timber was harvested in the mid-90s. The seedlings growing back are still mostly less than 4 feet tall, so this opening in the forest allows for some good views of Russell Ridge to the

The Kootenai River Valley near Creston, British Columbia as seen from Fisher Peak

south. As you gain in elevation, lodgepole pine becomes more common until at one point the overstory is almost pure lodgepole. The forest here is beautiful and open with mostly beargrass and grouse whortleberry carpeting the forest floor. Then subalpine fir takes over and finally whitebark pine at the highest elevations. From time to time the trail switchbacks close to a ridgeline overlooking Farnham Peak, then it finally gains the top of that ridge and Fisher Peak can be seen maybe a mile off in the distance. The trail cuts across the east side of a mountain, then gains the ridge climbing to the summit. The remains of a lookout are still there, and the views of the Kootenai Valley and Parker Peak are fabulous. Creston, British Columbia can be seen from this mountaintop.

USGS Map: Pyramid Peak, Farnham Peak

Trailhead: In Bonners Ferry, Idaho, turn off Highway 95 next to the Kootenai River Bridge onto Riverside (County Road No. 18) and head for the Kootenai Wildlife Refuge. After about 5.4 miles the road bears right past the wildlife refuge headquarters. Continue about 10 miles to Trout Creek Road No. 634. Turn west and go 5.4 miles to the signed trailhead on the north side of the road. There is no good turnaround here and the only parking is a wide spot in the road good for two or three vehicles. Another 0.9 mile up Road 634, there is a good turnaround for horse trailers at the trailhead for Russell Peak.

Trail Length: 7 miles one-way

Trail Condition: fair

Elevation: Trailhead – 4,410', High/Low Point – 4,410'-7,580', End – 7,580'

Estimated Duration of Hike: 3 to 4 hours up, 2.5 to 3.5 hours down

Sweat Index: bathed in sweat (strenuous)

Mountain Bike Sweat Index: not suitable

Best Features: high mountain top, fantastic views of the Kootenai Valley and other high peaks in the Selkirks and Purcells

Availability of Water Along the Trail: There is a good stream about 1 mile or so up the trail. There is no water after that.

Stream Crossings: one easy rock hop

Campsites: none

Alternate Hikes: Trail 27 once continued over Fisher Peak and down into the Parker Creek drainage, but that section of the trail has been abandoned. The forest map shows Trail 93 out to Eneas Peak descending from Fisher Peak, but I could find no evidence of that trail. And Farnham Ridge Trail No. 202 may have been abandoned as well. An old metal sign about 5 miles up Trail 27 at a switchback has some hand-scrawled writing on it pointing the way to Fisher Creek and Farnham Ridge, but there is no sign of a trail leading off that way. It might be accessible about 3 miles up Road 2426, but that road is gated at its junction with Trout Creek Road 634.

Pyramid Pass Trail No. 13

Destination: Pyramid Pass and trails to Pyramid, Ball, Trout and Big Fisher lakes and to Parker Ridge and Long Canyon. *Map, page 228.*

Best Suited For: hiking, horseback riding (and rugged mountain biking for hearty bikers)

How Much Use: A Little * A Little More * A Lot * A Lot More * **EXCESSIVE**

What's it like? This may well be one of the most heavily used areas in the Selkirks. Trail 13 provides access to several different destinations, the easiest of which to get to are Pyramid and Ball lakes. It begins in an area that was clear-cut years ago, and is now grown back into a stand of young trees, but soon the trail enters a mature forest of spruce and subalpine fir and meanders for one-half mile to the junction with Trail 43.

The author, right, with long-time hiking companion Jack Ferrell, on Pyramid Peak

There you will find a registration box. Be sure to fill out a card, no matter where you are heading in the upper Trout Creek/Long Canyon/Parker Ridge area. Another one-half mile or so farther on is the junction with Trail 41. There is a pretty good water source here where a footbridge spans a small stream. From this point the trail climbs more aggressively for a mile or more to the pass. Many people strike off from here to the summit of Pyramid Peak, 7,355 feet. It is a rugged climb but well worth the effort. The trail continues downhill for close to a mile at its junction with Trails 7 and 221.

USGS Map: Pyramid Peak

Trailhead: In Bonners Ferry, Idaho, turn off Highway 95 next to the Kootenai River Bridge onto Riverside (County Road No. 18) and head for the Kootenai Wildlife Refuge. After about 5.4 miles the road bears right past the wildlife refuge headquarters. Continue about 10 miles to Trout Creek Road No. 634. Turn west and go 9 miles to the trailhead and a parking area with 10 designated parking sites (if the parking lot is full you are asked to return another day or park at least 3 miles away).

Trail Length: 2.9 miles one-way from the trailhead to the junction with Trails 7 and 221).

Trail Condition: good

Elevation: Trailhead – 5,410', High/Low Point – 6,500' (Pyramid Pass), End – 6,440' (junction with Trail 7 and trail 221)

Estimated Duration of Hike: 1 to 1.5 hours to the pass

Sweat Index: break a sweat (moderate)

Mountain Bike Sweat Index: I would think not suitable; however, some hard-core bikers have been known to ride/carry their bikes to the pass, then ride down Long Canyon, a strenuous outing.

Best Features: access to high mountain lakes and spectacular peaks

Availability of Water Along the Trail: Several springs and brooks contain at least a trickle along this trail on the south side of the pass.

Stream Crossings: minor crossings of small streams and wet areas, some with boardwalk and some without

Campsites: This trail connects to other trails in the area that lead to lakes and primitive campsites.

Alternate Hikes: Pyramid Pass Trail No. 13 is the major access point to trails leading to Pyramid Lake and Ball Lakes (Trail 43), Trout Lake and Big Fisher Lake (Trail 41) and to Parker Ridge Trail No. 221 that provides a route to Parker Peak. It also connects to Trail 7, which connects to Long Canyon Trail No. 16.

Pyramid-Ball Lakes Trail No. 43

This is a Family Fun Hike

Destination: Pyramid Lake, Ball Lakes. *Map, page 228.*

Best Suited For: hiking, horseback riding, mountain biking

How Much Use: A Little * A Little More * A Lot * A Lot More * **EXCESSIVE**

What's it like? An easy stroll on a wide path through a beautiful spruce-alpine fir forest leads to Pyramid Lake, an hourglass-shaped body of water tucked up against a stony mountainside on one end with forest and reeds at the other end. Boardwalks in several places help protect marshy and streamside areas along the way. Shallows at the northeast end of the lake extend to a narrow strait between points of rock, but the southwest end is much deeper and reflects the cliffs towering above. Much of the shoreline is brushy, but there are numerous areas of rock at the water's edge. The trail to Ball Lakes forks to the left just before reaching the first campsite at Pyramid and climbs a steep-sided ridge. The views become increasingly dramatic, not only of the lake but of Pyramid Peak as well. At the top of the ridge the trail winds pleasantly through an open forest of alpine trees and brush. Be sure to check for huckleberries all along the way. It forks before the lakes come into view and a wooden sign indicates the direction to the upper and lower lakes. Each lake sits in stunningly beautiful rocky cauldrons. All of these lakes have some small cutthroat trout.

A refreshing drink from Ball Lake

USGS Map: Pyramid Peak

Trailhead: In Bonners Ferry, Idaho, turn off Highway 95 next to the Kootenai River Bridge onto Riverside (County Road No. 18) and head for the Kootenai Wildlife Refuge. After about 5.4 miles the road bears right past the wildlife refuge headquarters. Continue about 10 miles to Trout Creek Road No. 634. Turn west and go 9 miles to the trailhead and a parking area with 10 designated parking sites (if the parking lot is full you are asked to return another day or park at least 3 miles away).

Trail Length: Including a portion of Trail 13, it is about 1.25 miles to Pyramid Lake and 2.5 miles to Ball Lakes.

Trail Condition: good

Elevation: Start – 5,910' (junction with Trail 13), High/Low Point – 6,050' (Pyramid Lake), End – 6,708' (Upper Ball Lake)

Estimated Duration of Hike: 1 hour or less to Pyramid Lake, 1.5 to 2 hours to Ball Lake

Sweat Index: no sweat (easy) to Pyramid Lake, break a sweat (moderate) to Ball Lakes

Mountain Bike Sweat Index: bathed in sweat (strenuous)

Best Features: beautiful alpine lakes

Availability of Water Along the Trail: Several small streams along the way have water.

Stream Crossings: Footbridges and boardwalk cross several small streams and wet areas.

Campsites: All three lakes have several primitive campsites with established fire rings. Please use existing sites, as creating new campsites and fire rings is prohibited in order to minimize impacts to these fragile, high-country lakes.

Precautions: Because of the spectacular beauty and the easy access, this area has been heavily impacted by human use. Be sure to do your best to protect these precious natural resources by packing out everything you pack in and stay on established trails and campsites to reduce compaction of the sensitive soils. If possible, plan your visit during the week when fewer people are likely to be around.

Alternate Hikes: There is good off-trail access to an unnamed peak (some refer to it as Ball Peak) from upper Ball Lake.

Wild Notes: What better way to refresh yourself on a hot summer day than to jump into a high mountain lake? You can bet the water is almost always cold, but that only adds to the invigoration. The day I hiked to Pyramid Lake a family group of nearly a dozen people were enjoying the lake in that way at the point where it narrows and resembles an hourglass. Just remember when at these high lakes to be very careful not to damage these fragile environments. Don't use soap in the lake, don't allow children (or adults for that matter) to pee in the lake, and pick up after yourselves when you are done.

Big Fisher Lake Trail No. 41

Destination: Trout Lake and Big Fisher Lake. *Map, page 228.*

Best Suited For: hiking, horseback riding

How Much Use: A Little * A Little More * A Lot * **A LOT MORE** * Excessive

What's it like? This scenic hike crosses a mountainside with open timber, rock outcrops and meadows affording fabulous views of Trout Creek, surrounding mountains and, higher up, the Kootenai River Valley far below. The junction with Trail 41 is about 1.25 miles from the trailhead on Trout Creek Road No. 634 for Trail 13. At the junction there is a footbridge over a small stream that can provide water. Another small stream is a short distance up Trail 41. As you wander out this trail don't forget to look back over your shoulder from time to time, as the view of Pyramid Peak and other high mountains is fantastic. The approach to Trout

Trout Lake

Lake drops a couple hundred feet down a stony wall to the lake's outlet stream and a short trail to a large boulder rising a dozen feet above the lake's rippled surface. On a sunny day this is a great resting rock and a fine diving platform into the refreshing waters. From here the trail climbs steadily to a saddle, then follows Nosebleed Ridge along a relatively steep climb (there's a story behind that name I will tell you about in Wild Notes). A fine ridge top meadow well above 7,000 feet offers tremendous views way down the valley to the Kootenai River just before gaining the top of a ridge overlooking Big Fisher Lake. A sharp descent exceeding 600 feet takes you to the lake and some beautiful forested campsites. Both lakes have populations of feisty cutthroat trout.

USGS Map: Pyramid Peak

Trailhead: In Bonners Ferry, Idaho, turn off Highway 95 next to the Kootenai River Bridge onto Riverside (County Road No. 18) and head for the Kootenai Wildlife Refuge. After about 5.4 miles the road bears right past the wildlife refuge headquarters. Continue about 10 miles to Trout Creek Road No. 634. Turn west and go 9 miles to the trailhead and a parking area with 10 designated parking sites (if the parking lot is full you are asked to return another day or park at least 3 miles away).

Trail Length: Including a portion of Trail 13, it is 3 miles to Trout Lake and 5.25 miles to Big Fisher Lake.

Trail Condition: good

Elevation: Start – 6,320' (junction with Trail 13), High/Low Point – 6,352' (Trout Lake), 7,390' (between Trout Lake and Big Fisher Lake), End – 6,732' (Big Fisher Lake)

Estimated Duration of Hike: 2.5 to 3.5 hours to Big Fisher Lake, 2 to 3 hours back out

Sweat Index: buckets of sweat (difficult)

Mountain Bike Sweat Index: not suitable

Best Features: beautiful alpine lakes, terrific mountain views

Availability of Water Along the Trail: Several trickles cross the trail out to Trout Lake, but there is none between Trout and Big Fisher lakes.

Stream Crossings: nothing significant (some boardwalk and footbridges in the

first 2 miles)

Campsites: Both lakes have primitive campsites.

Alternate Hikes: Some difficult ridgeline hiking can lead out to Fisher Peak or to the top of unnamed peaks west of Trout Lake.

Wild Notes: Who doesn't enjoy a sunny, warm, dry day in the mountains? We all do. But an unfortunate calamity for some of us is the drying up of nasal passages when the relative humidity drops to as low as 10 percent or 15 percent, as it often does in the summertime here. When hiking with a couple of friends of mine out to Big Fisher Lake, one of them experienced just such an unexpected nosebleed. It came out of nowhere. As far as I know, he didn't have his finger in his nose and he didn't walk into a tree. It just started bleeding, and it would not stop, the poor guy. The other hiker and I finally got concerned that he was actually losing too much blood. We slowed our hiking pace at first, then stopped altogether while he rested with his head tilted back. It was a full hour later before the flow subsided. Weak and actually trembling, he finally got to the lake and we set up camp. We came to call that section of the trail Nosebleed Ridge.

Pyramid Trail No. 7

Destination: Pyramid Pass. *Map, page 228.*

Best Suited For: hiking, horseback riding (mountain bikers use it as a means to access Long Canyon for a long, strenuous ride)

How Much Use: A Little * A Little More * **A LOT** * A Lot More * Excessive

What's it like? From the bottom this trail switchbacks numerous times

A view of the rugged Selkirk Crest from Long Mountain, looking south

through old-growth cedar and hemlock, spruce and subalpine fir and whitepine. It climbs steadily out of the heavier forest to more open lodgepole pine, then into the rocks and scattered trees of the upper slopes. Views of Smith Peak across Long Canyon Creek are impressive. Also higher up, Pyramid Peak comes into view. Parts of this trail have been reconstructed in recent years and have a wide, smooth tread, while other parts are narrow and rutted. Unlike what appears on the forest map, this trail joins Long Canyon Trail No. 16 on the east side of Long Canyon Creek about one-half mile south of a stream crossing and the remains of an old cabin.

USGS Map: Smith Peak, Pyramid Peak

Trailhead: This is a connecting trail between Trails 13, 221 and 16 (Pyramid Pass, Parker Ridge and Long Canyon). See the directions to those trailheads for access.

Trail Length: 4 miles one-way

Trail Condition: good

Elevation: Start – 4,520' (junction with Trail 16), High/Low Point – 4,520'-6,440', End – 6,440' (junction Trail 221 and Trail 13)

Estimated Duration of Hike: 1.5 to 2.5 hours either way

Sweat Index: buckets of sweat (difficult)

Mountain Bike Sweat Index: buckets of sweat (difficult): Ardent bikers seem to access this trail via Pyramid Pass Trail No. 13 for a heck of a ride down Long Canyon.

Best Features: old-growth forest, connects other popular trails

Availability of Water Along the Trail: a small stream flows close to several of the switchbacks on this trail

Stream Crossings: none

Campsites: none

Alternate Hikes: This trail connects Long Canyon and Parker Ridge to Pyramid Pass, making for a wonderful opportunity for a loop hike of 50 to 60 miles.

Russell Mountain Trail No. 12 and Russell Ridge Trail No. 92

Destination: Russell Peak, 6,618 feet. *Map, page 228.*

This is a Family Fun Hike

Best Suited For: hiking, horseback riding

How Much Use: A LITTLE * A Little More * A Lot * A Lot More * Excessive

What's it like? From Trout Creek Road No. 634, an old roadbed now serving as the trail crosses the creek then bears right. The trail forks to the left and enters a magical world of old-growth cedar and hemlock with spruce, larch and Douglas fir. A Forest Service sign indicates it is 2.5 miles to Russell Peak and 2.75 miles to the junction with Trail 92; however, it perhaps means the distance to the Russell Peak spur trail is 2.5 miles, and from there it is another one-half mile to the summit. Beyond that junction it is only a hundred yards downhill to Trail 92, which forks rather obscurely to the east. This fantastic forest of ancient trees continues up the mountainside for quite a ways, punctuated by large boulder fields and steep cliffs in a couple places. The trail gains the ridge top in a shallow notch where the spur trail to the peak is obvious. It climbs rather steadily to the rocky pinnacle upon which rests an old cabin and the remains of what was once a lookout tower. The views are outstanding. From the Ball Creek side, after a mile and a half or more on a logging road, the trail meanders through an area that was harvested maybe 10 years ago. Some of the big old Western larch were left standing, and now a thick stand of young sapling larch is growing nicely. The trail then enters the woods and climbs among old-growth spruce and larch to the ridge. On the higher slopes you might notice the proliferation of dead lodgepole pine and whitebark pine from an outbreak of bark beetles a couple years ago.

The old cabin on Russell Mountain

USGS Map: Pyramid Peak, Farnham Peak

Trailhead: In Bonners Ferry, Idaho, turn off Highway 95 next to the Kootenai River Bridge onto Riverside (County Road No. 18) and head for the Kootenai Wildlife Refuge. After about 5.4 miles the road bears right past the wildlife refuge headquarters. Continue about 10 miles to Trout Creek Road No. 634. Turn west and go 6.3 miles to the unsigned trailhead. It is located at a junction with Road 2424, which has been ripped and revegetated. There is a large parking area and turnaround. This trail can also be accessed from Ball Creek Road No. 432 by way of gated Road 2276.

Trail Length: 3 miles to Russell Peak one-way

Trail Condition: fair

Elevation: Trail 12 Trailhead – 4,634' (at Road 634), High/Low Point – 6,300' (junction with Trail 92), End – 4,700' (junction with gated Road 2276B)

Elevation: Trail 92 Start – 6,300' (junction with Trail 12), High/Low Point – 6,818' (Russell Mountain), End – 6,285' (Russell Ridge)

Estimated Duration of Hike: 1.5 to 2.5 hours up, 1 to 2 hours down

Sweat Index: buckets of sweat (difficult)

Mountain Bike Sweat Index: not suitable

Best Features: old-growth forest, historical old cabin at the summit

Availability of Water Along the Trail: The trail crosses Trout Creek about 50 yards from the parking area; otherwise, there may only be a trickle in a small draw late in the summer farther up the trail.

Stream Crossings: A log spans Trout Creek, or at low water the stream can easily be jumped; the trail crosses a draw several times on the way up, though the draw will be dry by midsummer.

Campsites: There is plenty of room for camping at the trailhead where there is a fire ring.

Alternate Hikes: Trail 12 goes all the way over the ridge between Trout Creek and Ball Creek. From Ball Creek Road No. 432, take gated road 2276 about 1.5 miles to road 2276B, then follow that less than one-quarter mile to the trail, which climbs initially through an area of timber harvest (coming back nicely with a thick stand of larch saplings). The trail then ascends the mountainside for about 1.5 miles to the ridge top. Only 100 yards or so from the spur trail leading west to the summit of Russell Peak, Russell Ridge Trail No. 92 heads out along the ridge to the east for about 4 miles. Along the way there are several rocky points and openings with fine views of the surrounding countryside. The trail peters out after leaving an apparent helispot.

Two Mouth Lake with Harrison Peak in the far background

Trails: Burton Peak No. 9, Snow Creek Falls, Myrtle Falls

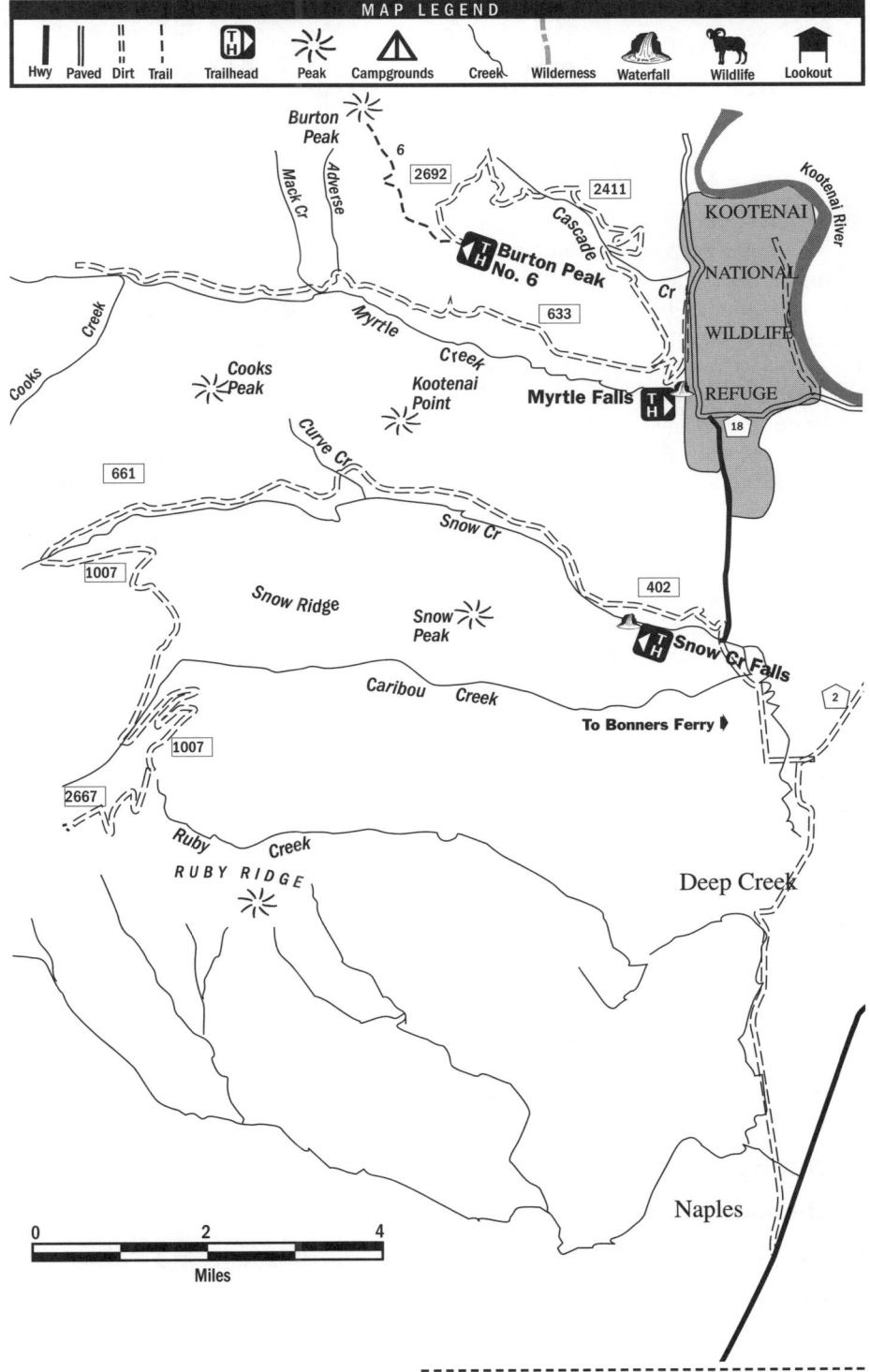

Burton Peak Trail No. 9

This is a Family Fun Hike

Destination: Burton Peak, 6,844 feet. *Map, page 239.*

Best Suited For: hiking, horseback riding

How Much Use: A Little * **A LITTLE MORE** * A Lot * A Lot More * Excessive

What's it like? This pleasant ridge hike begins in heavy timber and climbs gently for a mile and a half. Along the way there are scattered old-growth larch among the younger lodgepole pine and Douglas fir. It gets steeper after a switchback leads the hiker back to the ridge and the start of rocky openings. The views out across Myrtle Creek improve dramatically as the trail climbs through grassy meadows and scattered trees. The final push to the top is a steep grunt, but if you've caught sight of the old lookout cabin from farther down, you'll hardly notice that last effort to the top. The 360-degree view is spectacular and the

Burton Peak, like many mountains in the Selkirks, has an old, deteriorating cabin

dilapidated lookout is as photogenic as any old building. A brief scramble to the next summit just west of Burton Peak only improves the view, and a small lake is visible in the basin below that slightly higher peak.

USGS Map: Farnham, Moravia, Pyramid Peak

Trailhead: In Bonners Ferry, Idaho, turn off Highway 95 next to the Kootenai River Bridge onto Riverside (County Road No. 18) and head for the Kootenai Wildlife Refuge. After about 5.4 miles the road bears right past the wildlife refuge headquarters. Go about 1.3 miles to Myrtle Creek Road No. 633. Turn left and follow it 2 miles to the junction of Road No. 2411 and turn right. Go 6.3 miles to a fork in the road and bear left on Road No. 2692 (2411 is gated at that junction). Follow 2692 for 1.5 miles to the end of the road and the trailhead. A small traffic circle allows for six to eight vehicles and makes for a good turnaround. On the way up you can't help but notice the effects of a wildfire that burned across 4,000 acres in lower Myrtle Creek in the summer of 2003.

Trail Length: 2.6 miles one-way

Trail Condition: good

Elevation: Trailhead – 5,120', High/Low Point – 5,120'-6,844', End – 6,844'

Estimated Duration of Hike: 1 to 2 hours up, 1 to 2 hours down

Sweat Index: break a sweat (moderate)

Mountain Bike Sweat Index: Hearty mountain bikers might be able to make it up the first 1.5 miles or so of this trail, but it might be a difficult ascent by pedaling. However, the ride back down could be sweet.

Best Features: historic lookout, mountaintop, excellent views

Availability of Water Along the Trail: none

Stream Crossings: none

Campsites: none

Precautions: The old lookout is in an advanced state of decay, and extreme caution should be taken if you choose to go inside.

Alternate Hikes: There is opportunity for some nice ridgeline, off-trail hiking along Cascade Ridge.

Snow Creek Falls Trail

This is a Family Fun Hike

Destination: Snow Creek Falls. *Map, page 239.*

Best Suited For: hiking, mountain biking

How Much Use: A Little * A Little More * **A LOT** * A Lot More * Excessive

What's it like? A wide, gentle trail slants downhill into the Snow Creek valley from Road 402. The timber is scattered across the open slope, so views of the valley are quite nice. There are some beautiful ponderosa pines along the trail, but two real dandies are located just below where the trail splits. One fork leads to the lower falls, and the other goes to the upper falls. Along the path to the lower falls is a short spur called Birch Rest, though in fact the trees immediately around the bench situated in this quiet forest are aspens. At the creek there are stairs to an observation platform for the lower falls. At the fork, follow the trail to the right for a meditative stroll through the forest of Quiet Creek. Here there are giant cedars and grand fir. Many have fire scars from a wildfire that burned through this area many years ago. The trail comes out onto the rocks at the upper falls. Notice a cedar lying across the creek, still rooted and growing despite its reclining position. Below that cedar you can step out onto rocks for a look

Lower Snow Creek Falls

down the continuation of the upper falls, but be extremely careful on the wet, slippery granite.

USGS Map: Moravia

Trailhead: About 2 miles south of Bonners Ferry, Idaho, on Highway 95 turn west onto County Road No. 2 and go past Mirror Lake Golf Course. After about 2.5 miles turn west again onto West Side Road and take it about 2 miles to Snow Creek Road No. 402. Travel about a mile or so to the trailhead and a parking area. It is essentially a wide turnout on the side of the road and will accommodate five to seven vehicles.

Trail Length: approximately one-half mile one-way to the lower or upper falls

Trail Condition: excellent

Elevation: Trailhead – 2,440', High/Low Point – 2,300' (upper falls), End – 2,250' (lower falls)

Estimated Duration of Hike: 15 to 30 minutes each way

Sweat Index: easy (no sweat)

Mountain Bike Sweat Index: moderate (break a sweat)

Best Features: beautiful waterfalls and old-growth trees

Availability of Water Along the Trail: plenty of water in Snow Creek

Stream Crossings: There are footbridges and boardwalk for streams and wet areas, but be careful at the creek next to the falls.

Campsites: none

Alternate Hikes: none

Myrtle Falls Trail

ACCESSIBLE: A paved trail accesses the bridge over Myrtle Creek.

This is a Family Fun Hike

Destination: Myrtle Falls. *Map, page 239.*

Best Suited For: hiking

How Much Use: A Little * A Little More * A Lot * **A LOT MORE** * Excessive

What's it like? A visit to the Kootenai Wildlife Refuge headquarters is not complete without seeing Myrtle Falls just across the road. A fine parking area and accessible trail facility has been developed. Unfortunately, the wheelchair-accessible trail does not reach a viewpoint of the falls, but it does go to a sturdy, steel bridge over the creek and makes for a short, pleasant stroll into the forest. The trail continues past the bridge and climbs steeply uphill to a narrow, level point of land thrust high above the creek. The view is right into the gorge from whence pours the water of Myrtle Creek over a nice waterfall. The trail begins on the refuge but crosses private property and private timberlands. Signs alert the visitor to steep drop-offs and that hiking the trail is at your own risk.

USGS Map: Moravia

Trailhead: In Bonners Ferry, Idaho, turn off Highway 95 next to the Kootenai River Bridge onto Riverside (County Road No. 18) and head for the Kootenai Wildlife Refuge. After about 5.5 miles the road bears right and comes to the wildlife refuge headquarters. Across the road from the headquarters is the parking area and trailhead for Myrtle Falls.

Trail Length: 150 yards of paved accessible trail to a bridge over the creek; another couple hundred yards up a steep hillside to a viewpoint

Trail Condition: excellent

Elevation: Trailhead – 1,800' (across from Kootenai National Wildlife Refuge Headquarters), High/Low Point – 1,800'-1,900', End – 1,900'

Myrtle Falls spills through a narrow, deep gorge

Estimated Duration of Hike: 15 minutes each way

Sweat Index: easy (no sweat)

Mountain Bike Sweat Index: not suitable

Best Features: waterfall

Availability of Water Along the Trail: Myrtle Creek flows nearby.

Stream Crossings: A wide, steel bridge crosses Myrtle Creek at the end of the paved accessible trail.

Campsites: none

Precautions: The path after the bridge becomes very steep with dangerous drop-offs into the gorge below. Parents should keep young children close at all times. A portion of the trail passes through private property. Exercise respect for the environment you are passing through.

Alternate Hikes: The trail continues upslope beyond the viewpoint, but it is steep and rutted. There are tour routes that can be explored elsewhere on the wildlife refuge. Ask about these opportunities at the visitors' center.

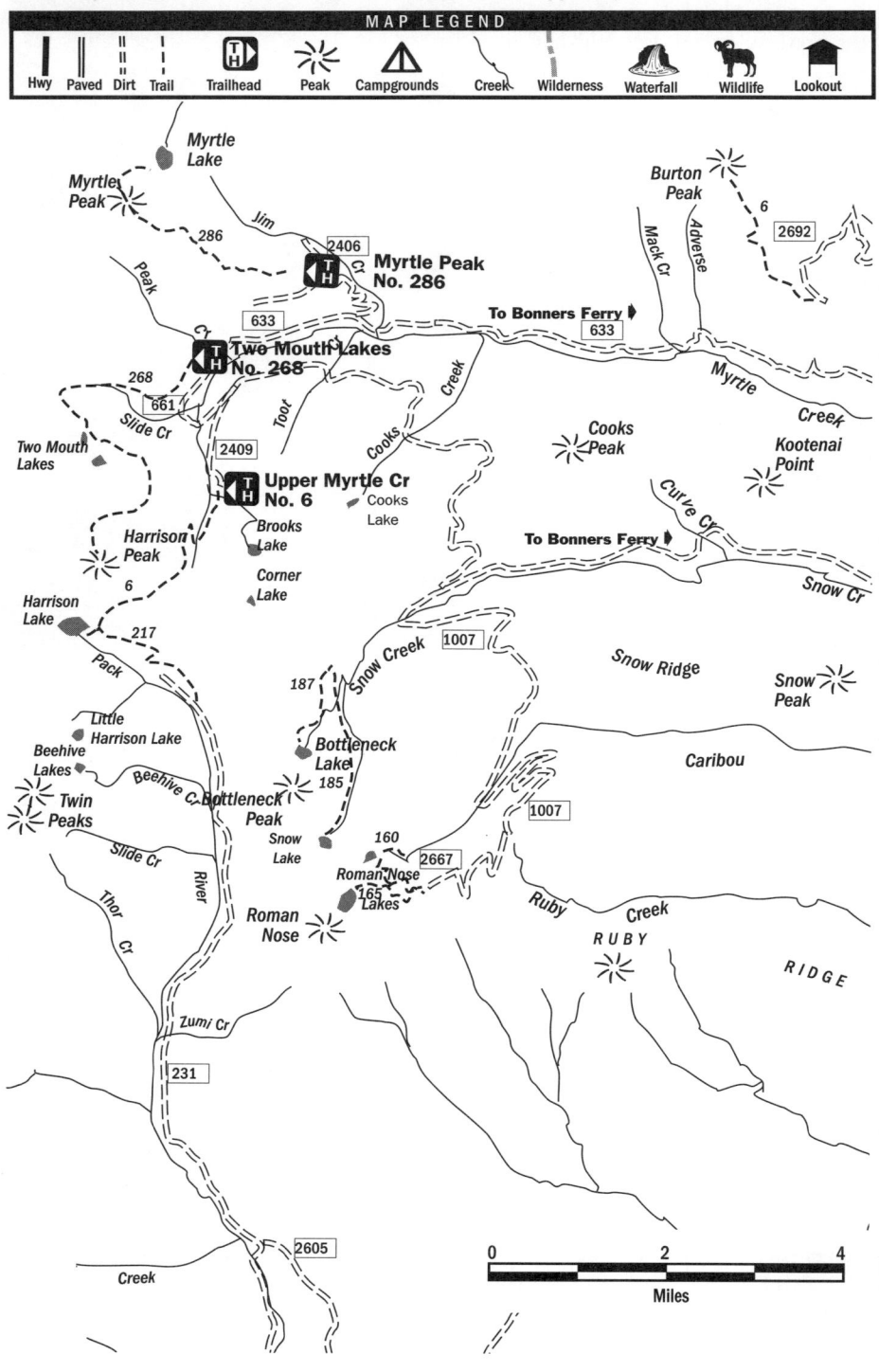

Myrtle Peak Trail No. 286

Destination: Myrtle Peak, 7,122 feet, and Myrtle Lake. *Map, page 245.*

Best Suited For: hiking, horseback riding

How Much Use: A Little * A Little More * **A LOT** * A Lot More * Excessive

What's it like? This trail begins on private timberlands that have been heavily logged, but after one-quarter mile the trail enters the forest and climbs steadily along a ridge. Maybe one-half mile from the trailhead a short, off-trail excursion to the north will take you into a basin cradling a lovely little lake at the head end of Jim Creek, but be prepared for thick brush if you take off cross-country. The trail continues to climb through open forest and rocky meadows with views of Harrison Peak and the Two Mouth Lakes basin to the south becoming increasingly awesome. Be on the lookout for Myrtle's Turtle as well. Where the trail finally breaks over the top, a short trail (100 feet or so) to the east accesses the summit of Myrtle Peak and the remains of the lookout that once sat there. The views in all directions are stupendous, particularly of The Lions Head and Smith Peak. The trail meanders down the north slope of the peak, then drops over the side toward the lake. It is a rather steep descent of about 1,000 feet. This is one of the larger lakes along the Selkirk Crest, and it has a good population of cutthroat trout.

On top of Myrtle Peak

USGS Map: Roman Nose, The Wigwams, Smith Peak

Trailhead: In Bonners Ferry, Idaho, turn off Highway 95 next to the Kootenai River Bridge onto Riverside (County Road No. 18) and head for the Kootenai Wildlife Refuge. After about 5.4 miles the road bears right past the wildlife refuge headquarters. Go about 1.3 miles to Myrtle Creek Road No. 633. Follow that nearly 10 miles to Road No. 2406. Turn right and go 3 miles to the end of the road. Road 2406 is rather rough and may require a high-clearance vehicle. There is a large turnaround at the trailhead that will accommodate eight to 10 vehicles.

Trail Length: about 3 miles one-way to the peak, 4.5 miles to the lake

Trail Condition: fair

Elevation: Trailhead –5,000', High/Low Point – 7,122' (Myrtle Peak), End –

5,946' (Myrtle Lake)

Estimated Duration of Hike: 1.5 to 2.5 hours to the peak, 2 to 3 hours to the lake, and the same back to the trailhead

Sweat Index: buckets of sweat (difficult)

Mountain Bike Sweat Index: not suitable

Best Features: mountaintop, remains of old lookout, beautiful lake

Availability of Water Along the Trail: a few small trickles in the first one-quarter mile, then nothing until the lake

Stream Crossings: nothing significant

Campsites: Primitive camping can be had at the trailhead, and there are several primitive sites with fire rings at the lake.

Alternate Hikes: Adventurous hikers head for Kent Lake to the southwest from Myrtle Peak. There is no trail and the going is tough.

Two Mouth Lakes Trail No. 268

Destination: Two Mouth Lakes. *Map, page 245.*

Best Suited For: hiking, horseback riding

How Much Use: A Little * A Little More * A Lot * **A LOT MORE** * Excessive

What's it like? The trail follows an old logging road for about 1.5 miles. A lot of this area has been logged, but some enormous trees remain, including several gigantic whitepine and one mammoth Western hemlock. The single-track trail then climbs along Slide Creek for another 1.5 miles through beautiful old-growth forest to a couple of tricky stream crossings and then on to a low ridgeline. From here a rocky knob just to the east of the trail affords terrific views of Harrison Peak and a peek at both lakes in the basin a couple hundred feet below. The trail gently descends into the basin and forks near a big granite slab. The

The pastoral creek and meadows between the Two Mouth Lakes

right fork goes a couple hundred yards to the lower lake. The left fork meanders about one-quarter mile to the upper lake. They are both beautiful, but the lower lake may be one of the most exquisite jewels in the Selkirks. Lots of exposed granite lines the lake, making for some good sunning opportunities in this serene setting. The lakes are connected by a series of meadows full of wildflowers and a meandering stream. It looks real "moosey" here, and you expect to see one behind every tree.

USGS Map: Smith Peak

Trailhead: In Bonners Ferry, Idaho, turn off Highway 95 next to the Kootenai River Bridge onto Riverside (County Road No. 18) and head for the Kootenai Wildlife Refuge. After about 5.4 miles the road bears right past the wildlife refuge headquarters. Go about 1.3 miles to Myrtle Creek Road No. 633. Turn left and travel just over 12 miles to the signed trailhead at a closed road. On the way up you can't help but notice the effects of a wildfire that burned across 4,000 acres in lower Myrtle Creek in the summer of 2003.

Trail Length: 4 miles one-way

Trail Condition: good

Elevation: Trailhead – 4,360', High/Low Point – 6,160', End – 5,831' (Lower Two Mouth Lake), 5,842' (Upper Two Mouth Lake)

Estimated Duration of Hike: 2 to 3 hours up, 2 to 3 hours down

Sweat Index: buckets of sweat (difficult)

Mountain Bike Sweat Index: not suitable

Best Features: beautiful alpine lakes and rugged mountain scenery

Availability of Water Along the Trail: There is good water about 3 miles along the trail at Slide Creek.

Stream Crossings: two crossings that are fairly easy rock hops

Campsites: There are several primitive campsites at the lakes.

Alternate Hikes: Some people strike off cross-country to summit Harrison Peak from the upper lake.

Wild Notes: Two Mouth Lakes has been the site of several efforts to augment the only remaining herd of woodland caribou in the Lower 48. During the 1990s wildlife biologists attempted to boost the population of these rare animals by transplanting several dozen individuals from British Columbia into the Two Mouth Lakes region. The plan has not worked too well as there are thought to be less than a dozen caribou in the U.S. portion of the Selkirks. These animals, which appear on the Endangered Species List, move a lot and mostly utilize the habitat in Stagleap Provincial Park north of the border. But from time to time some of them cross over into the United States and are seen in the Salmo-Priest Wilderness or as far south as Harrison Lake.

Upper Myrtle Creek Trail No. 6

Destination: Harrison Lake. *Map, page 245.*

Best Suited For: hiking, horseback riding

How Much Use: A Little * **A LITTLE MORE** * A Lot * A Lot More * Excessive

What's it like? This route to Harrison Lake is not nearly so well traveled as the shorter trail just over the divide, but it is a beautiful trail in its own right. The path follows an old roadbed for a little over half a mile, then crosses Myrtle Creek on a sturdy wooden footbridge. From here the trail climbs through 11 switchbacks among old-growth spruce and subalpine fir, brush and lush vegetation and beneath some steep rocky cliffs. Some giant Engelmann spruce occur high on this mountainside. The ridge up above is a fabulous granite dome that is best viewed from the access road to the trailhead. Once on the saddle between Pack River and Myrtle Creek, the trail meanders through a quiet basin full of white rhododendron. Glimpses of Harrison Peak are awesome. The trail then crosses some slab rock and, after about 4 miles, joins Trail 217 not far from the lake.

Harrison Peak

USGS Map: Smith Peak

Trailhead: In Bonners Ferry, Idaho, turn off Highway 95 next to the Kootenai River Bridge onto Riverside (County Road No. 18) and head for the Kootenai Wildlife Refuge. After about 5.4 miles the road bears right past the wildlife refuge headquarters. Go about 1.3 miles to Myrtle Creek Road No. 633. Turn left and travel just over 12 miles to where Road 633 becomes Road No. 661 at the Two Mouth Lakes trailhead. Continue another 1.5 miles or so to the junction of Road No. 2409, then take it about 1.3 miles to the end of the road and the trailhead. There is room for four to six vehicles in a fairly tight turnaround area. On the way up Road 633, you can't help but notice the effects of a wildfire that burned across 4,000 acres in lower Myrtle Creek in the summer of 2003.

Trail Length: 4 miles one-way to the junction with Trail 217, 4.5 miles to Harrison Lake

Trail Condition: fair

Elevation: Trailhead – 4,800', High/Low Point – 6,080', End – 6,000' (junction with Trail 217)

Estimated Duration of Hike: 2 to 3 hours up, 2 to 3 hours down

Sweat Index: buckets of sweat (difficult)

Mountain Bike Sweat Index: not suitable after the first mile

Best Features: old-growth alpine forest, alpine lake, mountain views

Availability of Water Along the Trail: Two small streams (one flowing out of Brooks Lake) cross the trail within a hundred yards of the trailhead, and Upper Myrtle Creek flows across the trail about a mile up the trail.

Stream Crossings: The first two crossings are easy rock hops, and the crossing at Upper Myrtle Creek has a wooden footbridge followed by some boardwalk.

Campsites: Primitive camping is available at the trailhead, and there are numerous campsites at Harrison Lake.

Alternate Hikes: This trail ties in with Harrison Lake Trail No. 217 less than one-half mile from the lake.

Kootenai National Wildlife Refuge

A century ago springtime was a violent time on the Kootenai River. Snow that had accumulated all winter high in the Canadian Rockies, in the Whitefish and Salish ranges of Montana, and deep in the heart of the Yaak Valley, would melt in the face of the strengthening sun. Water rushed from the high country in every brook, draw and stream, pouring into the Kootenai as it flowed down its big river valley. The river would rise and overflow its banks year after year. Floods would inundate the broad Kootenai valley. It was the rite of passage each spring.

For thousands of years this process had come to benefit hundreds of species of wildlife – 230 species of birds, 45 different mammals, plus fish, amphibians and reptiles. A natural system that seemed so out of balance in spring was the force that brought balance to the habitat that was home all year or part of the year to each of these creatures.

Then the balance of power shifted when, as early as the 1920s, human activities began to change the course of the river. Dikes were built to contain the spring floods; the mighty cottonwoods lining the river's banks mile after mile were removed and the wetlands that had been nourished by the spring torrents were drained. Agriculture came to characterize the valley, replacing the marshes and ponds and grasslands with wheat and oats and barley.

In 1975 the great river was finally harnessed, choking the last of the wildness from its gargantuan flow, with the construction of Libby Dam in Montana. The taming of the river was complete, and today it meanders meekly among fields and forests and past the towns that men have built in little over a hundred years of settlement.

There were those who foresaw the plight of migrating birds and waterfowl, though, if something was not done to restore at least a portion of the habitat lost to man's wiles. And so in 1934 the U.S. Congress passed the Migratory Bird Hunting Stamp Act. From then on every waterfowl hunter over the age of 16 was required to purchase an annual federal Duck Stamp. Since then, over the course of 70 years, proceeds from this stamp have contributed to preserving approximately 4 million acres of wetlands and adjacent habitats across the nation in a unique series of preserves called national wildlife refuges. Among them is the Kootenai National Wildlife Refuge, a mere 5 miles west of Bonners Ferry, Idaho.

Established in 1964, it was created to reclaim some of the habitat lost to development in the Idaho Panhandle. With funds generated from the sale of Duck Stamps, 2,774 acres were purchased alongside the Kootenai River and Deep Creek on the east. The west side of the refuge rises a short way into the foothills of the Selkirk Mountains where Myrtle Creek and Cascade Creek tumble from the rugged highlands. Myrtle Creek is the principal supply of water for the refuge, but water is also pumped from the Kootenai River and Deep Creek in order to maintain permanent ponds and to flood waterfowl food plots each fall.

The primary goal of the Kootenai National Wildlife Refuge, which is managed by the U.S. Fish and Wildlife Service, is to provide resting and feeding habitat for migrating waterfowl. In achieving that goal, many other species of birds and

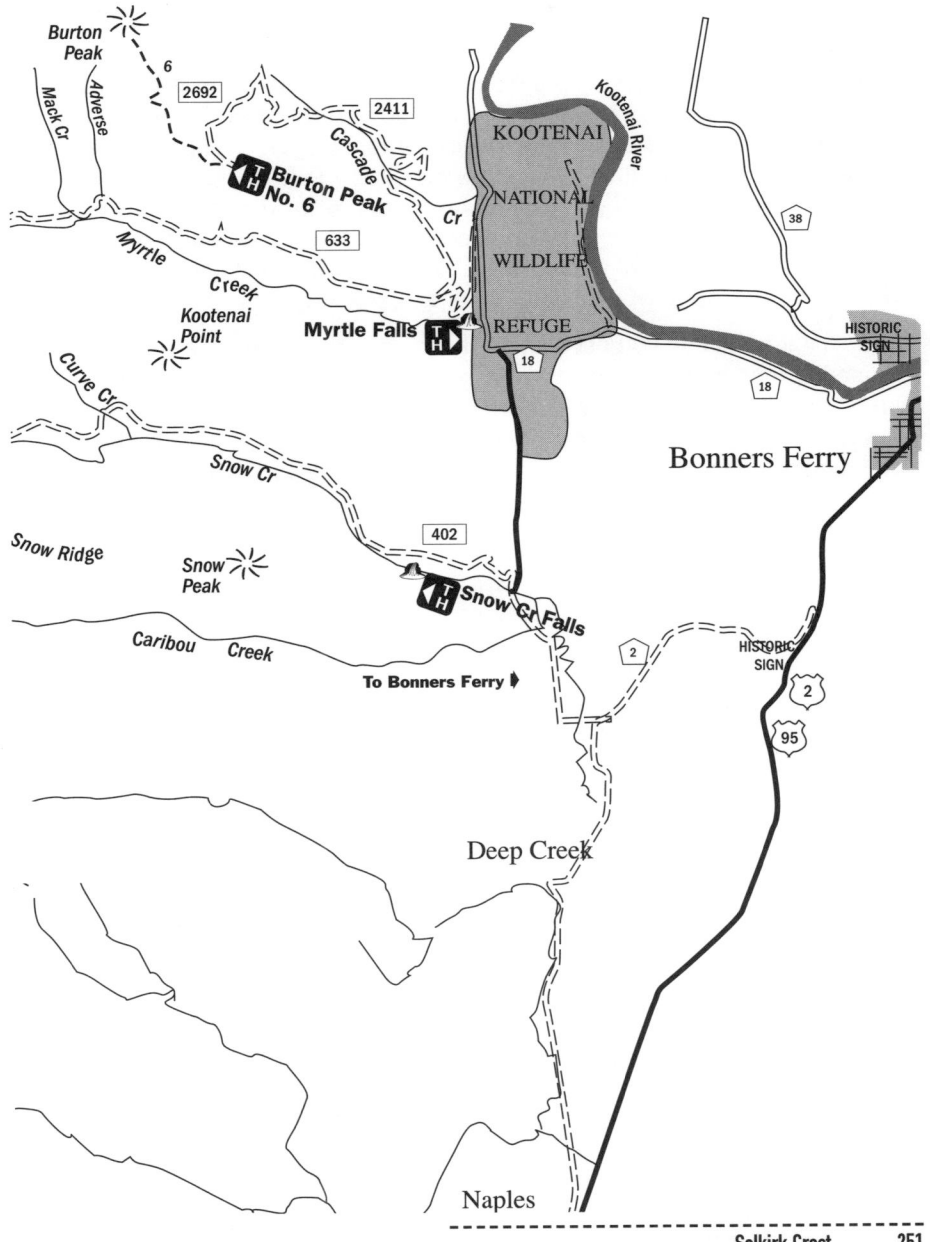

wildlife, plus fish and other creatures, benefit from the habitat that has been preserved on the refuge.

Visitors are welcomed at the refuge and are encouraged to explore its four square miles of wetlands, ponds and fields. There are observation blinds, overlooks, several miles of foot trails and a 4.5-mile-long auto tour road. There is a new element to see on the west edge of the refuge as well: a wildfire in 2003 burned down out of the mountains into Myrtle Creek barely a hundred yards from the refuge's visitors' center. The inferno was stopped by the heroic efforts of firefighters, but nearly 4,000 acres of forests and brushfields were charred by the flames.

At any time of the year there are exciting discoveries to make in this wildlife-rich corner of the Kootenai Valley. Go see for yourself the mallards and pintails, the tundra swans and Canada geese, the cinnamon teal, blue-winged teal and pied-billed grebe; go see the eagles and osprey, the winnowing snipe and the drumming grouse; go see if you'll be lucky enough to spy a black bear, a moose, an elk or most certainly a white-tailed deer. It doesn't take much luck to see some of the nearly 300 species of wildlife at the Kootenai National Wildlife Refuge, just a bit of patience and maybe a handy set of binoculars.

All the information you need about this oasis of wildlife habitat may be obtained at the refuge headquarters. To get there turn off Highway 2 in Bonners Ferry at the south end of the bridge over the river onto River Road. Follow it 5.5 miles to West Side Road and bear right to the visitors' center. New construction was taking place there during the summer of 2003. You can also go online for a wonderful virtual tour of the refuge at http://kootenai.fws.gov or call 208-267-5570. Additional information about National Wildlife Refuges can be obtained by calling 1-800-344-WILD.

Essay:

Gifts

July 25, 1956. My mom remembers that date well. She lay in a bed in Johnston-Willis Hospital in Richmond, Virginia and gave birth to a beautiful baby boy. Me. What a gift, huh? Of course, the "beautiful" may be subjective, but I bet if you were to ask her she'd say, "My goodness, yes, he was a beautiful baby boy! I don't know what happened to him when he grew up."

Well, anyway, on with the story.

July 25, 1975. Perhaps my dad, if he was still with us, would remember that date, or at least that period of time. He took me to the Greyhound bus station a couple of weeks before that and off I went to Rocky Mountain National Park in Colorado. On exactly that date 17 other people, including two adults and 15 high school kids I hardly knew, sang happy birthday to me, and the tune echoed off the cliffs surrounding Pawnee Lake. It still ranks as one of the most memorable birthdays of my life.

July 25, 1996. I bet my oldest brother Archie remembers that date. I was back in Rocky Mountain National Park with him, my hiking buddy Jeb Williamson and a friend from England, Chris Richardson. We backpacked for seven days covering something like 55 miles in celebration of my 40th birthday. On that day Jeb and I left Archie and Chris in camp at the July 4th campsite and climbed to the top of Taylor Peak, a "thirteener," my first and only one so far.

July 25, 2003. No one will remember that day but me. There I was in the Pack River valley north of Sandpoint, Idaho, doing what I love to do most of all – eating and drinking beer. No, seriously, I was hiking. And hiking on my birthday, which has been a habit I've developed over the past 10 years or so. Doesn't matter what day of the week it is, I'll drop everything and disappear into the mountains, usually just for the day, but sometimes for an entire week. This was one of those occasions when I took the whole week. It seemed silly to go all the way up Pack River for one simple day hike, so I just stayed there and went to Caribou Lake and Keokee Lake, Mount Casey and Dodge Peak, Harrison Lake, Beehive Lake and for that day, my birthday, I saved what I thought might be the best of them all, Chimney Rock. It was sort of a gift to myself.

Six miles into the basin below the granite face of the most recognizable landmark in the Selkirks, it is. Steadily up and up the trail climbs, but I hardly noticed the grade. The sun was shining in an absolutely gorgeous, cloud-free sky. The morning air was warm, hinting it would be hot later in the afternoon. Penstemons bloomed on the exposed soil of the old road-cut the trail followed for the first few miles. I had not a care in the world. All that concerned me was getting into the high country and exploring the wildness it harbored.

The first indication I was not alone came when I noticed something else on the trail a hundred yards out in front of me. A coyote was loping casually in my direction. I stopped and watched as it came on. At about 50 yards it veered to the side of the old road, put its head down and looked as though it was eating something. Its grayish-brown coat glistened in the clear morning air and a huge fluffy tail stuck straight out in line with its backbone. After a few moments of undisturbed reverie, I advanced slowly, but this wild dog was not to be crept up on. It swung its muzzle toward me, took all of one second to size up the situation, then hightailed it up the road, stopped twice to look back, and then disappeared from sight.

I picked up my pace once again and continued the hike toward Chimney Rock. The road swings around into a narrow canyon flanking the West Branch of Pack River and the brush crowding the shoulder gets thicker. I walked nonchalantly along the wide path until a slight disturbance below the trail caught my attention. Easing to the side, I peered over the head-high alder and staring back at me from all of 6 feet away were a pair of eyes set wide in a hairy, black face with a snout pointed up at me and nostrils flared. A miniature canoe paddle stuck out one side of the lopsided head, matched by an identical protrusion on the other. The eyes blinked once, twice and then a sudden release of pent-up tension caused snot to blow from its nose. Before the young bull moose could lunge up the slope through the brush, I figured I best move along.

The trail was easy and my eyes wandered. An eagle soaring high on air currents sweeping upward from the shadowed valley, buoyed by intensifying rays of the sun, made me wish I had wings to fly. The big bird was already over Chimney Rock and sailed on to Mount Roothaan and out of sight, but as soon as it was gone, something a bit closer at hand made me stop dead in my tracks. A bear had spotted me and seemed to be slightly annoyed. It was in the trail maybe 75 yards away facing toward me. I didn't breathe and only rolled my eyes from side to side to see if I could spot a suitable climbing tree. A limby, prickly spruce was the only one close enough, but if that bear charged, no tree was really close enough.

The sun stood still, the air grew stagnant, not another sound from the forest reached my buzzing ears. Only two things existed in the world at that moment – me, and the bear. And then he didn't exist anymore, or so it seemed. He whipped around as fast as a high-schooler spinning brodies in the high school parking lot and was gone from sight. When I decided to breathe again my throat was as dry as the dust my boots had been kicking up all morning. I took a short break, drank some water, ate a granola bar, then resumed my determined hike to Chimney Rock.

An hour later I stood transfixed at the toe of the most spectacular chunk of real estate I've ever seen. The pockmarked wall rose straight up, towering over a basin littered with fragments of granite, pockets of beargrass and sedges and a smattering of subalpine firs. If anyone else was on the earth at that moment, I didn't know it. I could've been the last of my race, bound to wander the wilds alone forever. Only the sky, the sun, the moon and stars at night and the wild creatures that had allowed me passage into this remote valley would ever offer me company again. It was a lonely sensation but an exhilarating one, too.

I struck off along the edge of smooth rock that had pushed its way from the grassy soil into the blinding turquoise sky overhead more than a hundred million years ago. From time to time I would stop and tilt my head back as far as it would go and gaze at the angular stone behemoth, unable to see the top. Three times I sat on a lip of the rock and placed my hands flat on its sun-warmed surface. Perhaps I hoped it would impart some assurance that I was not alone in the world, but all I got was the cold, reverberating echo of days and years and millennia, and whispers of time with no beginning and no end.

At a high point where the giant glacial bowl turned upward into solid rock, I angled out into the open basin. The walking was as easy as following the old roadbed into the West Branch. Wildflowers bloomed in profusion, bobbing their colorful heads against a gentle breeze blowing in off Pack River far below. Several snow banks tucked tight against the granite edifice offered virgin water where snowmelt dripped a molecule at a time into a holding basin big enough for one drink. I sipped, then sat and soaked it all in. The beauty was astonishing, the silence deafening. Knowing better, I still pretended no one had ever been here before.

And then I saw it, a moment later, as I was stepping from rock to rock so as not to disturb the fragile elegance of this alpine sanctuary. I stooped and picked it up. On its face it said Casio and Water Resistant. It was a digital wristwatch and it indicated the time was 10:47:25 AM on 7-25-03, and still ticking, or whatever those new digitals do if they don't tick. Odd, I thought, how the time reflected the date, the 25th, my age on that date, 47, and, on a scale of 1 to 10, what I would have rated the hike that day to Chimney Rock.

Hours later, with the sun sagging low in the west, I turned my face back toward the lowlands. My day in the high country was closing in around me, and it was time to return to my pickup and to home and a birthday dinner with friends. Ladened with gifts, I happily descended the mountain. I carried with me the gifts of solitude, a menagerie of wilderness art painted on the canvas of my mind, and a Casio wristwatch that perhaps someday the real owner will come and reclaim. I'll gladly hand it over, as gladly as Chimney Rock offered it up to me on a day in July that I, if no on else, will always remember.

The South End
Harrison Lake to Caribou Lake

The south end of the Selkirk Crest is bisected by Pack River. A high-gradient stream that pounds its way through granite boulders until it reaches the flatlands near Samuels, Pack River drops more than 4,000 feet in 20 miles from its source at Harrison Lake to the swimming hole adjacent to Highway 95 beneath the railroad trestle. From there the lower Pack River snakes through fields and forests and between homes and ranchettes on its way to Lake Pend Oreille.

Some of the most dramatic terrain found in the Selkirk Mountains flanks either side of this river. Harrison Peak, 7,292 feet, stands like a hook-nosed sentinel at the headwall, and fanning out southeast and southwest from that ragged peak are eight more summits that surpass 7,000 feet. The north tower of Twin Peaks, among the Seven Sisters, is the highest at 7,607 feet, according to a USGS survey marker atop its lofty ramparts. It is one of just three named mountains that reach above 7,600 feet in all the American Selkirks.

What is probably the most imposing and awe-inspiring geologic feature of them all is located in the southern part of the Selkirk Crest – Chimney Rock. A granitic spike that pulled away from a ridge of uplifted rock during the birth of these mountains 135 million years ago, Chimney Rock is a vertical spire jutting 500 feet above the glacial basins surrounding it. Almost due east of this feature rises Roman Nose (7,260 feet), one of the most recognizable mountains south of the Canadian border.

Sweeping across the Pack River Valley and over Roman Nose is the 4-mile wide swath of destruction created by the inferno known as the Sundance Fire. In 1967 flames consumed 56,000 acres in this part of the Selkirks, killing two firefighters in the process. The landscape is well on its way to recovering, but the memories will always remain of the sacrifices that were made to stop the hungry monster that threatened homes and lives for two terrifying weeks that summer.

At the far south end of this part of the range is Schweitzer Mountain Resort, one of the premier ski mountains of the Pacific Northwest, and Caribou Lodge, a gateway to the backcountry anytime of the year. In the heart of the Upper Pack River was formerly a well-known watering hole called Edna and Buck's Tavern, now burned and gone.

More than a dozen lakes dot the high country on either side of Pack River, helping make this portion of the Selkirks one of the most popular with outdoor enthusiasts of all kinds.

Trails: Bottleneck Lake No. 187, Snow Lake No. 185, Roman Nose Lakes No. 165

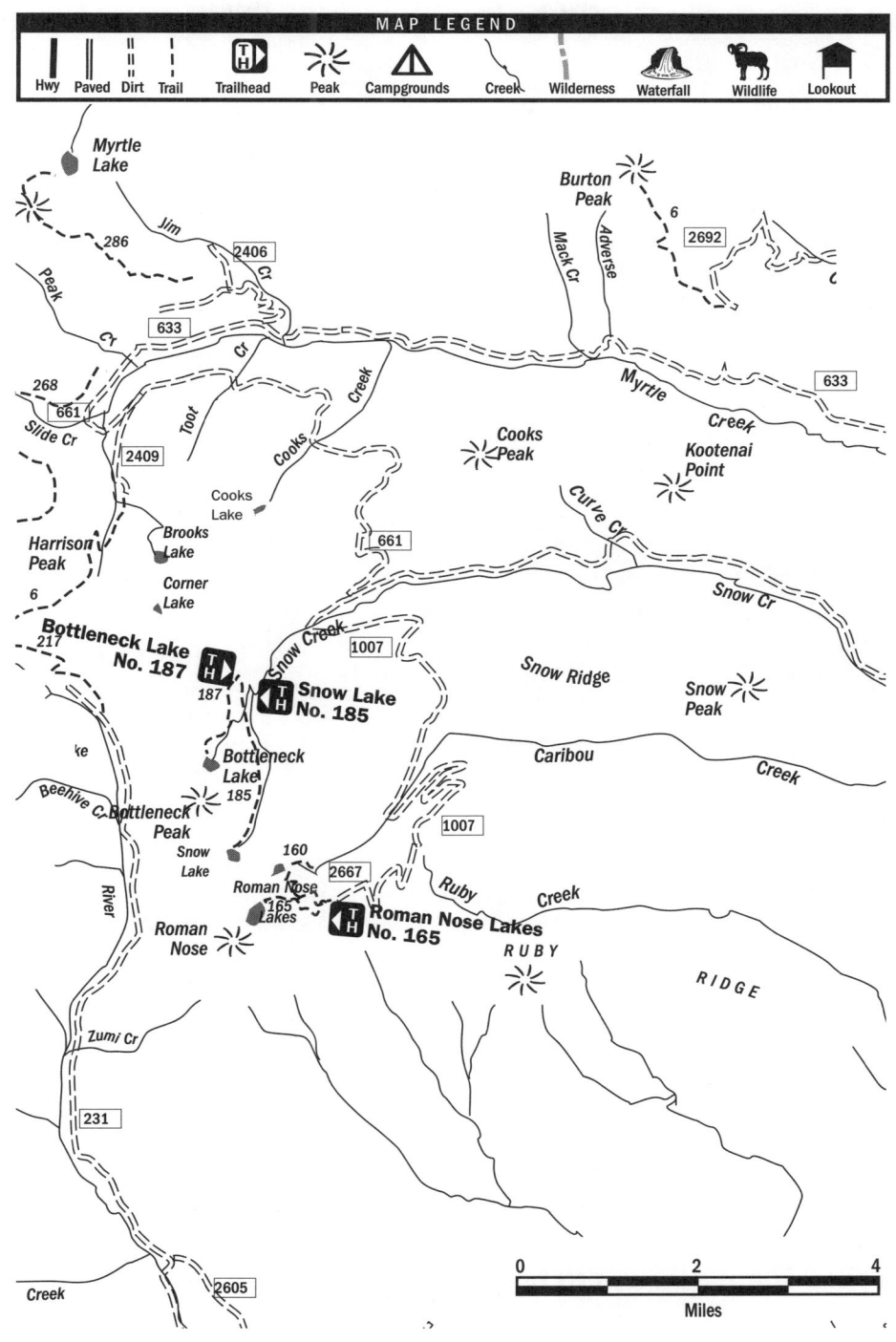

Bottleneck Lake Trail No. 187

Destination: Bottleneck Lake. *Map, page 257.*

Best Suited For: hiking, mountain biking, horseback riding

How Much Use: A Little * A Little More * **A LOT** * A Lot More * Excessive

What's it like? As with Trail 185 and Snow Lake, an old logging road goes nearly all the way to Bottleneck Lake. The first mile or so of this trail is shared with Trail 185, then you come to a signed junction. To continue to Bottleneck go right. The road rounds a switchback after a few hundred yards and climbs gently into a basin below the lake. After crossing the creek for the second time, the road gives way to a rutted, eroded, muddy trail that climbs steeply for 200 vertical feet. Mountain bikers and horses can easily make it to this point but may have to walk from here. The lake is surrounded by heavy timber with Bottleneck Peak in the background. There are some small fish here.

Bottleneck Lake glimpsed from Bottleneck Peak

USGS Map: Roman Nose

Trailhead: From Bonners Ferry, Idaho, go south on Highway 95 about 2 miles and turn west by the Mirror Lake Golf Course. Follow that between 2 and 3 miles to County Road No. 13. It goes west at first, then turns sharply north. After about 2 miles turn west again onto Snow Creek Road No. 402 and take it some 8 miles to its junction with Cooks Pass Road No. 661. Another hundred yards beyond that junction is a narrow road to the right that is gated after a couple hundred yards. That is actually the continuation of Road 402. The main route becomes Road No. 1007. It is best not to drive up to the gate, as there is no turnaround. It is better to park in the wide spot at the Road 661 junction, or two to three vehicles can park on 402 before the gate.

Trail Length: 3.3 miles one-way

Trail Condition: good at first, poor the last one-quarter mile

Elevation: Trailhead – 4,360', High/Low Point – 4,776' (junction with Trail 185), End – 5,622'

Estimated Duration of Hike: 1.5 to 2.5 hours up, 1 to 2 hours down

Sweat Index: break a sweat (moderate)

Mountain Bike Sweat Index: break a sweat (unsuitable the last one-quarter mile)

Best Features: nice mountain lake, good view of Bottleneck Peak

Availability of Water Along the Trail: Bottle Creek is a perennial stream.

Stream Crossings: The trail twice crosses the creek, but each time is easy; early in the season water flows in the upper part of the trail making it very tricky to negotiate.

Campsites: There is an established campsite with a fire ring at the lake.

Alternate Hikes: Snow Lake Trail No. 185 shares the trailhead with this trail.

Snow Lake Trail No. 185

Destination: Snow Lake. *Map, page 257.*

Best Suited For: hiking, mountain biking, horseback riding

How Much Use: A Little * A Little More * **A LOT** * A Lot More * Excessive

What's it like? An old logging road goes nearly all the way to Snow Lake. It has been closed back where Roads 402 and 1007 split, adding more than a mile to the overall hike. The upper reaches of Snow Creek were burned in 1967 by the Sundance Fire, so the panoramas really open up in the high country, partly because of the fire and partly because of the extensive logging that has been done in years past in this drainage. Despite that, the hike is a pleasant one and the lake is glorious. There is a difficult climb of about 400 feet to negotiate to get into the lake basin. Here the trail is heavily eroded and very steep. But once over the lip of the basin, the trail is level and you walk into a stunning amphitheater of high cliffs and open grassy slopes. Mountain bikers may find the going a bit rough through areas of deep coarse sand along the way, but horses should have no problem except on that final steep approach to the basin.

Snow Lake

USGS Map: Roman Nose

Trailhead: From Bonners Ferry, Idaho, go south on Highway 95 about 2 miles and turn west by the Mirror Lake Golf Course. Follow that between 2 and 3 miles to County Road No. 13. It goes west at first then turns sharply north. After about 2 miles turn west again onto Snow Creek Road No. 402 and take it some 8 miles to its junction with Cooks Pass Road No. 661. Another hundred yards beyond that junction is a narrow road to the right that is gated after a couple hundred yards. That is actually the continuation of Road 402. The main route becomes Road No. 1007. It is best not to drive up to the gate, as there is no turnaround. It is better to park in the wide spot at the Road 661 junction, or two to three vehicles can park on 402 before the gate.

Trail Length: 5.6 miles one-way

Trail Condition: good most of the way, poor the last one-quarter mile to the lake

Elevation: Trailhead – 4,360', High/Low Point – 4,776' (junction with Trail 187), End – 5,921'

Estimated Duration of Hike: 2.5 to 3.5 hours up, 2 to 3 hours down

Sweat Index: buckets of sweat (difficult)

Mountain Bike Sweat Index: buckets of sweat (the final one-quarter mile is not suitable). There are areas of deep, coarse sand along this trail.

Best Features: beautiful mountain lake, rugged mountain scenery

Availability of Water Along the Trail: There are three good streams along the last 2 miles of trail that offer good water.

Stream Crossings: The old roadbed crosses Snow Creek three times on the way up, and each is relatively easy to cross later in the year (during spring runoff they may be much more difficult).

Campsites: Primitive campsites are located at the lake.

Alternate Hikes: Bottleneck Lake Trail No. 187 shares the trailhead with this trail.

Roman Nose Lakes Trail No. 165

ACCESSIBLE: The lower lake has a great boardwalk trail leading a hundred yards or so to its edge.

This is a Family Fun Hike

Destination: each of the three Roman Nose Lakes. *Map, page 257.*

Best Suited For: hiking, horseback riding

How Much Use: A Little * A Little More * A Lot * A Lot More * **EXCESSIVE**

What's it like? The driving directions to Roman Nose Lakes may be a little complicated, but the roads are good and the destination is a worthy one. The high country around these magnificent lakes is some of the most beautiful in the Selkirks. A fine parking area and trailhead facility has been developed by the

Barb Perusse with Duke near Lower Roman Nose Lake

Forest Service that includes a vault toilet and a rustic camping area. From the parking lot to the lower lake is a short, simple stroll on boardwalk that is accessible to wheelchairs. The terrain around the lower lake was intensely burned during the Sundance Fire of 1967. That has had the beneficial effect of enhancing the blooming of prolific wildflowers well into the summer and huckleberries are often plentiful. Interestingly, the fire skipped around the middle lake and most of the upper lake, burning on the ridges above both but barely singing the lake basins. The trail to these two lakes begins at the parking lot and passes over a footbridge across a creek, then climbs along a boardwalk to the dirt and rock path. It climbs steadily among granite rocks and scattered, small subalpine fir trees. A spur trail accesses an overlook that offers a dramatic view of the glacial cirque below the middle lake. Farther on another spur trail leads to the middle lake, descending about 200 feet in half a mile. A third spur trail meanders to the upper lake with only minimal change in elevation. A scenic loop trail with interpretive signs can also be enjoyed on the rocky slopes above the lower lake. At the parking area is a descriptive sign about all these trails. Because of the relative ease of access, impacts have been severe on this fragile alpine environment. Visitors are urged to use the utmost care while exploring this remarkable place.

USGS Map: Roman Nose

Trailhead: From Bonners Ferry, Idaho, go south on Highway 95 about 2 miles and turn west by the Mirror Lake Golf Course onto County Road No. 2. Follow that between 2 and 3 miles to County Road No. 13. It goes west at first, then turns sharply north. After about 2 miles turn west again onto Snow Creek Road No. 402 and take it some 8 miles to its junction with Road No. 1007. Follow it across Snow Creek, over Caribou Pass, across Caribou Creek and over Ruby Pass – a distance of about 7.5 miles. Then turn right onto Road 2667 and take it about

1.5 miles to the trailhead parking area. You can also get on County Road No. 2 at Naples and follow it north about 6 miles to Road No. 13. The parking area accommodates 10 vehicles and there is an overflow parking area about one-half mile back along the road.

Trail Length: 4.1 miles of trail altogether; about 100 yards of accessible boardwalk to the lower lake; about 1 mile to each of the middle and upper lakes; plus an interpretive scenic loop trail of about 2 miles

Trail Condition: good

Elevation: Trailhead – 5,900', High/Low Point – 5,891' (lower lake), 5,921' (middle lake), End – 6,194' (upper lake) – Note: the loop trail tops out at 6,400'.

Estimated Duration of Hike: 30 minutes to 1 hour to the middle or upper lake, 1 to 2 hours for the scenic loop

Sweat Index: no sweat (easy) to break a sweat (moderate)

Mountain Bike Sweat Index: not suitable

Best Features: beautiful alpine lakes, high peaks, close-up look at the effects of the 1967 Sundance forest fire

Availability of Water Along the Trail: The outlet stream from the lower lake flows by the parking area.

Stream Crossings: Bridges and boardwalk make crossing the stream and marshy areas no problem.

Campsites: A campground near the lower lake will accommodate tent and vehicle campers, and the middle and upper lakes have several primitive campsites.

Alternate Hikes: Off-trail hikers love to summit Roman Nose, 7,260 feet, from the upper lake.

Wild Notes: When the Sundance Fire roared over the summit of Roman Nose on September 1, 1967, a Sandpoint High School graduate, 18-year old Randy Langston, was stationed at the lookout. He found a safe hiding place beneath an overhanging rock ledge as firebrands as long as his arm whistled by on winds gusting as high as 95 miles an hour. He emerged unscathed the next day, unlike two fellow firefighters in the Pack River Valley below. Lee Collins and Luther P. Rodarte were overrun by the flames and lost their lives during that firestorm.

Wildlife Sighting: Once back at the trailhead, a fellow and his wife wandered over to me and my hiking companion, Taneesha Smith, and explained they had seen a grizzly bear just down the road near the overflow parking area only moments ago. We all went back to see if the creature was still there, which of course it was not. Grizzlies are rare in the Selkirks, but with the great huckleberries that are produced each year on Roman Nose, it is not surprising to hear of one visiting that area in late summer.

Trails: Harrison Lake No. 217, Beehive Lakes No. 279, Chimney Rock No. 256, Fault Lake No. 59

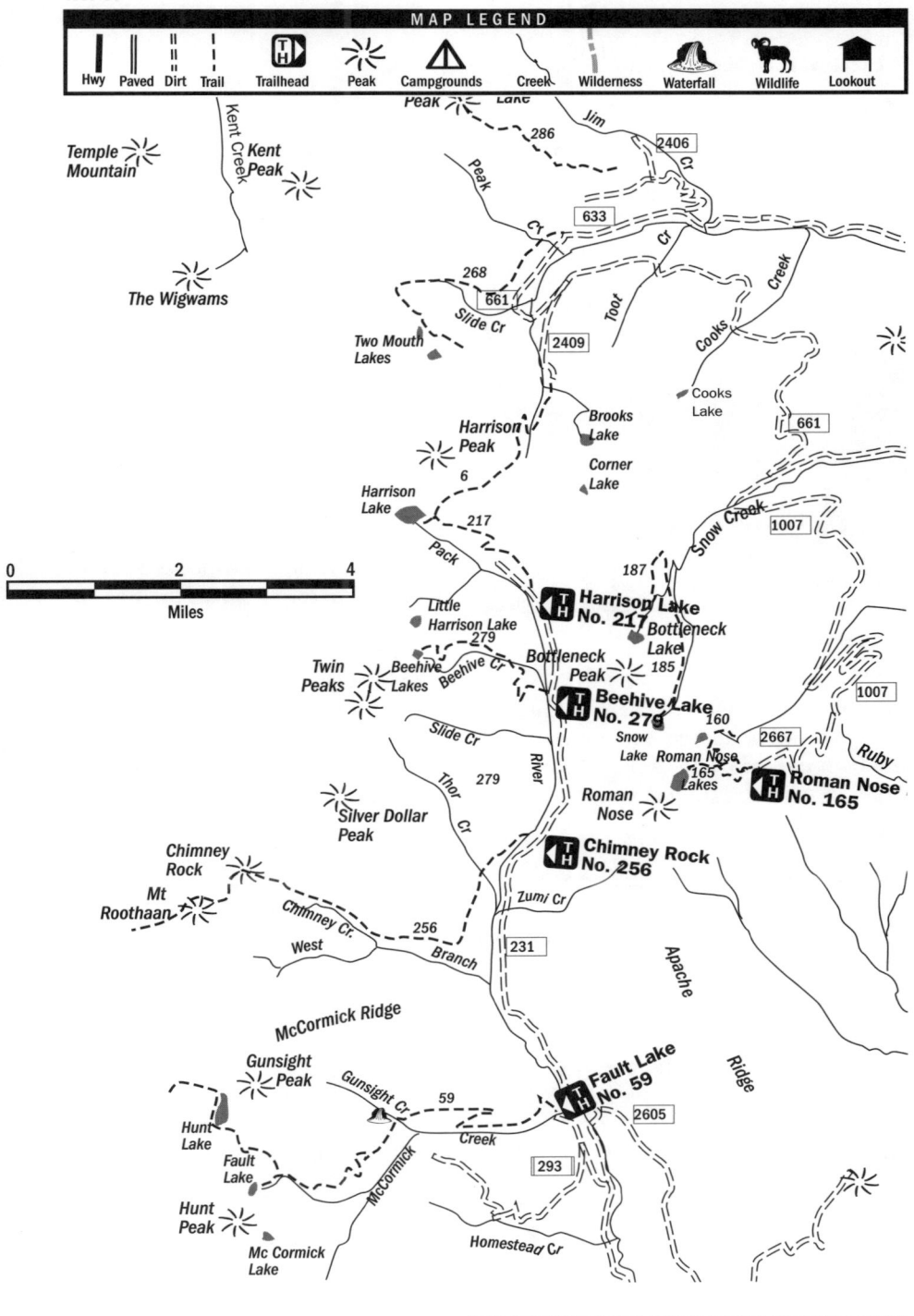

Harrison Lake Trail No. 217

This is a Family Fun Hike

Destination: Harrison Lake. *Map, page 263.*

Best Suited For: hiking

How Much Use: A Little * A Little More * A Lot * A Lot More * **EXCESSIVE**

What's it like? Harrison Lake is probably the most visited destination in the Selkirks. The trail, though relatively steep in places, is fairly short and accesses a stunningly beautiful alpine cirque cradling the lake in a basin ringed by granite cliffs and peaks. The trail follows an old logging road for a mile or so, then climbs through subalpine fir and spruce into the rocks. The Forest Service has cleared a few spots along the way that help provide excellent views of The Beehive, Bottleneck Peak and Roman Nose. Also, keep an eye out above the trail for glimpses of Harrison Peak's dramatic hooked summit. But if you miss it along the trail you sure can't miss it once at the lake. It raises its head to the north above a timbered ridge. Snow lingers a long time along the southern shore of the lake since it is protected by high-rise cliffs. Campsites are scattered among gigantic boulders at the east end of the lake. This is a high-use area, and great caution needs to be exercised by every visitor in order to minimize human impacts to this fragile environment.

Harrison Lake and Peak

USGS Map: The Wigwams

Trailhead: Drive 13 miles north of Sandpoint, Idaho, on Highway 95 and turn west onto Pack River Road No. 231. Travel about 20.5 miles, the last 6.5 of which are extremely rough, requiring a high-clearance vehicle. The trailhead is near the end of the road and has a vault toilet. Directions to this trailhead are well signed in the Upper Pack River. Pack River Road No. 231 is not suitable for horse trailers after the Pearson Creek Road No. 2605 junction.

Trail Length: 2.3 miles one-way

Trail Condition: good

Elevation: Trailhead – 4,746', High/Low Point – 4,746'-6,182', End – 6,182'

Estimated Duration of Hike: 1 to 2 hours up, 1 to 2 hours down

Sweat Index: break a sweat (moderate)

Mountain Bike Sweat Index: not suitable

Best Features: beautiful mountain lake, rugged peaks

Availability of Water Along the Trail: There are more than a dozen trickles across this trail in midsummer.

Stream Crossings: There is nothing significant, though early in the season there might be water in the trail in places.

Campsites: Half a dozen established primitive sites are at the lake; there is a bear-proof food storage container at the lake that campers should use.

Alternate Hikes: Upper Myrtle Creek Trail No. 6 ties in with this trail about one-quarter mile from the lake. Off-trail hikers climb Harrison Peak, 7,292 feet, from here or clamber cross-country to Little Harrison Lake and Upper Beehive Lake.

Beehive Lakes Trail No. 279

Destination: Upper Beehive Lake. *Map, page 263.*

Best Suited For: hiking

How Much Use: A Little * A Little More * A Lot * **A LOT MORE** * Excessive

What's it like? An old logging road takes the hiker the first mile and a half toward Upper Beehive Lake. Once over a somewhat tedious stream crossing, the trail narrows to a single track and switchbacks through the forest and some brushy areas until it runs into slab rock. Which way to go could be a little confusing as rock cairns indicate continuing sideways across the hill or turning up and climbing steeply. The way to the upper lake is to head uphill across vast exposed granite. It is frequently marked with rock cairns. Though this portion of the trail is strenuous, the rock, when dry, is easy to walk on. And the views that unfold as you climb are fabulous. You may not notice the lower lake at all as it is pretty much a small marshy pond tucked into a meadow in the creek valley below, but the upper lake is one of the more spectacular lakes in the Selkirks. The north Twin rises starkly above the pristine waters of the lake, sheltering a basin that looks and feels as wild as any place on the continent. Despite the difficulty in hiking to this lake, it is a popular destination and impacts have been severe. Please use established campsites, of which there are several, and always remember to pack out everything you pack in.

The Beehive in Upper Pack River

USGS Map: The Wigwams

Trailhead: Drive 13 miles north of Sandpoint, Idaho, on Highway 95 and turn west onto Pack River Road No. 231. Travel about 19 miles, the last 5 of which are extremely rough, requiring a high-clearance vehicle. A spur road branches off to the left and goes a couple hundred yards to the trailhead parking area, which has room for four to six vehicles. Directions to this trailhead are well signed in the Upper Pack River. Pack River Road No. 231 is not suitable for horse trailers after the Pearson Creek Road No. 2605 junction.

Trail Length: 4.4 miles one-way

Trail Condition: fair

Elevation: Trailhead – 4,450', High/Low Point – 4,450'-6,457', End – 6,457'

Estimated Duration of Hike: 2 to 3 hours up, 2 to 3 hours down

Sweat Index: buckets of sweat (difficult)

Mountain Bike Sweat Index: not suitable (except for the first mile and a half along the old logging road)

Best Features: spectacularly beautiful mountain lake, rugged peaks

Availability of Water Along the Trail: Several streams cross the trail in the first 2 miles and have water most of the year.

Stream Crossings: Most of the creeks to be crossed are easy to negotiate; the stream where the road becomes a trail might be challenging to get across early in the season.

Campsites: This lake is a popular destination, and several campsites have been established in places along the lakeshore. Please use established campsites in order to minimize additional impacts.

Alternate Hikes: Off-trail hikers love to explore the higher terrain by climbing Twin Peaks, 7,607 feet, which is strenuous with some exposure, but not technical. Also, cross-country hiking to Little Harrison Lake or all the way over to Harrison Lake is feasible from here.

Wild Notes: The name "Beehive" comes from a dramatic topographic feature looming above Pack River. It is a granite dome called The Beehive because it has been likened to a hornet's nest; those that resemble a papier-mâché creation found dangling from tree limbs or tucked into the tangled branches of a bush.

Chimney Rock Trail No. 256

Destination: Chimney Rock, 7,124 feet, and Mount Roothaan, 7,326 feet. *Map, page 263.*

Best Suited For: hiking

How Much Use: A Little * A Little More * **A LOT** * A Lot More * Excessive

What's it like? The most stunning geologic feature in all the Selkirks is

Chimney Rock. Its vertical walls rise nearly 500 feet above the alpine cirques where Chimney Creek and the North Fork of Indian Creek are born. But it is not a particularly easy task getting there. The trail from Pack River follows an old logging road for several miles. You might notice evidence of a battle against noxious weeds along this road, especially knapweed and tansy. The road eventually gives way to a trail near Chimney Creek, where the trail is rutted and washed out from years of spring runoff. A nice waterfall below the road can be glimpsed from the side of a giant boulder on the side of the road near this point. Farther along, the trail crosses a lot of slab rock, and so one must keep an eye out for rock cairns. Perhaps 3.5 miles along, at the top of a stiff climb to a granite bench, is the first

Chimney Rock seen from Mount Roothaan

good view of Chimney Rock. To this point it is not too difficult of a hike, and it is well worth the view if this is as far as you get. However, go a little farther through some brush and scattered trees on this flat ridge and you will find an equally majestic view of the West Branch of Pack River and Gunsight Mountain to the south. The terrain is awesome. But the best of this hike is in the basin below Chimney Rock and onto the ridge that radiates from its eastern wall. From here a rugged trail creeps along its north face to the backside of the rock and a U-shaped saddle that separates it from the rest of the knife-edged ridge it broke away from eons ago. The basin below is spectacular and allows good access to Mount Roothaan a mile to the southwest.

USGS Map: Mount Roothaan

Trailhead: Drive 13 miles north of Sandpoint, Idaho, on Highway 95 and turn west onto Pack River Road No. 231. Go about 16 miles to West Branch Road No. 2653, turn left and go one-half mile to the trailhead.

Trail Length: 6 miles one-way

Trail Condition: fair

Elevation: Trailhead – 4,020', High/Low Point – 4,020'-6,700', End – 6,700' (at the toe of Chimney Rock's vertical wall)

Estimated Duration of Hike: 3 to 4 hours up, 2.5 to 3.5 hours down

Sweat Index: bathed in sweat (strenuous)

Mountain Bike Sweat Index: break a sweat (moderate) for 2 to 3 miles along the old logging road, then not suitable

Best Features: spectacular mountain scenery and peaks

Availability of Water Along the Trail: Several streams are flowing mid-summer, including Chimney Creek about 3 miles from the trailhead.

Stream Crossings: only one significant crossing, an easy rock hop

Campsites: A few sites are scattered along the latter half of the trail where you find old fire rings.

Alternate Hikes: Though not clearly marked, this trail connects to the Mount Roothaan trail that comes in from the Priest Lake State Forest to the west. By circling through the basin below Chimney Rock and going through two passes, you can find the trail on the north flank of Mount Roothaan.

Wild Notes: Chimney Rock is a huge attraction among those who get their thrills climbing vertical terrain. It is a technical ascent requiring the use of specialized equipment. Only experienced climbers should attempt it, and as with hiking, it is wisest to never climb alone.

Fault Lake Trail No. 59

This trail is part of the 1,200-mile long Idaho Centennial Trail

Destination: Fault Lake. *Map, page 263.*

Best Suited For: hiking, mountain biking, horseback riding

How Much Use: A Little * A Little More * **A LOT** * A Lot More * Excessive

What's it like? For about 4 miles this trail follows an old roadbed. It is now maintained as a trail, but it gets brushy from near Gunsight Creek to where the single track takes off uphill toward the lake basin. The climb is a gentle one until that last mile or so. Along the entire length of the trail, the effects of the 1967 Sundance Fire are evident. Snags still stick up like gray skeletons from the young forest that has regenerated across the mountainsides. The views out over McCormick Creek to the ridges beyond are fabulous. Be on the lookout for some nice waterfalls beyond the Gunsight Creek crossing. Once into the basin below the lake, the magic of the high country casts its spell. Sparse, stunted trees dot the open terrain. High peaks rise before you on the ascent into the slot that drains the lake. A magical cirque cradles Fault Lake. Cliffs sheltering it to the west and stony ledges rising on the east frame the summit of Hunt Peak. From a vantage point just southwest of the lake, the fault line for which the lake is named is obvious. Hardy mountain bikers can make it most of the way to the lake, but the first 3 miles or so are the easiest.

USGS Map: Mount Roothaan

Trailhead: Drive 13 miles north of Sandpoint, Idaho, on Highway 95 and turn west onto Pack River Road No. 231. Travel just over 12 miles to the junction of Road No. 293 and bear left. At a switchback take the spur road straight ahead to the parking area, which will accommodate eight to 10 vehicles. A section of the 1.2 miles to the trailhead along this road is steep and rugged and requires high-clearance vehicles. The trail begins at a bridge over McCormick Creek.

Trail Length: 6.5 miles one-way

Trail Condition: fair to good, very dense brush in places

Elevation: Trailhead – 3,200', High/Low Point – 3,200'-5,980', End – 5,980'

Estimated Duration of Hike: 3 to 4 hours up, 2.5 to 3.5 hours down

Sweat Index: buckets of sweat (difficult)

Mountain Bike Sweat Index: break a sweat (moderate) first 3 miles, then virtually unsuitable due to brush

Best Features: alpine lake with fish, waterfall, close-up look at the effects of the 1967 Sundance Fire

Availability of Water Along the Trail: Two creeks splash across the trail between 3 and 4 miles up.

Stream Crossings: There are several springs and boggy areas along the trail and a couple of creeks to jump across.

Campsites: There are several primitive sites near the outlet and on the rock ledges to the north.

Alternate Hikes: This is a good place to initiate a climb to the tops of Hunt Peak, 7,058 feet, to the south and Gunsight Mountain, 7,352 feet, to the north.

McCormick Lake with a rim of ice on the first day of summer

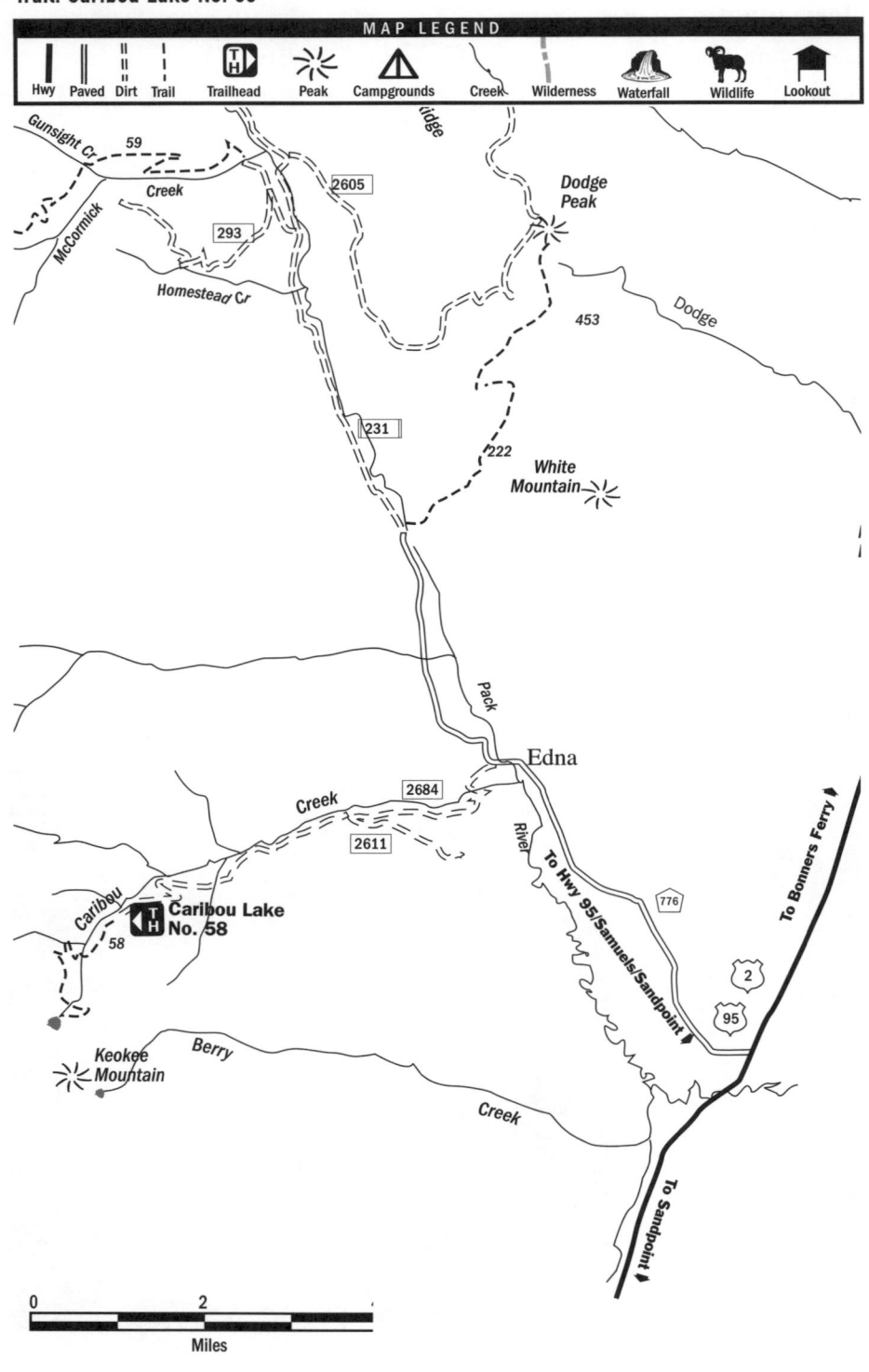

Caribou Lake Trail No. 58

This is a Family Fun Hike

Destination: Caribou Lake. *Map, page 270.*

Best Suited For: hiking, horseback riding, mountain biking

How Much Use: A Little * A Little More * **A LOT** * A Lot More * Excessive

What's it like? A logging road once crossed Caribou Creek, but what's left now is a deteriorating bridge and a roadbed becoming crowded by alders. It is a gentle grade along the road, which is so overgrown with brush it is often like walking through a tunnel. This may make it difficult for horses. Watch closely for the trail branching off to the right (there is an arrow pointing the way) and follow this less than one-half mile through a forest of spruce and fir to the lake. Heavily timbered ridges encircle the lake, and just beyond that to the south you can glimpse the top of Keokee Mountain. There are fish in the lake and moose frequent this area.

A short climb and a ridge away from Caribou Lake is a fine view of Keokee Lake from Keokee Mountain

USGS Map: Mount Casey

Trailhead: Drive 13 miles north of Sandpoint, Idaho, on Highway 95 and turn west onto Pack River Road No. 231. Go about 5 miles, or just a tenth of a mile past the former site of Edna and Buck's (burned in Winter 2004), and turn left on Caribou Creek Road No. 2684. After 4.1 miles bear left and go 2.5 miles to the end of the road at a deteriorating bridge over the creek. There is room for four to six vehicles with a fairly good, though a bit tight, turnaround area.

Trail Length: 1.5 miles one-way

Trail Condition: fair

Elevation: Trailhead – 4,270', High/Low Point – 4,270'-5,192', End – 5,192'

Estimated Duration of Hike: 1 hour up, 1 hour down

Sweat Index: no sweat (easy)

Mountain Bike Sweat Index: bathed in sweat (strenuous)

Best Features: pleasant mountain lake

Availability of Water Along the Trail: Caribou Creek flows by the trailhead and crosses the trail about a mile up.

Stream Crossings: There are two stream crossings; the first over a dilapidated bridge at the trailhead and the second is an easy rock hop.

Campsites: There is a primitive campsite at the end of the trail next to the lake. It is used heavily, and some people don't pack out their garbage. Please respect the land and other visitors to this pretty little lake by packing out whatever you pack in.

Alternate Hikes: This trail and destination are located in an isolated section of Forest Service lands surrounded by state and private timberlands. However, there is some terrific off-trail hiking opportunities here to the tops of Mount Casey, 6,706 feet, and Keokee Mountain, 6,448 feet, and to Keokee Lake (these are the landmarks for which the publishing company that produced this book are named).

Mickinnick Trail

This trail is under construction in 2004

This is a Family Fun Hike

Destination: a ridge between Syringa Creek and Little Sand Creek north of Sandpoint, Idaho, and south of Schweitzer Mountain Resort, sometimes called Greenhorn Mountain

Best Suited For: hiking

How Much Use: Since the trail was only just becoming a reality at the time this book was printed, it's hard to say how much use it will get, but I'm betting it will become very popular.

What's it like? A cooperative effort on the parts of a private landowner, the City of Sandpoint and the Forest Service has made this brand-new trail a reality. It is under construction in Summer 2004, but visitors are welcome to check it out. This trail will climb high onto a ridge north of Sandpoint and provide most extraordinary views of the Pend Oreille River and Lake Pend Oreille, Sandpoint and the Cabinet Mountains to the east. Traversing various habitats, the trail will sometimes be in timber and at other times in open meadows. It will navigate among giant boulders and through forests of huge cedars, ponderosa pines and other evergreen and deciduous trees. Wildflower lovers will love this hike, and those wanting to marvel at the magnificent, scenic setting of the town of Sandpoint will want to go as high as they possibly can, as the views get better with each step up. Contact the Sandpoint Ranger Station for an update on the progress of this exciting new trail.

USGS Map: Sandpoint

Trailhead: From Sandpoint, Idaho, follow the signs on Highway 95 North to Schweitzer Mountain Resort. At the light turn left (west) on Schweitzer Cutoff Road, go one-half mile to N. Boyer Road and at the "T" turn right at the Mormon church. Go 1 mile, turn left onto Schweitzer Mountain Road and go one-half mile to Woodland. Turn left and go one-half mile to trailhead on right with vault toilet and parking.

Trail Length: The first phase of construction will cover roughly 3.5 miles one-way, but ultimately the trail will cover about 9 miles one-way.

Trail Condition: As of press time, pending construction

Elevation: Trailhead – 2,150', High/Low Point – 2,150'-4,300', End – 4,300'

Estimated Duration of Hike: Viewpoints are plentiful along this trail; hikers can go for about any length of time they choose, from an hour or two up to an entire day.

Nicky Pleass at the top of the proposed route for the new Mickinnick Trail

Sweat Index: buckets of sweat (difficult) with some moderate sections

Mountain Bike Sweat Index: not suitable

Best Features: unequaled views of Sandpoint, the Pend Oreille River, Lake Pend Oreille, the Cabinet and Monarch Mountains

Availability of Water Along the Trail: Several small, seasonal streams carry water early in the summer, but don't expect any later in the year.

Stream Crossings: nothing significant

Campsites: none

Alternate Hikes: Someday this trail might tie in with a trail coming from Baldy Mountain.

Wild Notes: Mick and Nicky Pleass moved to Sandpoint from Maryland in the early 1990s, having fallen in love with the wonderful recreational opportunities of northern Idaho. They both loved to hike, ski and be outdoors any chance they got. Mick passed away in 1996 but not before he and his wife, Nicky, decided to donate 160 acres of the large property they had purchased just north of Sandpoint city limits to the Forest Service in 1997. The reason they did so was to make it possible for a scenic trail close to town to be constructed for the enjoyment of all. This is their way of preserving this land for future generations. The result is the Mickinnick Trail scheduled for initial construction in Summer 2004. A joint effort of the USFS and the City of Sandpoint, the trail will wend from Sandpoint's water tower on Schweitzer Cutoff Road to the top of a ridge between Little Sand Creek and Syringa Creek. It is a testament to this couple's devotion to the outdoors and to the community they adopted a decade ago as their home. "Mickinnick" is derived from "Mick and Nicky" and the kinnikinnick plant that is native and plentiful in northern Idaho. The Friends of the Mickinnick Trail have adopted both the trail and trailhead.

Essay:
Lost Summer: 1967

It was a summer like no other, a summer like every other. Snowy winter. Wet spring. Hot dry July. Windy, parched August. Fire.

It was the summer when all eyes were on North Idaho.

It was 1967, and it was the year North Idaho burned.

"It seemed like a long, wet spring," recalled Bill Stockman, "that suddenly dried up." Stockman worked on the Bonners Ferry Ranger District of the Kaniksu National Forest more than 35 years ago. During an interview he vividly recounted how the woods heated up, dried out and then burned with a ferocity seldom seen anywhere.

The result is well-known today as the Sundance Fire. But it was not alone. Lightning pounded the Selkirk and Cabinet mountains from mid-July until late August 1967, causing dozens of forest fires; most were extinguished by a burgeoning firefighting force before they could escape and grow; some weren't. By late August thousands of firefighters from across the country had converged on Bonner and Boundary counties to battle the fiercest blazes in the nation.

"The fire season in northern Idaho developed quite normally (in 1967), and in the first three months showed characteristics of an average fire season," wrote Hal E. Anderson in a report for the Intermountain Forest and Range Experiment Station in Missoula, Montana. He authored a study of the Sundance Fire to figure out what happened and why.

The first critical date was August 11 when, Anderson observed, the fire danger index reached its highest level in 13 years on its way to a level rivaling the storied 1910 fire season. Also on August 11, a thunderstorm shattered the serene North Idaho skies and left five smoldering fires on the flanks of Sundance Mountain straddling the county line west of the Selkirk Divide.

Two of the five were spotted and contained that same day; a third was declared out four days later. A fourth fire from that storm wasn't discovered until August 20, and it too was extinguished promptly. Those four strikes accounted for less than 3 acres of charred terrain.

Then three days later a fifth smoke was spotted on Sundance Mountain near the lookout. Because of increasing fire danger due to severely dry conditions, the fire sprang to 35 acres by the next afternoon, but it was quickly surrounded by fire lines and crews worked on suppressing the blaze for the next five days.

While other fires in the Panhandle had raced out of control – Trapper Peak at more than 18,000 acres, Plume Creek on another 1,200 acres and Kaniksu Mountain which threatened to burn into Canada in the Upper Priest ("We were afraid it was going to cause an international incident!" Bill laughed) – Sundance seemed to be well in hand on August 29.

A little after 10 o'clock that night, however, word came into the headquarters of the Priest Lake Timber Protective Association at Coolin that fire activity had increased throughout the evening – a rare occurrence on wildland fires – and Sundance had jumped its containment lines. Over the next eight dark hours it grew to more than 2,000 acres.

From the town of Dover, the initial blowup of the Sundance Fire was "an awesome sight," remarked Bud Moon who lived there at the time. "Smoke was coming up over Schweitzer and you could see the glow in the dark sky, a dull red glow."

That night's fire activity, however, proved only to be a spark compared to what was coming on the wind two days later.

Vern Eskridge was transportation dispatcher for many of the northern Idaho fires in 1967. He was up Pack River doing reconnaissance the day before Sundance first jumped its perimeter. At 3 o'clock on the morning of the 30th he got word that it was making a run. Strengthening winds pushed embers into Lost Creek that afternoon where a spot fire roared across the lower part of the drainage. Residents in Naples far to the northeast reported ash falling from the smoky skies.

Sundance had doubled in size by early morning on the first of September, the second critical date in the life of this fire. Though the flames were still confined to Sundance Mountain south of Soldier Creek at noon, the temperature was climbing, the relative humidity was dropping and a strong southwest wind blew in.

Two hours later one of the most spectacular fire runs ever witnessed began its deadly tear to the northeast.

On the back of fire-induced winds gusting to as much as 95 mph, the brewing firestorm angrily churned smoke and dust 30,000 feet into the atmosphere. It took only nine hours for the Sundance Fire to travel 16 miles. Once it crested the Selkirk Divide, a wall of hungry flames 4 miles wide burned across the entire Pack River drainage and over Apache Ridge – a distance of more than 10 miles – in a matter of three hours. The radiant heat from the marching inferno was so intense that the west side of Roman Nose erupted in spontaneous combustion so violently that entire trees were ripped from the ground and hurled over the top of the mountain into the tinder-dry forest below.

It was during the height of this firestorm that Luther P. Rodarte of Santa Maria, California, and Lee Collins of Thompson Falls, Montana, were killed while hiding beneath a bulldozer, seeking a safe place where there was none.

Stationed at the lookout tower on Roman Nose high above Pack River, young Randy Langston, just 18 years old and a graduate of Sandpoint High School, was

A firefighter hoses down a smoldering log during the Sundance Fire

forced to seek cover from the rapidly advancing wall of flames. He was quoted in *National Geographic* a year later describing his hiding spot: "The rock shelf had an overhang, and I wedged back under it as far as I could. Flames began roaring over it. I saw blazing branches as long as my arm fly past the overhang and down into the forest around the Roman Nose lakes."

He was rescued by helicopter the next day amidst the smoldering ruins of a vast, blackened landscape while Bud Moon, as county coroner, traveled up Pack River to transport the dead men's bodies back to Sandpoint. Overwhelmed by the desolation, he exclaimed, "It was an awesome sight, like lava hot springs. Everything was denuded. Pack River Bridge was just a mass of twisted steel. The heat must've been tremendous."

Miraculously, the advancing flames died in the fields a mile southwest of Bonners Ferry and on the slopes west of Naples that night as the winds blew themselves into the Cabinets to the east. No serious damage was done to private property and no other injuries were sustained from the monster that devoured so much of the Selkirk Mountains those fateful days long ago.

In the end, the Sundance Fire consumed 55,910 acres. Yet, it was just one of a host of fires that threatened homes and lives throughout the summer of 1967, demanding the heroic actions of thousands of men and women day after day.

"It was a lost summer," sighed Eskridge, "when it seemed like the world was on fire."

For seven straight weeks people like Eskridge and Stockman worked long, hard hours in the battle against Mother Nature at her fiercest. Twice Stockman remembers putting in 36-hour shifts and not having a single day away from the fire effort for seven consecutive weeks.

For years following the blaze, the area burned by the Sundance Fire sprouted new life in the midst of the death and devastation it brought to northern Idaho. The blackened forest produced millions upon millions of mushrooms – particularly morels, which typically follow the path of wildfire. Bumper crops of huckleberries are still harvested today in the upper Pack River, and the vast landscape in the high country of the Selkirks made naked by the flames has become a premier destination for backcountry snowmobilers and skiers.

The effects of the Sundance Fire were tragic, in that lives were lost and a forest was blackened beyond recognition. But life springs anew, and though for many the summer of 1967 was lost to Mother Nature's fury, the memories remain and with them the hope that a fair wind will blow and the thunder will be silent.

Priest Lake State Forest

In 1890 the newly formed state of Idaho was granted sections 16 and 36 of each township from the federal government as Endowment Lands. These lands were entrusted to state management primarily for the purpose of building and funding schools. By 1917 a process of exchanging lands to better consolidate both the federal government's and state's holdings commenced. Thirty-three years later Priest Lake State Forest was one of the results of that consolidation. Land exchanges took place in the 1980s as well when the state traded properties with private timber companies and the present state forest took shape. Today it covers 186,000 acres from the west shores of Priest and Upper Priest lakes to the spine of the Selkirk Crest, from The Mollies in the north to Johnny Long Mountain in the south. It is among the most beautiful landscapes in the Rocky Mountains.

The forest's namesakes are the fantastic lakes hugging its western boundary. The largest lake in the American Selkirks, Priest Lake, is 18.7 miles long, has a maximum width of 4.5 miles, is circumscribed by 72 miles of shoreline, covers 23,800 acres and is 369 feet deep. The smaller lake, rippling across 1,338 acres, is 3.3 miles long, a mile wide and 112 feet deep. Together with the lands surrounding them they form one of the most popular recreational sites in the Inland

A view of Priest Lake from the shoulder of Lookout Mountain

Northwest. Aside from all the fun to be had on the water, the Priest Lake State Forest offers, even if unintentionally so, some mighty fine hiking opportunities. The agency responsible for its management makes no bones about their sole mission on state-owned forested lands – the harvesting of timber. A huge network of roads and widespread cutting units dominate the rugged west side of the Selkirk Crest.

Nonetheless, a nice network of trails has survived, and though they are not maintained by the state, someone has been taking care of many of them, and there are some magnificent destinations to explore on the Priest Lake State Forest. The best access is from Priest River, Idaho, on Highway 57 to the Coolin turnoff. Then follow the roadways to East Shore Road, also Road No. 1, through the length of the forest going south to north. The far north end of this road, at milepost 36, can also be reached from Forest Roads 1013 and 655 in the Upper Priest River. A few trails I heard about but did not explore included Two Mouth Creek, a trail that follows that drainage supposedly all the way to Two Mouth Lakes. I also heard of a trail connecting to that from The Wigwams. I earnestly wanted to go explore The Lions Head but because I knew of no trail and none was shown on any map I had, I never got the time to check it out. However, I later heard that there might be a trail in Abandon Creek leading into that most rugged of all the backcountry in the southern Selkirks. A handout I got from Wayne Kopischke at Priest Lake Ranger Station identified a number of other trails on the state forest, but their status was unknown. Even the state's map of the forest shows more trails than included here, but many of them are questionable as to whether they can now be found. This west side of the Selkirk Crest definitely warrants more exploration. Anyone want to go?

Trails: Trapper Creek, Mollies Lake and The Mollies, Lookout Lake and Lookout Mountain

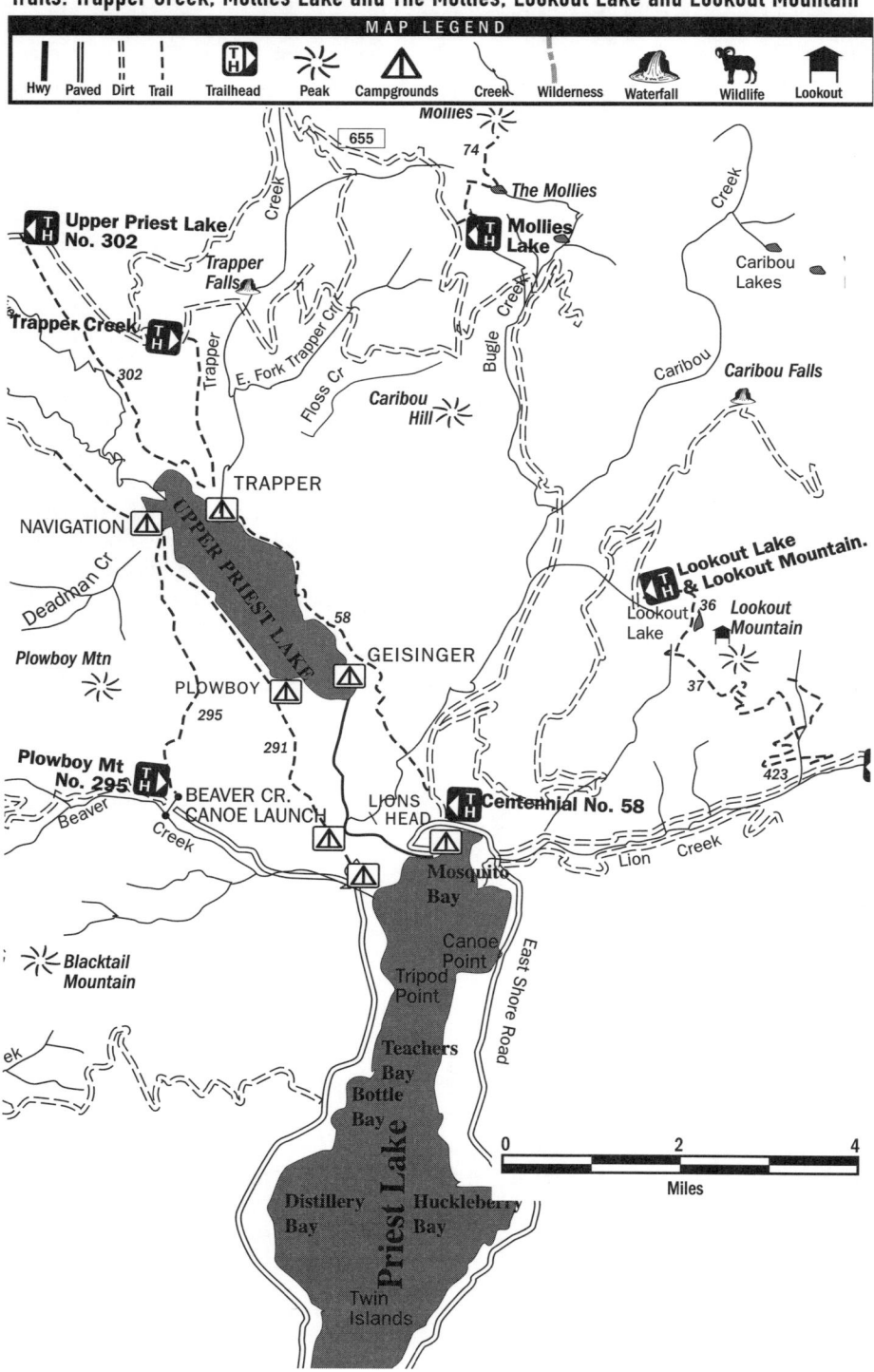

Trapper Creek Trail

Destination: Upper Priest Lake and Trapper Campsite. *Map, page 280.*

Best Suited For: hiking, horseback riding, mountain biking

How Much Use: A Little * **A LITTLE MORE** * A Lot * A Lot More * Excessive

What's it like? What was once a trail is now mostly a roadbed that was cut through the forest, but it doesn't look like it has been used as a road for many years. Brush and sapling trees are growing back into the roadbed, but it has been used enough to keep a path open. Beware of a couple of forks as you go downhill and stay to the left each time. Though it was a road it feels a lot like a wide trail and there are some nice views. Be sure to turn around from time to time for glimpses of Phoebe Tip and The Mollies. Near the end of the road cut, about a mile and a half from the trailhead, a single-track trail heads sharply to the right. It is marked with blazes and white paint on a couple of trees. The trail enters heavy timber and follows a terrace high above an impressive gorge through which Trapper Creek roars. At the lake this trail joins Trail 302 next to a giant whitepine with a dead larch leaning into it.

USGS Map: Upper Priest Lake

Trailhead: From Priest River, Idaho, go north on Highway 57 to Nordman, a distance of 36.5 miles. Continue north until Highway 57 turns into Road 302 and go 14 miles to Granite Pass and the junction with Road 1013. Travel Road 1013 for 10.3 miles to Road 655 and turn east. Go about 2.25 miles to the junction with state Road No. 1 and take it about 1.1 miles to the unmarked trailhead at a spur road taking off downhill at a sharp angle from the main road. There is room for only one vehicle in a wide spot.

Trail Length: approximately 2.5 miles one-way

Trail Condition: fair

Elevation: Trailhead – 2,820', High/Low Point – 2,820'-2,450', End – 2,450' (Trapper Campground on Upper Priest Lake)

Estimated Duration of Hike: 1 to 2 hours each way

Sweat Index: break a sweat (moderate)

Mountain Bike Sweat Index: break a sweat

Best Features: access to the lake

Availability of Water Along the Trail: none until reaching the lake

Stream Crossings: none

Campsites: Trapper Campground on the lake offers several semi-primitive campsites with picnic tables, fire pits and pit toilets.

Alternate Hikes: This trail is the shortest distance by foot to Trapper Campground on Upper Priest Lake and it connects to Trails 58 and 302.

Mollies Lake and The Mollies Trail

Destination: Mollies Lake and The Mollies, 6,512 feet (also called Mollies Tip). *Map, page 280.*

Best Suited For: hiking

How Much Use: A Little * **A LITTLE MORE** * A Lot * A Lot More * Excessive

What's it like? Brushy and sometimes steep characterize the trail to Mollies Lake. Brushier, but maybe not quite so steep, characterize the trail as it continues to the top of The Mollies. Evidently not used a lot, this trail accesses a fabulous destination in the northern end of the Selkirk Crest. Be prepared for rhododendron slapping mercilessly at your legs (you may want to wear long pants). The trail climbs a steep slope through the brush to a small saddle, then wraps around to the south side of the ridge just above the lake. When it comes into view, stop to appreciate the magnificent backdrop to this little forested lake. The trail forks and the right-hand path descends to a sedgy meadow at the head of the lake. It is a small, marshy, delicate site so take care not to cause unnecessary impacts by wandering across the spongy ground. Notice a path beaten through the grasses to the left. It accesses a campsite about 50 feet

Mollies Lake nestles in a dense forest of fir and spruce

away among tall spruce trees. The lake is shallow and silty and surrounded by trees and brush, but it has fish. The left fork continues up the ridge to the top of the Mollies, a collection of four pinnacles separating Bugle Creek from Trapper Creek. Cement footings that once supported a lookout are still there. Watch and listen carefully for the sounds of cows to the northeast in the headwaters of a drainage called, of all things, Cow Creek. A herd of Black Angus was there when I visited this peak.

USGS Map: Caribou Creek, Grass Mountain

Trailhead: Take Highway 57 north from Priest River, Idaho, approximately 23 miles and turn east toward Coolin. Go about 5.25 miles to Coolin and turn east on Cavanaugh Bay Road. Travel another 3.3 miles to East Shore Road (Priest Lake State Forest Road No. 1). Travel north on that road 29 miles. Past Lions Head Campground it leaves the lake and heads up Caribou Creek. Turn north on Road 46 and go 1.7 miles to a prominent saddle (this is a rough road requiring high-clearance vehicles). A narrow, brushy road veers off to the right to a primitive campsite and the trailhead, only about 100 feet away. It is best to park on the main road, as the turnaround is very tight among the big spruce trees at the trailhead.

Trail Length: approximately 1.5 miles one-way to Mollies Lake and 2.5 miles to The Mollies

Trail Condition: poor

Elevation: Trailhead – 4,860', High/Low Point – 5,529' (Mollies Lake), End – 6,511'

Estimated Duration of Hike: about 1 hour to the lake, 2 hours to The Mollies

Sweat Index: buckets of sweat (difficult)

Mountain Bike Sweat Index: not suitable

Best Features: a mountain lake, mountaintop and fabulous views

Availability of Water Along the Trail: one tiny spring with barely a trickle in late summer; otherwise nothing except the lake, which is not a good source of water

Stream Crossings: none

Campsites: There is a fire ring at the trailhead and a primitive site at the lake.

Alternate Hikes: The Mollies is a good place to head out to Phoebe Tip, 6,658 feet. The ridgeline hiking is relatively easy (except for the laborious climb up steep rock to the summit) and the rewarding views are well worth the effort.

Wild Notes: The Mollies are on the edge of the Trapper Peak Fire of 1967, the same year Sundance burned so much of the Selkirk Crest and Pack River to the south. More than 18,000 acres burned in upper Trapper Creek, Bugle Creek and over the divide into Cow Creek.

Lookout Lake and Lookout Mountain Trail

Destination: Lookout Lake, Lookout Mountain, 6,727 feet. *Map, page 280.*

Best Suited For: hiking, horseback riding

How Much Use: A Little * A Little More * **A LOT** * A Lot More * Excessive

What's it like? The long road journey to this trailhead is rewarded with a nicely cleared trail beginning in an old clear-cut. But it soon enters an open forest of big spruce with dense brush. The trail's gentle grade meanders through this high-elevation forest for barely a mile before reaching the lake, a beautiful sparkling gem with a magnificent backdrop. The cliffs and pinnacles of Lookout Mountain rise starkly to the southeast, and the lookout itself can be seen on one of those rocky summits. Beyond the lake the trail climbs easily to a ridgeline where it apparently forks. However, to the right the trail quickly becomes overgrown and impassable. To the left the trail slants downhill until it skirts the end of a road, then turns sharply eastward and starts the long ascent to the top. The higher up, the more stunted and sparse the trees become and the more magnificent the views are of Priest Lake. The last few hundred yards of the trail are along the roadbed that accesses the lookout. However, this portion of the road is steep and full of loose rock. At the summit you will be delighted with the restored, historic lookout and its storage building and you will be in awe of the incredible scenery surrounding this peak. The lookout is still manned at times during fire season.

The historic lookout on Lookout Mountain has a spectacular view of The Lions Head

USGS Map: Caribou Creek

Trailhead: Take Highway 57 north from Priest River, Idaho approximately 23 miles and turn east toward Coolin. Go about 5.25 miles to Coolin and turn east on Cavanaugh Bay Road. Travel another 3.3 miles to East Shore Road. Follow that road approximately 23.5 miles to Road 44 and turn right. Go 2.5 miles to the junction with Road 43 and go 1.5 miles to a fork. Keep right and go another 1.7 miles to a fork. The left fork is gated so go right about 0.1 mile to another gate and the trailhead. There is a decent turnaround area and the parking space will accommodate five to seven vehicles.

Trail Length: approximately 1 mile to the lake, approximately 3 miles to the lookout

Trail Condition: good

Elevation: Trailhead – 4,500′, High/Low Point – 5,564′ (Lookout Lake), End – 6,787′

Estimated Duration of Hike: 30 to 45 minutes to the lake, about 1 to 2 hours to the lookout

Sweat Index: no sweat (easy) to the lake, buckets of sweat (difficult) to the lookout

Mountain Bike Sweat Index: It is not suitable for bikes; however, an old road coming out of Lion Creek switchbacks up the south side of Lookout Mountain and provides a good route.

Best Features: beautiful mountain lake, historic lookout, spectacular views

Availability of Water Along the Trail: The lake and its outlet stream offer the only water along the trail. There is none after the lake on the way to the top.

Stream Crossings: one easy rock hop

Campsites: The trail passes through a couple of primitive sites near the lake.

Alternate Hikes: The national forest map shows the trail into the lake as Trail No. 36 and the trail to the lookout as No. 37. Trail 37 is shown on the map as continuing in a southwesterly direction toward the Lions Head Campground on Priest Lake, but that trail seems to have been abandoned and is no longer maintained.

Trails: Devil Falls, The Wigwams, Upper Standard Lake, Goblin Knob, Mount Roothaan, Hunt Lake, Hunt Creek Falls

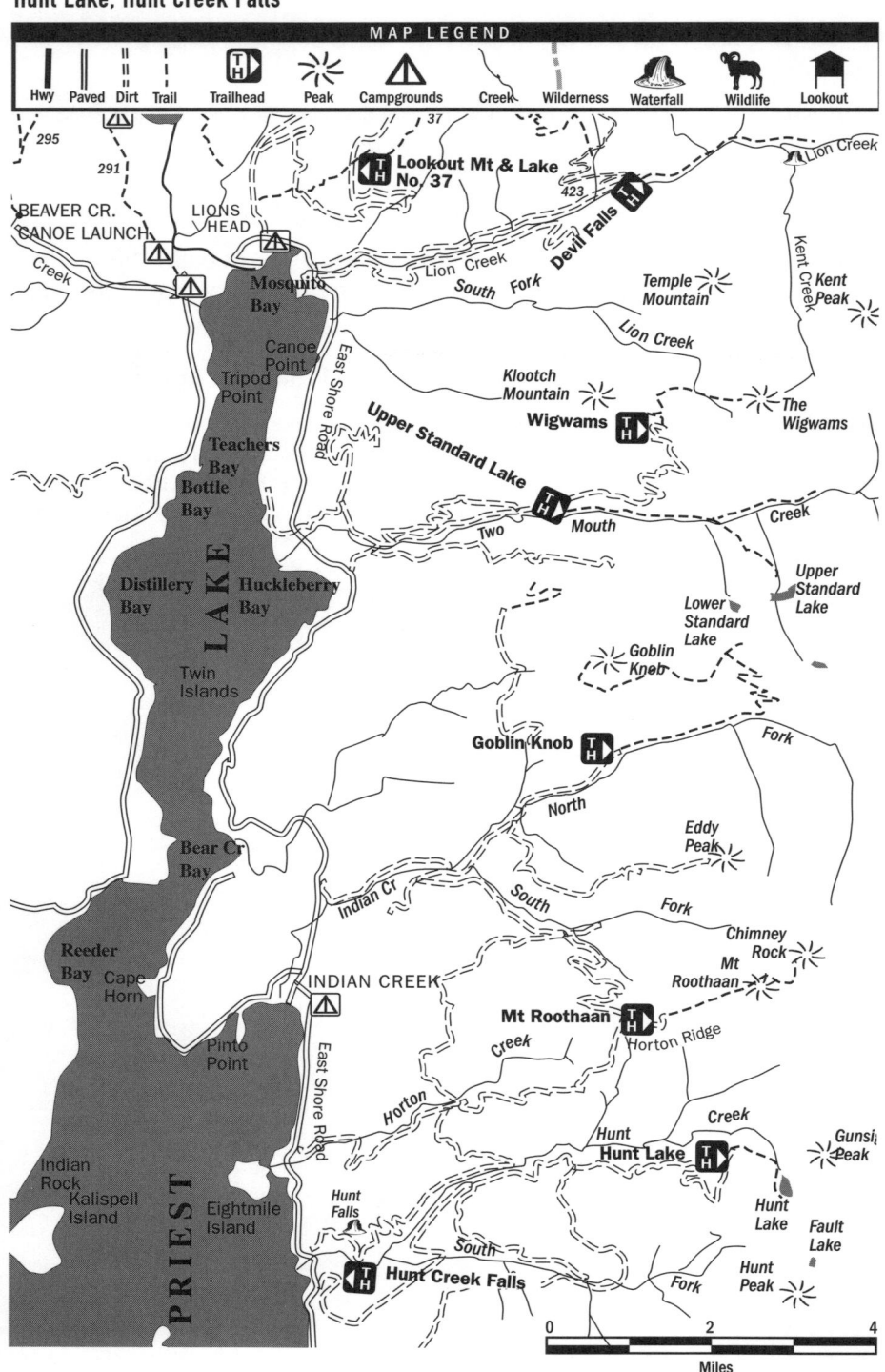

Devil Falls Trail (The Natural Rock Slide)

This is a Family Fun Hike

Destination: Devil Falls. *Map, page 286.*

Best Suited For: hiking, mountain biking

How Much Use: A Little * A Little More * A Lot * **A LOT MORE** * Excessive

Devil Falls

What's it like? The destination of this easy trail may be well-known to locals, but it has been a well-kept secret from many visitors. The falls of the Natural Rock Slide, also called Devil Falls, according to a fellow I met on the trail, are among the most beautiful anywhere in the region. The trail follows a closed road for about a mile and a half, at first through a stand of young trees growing back in a clear-cut, but then through a magnificent forest of old-growth cedar and hemlock. At the crossing of Lion Creek, there are several trees exceeding 15 feet in circumference. Once across the stream the trail follows a rooty footpath through the dark forest of towering trees close to the creek. The nature of this falls becomes apparent once you notice the stream bottom is slab rock. The creek is beautiful as its waters flow in glistening sheets across the granite. But the real treat is at the end of the trail, which comes to a pool one-quarter mile from the end of the road. Splashing noisily into this catch basin are waters cascading a hundred feet down the face of a steeply ascending natural rock slide of smooth-faced granite. A path has been beaten up one side of the falls for views from on top, but be careful when making this climb.

USGS Map: The Wigwams

Trailhead: Take Highway 57 north from Priest River, Idaho approximately 23 miles and turn east toward Coolin. Go about 5.25 miles to Coolin and turn east on Cavanaugh Bay Road. Travel another 3.3 miles to East Shore Road. Take it approximately 22 miles to Lion Creek Road 42. Follow that road almost 5 miles to a barricade on a spur road branching off at a switchback. There is a good turn-around and the parking will accommodate three to five vehicles.

Trail Length: approximately 1.75 miles one-way

Trail Condition: good

Elevation: Trailhead – 3,350', High/Low Point – 3,350'-4,200', End – 4,200'

Estimated Duration of Hike: 30 minutes to 1 hour each way

Sweat Index: no sweat (easy)

Mountain Bike Sweat Index: easy to the Lion Creek crossing

Best Features: waterfall, old-growth forest

Availability of Water Along the Trail: plenty of water

Stream Crossings: There are three plank bridges across small streams along the way, but then Lion Creek is crossed either on a narrow log, by rock hopping or wading.

Campsites: There is a site with a fire ring at the Lion Creek crossing.

Precautions: The temptation is to wear a swimsuit and go down the natural water slide found at this falls, but it can be very dangerous and serious accidents have occurred. This area is receiving more and more visitors because of its extraordinary beauty, so please help protect it by staying on established trails to minimize compaction of the sensitive forest soils. And take out all your trash.

The Wigwams Trail

This is a Family Fun Hike

Destination: The Wigwams, 7,033 feet. *Map, page 286.*

Best Suited For: hiking

How Much Use: A Little * **A LITTLE MORE** * A Lot * A Lot More * Excessive

What's it like? The drive to this trailhead is exhausting in and of itself, but the effort is well worth it. The parking area, which will accommodate four to six vehicles, is on a saddle between Klootch Mountain and the ridge up to The Wigwams. The trail rises gently in a forest of spruce and subalpine fir, meandering through a broad basin cupped by a remarkable ridge of sawtooth granite. A small, muddy-bottomed lake rests at the base of this granite and is the source of the South Fork of Lion Creek, but you cannot see it until on top. After a little over a mile the trail comes to a precipice overlooking the incredible valley of Kent

The granitic headwall of Kent Creek from The Wigwams

Creek and its headwall of smooth granite sweeping upwards to a rugged ridge of gnarly, rocky teeth and pinnacles. Across the valley is the bulk of Kent Peak, 7,243 feet. From here the trail switchbacks to a shallow notch between the rock formations for which this peak gets its name and a primitive campsite, as well as an area that serves as a helispot. To the west a couple hundred feet is the summit with the remains of a lookout; all that's left are two concrete footings. The ridge that descends to the south and west encircling the South Fork of Lion Creek is an awesome spectacle to behold. To the east are the more rugged rocks seemingly impossibly perched on the ridge above Kent Creek. The view north is breathtaking, especially of the jagged peaks of The Lions Head.

USGS Map: The Wigwams

Trailhead: Take Highway 57 north from Priest River, Idaho, approximately 23 miles and turn east toward Coolin. Go about 5.25 miles to Coolin and turn east on Cavanaugh Bay Road. Travel another 3.3 miles to East Shore Road and take it just over 15 miles to Two Mouth Road No. 32. Follow that road about one-half mile to a fork and go left, cross the creek and continue to another fork about 2.5 miles up and go right. At about 2.9 miles there is a sign about Idaho Endowment Lands at a fork. Go left, continuing on Road 32, which now becomes increasingly rough and switchbacks numerous times up toward Klootch Mountain. It is 4.4 miles to yet another fork. Stay to the right on Road 325 and proceed steeply almost another mile to the trailhead at the end of the road. The last 4 miles require a high-clearance vehicle and perhaps four-wheel drive; also be sure to have good tires and brakes.

Trail Length: approximately 2 miles one-way

Trail Condition: fair

Elevation: Trailhead – 5,680', High/Low Point – 6,640' (overlook into Kent Creek), End – 7,033'

Estimated Duration of Hike: 1 to 2 hours up and 1 to 2 hours down

Sweat Index: break a sweat (moderate)

Mountain Bike Sweat Index: not suitable

Best Features: fabulous high-mountain views, panorama of Priest Lake and Upper Priest Lake

Availability of Water Along the Trail: The South Fork of Lion Creek seems to flow year-round.

Stream Crossings: There is one easy crossing on a narrow log; near this crossing there is likely water in the trail early in the year.

Campsites: There is a pleasant, primitive campsite at the stream crossing about three-quarters of a mile from the trailhead and another on top.

Alternate Hikes: Rugged off-trail ridge hiking to Two Mouth Lakes is possible from here.

Upper Standard Lake Trail

Destination: Upper Standard Lake, 5,318 feet. *Map, page 286.*

Best Suited For: hiking, horseback riding

How Much Use: A Little * **A LITTLE MORE** * A Lot * A Lot More * Excessive

What's it like? This hike proves to be a pleasant surprise. The trail follows a closed road for 2 miles, much of it through an old-growth forest of Western hemlock, cedar and larch. A couple of nice cataracts cross the road, offering a good water source and the pleasing, cooling mist of a mountain stream. After a long stretch along the road, it switchbacks and at the third switchback the trail takes off to the east. It is marked with orange flagging. Snaking through the fabulous old-growth forest like it does, this trail provides a primal sensation among these ancient trees. Spruce and subalpine fir eventually dominates the canopy, but some big old larch and hemlock remain all the way to the lake. The trail intersects an old road at one point, but the road has become so overgrown that it is hardly recognizable as a road but for the old skidder cable you might notice at a switchback. The lake is a beautiful, crescent-shaped gem with a few fish and a shoreline strewn with boulders and brush. It appears a helispot has been cleared near the west end of the lake.

Upper Standard Lake

USGS Map: The Wigwams

Trailhead: Take Highway 57 north from Priest River, Idaho, approximately 23 miles and turn east toward Coolin. Go about 5.25 miles to Coolin and turn east on Cavanaugh Bay Road. Travel another 3 miles or so to East Shore Road and take it just over 15 miles to Two Mouth Road No. 32. Follow that road about one-half mile to a fork and go left, cross the creek and continue to another fork about 2.5 miles up and go right. At about 2.9 miles there is a sign about Idaho Endowment Lands at a fork. Road 32 continues left. Take Road 2 to the right, cross Two Mouth Creek and almost immediately there is a fork. Follow the switchback onto Road 325 and go about one-half mile to the trailhead. It is a tight turnaround area suitable for two to four vehicles.

Trail Length: approximately 4.5 miles one-way

Trail Condition: fair

Elevation: Trailhead – 3,600', High/Low Point – 3,600'-5,318', End – 5,318' (Upper Standard Lake)

Estimated Duration of Hike: 2 to 3 hours up, 2 to 3 hours down

Sweat Index: break a sweat (moderate)

Mountain Bike Sweat Index: first 2 miles are easy but the trail becomes less suitable after that

Best Features: old-growth hemlock forest, nice mountain lake

Availability of Water Along the Trail: Several streams offer water along the way.

Stream Crossings: One crossing along the old road has several big logs over it, which may be tricky for horses.

Campsites: Where the trail first approaches the lake, there is a campsite on a knoll up above it, but continue along the trail through the brush to the east to a beautiful site adjacent to the lake.

Alternate Hikes: Trail 321 between Upper and Lower Standard lakes, as it appears on the Kaniksu National Forest map, does not exist anymore, or at least I could not find it.

Goblin Knob Trail

Destination: Goblin Knob, 6,606 feet. *Map, page 286.*

Best Suited For: hiking

How Much Use: A LITTLE * A Little More * A Lot * A Lot More * Excessive

What's it like? From a barricade at the end of the road, the trail follows an old roadbed for maybe one-half mile, then becomes a single-track trail. Dense, small trees – mostly Western hemlock overtopped by skinny Western larch – crowd the trail in an almost claustrophobic manner, but the forest changes from the doghair hemlock to an impressive grove of big cedar and spruce for a short way. This section of trail is fairly well used by ATVs to where the trail splits. Take the left fork, which begins the climb up to a high ridge. The right fork stays in the creek bottom but does not seem to be used much. The ascent, though it covers quite a change in elevation, is gradual along a steady grade. The slope is heavily timbered, and views are limited until high on the mountainside. Then suddenly the panoramas become spectacular. Between gaps in the trees, be sure to watch for the appearances of Chimney Rock and Mount Roothaan, Silver Dollar Peak and the Twins, all to the south and southeast. Several springs cross the trail on the way up, but they mostly contain a bare trickle of water late in the summer. On

On the rocky summit of Goblin Knob

the ridge top the trail forks. Don't go right, even though the tread seems well worn. It quickly disappears into thick rhododendrons and angles downhill toward Two Mouth Creek. Perhaps there was once a trail that went to Standard Lakes from this ridge. To the left the trail goes over a shoulder of the mountain, then slants downhill for more than a mile before climbing slowly back to the ridge west of Goblin Knob. This portion of the trail has not been traveled much in recent years. There are a lot of logs down across the trail and the tread is in poor shape. Once back on the ridgeline the trail becomes even more difficult to follow, but by then the top is so close that it is no problem bushwhacking the final one-half mile. And it is definitely worth the effort. The views of Priest Lake, Upper Priest Lake and the surrounding mountains of the Selkirk Crest are fabulous. Evidence of a lookout is still on the summit.

USGS Map: The Wigwams

Trailhead: Take Highway 57 north from Priest River, Idaho, approximately 23 miles and turn east toward Coolin. Go about 5.25 miles to Coolin and turn east on Cavanaugh Bay Road. Travel another 3.3 miles to East Shore Road and take it 9.1 miles to Road 2/27 and turn right. Follow Road 27 a little over 3 miles, crossing Indian Creek twice, to its junction with road 272. Continue on Road 272 about 1.5 miles to a barricade and the trailhead. The turnaround is tight, but there is room for four to six vehicles.

Trail Length: approximately 7 miles one-way

Trail Condition: good to the ridgeline, poor out to Goblin Knob

Elevation: Trailhead – 3,870', High/Low Point – 5,841' (ridge top), End – 6,606'

Estimated Duration of Hike: 3 to 4 hours up, 2.5 to 3.5 hours down

Sweat Index: bathed in sweat (strenuous)

Mountain Bike Sweat Index: not suitable most of the way

Best Features: excellent views of Priest and Upper Priest lakes and surrounding mountains

Availability of Water Along the Trail: There are two small streams within the first one-half mile then six springs along the trail, three of them up high. Only one will likely have enough of a flow for good water late in the summer.

Stream Crossings: all easy to cross

Campsites: Indian Creek Campground, a state park, is located on East Shore Road near the turnoff up Indian Creek and there is a fire ring at the trailhead.

Wild Notes: A hot fire burned the lower reaches of this mountainside perhaps 50 years ago and left behind a forest that has grown back into what is commonly called "doghair." The phrase is in reference to a forest condition where "trees are as thick as hair on a dog's back." Sapling and pole-sized Western hemlock dominate much of the first mile of trail along Indian Creek and may number as high as 20,000 stems per acre. Farther upslope there is an area of thick lodgepole pine that may also qualify for the dubious honor of being called "doghair."

Mount Roothaan Trail

Destination: Mount Roothaan, 7,326 feet, and Chimney Rock. *Map, page 286.*

Best Suited For: hiking, horseback riding

How Much Use: A Little * A Little More * **A LOT** * A Lot More * Excessive

What's it like? This route provides a much shorter and easier way to Chimney Rock than hiking in from Pack River on Trail 256. The drive to the trailhead is long and arduous and the trail is not well maintained, but it is a great hike along Horton Ridge to the shoulder of Mount Roothaan. From the trailhead, the path enters the forest and follows a gentle ridge until the trees thin out and open meadows afford fantastic views of Gunsight Mountain, Hunt Peak and Sundance Mountain to the south. The ridge then climbs more steeply, and the trail with it, to the rocky shoulder just a few hundred feet below the summit of Mount Roothaan. The trail is braided in places, but each path ends up in the same place. Enough people have made their way to the top to wear a tread through the stunted trees and out onto the rocks, making the climb up relatively easy. From the ridgeline where the trail crosses over onto the north side of Roothaan, the trail descends a short ways then cuts unevenly across the steep face. And right out in front of you will be Chimney Rock. The vista is priceless. The trail essentially

Looking up at Mount Roothaan

ends in a saddle between Roothaan and the Chimney Rock ridge at a nice campsite, but some boulder hopping to another saddle a bit farther east will take you to the edge of the high basin at the very toe of the rock. The scenery is some of the best in the west, guaranteed. It is a pretty easy dash across this basin to the bottom of Chimney Rock itself.

USGS Map: Mount Roothaan

Trailhead: Take Highway 57 north from Priest River, Idaho, approximately 23 miles and turn east toward Coolin. Go about 5.25 miles to Coolin and turn east on Cavanaugh Bay Road. Travel another 3 miles or so to East Shore Road and take it about 4.5 miles to Hunt Creek Road No. 24, just across the bridge over Hunt Creek. Go 4 miles on Road 24 to its junction with Road 2, bear left and go 1.6 miles to Road 25. Keep straight for about a mile to a fork, bear right, then go 0.3 mile to another fork and bear left. About 2 miles up Road 25 you will enter the area burned by the Hunt Creek Fire of 2003. The 4.25 miles up Road 25 are very rough and require high-clearance vehicles and perhaps four-wheel drive to the trailhead. There is a large parking area suitable for 10 vehicles or more. It may be unsuitable to get horse trailers to the trailhead.

Trail Length: approximately 2.5 miles one-way

Trail Condition: fair

Elevation: Trailhead – 6,091', High/Low Point – 7,326' (Mount Roothaan), End – 6,950' (saddle between Mount Roothaan and Chimney Rock)

Estimated Duration of Hike: 1 to 2 hours to the saddle between Mount Roothaan and Chimney Rock and an hour or 2 back

Sweat Index: break a sweat (moderate)

Mountain Bike Sweat Index: not suitable

Best Features: high mountain peaks, rock scrambling opportunities, incredible views of the Selkirk Crest, panorama of Priest Lake

Availability of Water Along the Trail: none

Stream Crossings: none

Campsites: Primitive campsites are located on the ridge tops near Roothaan.

Alternate Hikes: This trail becomes obscure beyond the Mount Roothaan-Chimney Rock saddle, where boulder hopping will get you into upper Chimney Creek, but you can connect to Chimney Rock Trail No. 256 coming out of Pack River below Chimney Rock.

Hunt Lake Trail

This is a Family Fun Hike

This trail is part of the 1,200-mile-long Idaho Centennial Trail. *Map, page 286.*

Destination: Hunt Lake

Best Suited For: hiking

How Much Use: A Little * A Little More * **A LOT** * A Lot More * Excessive

What's it like? From the end of Road 241, you will follow a trail for all of 30 feet before hitting the rocks. It is a scramble from there just about all the way to Hunt Lake. But take your time and enjoy the challenge of negotiating a major boulder field for nearly a mile. It can actually be a lot of fun. Follow the orange and red dots and arrows painted on rocks along the route and you won't get lost. At times you can actually skirt the boulders on segments of trail through the brush, but for the most part the best route is on the rocks. Eventually you will top a high spot, then descend steeply less than 100 feet to a small pond nestled in some trees. Don't mistake this for the lake, which is another 100 yards or so through a strip of timber. Tucked tightly against cliffs

Hunt Lake makes a beautiful destination

and talus, with Gunsight Mountain rising sharply to the east, this is one of the more beautiful lakes in the Selkirks. It has a good population of hungry trout. At the far end of the lake, there is a small cave beneath fractured rock, one end of which has been enclosed by a handy mason to provide shelter in case of sudden inclement weather. And don't miss the view of Mount Roothaan and Chimney Rock from the south end of the lake. It is an interesting perspective.

USGS Map: Mount Roothaan

Trailhead: Take Highway 57 north from Priest River, Idaho, approximately 23 miles and turn east toward Coolin. Go about 5.25 miles to Coolin and turn east on Cavanaugh Bay Road. Travel another 3 miles or so to East Shore Road and take it about 4.5 miles to Hunt Creek Road No. 24, just across the bridge over Hunt Creek. Go 4 miles on Road 24 to its junction with Road 2, but bear right on 24 for 1.25 miles to a fork and go steeply uphill to the left on Road 241. It is 3.5 miles along this rough and rutted road to the trailhead. There is parking for four to six vehicles. Road 241 offers some interesting views of the Hunt Creek Fire of 2003.

Trail Length: 1 mile one-way

Trail Condition: poor (mostly boulder hopping)

Elevation: Trailhead – 5,300', High/Low Point – 5,800' (pothole just below the lake), End – 5,813'

Estimated Duration of Hike: 1 to 2 hours each way

Sweat Index: break a sweat (moderate)

Mountain Bike Sweat Index: not suitable

Best Features: marvelous, high-mountain lake

Availability of Water Along the Trail: none until reaching the lake

Stream Crossings: none

Campsites: There are several primitive sites at the lake.

Precautions: Small children should be watched carefully while proceeding among the boulders. It is a fun climb to Hunt Lake, but broken legs or other injuries are possible if due care is not taken.

Alternate Hikes: The trail continues around the west side of the lake to a "man-way" that climbs to a saddle north of Gunsight Mountain. This provides access to Fault Lake and Trail No. 59.

Hunt Creek Falls Trail

ACCESSIBLE: Though there is not good parking at the falls overlook, a dirt road goes all the way to the bluff. The road is an easy walk and may be suitable for wheelchairs if you park at one of the turnouts closer to the end.

This is a Family Fun Hike

Destination: Hunt Creek Falls. *Map, page 286.*

Best Suited For: hiking, mountain biking

How Much Use: A Little * A Little More * A Lot * **A LOT MORE** * Excessive

What's it like? The walk into Hunt Creek Falls is an easy stroll along a dirt road through a forest of Douglas fir, larch, pines, cedar and hemlock. Though the road is rough and the overlook is undeveloped, this trail is accessible to those in wheelchairs with help from family or friends. The falls seem to be in two tiers with the upper tier the most visible from the well-worn path at the end of the road.

Beware of the steep drop into the gorge. Rocks covered with duff and forest debris overhang the creek and are dangerous to stand on. The upper tier descends about 30 to 40 feet while the lower part of the falls crashes down the gorge for perhaps another 30 feet or more.

USGS Map: Mount Roothaan

Trailhead: Take Highway 57 north from Priest River, Idaho, approximately 23 miles and turn east toward Coolin. Go about 5.25 miles to Coolin and turn east on Cavanaugh Bay Road. Travel another 3.3 miles to East Shore Road. Take it nearly 4 miles to Road 23 bearing right at a steep uphill angle. Go less than one-quarter mile to the first left. A dirt road goes all the way to the falls but it is best to park in the area that has been used as a makeshift campground. There is not a suitable turnaround at the end of the road. The campground area has lots of parking and turnaround space.

Trail Length: One-half mile one-way

Trail Condition: excellent

Elevation: 2,560 feet

Estimated Duration of Hike: 15 to 30 minutes each way

Sweat Index: no sweat (easy)

Mountain Bike Sweat Index: no sweat

Best Features: waterfall

Availability of Water Along the Trail: none

Stream Crossings: none

Campsites: There are several primitive sites with fire rings at the parking area.

Precautions: The overlook at the falls is extremely steep and has no protections in place. Use the utmost caution, especially with children, when viewing.

Essay:
Caribou Conundrum

Sunrise was still a mountain ridge away, but the dawn was already beckoning me out of bed for a day's hike in the Selkirks.

"No," I said out loud to no one but myself. "I can't go. I've got too much work to do."

I stuck by those words for half a day, but by noon the clear blue sky lured me out of the office, and the sun guided me into the mountains. I chose what I thought would be a quick and easy destination: Harrison Lake at the headwaters of Pack River. That was in the days before I knew the upper Pack River Road was like driving through a war zone. Turned out the drive to the trailhead took longer and was more difficult than the hike itself.

It also turned out that half the population of northern Idaho had been drawn into the mountains by the sky and sun and the majority of them had selected Harrison Lake as their destination, too. My fondness for being alone in the woods evaporated by the lakeshore where dozens of people engaged in various forms of backcountry recreation, including noisily rolling rocks off the cliffs to the south. So I climbed the mountainside north of the lake to get away from the crowds enjoying a classic summer day in the high country.

Though their noise reverberated throughout the granite-walled basin, all conscious thought of the other people frolicking among the boulders and along the lakeshore ceased when the movements of a feeding animal caught my attention. I crouched low and began to sneak from one clump of alpine fir to another in order to get a closer look. And the closer I got, the less I could believe my eyes.

Belly deep in skunkbrush and white rhododendron a mere 40 yards away, a fantastic bull woodland caribou contentedly browsed as though nothing in the world was of any concern to him. Undetected, I watched his every move through binoculars in awestruck silence. After half an hour of spying on the unsuspecting animal, I quietly left so as not to disturb the magnificent creature that had rewarded my instinct to obey orders from the sky and sun to go for a hike that fine Sunday afternoon.

It is quite likely the woodland caribou (*Rangifer tarandus caribou*), also called mountain caribou, is the rarest mammal in the continental United States today. In 2002 only 34 of these hearty, high-country survivors inhabited the United States along the Canadian border. An animal that once roamed coniferous forests in New England, adjacent to the Great Lakes and in the rugged wilds of the Pacific Northwest, from the Continental Divide in Montana to the Cascades towering over Puget Sound, the caribou is now confined to one small area in the Selkirk Mountains of northern Idaho and northeastern Washington.

In 1984 the Selkirk population of woodland caribou was listed as an endangered species under the Endangered Species Act. Though it is probable they have never been abundant in the Lower 48, they were once known in the Kettle River Range and as far south in Idaho as the Salmon River. But by 1984 their numbers had dwindled to less than 30 animals anywhere south of Canada. The U.S. Fish and Wildlife Service developed a recovery plan for the Selkirk caribou, as required by the ESA, which began with a population augmentation project. Between 1987 and 1990, 60 animals were translocated from central British Columbia where they thrived in Ball Creek northwest of Bonners Ferry, Idaho. The effort resulted in the establishment of a new herd in the Selkirks.

The surviving caribou at the time of the ESA listing were known as the Stagleap herd and primarily inhabited the country north of the border in and around British Columbia's Stagleap Provincial Park. Some of the released animals moved north and ultimately joined that herd, but others stayed near the release site and formed what became known as the Two Mouth Lakes herd. Two Mouth Lakes are located just 2 miles north of Harrison Lake and the site of the encounter described above.

Of the 60 individuals that were released up until 1990, at least 36 of them were dead by 1997 from a variety of causes. The population held stable for several years from 45 to 51 animals between the two herds, but in 1994 the winter census counted only 39 caribou altogether.

The state of Washington joined in the recovery effort by transplanting 32 caribou over a two-year period in 1994 and 1997. But of 10 animals that were radio-marked in the spring of '97, five were dead within seven months. Through the decade of the '90s ongoing studies indicated survival and reproductive rates were too low to sustain the herds naturally, so augmentation has been necessary in order to keep hope alive for a self-supporting population of woodland caribou in the backcountry of the Selkirk Mountains. Altogether, in 16 years six transplant efforts brought 103 caribou to the Selkirk Mountains, and still the herd struggles with less than three-dozen individual survivors.

A problem with augmentation is that British Columbia, the source of those transplanted animals, no longer wants to share. That's because their own herds have dwindled precipitously over the past decade. In 1997 woodland caribou numbered 2,450 in the B.C. interior, but just five years later the population numbers had dropped 25 percent. In the southern Purcell Mountains east of the Selkirks, a resident herd there had shrunk from 78 to 18 members.

The biggest problem facing woodland caribou in the Selkirks is people. Everyone wants access, whether it is for hiking, mountain biking, on horseback or on the back of an ATV, a dirt bike or a snowmobile. In addition, caribou love old-growth forests where there are lots of big trees. The timber industry loves those trees, too. Between roads and logging and widespread recreation, too much caribou habitat has become degraded and next to useless for them. Yet, there is still enough that the herd could be saved, at least in this one small area, which may not seem so small considering some people believe there are more than 7,000 square miles of critical habitat that could be designated in a four-county area straddling the Washington-Idaho border adjacent to British Columbia for the purpose of recovering this nearly extinct animal. Extinct in the mainland U.S., that is, and that's the conundrum.

There are plenty of caribou in Alaska and a lot of caribou in northern Canada. They aren't endangered. We just don't want them here. We'd rather be able to go where we please, how we please with no interference from anyone or anything.

That attitude, if it prevails, may well be what drives the Selkirk woodland caribou over the brink. And what will follow next? Grizzly bears? Bighorn sheep? Elk? They all need habitat, places to live and raise their young and be secure. We all need that, people too. But only people have the power to take all that away from other creatures. What will we do?

In early September 2003 I took a hike. I drove up the North Fork of Indian Creek on the Priest Lake State Forest as far as I could go then started walking. An old logging road continued for a mile, then narrowed to a single-track trail. The stream it followed was beautiful, but it was impossible to see much because of the dense thicket of doghair hemlock, cedar and larch that seemed to be choking on each other. But once the trail began to climb up the mountainside, the timber thinned out some and the forest opened up, and I could glimpse Eddy Peak to the south.

At the top of the ridge the trail forked. I wasn't quite sure of my location so I went right, which seemed to be the better trail. But within a hundred yards the trail had slid over onto the north side of the slope, and the rhododendron became so thick the trail was nearly impassable. I turned back and went left instead. For the next several miles the trail stayed on the south side of the mountain, which meant it was much freer of brush even though the downfall had not been cleared in years.

As the path angled up through the lodgepole and subalpine fir, I could see it was going to come out on the western shoulder of Goblin Knob, then turn east and lead me to the summit. Where the trail made its wide bend back to the east, it became more obscure and I lost it in the huckleberry and skunkbrush. Thinking I might as well just strike off up the ridge, I took about five steps off what was left of the trail, then stopped dead in my tracks, amazement welling up inside me.

There on the ground, bleached white and chewed to a few stunted nubs, was a caribou antler.

It was obviously pretty old. I supposed it had been shed three, four, even five years earlier, and in my mind I tried to imagine the bull that had stood in that spot one late winter or early spring day, and with the shake of his head an antler fell off. I was over 6,000 feet, so the big fella was up high in the snow at the time, but then, that's where they like it best. They are adapted to harsh terrain at high elevations where the snow piles deep and melts late.

The discovery gave me pause to think about the plight of these creatures, and what part did I play in that by simply being there? We should all ask ourselves that question when we are playing or working in the wilds of the Selkirk Mountains. The answers we come up with will determine the fate of woodland caribou in this magnificent landscape.

North of the Border: A Hike in West Arm Provincial Park

"There's kind of a tricky spot right there. You gotta scale that rock face."

"Kind of tricky" seemed an understatement to me, so I studied that rock face for a moment. The peak on which I precariously perched was narrower than a Creston sidewalk. Broken rocks heaved in all directions. A shallow notch split the peak in two, and in order to ascend the farther rocky knob where Josh danced in the wind would require me to hang out over a thousand-foot cliff above this gnarly terrain eager to break me into a thousand pieces should I slip and fall.

I sat down, studied the steeply sloping rock face for another moment, then took off my pack and dug around for some dried fruit and my water bottle. Josh disappeared beyond the jumbled boulders atop what we had been calling Burnim's Spire for the past couple of days. He was a little embarrassed at having a mountain as awesome as this one labeled with his own name, but it seemed only fitting to me. His trek from the Sawtooth Mountains of central Idaho to the Canadian Selkirks was about to culminate. One mountain along the way named in honor of this fearless hiker seemed appropriate.

He skipped back into view, a 6-foot, 4-inch beanpole standing stark against a blue sky with nothing but open, dizzying space on all sides. "Is that as far as you're coming?" he asked. "Yep," I replied. "Okay."

That's what I liked about hiking with Josh Burnim. After four and a half months and 850 miles on the trail, he could sprint circles around me, even with his 60-pound pack on. He never pushed me beyond what I was capable of and comfortable with. Though we were virtually total strangers when we started, it turned out we hiked well together.

I first met Josh at City Beach in Sandpoint, Idaho, one hot afternoon in August, three-fourths of the way into his epic hike. Enjoying a short rest break from life on the trail, he had called and wondered if I'd like to meet him and find out more about his journey through the wildest country remaining in the Lower 48. Intrigued, I sat in the cool grass and listened to his soft-spoken passion for wilderness, wildlife and the magnificence of the wild country cloaking range after range of mountains from Stanley to Sandpoint. And when he was done, though he had related only the smallest fraction of his adventures, he invited me to hike with him if I could. It took all of three seconds for me to decide I most certainly could.

My first attempt to join him a couple weeks later was foiled by a freak accident. While concentrating on getting a good photo of the bed races taking place in Noxon, Montana, one Saturday afternoon, a bed careened out of control when its left front wheel buckled. The bed crashed right into me. I was hobbled with bruises and aches for weeks and, dispiritedly, had to inform Josh I would miss the opportunity to hike with him.

Then an even better opportunity came along a month later, when my injuries were sufficiently healed to allow me to tote a pack. Josh said I could join him in Canada.

Porcupine Pass is a broad, heavily forested divide between Porcupine Creek and Cultus Creek. It is about 12 miles along a dusty road to the top from Highway 6 just north of Salmo, British Columbia. That's where I hooked up with Josh on a Saturday that must have blown in off the South Pacific. Not a cloud marred the emerald sky and a welcome breeze stirred through the treetops. By 2:00 in the afternoon, Josh and I were striding along a road – a necessary part of the route in order to get to wilder country. We located our first camp a few hours later amidst the rhododendrons choking the banks of North Cultus Creek and chose to sleep out under the stars that night.

As we hiked that first day and throughout the week, we spoke of Josh's purpose in spending an entire summer traipsing on trails, bushwhacking through wicked brush and summiting some of the gnarliest peaks in the Rockies. He was on a journey of discovery from the Sawtooths to the Selkirks to see first hand what obstacles lay in the paths of wide-ranging animals seeking to move along the spine of the continent. Josh was intent on helping raise awareness of the need for wildland corridors connecting the remaining fragments of Rocky Mountain wilderness in order to benefit the wildlife dependent on large, undeveloped tracts of land.

Josh Burnim hiked more than 900 miles from the Sawtooth Mountains in Idaho to Kokanee Glacier Provincial Park in British Columbia

He began the trek at Redfish Lake outside Stanley, Idaho, in early May. In week after week of hiking, he crossed the Salmon River, the Selway, the Lochsa, and scaled mountains in the Frank Church-River of No Return Wilderness and the Selway-Bitterroot. At Lookout Pass, Josh traversed into Montana and found his way to the small town of Trout Creek. From there, he crossed the mightiest of rivers in Montana, Clark's Fork of the Columbia, then entered the Cabinet Mountains Wilderness, forded Bull River and embarked on what he called the most difficult leg of the entire trip, the Scotchman Peaks.

This part of the journey brought him back into Idaho, where he skirted the shores of MacArthur Lake and scrambled over the granitic highlands of Roman Nose, Myrtle Peak and down the lush valley of Long Canyon. On the edge of the Salmo-Priest Wilderness where Washington, Idaho and British Columbia meet, Josh stepped uneventfully into Canada and trudged through a clear-cut on his way to Stagleap Provincial Park and Highway 3. An official refusal to enter the country and several days later, I joined him at Porcupine Pass.

You see, when Josh and his companions at the time reported to Canadian customs subsequent to reaching Highway 3 at Kootenay Pass, there was some disgruntlement that they had entered Canada the way they did. Josh had sent a letter requesting permission to do so, but the authorities refused the hikers entry into the country and sent them packing. The next day, however, the officials reversed their decision and allowed Josh to continue his pilgrimage.

Thank goodness for me, because the grueling, 30-plus miles along which I accompanied him were among the best miles of backpacking I've ever done. Though we encountered roads and clear-cuts two of the first three days out, once we negotiated the treacherous flank of Burnim's Spire, we entered a land of rugged wilderness at the edge of West Arm Provincial Park. To the east lay Kootenay Lake, westward snaked the silvery Salmo River, and to the north glistened the narrow, fjord-like bay of Kootenay Lake called the West Arm.

Burnim's Spire, left, in the Canadian Selkirks

Our greatest concern, following the successful traverse of the spire, was where to find water. We were high in the mountains and preparing to cross miles of open, barren rock and meadows. The highest peak in the area, Ymir Peak, towered to more than 8,000 feet above us, and the valleys, where water might be found, were far below, lost in shadow.

But one of those meadows yielded a tiny trickle and one small pool and we rejoiced at our good fortune. We were equally rewarded that evening when, dead tired and on our last legs, we stumbled upon a glade surrounded by yellowing alpine larch below a remnant snow bank tucked close in against a high cliff. Snowmelt surfaced among the grasses and sedges cushioning our campsite at the humble headwaters of Lasca Creek, and we had ample water once again.

Spectacular would be an inadequate word to describe the country we hiked through those seven days in September. High above the towns of Salmo, Ymir, Nelson, and Harrop-Proctor, we wandered in a magical land gripped tenderly in the colors of autumn. Signs of wildlife – bears, cougars, bobcat, lynx, wolverines, moose, elk and maybe even wolves – were to be found everywhere, offering us the encouragement that in the remote landscape of the Canadian Selkirks, Nature still thrives and seeks only how to connect with wild spaces far to the south.

Josh Burnim has an idea of how that can be done. He did it; he connected the Sawtooths with the Selkirks, though not without encountering the obstacles man has placed in the animals' way, and not without sharing the same fear and trepidation man's intrusion into the wilderness instills in the hearts of its inhabitants.

Our final day took us down the only trail we followed that whole week from a small lake. Clouds had moved in and rain fell softly but steadily. We descended from the alpine heaven where we had found sanctuary alongside the wild creatures living there into a dark forest. At the end of the trail we found ourselves in Harrop where friends and took us in then took us back to my truck left on Porcupine Pass.

In reflecting on those days of backcountry splendor, Josh and I agreed the experience was fabulous, but only served to whet our appetites for more of the mountains north of the border. From the high country of West Arm Provincial Park, we had seen farther north and west where peaks split the clouds and the sky at Kokanee Glacier and in the land of the Valhallas. So many mountains, so little time. But they will be there; it seems like they will always be there, just waiting for the adventurous to go for hike, to go explore the magnificent Canadian Selkirks.

Alpine larch decorates the high country of West Arm Provincial Park above the town of Nelson, B.C.

Appendix 1: Leave No Trace and Outdoors Ethics

For comprehensive information on outdoors ethics and "Leave No Trace" practices, log onto the Internet at www.LNT.org.

Plan Ahead and Prepare
- Know the regulations and special concerns for the area you plan to visit.
- Prepare for extreme weather, hazards and emergencies.
- Schedule your trip, if possible, to avoid times of high use.
- Visit in small groups, splitting larger parties into groups of four to six.
- Repackage food to minimize waste.
- Use a map and compass to travel the backcountry, thereby minimizing the need to use rock-cairns, flagging or paint for marking routes of travel.

Travel and Camp on Durable Surfaces
- Durable surfaces include established trails and campsites, rock, gravel, dry grasses or snow.
- Protect riparian areas by camping at least 200 feet from lakes and streams.
- Good campsites are found, not made. Altering a site is not necessary.
- Concentrate use on existing trails and campsites.
- Walk single file in the middle of trails, even when wet or muddy.
- Keep campsites small. Focus activities where vegetation is scarce or absent.
- Disperse use to prevent the creation of campsites and trails in sensitive pristine areas.
- Avoid places where impacts are becoming apparent.

Dispose of Waste Properly
- Pack it in, pack it out. Inspect your campsite for trash and spilled foods and pack out all trash, leftover food and litter.
- Deposit solid human waste in "catholes" dug 6 to 8 inches deep at least 200 feet from water, camp and trails. Cover and disguise the cathole when finished.
- Pack out toilet paper and hygiene products.
- To wash yourself or dishes, carry water 200 feet away from streams or lakes and use small amounts of biodegradable soap. Scatter strained dishwater.

Leave What You Find
- Preserve the past: Examine but do not touch or remove cultural or historic structures and artifacts.
- Leave rocks, plants and other natural objects as you find them.
- Avoid transporting non-native species into wild areas.
- Do not build structures, furniture or dig trenches.

Minimize Campfire Impacts
- Instead of constructing new campfire rings, use lightweight cookstoves to

prepare meals and candles or lanterns for light.
- Where fires are permitted, look for and use existing fire rings.
- Keep fires small.
- Burn all wood and coals to ash, put campfires out completely then scatter cool ashes over a wide area.

Respect Wildlife
- Observe wildlife from a distance. Do not follow or approach wild animals.
- Never feed animals, as it can alter natural feeding habits and potentially damage their health.
- Protect wildlife and your food by storing rations and trash securely.
- Control pets at all times, or leave them at home.
- Particularly avoid wildlife during sensitive times: mating, nesting, raising young, in winter.

Be Considerate of Other Visitors
- Respect other visitors and protect the quality of their experience.
- Be courteous. Yield to other users on the trail.
- Step to the downhill side of the trail when encountering pack stock or trail users on horseback.
- Camp away from trails and other visitors.

Avoid loud voices and noises so other's enjoyment of natural sounds is not disrupted.

"Ten Essentials" when out on the trail:
1. extra food and water
2. extra and appropriate clothing
3. map
4. compass
5. knife
6. matches
7. fires starter
8. first aid kit
9. sunglasses
10. flashlight

Appendix 2: Who to Contact for Recreation Information

The Selkirks cover a lot of territory and there a lot of people who have an interest in how public lands in this mountain range are managed. This section lists contact information for federal and state government offices, tribal offices and non-profit organizations from which hiking and recreational information can be obtained.

Federal Agencies

U.S. Department of Agriculture, U.S. Forest Service
Idaho Panhandle National Forests
www.fs.fed.us/ipnf

Supervisor's Office
3815 Schreiber Way
Coeur d'Alene, ID 83815
(208) 765-7223

Bonners Ferry Ranger District
Route 4 Box 4860
Bonners Ferry, ID 83805
(208) 267-5561

Sandpoint Ranger District
1500 Highway 2 Suite 110
Sandpoint, ID 83864
(208) 263-5111

Priest Lake Ranger District
32203 Highway 57
Priest River, ID 83856
(208) 443-2512

Colville National Forest
Supervisor's Office
765 S. Main
Colville, WA 99114
(509) 684-7000
www.fs.fed.us/cvnf

Colville Ranger District
755 S. Main
Colville, WA 99114
(509) 684-7000

Newport Ranger District
315 North Warren
Newport, WA 99156
(509) 447-7300

Sullivan Lake Ranger District
12641 Sullivan Lake Road
Metaline Falls, WA 99153
(509) 446-7500

Kootenai National Wildlife Refuge
HCR 60 Box 283
Bonners Ferry, ID 83805
(208) 267-3888
http://kootenai.fws.gov

Little Pend Oreille National Wildlife Refuge
1310 Bear Creek Road
Colville, WA 99114
(509) 684-8384
http://littlependoreille.fws.gov

Lake Roosevelt National Recreation Area
1008 Crest Drive
Coulee Dam, WA 99116
509-633-9441
www.nps.gov/laro

State Agencies

Idaho Department of Lands
Priest Lake Supervisory Area (Priest Lake State Forest)
4053 Cavanaugh Bay Road
Coolin, ID 83821
(208) 443-2516
http://www2.state.id.us/lands/Areas/PriestLake.htm

Idaho Parks and Recreation
Priest Lake State Park
314 Indian Creek Park Road
Coolin, ID 83821
www.idahoparks.org/parks/priest.html

Washington State Parks
Crawford State Park
General Delivery
Metaline Falls, WA 99153
(509) 446-4065
www.parks.wa.gov/parks/

Mount Spokane State Park
26107 N. Mount Spokane Park Drive
Mead, WA 99021
(509) 238-4258
www.parks.wa.gov/parks

Riverside State Park
9711 West Charles
Nine Mile Falls, WA 99026
(509) 465-5064
www.riversidestatepark.org

Recreation and Other Groups
Spokane Backpacking Club
P.O. Box 9142
Spokane, WA 99209
(509) 467-8099
www.host33.com/backpack

Spokane Mountaineers
PO Box 1013
Spokane, WA 99210-1013
(509) 838-4974
www.spokanemountaineers.org

The Friends of Mount Spokane State Park
621 W. Mallon, Suite 509
Spokane, WA 99201
(509) 467-9343
www.mtspokane.org

Pacific Northwest Trail Association
P.O. Box 1817
Mount Vernon, WA 98273
1-877-854-9415
www.pnt.org

Idaho Trails Council
P.O. Box 1629
Sun Valley, ID 83353

International Selkirk Loop
P.O. Box 920
Bonners Ferry, ID 83805
1-888-823-2626
www.selkirkloop.org

Priest River Valley Backcountry Horsemen
4827 Gleason-McAbee Road
Priest River, ID 83856
www.prvbch.com

North Idaho Backcountry Horsemen
1494 Beers-Humbird Road
Sagle, ID 83860

Panhandle Backcountry Horsemen
3595 Greensferry Road
Post Falls, ID 83854
www.pbch.org

Inland Empire Backcountry Horsemen of Washington
P.O. Box 30891
Spokane, WA 99223
www.iebch.com

Northeast Chapter of Backcountry Horsemen of Washington
P.O. Box 3094
Deer Park, WA 99006
www.nebchw.com

Sandpoint Online visitor and recreation information
www.sandpointonline.com

Tribal Groups

Kalispel Tribe and the Camas Institute
P.O. Box 39
Usk, WA 99180
1-800-561-7714
www.kalispeltribe.com
www.camasinstitute.com

Spokane Tribe
Alex Sherwood Memorial Center
6208 Ford-Wellpinit Road
P.O. Box 100
Wellpinit, WA 99040
(509) 258-4581 or 1-888-201-4324
www.spokanetribe.com

Coeur d'Alene Tribe
850 A Street
P.O. Box 408
Plummer, ID 83851
(208) 686-1800
www.cdatribe.org

Confederated Tribes of the Colville Reservation
P.O. Box 150
Nespelem, WA 99155
(509) 634-2200
www.colvilletribes.com

Also see regional conservation groups on page 42.

Appendix 3: Family Fun Hikes

A question I often get asked is, "Where is there a good place to take my mother for an easy hike?" or the children, or the grandparents, or the elderly aunt and uncle visiting for a week? Well, here is a handy-dandy reference chart listing the trails contained in this book that I identified as *Family Fun Hikes*, meaning they are suitable, for the most part, for just about anyone of any age. Many of the hikes are easy or moderate (or, as so aptly expressed in the Sweat Index, "no sweat" and "break a sweat"), and some are difficult (buckets of sweat). I generally tried to keep this list to trails under 6 miles round-trip and with less than 2,000 feet in elevation gained, which does seem a bit ambitious. But who is to say who can hike any or all of these trails? Many of them are easy with little elevation gain involved and some are less than 2 miles round trip. This doesn't mean, however, that more difficult hikes might not be suitable for your mother. This is just a guide to help you select a trail that might be enjoyable to your whole family. For more details, go to the trails description on the page given, then decide for yourself who in your family any of these trails might be suitable for. Here are the hikes I call *Family Fun Hikes*:

Between the Columbia River and Pend Oreille River
  Abercrombie Mountain Trail No. 117
  Sherlock Peak Trail No. 139
  Big Meadow Lake Trail No. 120
  Meadow Creek trail No. 125
  Crawford State Park and Gardner Cave
  Little Pend Oreille National Wildlife Refuge
  Frater Lake Trail No. 150
  Lake Leo Trail No. 155
  Springboard Trail No. 149
  Sherry Trail No. 147
  Crystal Falls Viewpoint
  Upper Wolf Trails
  Lower Wolf Trail Nos. 304 and 305
  Spokane River Centennial Trail
  Little Spokane River Natural Area Trail
  Old Kettle Townsite Trail
  St. Paul's Mission
  Sentinel Trail at Fort Spokane
  Mount Spokane State Park

Pend Oreille-Priest Divide
  Upper Priest River Trail No. 308
  Salmo Divide Trail No. 535
  Hughes Ridge Lookout Trail No. 314
  Mill Pond Flume Trail No. 520
  Mill Pond Trail No. 550
  Elk Creek Trail No. 560

Sullivan Lakeshore National Recreation Trail No. 504
Sullivan Nature Trail No. 509
Hall Mountain Trail No. 540
Muskegon Lake Trail
Granite-Roosevelt Trail No. 301
Cedar Grove Trail No. 301A
Huff Lake Trail
Blacktail Mountain Trail No. 292
Kalispell Rock Trail No. 370
Hanna Flats National Recreation Trail No. 600
North Fork Lamb Creek Trail No. 204
Binarch Creek Trail No. 220
Browns Lake Trail No. 320
South Skookum Lake Trail No. 138
Bead Lake Trail No. 127
Newport Geophysical Trails
Nok-OSH-Kol Heritage Trail at Pioneer Park

Upper Priest Lake Trail No. 302
Centennial Trail No. 58
Navigation Trail No. 291
Portage Trail
Priest Lakeshore National Recreation Trail No. 294
Beach Trail No. 48
Kalispell Island Trail No. 49
Vinther-Nelson Cabin Historic Site

Selkirk Crest
Italian Ridge Trail No. 95
Red Top Trail No. 102
Smith Creek-Red Top Ridge Trail No. 21
Pyramid-Ball Lakes Trail No. 43
Burton Peak Trail No. 9
Roman Nose Lakes Trail No. 165
Harrison Lake Trail No. 217
Caribou Lake Trail No. 58
Devil Falls Trail (The Natural Rock Slide)
The Wigwams Trail
Hunt Lake Trail
Hunt Creek Falls Trail

Now, if you ask me, that's a heck of a choice of trails for Mom. Though some listed here will be too difficult for some people, I am quite certain there are others not in this list that would be suitable for some elderly or youthful hikers. So, check out the ones that most interest you, then judge for yourself how suitable they are for your circumstances.

Appendix 4: Americans with Disabilities Act Accessibility Guidelines

On July 26, 1990, landmark legislation was signed into law by President George Herbert Bush. It marked the beginning of a new era for disabled people and was called the Americans with Disabilities Act (ADA). Aside from the wheels it set into motion for making buildings, businesses and facilities more accessible to disabled people, passage of the ADA also announced a new era of recreational opportunities on public lands. The phrase that came to ring across national forests and recreation areas, campgrounds, boat launches and picnic sites was "barrier-free," and in little more than a decade astounding progress has been made in accommodating the disabled in the Great Outdoors.

The boardwalk to lower Roman Nose Lake

In terms of recreation, the "barrier-free" concept promotes the elimination of physical barriers that inhibit access to sites and facilities designed to provide recreational experiences. This concept addresses the two primary categories of people with disabilities – those who are disabled but are ambulatory and those who must use wheelchairs because of their disability. As new recreation sites on federal and state lands are developed or others are upgraded, the need to expand the recreational experience to those who cannot enjoy traditional opportunities has been more carefully addressed. The Americans with Disabilities Act Accessibility Guidelines (ADAAG) goes a long ways in directing this progress.

In the context of this book, which describes trails primarily used for hiking, mountain biking and horseback riding, accessibility issues are complex. Much of the landscape accessed by the trails covered in these pages is primitive backcountry or outright wilderness. However, a growing list of trails and recreation sites in the Selkirk Mountains are now welcoming people with disabilities. Mind you, the degree of accessibility will vary. Not everyone with a disability will be able to access portions of some accessible sites or trails.

What determines the level of accessibility is largely dictated by four criteria: the width of the path of travel, the slope of that path, its surface texture and the presence of obstacles in the path or overhead. For instance, the accessible trail at Mill Pond is wide enough for wheelchairs, has little or no grade, and few overhanging tree limbs, but it is surfaced with gravel. An accessible trail at Big Meadow Lake west of Ione, Washington, has the same characteristics except it is also paved, which helps it meet the highest level of accessibility for a trail. At Roman Nose Lakes north of Sandpoint, Idaho, a boardwalk suitable for wheelchairs provides access to the lower lake.

The key to identifying accessible trails and recreation sites is simply the transmittal of enough information so that someone with a disability can determine whether a trail or site is accessible to them. As accessibility guidelines have evolved, so have the terms used to describe accessibility. At one point a system of three symbols was developed to help identify recreation sites that meet ADAAG criteria. They are shown in the chart below. The circle is blue, the square green and the diamond brown.

Symbol Key:

● Accessible: Based on criteria within the Americans with Disabilities Act Accessibility Guidelines (ADAAG). Facility is connected with barrier-free-route-of-travel from an accessible parking area. Due to topography and the primitive nature of some sites, these routes may not be accessible to all with disabilities.

■ Useable: Facility allows significant access. Some individuals with disabilities may have difficulty and need assistance.

◆ Non-Accessible: Does not meet ADAAG criteria.

A variation of these symbols can be found in a fine publication produced by the state of Washington and the U.S. Forest Service. Called Accessible Outdoor Recreation Guide (for Washington), it replaces the blue circle with a blue square, the green square with a brown square and a blue asterisk and the brown diamond with a brown square.

In the publication Universal Access to Outdoor Recreation, a series of four symbols are used to denote various levels of accessibility, ranging from easy to most difficult. And in a Forest Service ring-binder called Access for the 90s there is information expressing accessibility in three different "challenge levels." That phrase is used in some Forest Service trails booklets. For instance, Lower Wolf Trail Nos. 304 and 305 on the outskirts of Newport, Washington, are described in the Newport Ranger District's trails booklet as "barrier free trails meet(ing) Challenge Level II Accessibility Standards." These levels basically represent the length, width and slope (running slope and cross slope) of any given path or trail connecting parking areas to other recreational elements at any given recreation site. Level 1 means accessible, level 2 means useable and level 3 means difficult. So the Lower Wolf trails are useable for disabled people but may not accommodate everyone with disabilities. The numbers seem to be interchangeable with Roman numerals when expressing challenge levels.

Below is a list of the trails included in this book that are specifically identified as accessible or may have some accessible characteristics. Read the descriptions and speak with local folks about trail conditions to determine for yourself how accessible they may be for you. Some of these trails are officially designated as barrier-free and accessible to people with disabilities, but not all of them. I took the liberty of identifying some trails as accessible if they seemed to have some characteristics that meet ADAAG criteria.

Between the Columbia River and the Pend Oreille River
    South Fork Silver Creek Trail No. 123
    Meadow Creek Trail No. 125
    Crawford State Park
    Little Pend Oreille National Wildlife Refuge
    Frater Lake Trail No. 150
    Sherry Trail No. 147
    Upper and Lower Wolf Trails
    Spokane River Centennial Trail

Pend Oreille-Priest Divide
    Salmo Divide Trail No. 535
    Mill Pond Historic Site and Mill Pond Flume Trail No. 520
    Muskegon Lake Trail
    Roosevelt Grove of Ancient Cedars and Cedar Grove Trail No. 301A
    Huff Lake Interpretive Site
    Hanna Flats National Recreation Trail No. 600
    Browns Lake Trail No. 320
    Bead Lake Trail No. 127
    Nok-OSH-Kol Heritage Trail at Pioneer Park
    Portage Trail at Beaver Creek Campground
    Beach Trail No. 48

Selkirk Crest
    Kootenai National Wildlife Refuge
    Roman Nose Lakes Trail No. 165
    Hunt Creek Falls Trail

Here are some sources to go to for more information on accessibility issues.

    U.S. Access Board
    1-800-872-2253
    www.access-board.gov

    National Center for Physical Activity and Accessibility
    1-800-900-8086
    www.ncpad.org

    Interagency Committee for Outdoor Recreation
    (360) 902-3000
    www.iac.wa.gov

    Accessible Outdoor Recreation Guide
    (360) 902-8844
    www.parks.wa.gov/ada-rec

    To contact the Disability and Business Technical Assistance Center in Colorado Springs, call 1-800-949-4232.

Appendix 5: The National Recreation Trails System

There are literally thousands and thousands of miles of hiking trails across America. Some are great, some are mundane, many are maintained; many more are not. As a way of recognizing trails of particular interest and special value, the National Trail System Act of 1968 authorized the creation of three categories of trails that could receive special attention and care. They were identified as National Recreation Trails, National Scenic Trails and National Historic Trails. The last two can only be designated by acts of Congress, but the first category, National Recreation Trails (NRT), can be designated by the Secretary of Interior (National Parks) or the Secretary of Agriculture (National Forest lands). The designation recognizes exemplary trails of local and regional significance. The benefits that go with these designations include governmental assistance in promotion and help with technical matters and networking, plus access to funding. These trails are also included in the online database. The goal is to enhance the use and care of existing trails and to stimulate the development of new trails.

There are more than 800 trails in all 50 states in the National Recreation Trail system. They range from less than a mile to 485 miles in length. In the Selkirk Mountains there are five National Recreation Trails. They are trails of extraordinary beauty, or they access areas of specialized habitats.

National Recreation Trails in the Selkirk Mountains
Colville National Forest, Washington
Grassy Top National Recreation Trail No. 503
Sullivan Lakeshore National Recreation Trail No. 504
Idaho Panhandle National Forests, Idaho
Chipmunk Rapids National Recreation Trail No. 192
Hanna Flats National Recreation Trail No. 600
Priest Lakeshore National Recreation Trail No. 294

Remember when visiting these trails, or any others on public lands, to take care of the environment you pass through. These trails often traverse areas sensitive to the impacts people have on the landscape. If we each take care of the places we visit, they will always be better off for the next visitor.

For more information visit these websites:

www.americantrails.org/nationalrecreationtrails

www.nps.gov/nts/nrt.html

Appendix 6: Idaho Centennial Trail and Pacific Northwest Trail

There are two long-distance trails (or routes) that pass through the Selkirk Mountains. In keeping with the traditions begun by the Appalachian Trail on the East Coast, the Pacific Crest Trail on the West Coast and the Continental Divide Trail along the spine of the Rockies, these two trails are destined to become magnets for cross-country hikers.

Idaho Centennial Trail

In 1990, in celebration of its 100th year of statehood, the state of Idaho adopted a 1,200-mile route as the official Idaho Centennial Trail. A combination of single-track trails, jeep trails and dirt roads were selected to form one of the most diverse and scenic recreation trails in the nation. In the Selkirk Mountains of the Idaho Panhandle, the Centennial Trail's northernmost segments traverse trails and terrain covered in this book, *Trails of the Wild Selkirks*.

The idea for such a trail came from two men who, in 1986, embarked on an epic journey through Idaho's most rugged and remote backcountry. Roger Williams and Syd Tate began their trek in the heart of the Owyhee Desert in Black Rock Canyon on the Idaho-Nevada border. For 86 days they averaged 14 miles per day en route to Upper Priest Falls less than one-half mile from the Canadian Border in the heart of the temperate rainforest country of the Upper Priest River.

Once this magnificent odyssey was completed, Williams, a long-time member and past president of the Idaho Trails Council, advanced the notion of the Centennial Trail at the Council's annual meeting in 1987. The picture slides he presented of his and Tate's remarkable journey easily swayed Council members to take up the cause. Three years later, after much debate and refinement of the exact route, the trail was adopted by the Idaho Parks and Recreation Board and the National Forests and BLM Districts that participated in its creation.

Establishment of the Idaho Centennial Trail was a monumental milestone in promoting recreation of all types. Unlike many other long-distance trails, this trail encourages and allows users of all stripes to enjoy this trail; hikers, mountain bikers, horseback riders, skiers, snowshoers and motorized users. Where the trail passes through wilderness or other areas off-limits to ATVs, dirt bikes and mountain bikes, an alternative route exists for those users.

In 1998, the Idaho Trails Council released Discover Idaho's Centennial Trail by Stephen Stuebner with photographs from Roger Williams. It is the first and most comprehensive book to date on these 1,200 miles. For more information about the Idaho Centennial Trail and any other questions you might have regarding trails and recreation in Idaho, contact the Idaho Trails Council at P.O. Box 1629, Sun Valley, ID 83353. To learn more about the trails in far northern Idaho that make up part of the Centennial Trail, refer to the descriptions in this book for Fault Lake Trail No. 59, Hunt Lake Trail, Upper Priest Lake Centennial Trail No. 58 and Upper Priest River Trail No. 308.

Pacific Northwest Trail

In 1970, Ron Strickland had a dream of creating a cross-country, national scenic trail from the Continental Divide in Montana to the Pacific coast on the Olympic Peninsula in Washington. His vision was for a route from Glacier National Park to Olympic National Park through the North Cascades. Thus was born the Pacific Northwest Trail (PNT), a route that follows trails and roads and goes terrain with neither for over 1,100 miles. Though some portions of the route are still to be definitively determned, the concept grew quickly through the 1990s and an association evolved that now promotes the care and use of the PNT.

The Selkirk Mountains from the Kootenai River in Idaho to the Columbia River in Washington is one section whose exact path for the PNT remains uncertain. Efforts are afoot to better establish the route through the Selkirks. At this time, the Pacific Northwest Trail more or less corresponds to the directions below from Bonners Ferry, Idaho to Northport, Washington. Some portions of this route are subject to change in the future.

- Cross the Kootenai River at Copeland Bridge about 15 miles north of Bonners Ferry and take West Side Road No. 417 to Parker Creek Trail No. 14.
- Follow that trail to its junction with Parker Ridge Trail No. 221 and follow it to its junction with Pyramid Pass Trail No. 13
- Take Trail 13 to Pyramid Lake-Ball Lakes Trail No. 43 and proceed to Ball Lakes.
- From Ball Lakes, the route strikes off cross-country to the ridge top, then bushwhacks down into Lion Creek to Lion Creek Road. At the junction with gated Road 423, the PNT follows this closed road to the summit of Lookout Mountain.
- From here, Trail No. 37 once descended to the southwest and connected to Road 43. That trail is not maintained and is difficult to follow. However, the trail does drop down to Lookout Lake and goes out to a road high on the mountain. The idea is to reach Centennial Trail No. 58 that leads to Upper Priest Lake.
- Once on Trail 58, follow it to Trail 302.
- Continue on Trail 302 to Forest Service Road No. 655 and follow it to Road No. 1013 and carry on to Upper Priest River Trail No. 308.
- Follow Trail 308 to its junction with Little Snowy Top Trail No. 349. Keep in mind, however, that Trail 349 was wiped out in an avalanche in 2003. However, a project is planned to be launched in the summer of 2004 to reconstruct this trail. An alternative is to take Cabinet Pass Trail No. 317 from Trail 308 to Hughes Ridge Trail No. 315.
- Go on Trail 315, which is an old logging road for miles, until it joins Shedroof Divide Trail No. 512. Here you can go two different directions – take Trail 512 north to its junction with Salmo Basin Trail No. 506 and that

trail to the Salmo Pass trailhead, or take Trail 512 south to its junction with Salmo Divide Trail No. 535 and that trail to Salmo Pass.

- From Salmo Pass, the route becomes less certain. There are several alternatives and a final route for the PNT from here to Northport is still in the formative stages. One option is to follow Sullivan Creek Road and other roads to the north end of Crowell Ridge Trail No. 515, a trailhead called Bear Pasture. Once on that trail, follow it to the junction with North Fork Sullivan Creek Trail No. 507, which in turn leads to Halliday Trail No. 522, which then comes out on Highway 31 a few miles north of Metaline Falls.

- Once on Highway 31, the best choice seems to be to stay on the highway going south until it crosses the Pend Oreille River, then get on Boundary Dam Road and follow it to Road No. 350 that climbs to the trailhead for Flume Creek Trail No. 502. Near the summit of Abercrombie Mountain this trail ties in with Abercrombie Mountain Trail No. 117. The other option at the end of Trail 522 is to go north on Highway 31 and cross the river at Boundary Dam, but then it is a long ways south to the access for Trail 502, or there are miles and miles of logging roads to follow all the way to Northport.

- If you go to Trail 117, follow it to its junction with North Fork Silver Creek Trail No. 119 and descend to the Silver Creek Trailhead. From there, take Silver Creek Road out to the Aladdin Highway and follow it all the way to Northport where you can cross the Columbia River.

There is a guidebook available for the PNT written by Ron Strickland. It was published in 2001 and contains a great deal of detail and history relating to the PNT. You may find the route through the Selkirks described in the book to be somewhat different from what I have outlined above, but information I received from the Pacific Northwest Trail Association suggests the final route through the Selkirks that will comprise this section of the PNT is still evolving.

For more information about this monumental cross-country trail go online to www.pnt.org or call 1-877-854-9415. The association is headquartered in Mount Vernon, Washington.

Appendix 7A: Mileage Chart

Distances between towns and cities in and around the Selkirks

The Selkirk Mountains have had people living in them for literally thousands of years, but cities and towns connected by roads are a relatively recent development. In 120 years the population of the area has exploded, and hundreds upon hundreds of miles of roads have been built to connect the communities that sprang up along the rivers and valleys of this mountain range. Below is a chart with the miles between many of those towns. Some are on the fringes of the range and some, like Nordman, Idaho, are in the heart of the range. It seemed valuable to me to have a quick reference chart noting the distances between many of these towns that provide access to the trails in the Selkirks.

TOWN	1.	2.	3.	4.	5.	6.	7.	8.	9.	10.	11.	12.	13.	14.	15.	16.	17.	18.	19.
1. Bonners Ferry ID	-	95	82	143	86	77	111	153	122	120	12	59	89	184	55	33	117	77	164
2. Chewelah WA	95	-	87	21	77	30	62	31	73	71	91	44	86	62	50	72	50	28	40
3. Coeur d'Alene ID	82	87	-	103	76	61	93	113	104	102	73	43	85	144	49	48	32	59	79
4. Colville WA	143	21	103	-	115	64	40	10	51	49	131	82	134	41	88	110	71	66	61
5. Coolin ID	86	77	76	115	-	51	83	125	94	92	65	33	19	156	27	49	81	49	128
6. Cusick WA	79	30	61	64	51	-	32	74	43	41	67	18	60	105	24	42	49	2	70
7. Ione WA	111	62	93	40	83	32	-	50	11	9	99	50	92	81	56	78	84	34	101
8. Kettle Falls WA	153	31	113	10	125	74	50	-	61	59	141	92	144	31	98	120	81	76	71
9. Metaline Falls WA	122	73	104	51	94	43	11	61	-	2	110	61	103	92	67	89	105	45	112
10. Metaline WA	120	71	102	49	92	41	9	59	2	-	108	59	101	90	65	87	103	43	110
11. Naples ID	12	91	73	131	65	67	99	141	110	108	-	47	77	172	41	21	105	45	152
12. Newport WA	59	44	81	82	33	18	50	92	61	59	47	-	42	123	6	28	48	16	95
13. Nordman ID	89	86	85	134	19	60	92	144	103	101	77	42	-	175	36	58	90	58	137
14. Northport WA	184	62	144	41	156	105	81	31	92	90	172	123	175	-	129	151	112	107	102
15. Priest River ID	55	50	49	88	27	24	56	98	67	65	41	6	36	129	-	22	54	22	101
16. Sandpoint ID	33	72	48	110	49	42	78	120	89	87	21	28	58	151	22	-	76	44	123
17. Spokane WA	117	50	32	71	81	49	84	81	105	103	105	48	90	112	54	76	-	50	47
18. Usk WA	77	28	59	66	49	2	34	76	45	43	63	16	58	107	22	44	50	-	68
19. Wellpinit WA	164	40	79	61	128	70	101	71	112	110	152	95	137	102	101	123	47	68	-

Appendix 7B: Mileposts

There is a large network of roads throughout the Selkirk Mountains, providing access to dozens of trailheads. Many of the trails are well signed and easy to find but some are not. The tables below will help you identify the approximate location of a trailhead. Most of the roads have milepost markers, but keep in mind that some of the miles and the decimals were taken from the odometer on my 1990 Dodge Dakota pickup. Your odometer might read slightly different from mine and give you a different milepost reading. In a few cases an odometer reading was unavailable so I estimated mileage as best I could. These tables are inteded to provide a good reference to the access for almost every trail in this book.

1. Tiger Highway (Washington State Hwy 20) – winding, paved 2-lane road

Mileposts go backwards from end of the highway at Newport, Washington.

MILEPOST	LANDMARK
437	Newport Ranger Station at Newport, WA
437	Warren Street access to Lower Wolf trails system
436.9	Larch Street access to Upper Wolf trails system
421	Junction with Flowery Trail Road to 49 Degrees North Ski Area and the road to Usk, WA and access to Browns Lake and South Skookum Lake
419	Cusick, WA
418.5	Junction with Kapps Lane and access to Batey-Bould trails system
390.4	Tiger Store and junction with Highway 31
384	Frater Lake Trail 150 and Lake Leo Trail 155
379.1	Access to Lake Thomas, Gillette Lake and Gillette Campgrounds and access to Trails 142, 148 and 149.
378.6	Sherry trailhead for Trail 147
373.8	Tacoma Creek Road and access to Flodelle Creek Campground, Tacoma Divide, Batey-Bould and Little Pend Oreille trails systems
360.3	Access to Little Pend Oreille National Wildlife Refuge
355.4	Junction with Aladdin Road
354.7	Junction with Highway 395 in downtown Colville, WA

2. Aladdin Highway (County Road No. 9435) – narrow, paved 2-lane road

This road does not have any mileposts that I saw, so the mileages given are what I read from my odometer.

MILEPOST	LANDMARK
0.0	Colville, WA
15.5	Clinton Creek Road No. 500 and access to Trails 130, 131 and 132
19.5	Meadow Creek Road No. 4702 and access to Big Meadow Lake and Trails 120 and 125
25.7	Junction with Deep Lake-Boundary Road No. 9445 and access to the Silver Creek trailhead and Trails 117, 119, 123, and 139
37.3	Junction with Highway 25 in Northport, WA

3. Ione Highway (Washington State Highway 31) – 2-lane paved road

MILEPOST	LANDMARK
0.0	Tiger, WA at junction with Highway 20
3.0	Sullivan Lake Road and access to Noisy Creek trail and campground
4.0	Ione, WA city center
6.9	Box Canyon Dam viewpoint
12.7	Metaline, WA
13.1	Junction with Boundary Road and access to mountain goat viewing area, Flume Creek Trail 502, Boundary Dam and Crawford State Park
14.0	Bridge over Pend Oreille River
14.1	Metaline Falls, WA city center
16.4	Sullivan Lake Road and access to Mill Pond Historical Site and Red Bluff Trail No. 553
20.6	Halliday Trail No. 522 trailhead
21.8	Slate Creek Road and access to Trail 525
27.0	Canadian Border

4. Sullivan Lake Road – a narrow, winding paved 2-lane highway

MILEPOST	LANDMARK
0.0	Ione, WA and junction of Highway 31
7.0	Harvey Creek Road 1935 and access to Grassy Top National Recreation Trail No. 503 and Kalispell Rock-North Baldy Trail No. 103
8.4	Noisy Creek Campground and access to Trails 504 and 588
8.5	Bridge over Harvey Creek inlet to Sullivan Lake
12.5	Bridge over outlet of Sullivan Lake
12.6	Sullivan Lake Ranger Station
13.0	Road 22 and access to Salmo Mountain and Pass Creek Pass and area trails
13.3	Highline Road and access to Sullivan Mountain Lookout and Crowell Ridge Trail No. 515
13.8	Trailhead for Trail 553
14.1	Mill Pond Campground
14.5	Mill Pond Historical Site
17.8	Junction with Highway 31, 2.3 miles north of Metaline Falls, WA

5. Pass Creek Pass Road No. 22 – a gravel road

MILEPOST	LANDMARK
0.0	Sullivan Lake Road near the Sullivan Lake Ranger Station
0.3	East and West Sullivan Campgrounds and access to Trail 504
6.0	Junction with road 2220 and access to Salmo Mountain and Trails 511 and 526
12.4	Trailhead for Grassy Top National Recreation Trail No. 503
12.5	Pass Creek Pass, road merges into road 302, Shedroof Divide Trail No. 512 is one-quarter mile over the pass

6. Priest Lake Highway (Idaho State Highway 57) – 2-lane paved road

MILEPOST	LANDMARK
0.0	Priest River, ID at junction with Highway 2
3.5	Peninsula Road and access to Peewee-Steep Creek Trails 175-179
8.7	Peterson Road and access to Peewee-Steep Creek Trails 175-179
21.5	Junction with Squaw Valley Road and access to Trails 162 and 164
22.1	Priest Lake Information Center and access to Chipmunk Rapids National Recreation Trail No. 192
22.5	Coolin Road and access to Priest Lake State Forest
24.2	Binarch Creek Road 639 and access to Trail 220
26.0	Outlet Road and access to Trails 48, 235 and 274 and Outlet and Osprey Campgrounds
28.6	Luby Bay Road and access to Trails 48, 235 and 274, Luby Bay Campground and Priest Lake Museum
28.9	Lamb Creek Road 310 and access to Trails 204 and 220
31.5	Kalispell Bay Road and access to Trails 48, 49 and 365 and Kalispell Bay Boat Launch
31.7	Hanna Flats Road and access to Hanna Flats Grove of Ancient Cedars National Recreation Trail No. 600 and Trails 204 and 232
32.2	Priest Lake Ranger Station
34.9	Kalispell Creek Road 308 and access to Trails 241 and 370
35-36	Bismark Meadows
35.7	Trailhead for Lakeview Mountain Trail No. 269
36.5	Nordman and junction with Reeder Bay Road and access to Trails 365 and 294, 291 and 295 and the Thorofare to Upper Priest Lake, plus Reeder Bay, Beaver Creek Ledgewood recreation sites
37.2	End Highway 57 and start Road 302

7. Forest Road 302 – a 2-lane improved gravel road

MILEPOST	LANDMARK
0.0	Three-quarters of a mile north of Nordman, ID at end of Highway 57
3.0	End of pavement, junction with Tango Creek Road 638; to Trail 292
6.8	State Line – leave Idaho enter Washington
9.4	The "Shoe Tree" at Tillicum Creek trailhead
10.5	Huff Lake Interpretive Site
11.8	Trailhead for North Fork-Grassy Top Trail 379
12.0	Stagger Inn and the Roosevelt Grove of Ancient Cedars and Trail 301
12.1	Trailhead for Trail 266 and access to Trails 256, 265 and 293
13.9	Granite Pass and junction with Road 1013
21.0	Approximate location of trailhead for Shedroof Divide Trail No. 512 about one-quarter mile from Pass Creek Pass

8. Forest Road 1013 – 1-lane dirt road with turnouts

MILEPOST	LANDMARK
0.0	Granite Pass at junction with Road 302 about 14.5 miles north of Nordman, ID
1.2	Muskegon Campsite and trail to Muskegon Lake

1.4	State Line – leave Washington enter Idaho
4.2	Junction with Road 662 and access to Hughes Meadows and Hughes Ridge and Trails 311, 312 and 314
5.2	Access to Navigation Trail 291
6.2	Bridge across the Upper Priest River
6.7	Junction with Road 655 and access to Trail 302, Trapper Creek Trail and Priest Lake State Forest
11.3	Trailhead for Trail 308 and access to Trails 317 and 315
22.6	Trailhead for Trail 28 and end of road (barricade)

9. East Lakeshore Road (Priest Lake State Forest Road 1 – part paved, part gravel)

MILEPOST	LANDMARK
0.0	Junction with Cavanaugh Bay Road at Coolin, ID
4.0	Road 23 and access to Hunt Creek Falls Trail
4.5	Hunt Creek Road 24 and access to Hunt Lake, Mt. Roothaan and Chimney Rock
8.0	Indian Creek Unit of Priest Lake State Park
9.1	Road 2/27 and access to Goblin Knob Trail
15.1	Two Mouth Creek Road 32 and access to Upper Standard Lake and The Wigwams
22.0	Lion Creek Road 42 and access to Devil Falls (the Natural Rock Slide)
22.0	Lions Head Unit of Priest Lake State Park
23.5	Caribou Creek Road 44 and access to Lookout Lake and Lookout Mountain trail
29.0	Road 46 and access to The Mollies and Mollies Lake trail
34.9	Trailhead for Trapper Creek Trail
36.0	Junction with Forest Service Road 655 and access to Trail 302 and Upper Priest River

10. Upper Pack River Road (County Road 776 and Forest Service Road 231) – 2-lane gravel road that becomes a rugged 1-lane dirt road (mileposts have been estimated)

MILEPOST	LANDMARK
0.0	Junction with Highway 95, 13 miles north of Sandpoint, ID
5.0	Edna and Buck's (burned down in early 2004)
5.1	Caribou Creek Road 2684 and access to Trail 58
7.5	Snowmobile Parking Area
8.0	Spur road access to Trail 222
12.5	Junction with Road 293 and access to Trail 59
14.0	Junction with Pearson Creek Road 2605 and access to Trails 222 and 453 and Dodge Peak Road
16.0	Junction with Road 2653 and access to Chimney Rock Trail No. 256
19.0	Trailhead for Beehive Lakes Trail No. 279
20.5	Trailhead for Harrison Lake Trail No. 217

11. **West Side Road** (County Road 18 on 2003 Kaniksu Forest Map; also identified as Forest Road 417 on 1988 Kaniksu Forest Map) – 2-lane paved road

   MILEPOST   LANDMARK
   0.0   Kootenai River Bridge in Bonners Ferry, ID at junction with Highway 95
   5.4   Kootenai Wildlife Refuge Headquarters and trailhead for Myrtle Falls
   6.7   Junction with Myrtle Creek Road 633 and access to Trails 6, 9, 268 and 286; can also access Roman Nose Lakes and Trails 165, 185 and 187
   15.5 Junction with Trout Creek Road 634 and access to Trails 7, 12, 13, 41, 43 and 92
   20.5 Junction with Copeland Road (County Road 45) – milepost approximated

12. **Copeland Road** (County Road 45 on 2003 Kaniksu Forest Map and also called West Side Road 417 on old road signs) – 2-lane paved road (mileposts have been approximated)

   MILEPOST   LANDMARK
   0.0   Junction with Highway 1 a mile north of Highway 1/95 fork about 15 miles north of Bonners Ferry, ID
   3.0   Copeland Bridge over the Kootenai River
   8.4   Trailhead for Parker Creek Trail No. 14 and access to Trail 221
   11.0 Trailhead for Long Canyon Trail No. 16
   15.0 Junction with Smith Creek Road 281 and access to Trails 17, 18, 95, 102, 21 and 347

Appendix 8: Index by Trail Name

Abercrombie Mountain Trail No. 117 48
Batey-Bould / Boulder Mountain Trail No. 311 77
Batey-Bould / Tacoma Peak Trail No. 309 77
Batey-Bould Trail No. 306 77
Batey-Bould Trail No. 307 77
Batey-Bould Trail No. 308 77
Batey-Bould Trail No. 310 77
Batey-Bould Trail No. 311 77
Batey-Bould Trail No. 312 77
Batey-Bould Trails System 77
Beach Trail No. 48 197
Bead Lake Trail No. 127 179
Beehive Lakes Trail No. 279 265
Bench Creek Trail No. 319 118
Big Fisher Lake Trail No. 41 233
Big Meadow Lake Trail No. 120 57
Binarch Creek Trail No. 220 172
Blacktail Mountain Trail No. 292 158
Bottleneck Lake Trail No. 187 258
Boulder Creek Trail No. 296 133
Boulder Mountain Trail No. 293 153
Browns Lake Trail No. 320 175
Bulldog Point Trail No. 274 200
Burton Peak Trail No. 9 240
Cabinet Pass Trail No. 317 121
Camp 15 Trail No. 232 171
Caribou Lake Trail No. 58 271
Cedar Grove Trail No. 301A 155
Centennial Trail No. 58 186
Chimney Rock Trail No. 256 266
Chipmunk Rapids National Recreation Trail No. 192 201
Continental Trail No. 28 101
Crowell Ridge Trail No. 515 124
Crystal Falls Viewpoint 75
Devil Falls Trail 287
Elk Creek Trail No. 560 136
Fault Lake Trail No. 59 268
Fisher Peak Trail No. 27 229
Flume Creek Trail No. 502 47
Frater Lake Trail No. 150 69
Gillette Ridge Trail No. 131 60
Goblin Knob Trail 291
Granite Peak Trail No. 145 70
Granite-Roosevelt Trail No. 301 155
Grassy Top National Recreation Trail No. 503 145

Hall Mountain Trail No. 540 144
Hall-Grassy Divide Trail No. 533 144
Halliday Trail No. 522 127
Hanna Cutoff Trail No. 232 171
Hanna Flats National Recreation Trail No. 600 170
Harrison Lake Trail No. 217 264
Helmer Creek Trail No. 303 99
Huff Lake Interpretive Site 151
Huff Lake Trail 150
Hughes Fork Trail No. 312 118
Hughes Ridge Lookout Trail No. 314 120
Hunt Creek Falls Trail 296
Hunt Lake Trail 295
Icy Springs Trail No. 197 167
Italian Ridge Trail No. 95 211
Jackson Creek Trail No. 311 117
Jackson Mountain Trail No. 309 99
John Wayne Trail No. 176 204
Kalispell Island Trail No. 49 199
Kalispell Rock Trail No. 370 162
Kalispell Rock-North Baldy Trail No. 103 163
Kalispell-Reeder Bay Trail No. 365 193
Kootenai National Wildlife Refuge Trails 250
Lake Leo Trail No. 155 69
Lakeview Mountain Trail No. 269 196
Little Grass Mountain Trail No. 265 153
Little Pend Oreille Lakes Trail No. 140 68
Little Pend Oreille Lakes Trail No. 142 68
Little Pend Oreille Lakes Trail No. 143 68
Little Pend Oreille Lakes Trail No. 144 68
Little Pend Oreille Lakes Trail No. 145 68
Little Pend Oreille Lakes Trail No. 146 68
Little Pend Oreille Lakes Trails System 68
Little Pend Oreille National Wildlife Refuge 65
Little Snowy Lookout Trail No. 14 104
Little Snowy Top Trail No. 349 104
Little Spokane River Natural Area Trail .85
Long Canyon Creek Trail No. 16 221
Lookout Lake and Lookout Mountain Trail 283
Lower Wolf Trail Nos. 304 and 305 80
Meadow Creek Trail No. 125 57
Mickinnick Trail 272
Middle Fork Calispell ORV Trail No. 313 66
Middle Fork Calispell ORV Trail No. 314 66
Middle Fork Calispell ORV Trail No. 315 66
Mill Pond Flume Trail No. 520 135
Mill Pond Trail No. 550 135

Mollies Lake and The Mollies Trail .282
Mount Rogers Loop Trail No. 130 .60
Mount Roothaan Trail .293
Mount Spokane State Park .91
Muskegon Lake Trail .145
Myrtle Falls Trail .242
Myrtle Peak Trail No. 286 .245
Natural Rock Slide Trail .287
Navigation Trail No. 291 .188
Newport Geophysical Trails .181
Noisy Creek Trail No. 588 .140
Nok-OSH-Kol Heritage Trail at Pioneer Park .182
North Blacktail Trail No. 324 .133
North Fork Lamb Creek Trail No. 204 .171
North Fork Silver Creek Trail No. 119 .51
North Fork Sullivan Creek Trail No. 507 .129
North Fork-Grassy Top Trail No. 379 .133
North Idaho Centennial Trail .83
Old Kettle Townsite Trail .88
Orwig Hump Trail No. 373 .133
Parker Creek Trail No. 14 .226
Parker Ridge Trail No. 221 .224
Peewee-Steep Creek Trail Nos. 175, 176, 177, 178, 179 .204
Plowboy Mountain Trail No. 295 .189
Portage Trail .188
Priest Lakeshore National Recreation Trail No. 294 .192
Pyramid Pass Trail No. 13 .230
Pyramid Trail No. 7 .235
Pyramid-Ball Lakes Trail No. 43 .232
Quartz View Trail No. 179 .204
Red Bluff Trail No. 553 .128
Red Top Trail No. 102 .212
Roman Nose Lakes Trail No. 165 .260
Roosevelt Trail No. 266 .153
Rufus Trail No. 148 .72
Russell Mountain Trail No. 12 .236
Russell Ridge Trail No. 92 .236
Salmo Basin Trail No. 506 .107
Salmo Cabin Trail No. 531 .107
Salmo Divide Trail No. 535 .109
Sema Creek Trail No. 241 .133
Sentinel Trail at Fort Spokane .88
Shedroof Cutoff Trail No. 511 .112
Shedroof Divide Trail No. 512 .110
Sherlock Peak Trail No. 139 .54
Sherry Trail No. 147 .74
Slate Creek Trail No. 525 .126

Smith Creek Trail No. 17 .218
Smith Creek-Red Top Ridge Trail No. 21 .214
Smith Ridge Trail No. 18 .218
Snow Creek Falls Trail .241
Snow Lake Trail No. 185 .259
South Fork Cutoff Trail No. 378 .133
South Fork Silver Creek Trail No. 123 .52
South Jackson Mountain Trail No. 321 .99
South Skookum Lake Trail No. 138 .176
Spokane River Centennial Trail .83
Springboard Trail No. 149 .72
Squaw Valley Trail No. 164 .166
St. Paul's Mission .88
Stateline Trail No. 162 .165
Steep Creek Trail No. 177 .204
Sullivan Lakeshore National Recreation Trail No. 504 .139
Sullivan Nature Trail No. 509 .139
Tacoma Peak Trail No. 309 .78
The Wigwams Trail .288
The Wigwams-Two Mouth Lakes Trail .279
Thunder Creek Trail No. 526 .113
Thunder Mountain Trail No. 313 .118
Tillicum Creek Trail No. 261 .133
Tillicum Peak Trail No. 284 .133
Trapper Creek Trail .281
Two Mouth Creek Trail .279
Two Mouth Lakes Trail No. 268 .246
Upper Hughes Trail No. 315 .121
Upper Myrtle Creek Trail No. 6 .248
Upper Priest Lake Trail No. 302 .185
Upper Priest River Trail No. 308 .102
Upper Standard Lake Trail .290
Upper Wolf Trail Nos. 304 and 305 .80
West Fork Mountain Trail No. 347 .216
Woodrat Trail No. 235 .200
Zero Creek Trail No. 256 .153

Appendix 9: Index by Trail Number

Note: Trails with no designated trail number are not included here. To locate those trails, see Appendix 8: Index by Trail Name, page 328.

Trail No. 6 Upper Myrtle Creek 248
Trail No. 7 Pyramid 235
Trail No. 9 Burton Peak 240
Trail No. 12 Russell Mountain 236
Trail No. 13 Pyramid Pass 230
Trail No. 14 Little Snowy Lookout 104
Trail No. 14 Parker Creek 226
Trail No. 16 Long Canyon Creek 221
Trail No. 17 Smith Creek 218
Trail No. 18 Smith Ridge 218
Trail No. 21 Smith Creek-Red Top Ridge 214
Trail No. 27 Fisher Peak 229
Trail No. 28 Continental 101
Trail No. 41 Big Fisher Lake 233
Trail No. 43 Pyramid-Ball Lakes 232
Trail No. 48 Beach 197
Trail No. 49 Kalispell Island 199
Trail No. 58 Caribou Lake 271
Trail No. 58 Centennial 186
Trail No. 59 Fault Lake 268
Trail No. 92 Russell Ridge 236
Trail No. 95 Italian Ridge 211
Trail No. 102 Red Top 212
Trail No. 103 Kalispell Rock-North Baldy 163
Trail No. 117 Abercrombie Mountain 48
Trail No. 119 North Fork Silver Creek 51
Trail No. 120 Big Meadow Lake 57
Trail No. 123 South Fork Silver Creek 52
Trail No. 125 Meadow Creek 57
Trail No. 127 Bead Lake 179
Trail No. 130 Mount Rogers Loop 60
Trail No. 131 Gillette Ridge 60
Trail No. 138 South Skookum Lake 176
Trail No. 139 Sherlock Peak 54
Trail No. 140 Little Pend Oreille Lakes 68
Trail No. 142 Little Pend Oreille Lakes 68
Trail No. 143 Little Pend Oreille Lakes 68
Trail No. 144 Little Pend Oreille Lakes 68
Trail No. 145 Granite Peak 70
Trail No. 145 Little Pend Oreille Lakes 68

Trail No. 146 Little Pend Oreille Lakes 68
Trail No. 147 Sherry 74
Trail No. 148 Rufus 72
Trail No. 149 Springboard 72
Trail No. 150 Frater Lake 69
Trail No. 155 Lake Leo 69
Trail No. 162 Stateline 165
Trail No. 164 Squaw Valley 166
Trail No. 165 Roman Nose Lakes 260
Trail No. 175 Peewee-Quartz Cutoff 204
Trail No. 176 John Wayne 204
Trail No. 176 Peewee 204
Trail No. 177 Steep Creek 204
Trail No. 179 Quartz View 204
Trail No. 185 Snow Lake 259
Trail No. 187 Bottleneck Lake 258
Trail No. 192 Chipmunk Rapids National Recreation Trail 201
Trail No. 197 Icy Springs 167
Trail No. 204 North Fork Lamb Creek 171
Trail No. 217 Harrison Lake 264
Trail No. 220 Binarch Creek 172
Trail No. 221 Parker Ridge 224
Trail No. 232 Camp 15 171
Trail No. 232 Hanna Cutoff 171
Trail No. 235 Woodrat 200
Trail No. 241 Sema Creek 133
Trail No. 256 Chimney Rock 266
Trail No. 256 Zero Creek 153
Trail No. 261 Tillicum Creek 133
Trail No. 265 Little Grass Mountain 153
Trail No. 266 Roosevelt 153
Trail No. 268 Two Mouth Lakes 246
Trail No. 269 Lakeview Mountain 196
Trail No. 274 Bulldog Point 200
Trail No. 279 Beehive Lakes 265
Trail No. 284 Tillicum Peak 133
Trail No. 286 Myrtle Peak 245
Trail No. 291 Navigation 188
Trail No. 292 Blacktail Mountain 158
Trail No. 293 Boulder Mountain 153
Trail No. 294 Priest Lakeshore National Recreation Trail 192
Trail No. 295 Plowboy Mountain 189
Trail No. 296 Boulder Creek 133
Trail No. 301 Granite-Roosevelt 155
Trail No. 301A Cedar Grove 155
Trail No. 302 Upper Priest Lake 185
Trail No. 303 Helmer Creek 99

Trail No. 304 and 305 Lower Wolf 80
Trail No. 306 Batey-Bould 77
Trail No. 307 Batey-Bould 77
Trail No. 308 Batey-Bould 77
Trail No. 308 Upper Priest River 102
Trail No. 309 Batey-Bould / Tacoma Peak 77
Trail No. 309 Jackson Mountain 99
Trail No. 310 Batey-Bould 77
Trail No. 311 Batey-Bould / Boulder Mountain 77
Trail No. 311 Jackson Creek 117
Trail No. 312 Batey-Bould 77
Trail No. 312 Hughes Fork 118
Trail No. 313 Middle Fork Calispell ORV 66
Trail No. 313 Thunder Mountain 118
Trail No. 314 Hughes Ridge Lookout 120
Trail No. 314 Middle Fork Calispell ORV 66
Trail No. 315 Middle Fork Calispell ORV 66
Trail No. 315 Upper Hughes 121
Trail No. 317 Cabinet Pass 121
Trail No. 319 Bench Creek 118
Trail No. 320 Browns Lake 175
Trail No. 321 South Jackson Mountain 99
Trail No. 324 North Blacktail 133
Trail No. 347 West Fork Mountain 216
Trail No. 349 Little Snowy Top 104
Trail No. 365 Kalispell-Reeder Bay 193
Trail No. 370 Kalispell Rock 162
Trail No. 373 Orwig Hump 133
Trail No. 378 South Fork Cutoff 133
Trail No. 379 North Fork-Grassy Top 133
Trail No. 502 Flume Creek 47
Trail No. 503 Grassy Top National Recreation Trail 145
Trail No. 504 Sullivan Lakeshore National Recreation Trail 139
Trail No. 506 Salmo Basin 107
Trail No. 507 North Fork Sullivan Creek 129
Trail No. 509 Sullivan Nature 139
Trail No. 511 Shedroof Cutoff 112
Trail No. 512 Shedroof Divide 110
Trail No. 515 Crowell Ridge 124
Trail No. 520 Mill Pond Flume 135
Trail No. 522 Halliday 127
Trail No. 525 Slate Creek 126
Trail No. 526 Thunder Creek 113
Trail No. 531 Salmo Cabin 107
Trail No. 533 Hall-Grassy Divide 144
Trail No. 535 Salmo Divide 109
Trail No. 540 Hall Mountain 144

Trail No. 550 Mill Pond 135
Trail No. 553 Red Bluff 128
Trail No. 560 Elk Creek 136
Trail No. 588 Noisy Creek 140
Trail No. 600 Hanna Flats National Recreation Trail 170

Trail's End

Have you ever noticed that food you would turn your nose up at when home is like a feast fit for a king when out on the trail? I've made some odd concoctions in my day and called it soup while out under the stars. I've taken everything I can find in my pack, no matter how long it has been there, or everything from the cupboards at home, no matter how long it has been there, and thrown it altogether and called it trail mix. I have cooked up some of the skankiest-looking grub when in the backcountry, and thought I was dining in a five-star restaurant. It never matters if a little dirt or grit or ash gets into the dish, and insects attracted by the firelight or the warmth of the cook stove that get caught up in the stirring of ingredients just add a bit of protein.

The wilderness is wonderful for that. We drop our defenses a little, let down our guard just a bit when we are most vulnerable to Nature. We become more natural. That is something missing in most of our everyday lives, and not just in what we eat, but in how we relate to one another. Honesty is a rare personality trait in our society. Oh, few of us are seldom outright dishonest, but Life is much simpler when we don't let others too far into our own weird, little worlds.

The wilderness, given time, breaks down those walls, and instead of discovering we are inferior to others or not as good as someone else, anyone else, we begin to see that we each simply seek to live life the best way we know how; usually with our defenses in place, our guard up. Going for a hike with others, being outside, is the best way to get to know them and yourself. So grab a friend or round up the family, and go hiking. You will have some of the best interaction you've ever had with the kids, your spouse and your friends.

But you might want to buy trail mix at the store.